Cat Tales

Timeless Stories of Our Favorite Feline Companions

Edited by Tom McCarthy

LYONS PRESS

Essex, Connecticut

An imprint of Globe Pequot, the trade division of The Rowman & Littlefield Publishing Group, Inc.
4501 Forbes Blvd., Ste. 200
Lanham, MD 20706
www.rowman.com
Distributed by NATIONAL BOOK NETWORK

British Library Cataloguing in Publication Information available

Library of Congress Cataloging-in-Publication Data
Names: McCarthy, Tom, 1952- editor.
Title: Cat tales : timeless stories of our favorite feline companions / edited by Tom McCarthy.
Description: Essex, Connecticut : Lyons Press, [2023] | Includes bibliographical references.
Identifiers: LCCN 2023014502 (print) | LCCN 2023014503 (ebook) | ISBN 9781493074235 (trade paperback) | ISBN 9781493077595 (epub)
Subjects: LCSH: Cats--Literary collections.
Classification: LCC PN6071.C3 C37 2023 (print) | LCC PN6071.C3 (ebook) | DDC 808.8/0362–dc23/eng/20230512
LC record available at https://lccn.loc.gov/2023014502
LC ebook record available at https://lccn.loc.gov/2023014503

∞™ The paper used in this publication meets the minimum requirements of American National Standard for Information Sciences—Permanence of Paper for Printed Library Materials, ANSI/NISO Z39.48-1992.

CONTENTS

Introduction vii

One: Kittenhood. 1
Alfred Elwes

Two: The Black Cat 7
Edgar Allen Poe

Three: Peter: A Cat O'One Tail .17
Charles Morley

Four: "Is Cats to be Trusted?" .35
W. Gordon Stables

Five: The Case for Cats 43
Charles H. Ross

Six: The Cat 51
Andrew Barton Paterson

Seven: The Greedy Cat. 55
G. W. Dasent

Eight: The Gray Cat 61
Arthur Christopher Benson

Nine: The Home Life of a Holy Cat. 77
Arthur Weigall

Ten: The Cats of Ulthar 85
H. P. Lovecraft

Eleven: The Empty Sleeve 89
Algernon Blackwood

CONTENTS

Twelve: The Watchers 101
Bram Stoker

Thirteen: The Cat of the Cane-Brake 111
Frederick Stuart Greene

Fourteen: The Brazilian Cat 123
Arthur Conan Doyle

Fifteen: The White Cat 143
W. W. Jacobs

Sixteen: Who Was to Blame? 155
Anton Chekhov

Seventeen: Plato: The Story of a Cat. 159
A. S. Downs

Eighteen: A Talk with Mark Twain's Cat, the Owner Being
Invisible: New York *Times*, April 9, 1905 163

Nineteen: The Cat and the King. 171
Ambrose Bierce

Twenty: How a Cat Played Robinson Crusoe. 173
Charles G. D. Roberts

Twenty-One: The Yellow Terror 183
W. L. Alden

Twenty-Two: Midshipman, the Cat 193
John Coleman Adams

Twenty-Three: The Philanthropist and the Happy Cat 203
Saki (H. H. Munro)

Twenty-Four: My Cat 209
Michel de Montaigne

Twenty-Five: Calvin: A Study of Character. 211
Charles Dudley Warner

Twenty-Six: The Cat That Walked by Himself 221
Rudyard Kipling

Twenty-Seven: The Achievement of the Cat 233
Saki (H. H. Munro)

Twenty-Eight: The Woman and the Cat 237
Marcel Prevost

Twenty-Nine: The Demon Cat 247
Lady Jane Wilde

Thirty: The Hypocritical Cat. 249
W. H. D. Rouse

Thirty-One: The Cat and the Dream Man 251
Charles J. Finger

Thirty-Two: Mr. Sweeney's Cat 271
Bill Nye

Thirty-Three: The Cat and the Mouse 275
John R. Neill

Thirty-Four: Johnny Reed's Cat 281
English Folk Tale

Thirty-Five: An Idyll of Summer 285
Anne E. P. Searing

Thirty-Six: The Man Who Disliked Cats 297
P. G. Wodehouse

Thirty-Seven: The Cat Came Back. 313
Virginia West

Thirty-Eight: How Diana Made the Stars and the Rain 317
Charles G. Leland

Thirty-Nine: Ye Marvellous Legend of Tom Connor's Cat 319
Samuel Lover

Forty: The Cat the Mouse in Partnership 329
Anonymous

Forty-One: On Cats and Dogs 333
Jerome K. Jerome

Forty-Two: Greta and the Black Cat. 345
Abbie Phillips Walker

Forty-Three: The Slum Cat. 351
Ernest Thompson Seton

Forty-Four: The Cat and the Fiddle 361
L. Frank Baum

Forty-Five: The Master Cat 367
Charles Perrault

Forty-Six: The Cat on the Dovrefell 373
George Webbe Dasent

Forty-Seven: Mistress Pussy's Mistake. 375
Abbie Phillips Walker

Forty-Eight: What About the Cat? 377
Edith Eaton

Forty-Nine: There Arose a King 381
E.F. Benson

Fifty: The Visitor from the Cellar 391
Amy Walton

Fifty-One: Uncle Wiggly and the Rich Cat. 409
Howard R. Garis

Sources. 415

INTRODUCTION

A cat will not read this stirring collection from the beginning as most readers would. A cat will instead read it in any damn order he chooses. That is simply the way cats operate, and why humans can't seem to get enough of them.

I suggest you do the same, choosing a story to match your mood. You won't be disappointed. Among the many stories in this collection, you'll find those that are life-affirming, chilling, amusing, interesting, wry, informative, dark, heartbreaking, powerful, haunting, and gleeful.

These stories are classics—tales that have stood the test of time and place, as meaningful and moving today as they were when they were written. For cat lovers, this collection will confirm why we love cats as much as we do.

Cats are the perfect companions for people. Chilled to the max, their general aloofness is what draws us to them. Many of us, if given the choice, would like to live a cat's life. We all want to sleep twenty hours a day, rising only when the urge to hunt, or eat, or perhaps cause a bit of innocent mischief overcomes us.

I am among the many cat lovers who think their noted nonchalance is feigned. I know they love a good stroking and conversation, but only on their own time and choosing.

Cats are far more mysterious and exotic than most other pets. They are usually awake and prowling while we sleep, which adds to their mystery, as if they are always on some sort of clandestine mission. Cats have their own agenda. They hide, emerging suddenly to surprise us, then seem to wonder why me make such a big deal over their appearance.

They keep us on our toes. We're drawn to their complexities, totally under their spell.

Cats are irresistible and have a great capacity to receive our affection, though they reserve the right to ignore that affection at any time. Cats can be finicky and predictably unpredictable.

One remark I read recently sums up the feelings of most cat lovers: "In ancient times, cats were worshipped as gods. They have not forgotten this."

Cats have been among us for possibly 12,000 years, when humans new to agriculture ended their nomadic existence and settled in the Fertile Crescent. It was here they discovered that feral cats would help eradicate rodents attracted to the grain they grew. It seemed to be a mutually beneficial partnership.

In Cyprus, archeologists found evidence of cats and humans living in peaceful harmony as far back as 9,500 years ago. Ancient Egyptians worshipped cats, and that makes perfect sense to me.

Cats made their way to America on ships sailed by Christopher Columbus, the colonists who settled Jamestown, and aboard the *Mayflower*.

Cats also made their way into literature, and this collection is proof that cats have inspired some phenomenal writing, from much-lauded authors such as Edgar Allan Poe, Saki (H. H. Munro), Arthur Conan Doyle, Bram Stoker, Ambrose Bierce, P. G. Wodehouse, and L. Frank Baum, whose non-feline writing is still attracting readers today.

But cats are not just the purview of noted authors. Cats have inspired folktales from Ireland and Persia and England, and they have sparked the interest of writers of all stripes, which you will find here as well.

It makes perfect sense for a writer to choose a cat as a subject. Their mystery, adorability, and guile make for perfect protagonists.

This is a collection even the most discriminating cat—or cat lover—will be pulled into and unable to put down.

The order in which you read it is up to you.

ONE

Kittenhood
Alfred Elwes

THERE IS NOTHING LIKE BEGINNING AT THE VERY COMMENCEMENT OF a story, if we wish it to be thoroughly understood; at least, *I* think so; and, as I wish *my* story to be clear and intelligible, in order that it may furnish a hint or a warning to others, I shall at least act up to my opinion, and begin at the beginning,—I may say, at the very tip of my tale.

Being now a Cat of some years' standing (I do not much like remembering how many), I was of course a Kitten on making my entry into life,—my first appearance being in company with a brother and three sisters.

We were all declared to be "the prettiest little darlings that ever were seen"; but as the old Puss who made the remark had said precisely the same thing at sight of every fresh Kitten she beheld, and she was accustomed to see ten or twelve new ones every week, the observation is no proof of our being very charming or very beautiful.

I cannot remember what passed during the first few days of my existence, for my eyes were close-shut till the ninth morning. I have an indistinct recollection however of overhearing a few words which passed between my mother and a friend of the family who had dropped in for a little chat, on the evening of the eighth day.

The latter had been remarking on my efforts to unclose my lids, to obtain a little peep at what was going on, when my good parent exclaimed,

"Ah! yes, she tries hard enough to stare at life now, because she knows nothing of it; but when she is as old as you or I, neighbour, she will wish more than once that she had always kept her eyes closed, or she is no true Cat."

I could not of course, at the time, have any notion what my mother meant, but I think, indeed I am *sure*, that I have discovered her meaning long ago; and all those who have lived to have sorrow,—and who has not?—will understand it too.

I had found my tongue and my legs, and so had my brother and sisters, before we got the use of our eyes. With the first we kept up a perfect concert of sounds; the legs we employed in dragging our bodies about our capacious cradle, crawling over each other, and getting in everybody's way, for we somehow managed, in the dark as we were, to climb to the edge of our bed and roll quickly over it, much to our astonishment and the amusement or annoyance of the family, just as they happened to be in the humour.

Our sight was at last granted us. On that eventful morning our mother stepped gently into our bed, which she had left an hour before; and, taking us one by one in her maternal embrace, she held us down with her legs and paws, and licked us with more affection and assiduity than she had ever bestowed on our toilet before. Her tongue, which she rendered as soft for the occasion as a Cat's tongue can be made, I felt pass and repass over my eyes until the lids burst asunder, and I could *see*!

And what a confusion of objects I first beheld! It seemed as if everything above was about to fall upon my head and crush me, and that everything around was like a wall to prevent my moving; and when, after a day or two, I began to understand better the distance that these objects were from me, I fell into the opposite error, and hurt my nose not a little through running it against a chair, which I fancied to be very much further off. These difficulties however soon wore away. Experience, bought at the price of some hard knocks, taught me better; and, a month after my first peep at the world, it seemed almost impossible I could ever have been so ignorant.

No doubt my brother and sisters procured their knowledge in a similar way: it is certain that it cost them something. One incident, which happened to my brother, I particularly remember; and it will serve to prove that he did not get *his* experience for nothing.

We were all playing about the room by ourselves, our mother being out visiting or marketing, I do not know which, and the nurse, who was charged to take care of us, preferring to chat to the handsome footman in the tortoise-shell coat over the way, to looking after us Kittens.

A large pan full of something sticky, but I do not remember what, was in a corner; and as the edge of it was very broad, we climbed on to it and peeped in.

Our brother, who was very venturesome, said he could jump over it to the opposite brim. We said it was not possible, for the pan was broad and rather slippery; and what a thing it would be if he fell into it! But the more we exclaimed about its difficulty, the more resolved he was to try.

Getting his legs together, he gave a spring; but, slipping just as he got to the other side, his claws could not catch hold of anything to support himself, and he went splash backwards into the sticky mess. His screams, and indeed ours, ought to have been enough to call nurse to our assistance; but she was making such a noise herself with the tortoise-shell footman, that my brother might have been drowned or suffocated before *she* would have come to his assistance. As it was, he managed to drag himself to the edge without any help at all; and as we feared that all of us would get punished if the adventure were known, my sisters and myself set to work and licked him all over; and then getting into bed, we cuddled up together to make him dry, and were soon fast asleep.

Although the accident was not known at the time, we all suffered for it; for my brother caught a dreadful cold, and myself and sisters were ill for several days, through the quantity of the stuff we had licked off my brother's coat, and one of us nearly died through it.

As we grew stronger and older, we were permitted, under the care of our nurse, to go into the country for a few hours to play. It may be perhaps thought, from what I have said, that nurse's care was not worth much, and that we might just as well have looked after ourselves, as the poorer Kittens of our city were accustomed to do. But this was not precisely the case; for when nurse had nobody to chat with, she was very strict with us, I assure you, and on such occasions made up for her inattention at other times. That unlucky fondness of hers however for gossiping, was the cause of a great deal of mischief; and about this time it partly occasioned a sad misfortune in our family. I said *partly*, because the accident was also due to an act of disobedience; and as the adventure may serve as a double warning, I will briefly relate it.

It was a lovely morning in early summer; the sun shone gaily upon the city, looked at his brilliant face in the river, danced about among the leaves of the trees, and polished the coats of every Cat and Dog which came out to enjoy the beautiful day he was making.

To our great delight we were allowed to take a long walk in the country. Two of our cousins, and a young Pussy who was visiting at our house, were to accompany us; and nurse had strict charge to prevent our getting into mischief. Before we started our mother called us and said, that, although she had desired nurse to look after us, and take care that no harm should happen while we were out, she desired also that we should take care of *ourselves*, and behave like Kittens of station and good-breeding, not like the young Cats about the streets, poor things! who had no home except the first hole they could creep into, no food but what they could pick up or steal, and no father or mother that they knew of to teach them what was good. Such creatures were to be pitied and relieved, but not imitated; and she hoped we would, by our behaviour, show that we bore her advice in mind. "Above all," she added, "do not let me hear of your climbing and racing about in a rude and extravagant way, for a great deal of mischief is often done by such rough modes of amusement."

We hastily promised all and everything. If we had kept our words, we should have been perfect angels of Cats, for we declared in a chorus that we would do only what was good, and would carefully avoid everything that was evil; and with these fine promises in our mouths, we started off in pairs under the guidance of nurse.

We soon came to the wood, situated at some distance from the city; and, walking into it, shortly arrived at an open space, where some large trees stood round and threw broad patches of shade over the grass.

We at once commenced our gambols. We rolled over one another, we sprang over each other's backs, and hid behind the great beech trunks for the pleasure of springing out upon our companions when they stealthily came to look for us.

In the midst of our fun we observed that nurse had gone. We had been so busied with our own diversions that not one of us had observed her departure; but now that we found it out, we set off to discover where she had strolled to. We observed her, after a few minutes, cosily seated on a bank of violets, near the very same tortoise-shell footman, who lived opposite our house, although how *he* came there we could not imagine. Nor indeed did we much trouble ourselves to guess. Seeing she was so engaged we returned at once to our sport, and played none the less heartily because nurse was not there to curb us.

I remember, as if it were only yesterday, the scene which followed. I was amusing myself with one of my pretty cousins, who was dressed in white, and was about my own age. I had thrown her down on the grass, and was patting her with my paws, when I heard a scream; I turned quickly round, just in time to see one of my sisters falling from a tall tree, to which she had climbed with our young visitor, when, all of us running up, we discovered that, on reaching the ground, she had struck her head against a sharp stone, and was now bleeding and without motion.

Our cries brought nurse to the spot, who, as soon as she discovered all the mischief that had been done, without saying a word started off with all swiftness, with her tail in the air. We thought she had gone to fetch assistance or to inform our mother of what had occurred; but as she did not come back, and evening was fast setting in, we thought it best to proceed towards home, although we did not much like meeting our parents after what had happened.

There was no help for it however; so, giving a last frightened look at our poor little sister, who was now quite dead and cold, we walked sadly homewards, and reached the house just as night was falling.

I pass over what ensued,—my mother's grief, and her anger against nurse, who, by the bye, never came back to express her sorrow; I pass over also my mother's remarks upon the occasion; but I may observe, that they, added to the sad accident itself, made so deep an impression upon me, that whenever I felt inclined to disobey my good mother's admonitions, the image of my dead sister would rise up before me, and, although it did not, alas! *always* prevent my being wicked, it often did so, and on every occasion made me feel repentance for my error.

Two

The Black Cat

Edgar Allen Poe

FOR THE MOST WILD, YET MOST HOMELY NARRATIVE WHICH I AM about to pen, I neither expect nor solicit belief. Mad indeed would I be to expect it, in a case where my very senses reject their own evidence. Yet, mad am I not—and very surely do I not dream. But to-morrow I die, and to-day I would unburden my soul. My immediate purpose is to place before the world, plainly, succinctly and without comment a series of mere household events.

In their consequences, these events have terrified—have tortured—have destroyed me. Yet I will not attempt to expound them. To me they have presented little but horror, to many they will seem less terrible than *barroques*. Hereafter, perhaps, some intellect may be found which will reduce my phantasm to the commonplace—some intellect more calm, more logical, and far less excitable than my own, which will perceive in the circumstances I detail with awe nothing more than an ordinary succession of very natural causes and effects.

From my infancy I was noted for the docility and humanity of my disposition. My tenderness of heart was even so conspicuous as to make me the jest of my companions. I was especially fond of animals, and was indulged by my parents with a great variety of pets.

With these I spent most of my time, and never was so happy as when feeding and caressing them. This peculiarity of character grew with my growth, and in my manhood I derived from it one of my principal sources of pleasure. To those who have cherished an affection for a faithful and sagacious dog, I need hardly be at the trouble of explaining the nature or the intensity of the gratification thus derivable. There is something in the unselfish and self-sacrificing love of a brute, which goes directly to the heart of him who has had frequent occasion to test the paltry friendship and gossamer fidelity of mere Man.

I married early, and was happy to find in my wife a disposition not uncongenial with my own. Observing my partiality for domestic pets she lost no opportunity of procuring those of the most agreeable kind. We had birds, goldfish, a fine dog, rabbits, a small monkey, and *a cat*.

This latter was a remarkably large and beautiful animal, entirely black, and sagacious to an astonishing degree. In speaking of his intelligence, my wife, who at heart was not a little tinctured with superstition, made frequent allusion to the ancient popular notion, which regarded all black cats as witches in disguise. Not that she was ever serious upon this point—and I mention the matter at all for no better reason than that it happens, just now, to be remembered.

Pluto—this was the cat's name—was my favorite pet and playmate. I alone fed him, and he attended me wherever I went about the house. It was even with difficulty that I could prevent him from following me through the streets.

Our friendship lasted, in this manner, for several years, during which my general temperament and character—through the instrumentality of the fiend Intemperance—had (I blush to confess it) experienced a radical alteration for the worse. I grew, day by day, more moody, more irritable, more regardless of the feelings of others. I suffered myself to use intemperate language to my wife.

At length I even offered her personal violence. My pets, of course, were made to feel the change in my disposition. I not only neglected them, but ill-used them. For Pluto, however, I still retained sufficient regard to restrain me from maltreating him, as I made no scruple of maltreating the rabbits, the monkey or even the dog, when by accident or through affection they came in my way. But my disease grew upon me— for what disease is like alcohol! And at length even Pluto, who was now becoming old, and consequently somewhat peevish—even Pluto began to experience the effects of my ill-temper.

One night, returning home much intoxicated from one of my haunts about town, I fancied that the cat avoided my presence. I seized him, when, in his fright at my violence, he inflicted a slight wound upon my hand with his teeth. The fury of a demon instantly possessed me. I knew myself no longer. My original soul seemed, at once, to take its flight from my body; and a more than fiendish malevolence, gin-nurtured, thrilled every fiber of my frame. I took from my waistcoat pocket a penknife, opened it, grasped the poor beast by the throat, and deliberately cut one of its eyes from the socket! I blush, I burn, I shudder while I pen the damnable atrocity.

When reason returned with the morning—when I had slept off the fumes of the night's debauch—I experienced a sentiment half of horror, half of remorse, for the crime of which I had been guilty; but it was, at best, a feeble and equivocal feeling, and the soul remained untouched. I again plunged into excess, and soon drowned in wine all memory of the deed.

In the meantime the cat slowly recovered.

The socket of the lost eye presented, it is true, a frightful appearance, but he no longer appeared to suffer any pain. He went about the house as usual, but, as might be expected, fled in extreme terror at my approach. I had so much of my old heart left as to be at first grieved by this evident dislike on the part of a creature which had once so loved me. But this feeling soon gave place to irritation. And then came, as if to my final and irrevocable overthrow, the spirit of perverseness. Of this spirit philosophy takes no account.

Yet I am not more sure that my soul lives than I am that perverseness is one of the primitive impulses of the human heart—one of the indivisible primary faculties or sentiments which give direction to the character of man. Who has not, hundreds of times, found himself committing a vile or silly action, for no other reason than because he knows he should not? Have we not a perpetual inclination, in the teeth of our best judgment, to violate that which is Law, merely because we understand it to be such? This spirit of perverseness, I say, came to my final overthrow. It was this unfathomable longing of the soul to vex itself—to offer violence to its own nature—to do wrong for the wrong's sake only—that urged me to continue and finally to consummate the injury I had inflicted upon the unoffending brute. One morning, in cold blood, I slipped a noose about its neck, and hung it to the limb of a tree; hung it with the tears streaming from my eyes and the bitterest remorse at my heart; hung it because I knew that it had loved me, and because I felt it had given me no offense; hung it because I knew that in so doing I was committing a sin—a deadly sin that would so jeopardize my immortal soul as to place it, if such a thing were possible—even beyond the reach of the infinite mercy of the most merciful and most terrible God.

On the night of the day on which this cruel deed was done, I was aroused from sleep by the cry of "fire!" The curtains of my bed were in flames. The whole house was blazing. It was with great difficulty that my wife, a servant and myself made our escape from the conflagration. The destruction was complete. My entire worldly wealth was swallowed up, and I resigned myself thenceforward to despair.

I am above the weakness of seeking to establish a sequence of cause and effect between the disaster and the atrocity. But I am detailing a chain of facts, and wish not to leave even a possible link imperfect. On the day succeeding the fire I visited the ruins. The walls, with one exception, had fallen in.

This exception was found in a compartment wall, not very thick, which stood about the middle of the house, and against which had rested the head of my bed. The plastering had here, in great measure, resisted the action of the fire—a fact which I attributed to its having been recently spread. About this wall a dense crowd were collected, and many persons seemed to be examining a particular portion of it with very minute and eager attention.

The words "strange!" "singular!" and other similar expressions excited my curiosity. I approached and saw, as if graven in bas-relief upon the white surface, the figure of a gigantic cat. The impression was given with an accuracy truly marvelous. There was a rope about the animal's neck.

When I first beheld this apparition—for I could scarcely regard it as less—my wonder and my terror were extreme. But at length reflection came to my aid. The cat, I remembered, had been hung in a garden adjacent to the house. Upon the alarm of fire this garden had been immediately filled by the crowd—by some one of whom the animal must have been cut from the tree and thrown through an open window into my chamber.

This had probably been done with the view of arousing me from sleep. The falling of other walls had compressed the victim of my cruelty into the substance of the freshly spread plaster, the lime of which with the flames, and the ammonia from the carcass, had then accomplished the portraiture as I saw it.

Although I thus readily accounted to my reason, if not altogether to my conscience, for the startling fact just detailed, it did not the less fail to make a deep impression upon my fancy. For months I could not rid myself of the phantasm of the cat; and, during this period, there came back into my spirit a half sentiment that seemed, but was not, remorse. I went so far as to regret the loss of the animal, and to look about me, among the vile haunts which I now habitually frequented, for another pet of the same species and of somewhat similar appearance, with which to supply its place.

One night as I sat, half stupefied, in a den of more than infamy, my attention was suddenly drawn to some black object, reposing upon the head of one of the immense hogsheads of gin, or of rum, which constituted the chief furniture of the apartment. I had been looking steadily at the top of this hogshead for some minutes, and what now caused me surprise was the fact that I had not sooner perceived the object thereupon. I approached it and touched it with my hand.

It was a black cat—a very large one—fully as large as Pluto, and closely resembling him in every respect, but only Pluto had not a white hair upon any portion of his body; but this cat had a large, although indefinite, splotch of white, covering nearly the whole region of the breast.

Upon my touching him he immediately arose, purred loudly, rubbed against my hand, and appeared delighted with my notice. This, then, was the very creature of which I was in search. I at once offered to purchase it of the landlord; but this person made no claim to it—knew nothing of it—had never seen it before.

I continued my caresses, and when I prepared to go home the animal evinced a disposition to accompany me. I permitted it to do so, occasionally stooping and patting it as I proceeded. When it reached the house, it domesticated itself at once, and became immediately a great favorite with my wife.

For my own part, I soon found a dislike to it arising within me. This was just the reverse of what I had anticipated; but—I know not how or why it was—its evident fondness for myself rather disgusted and annoyed me. By slow degrees these feelings of disgust and annoyance rose into the bitterness of hatred.

I avoided the creature; a certain sense of shame, and the remembrance of my former deed of cruelty, preventing me from physically abusing it. I did not, for some weeks, strike, or otherwise violently ill use it; but gradually—very gradually—I came to look upon it with unutterable loathing, and to flee silently from its odious presence, as from the breath of a pestilence.

What added, no doubt, to my hatred of the beast, was the discovery, on the morning after I brought it home, that, like Pluto, it also had been deprived of one of its eyes. This circumstance, however, only endeared it to my wife, who, as I have already said, possessed, in a high degree, that humanity of feeling which had once been my distinguishing trait, and the source of many of my simplest and purest pleasures.

With my aversion to this cat, however, its partiality for myself seemed to increase. It followed my footsteps with a pertinacity which it would be difficult to make the reader comprehend. Whenever I sat it would crouch beneath my chair or spring upon my knees, covering me with its loathsome caresses.

If I arose to walk it would get between my feet, and thus nearly throw me down, or, fastening its long and sharp claws in my dress, clamber, in this manner, to my breast. At such times, although I longed to destroy it with a blow, I was yet withheld from so doing, partly by a memory of my former crime, but chiefly—let me confess it at once—by absolute dread of the beast.

This dread was not exactly a dread of physical evil—and yet I should be at a loss how otherwise to define it. I am almost ashamed to own—yes, even in this felon's cell, I am almost ashamed to own—that the terror and horror with which the animal inspired me had been heightened by one of the merest chimeras it would be possible to conceive. My wife had called my attention more than once, to the character of the mark of white hair, of which I have spoken, and which constituted the sole visible difference between the strange beast and the one I had destroyed.

The reader will remember that this mark, although large, had been originally very indefinite; but, by slow degrees—degrees nearly imperceptible, and which for a long time my reason struggled to reject as fanciful—it had, at length, assumed a rigorous distinctness of outline. It was now the representation of an object that I shudder to name—and for this, above all, I loathed and dreaded, and would have rid myself of the monster had I dared—it was now I say the image of a hideous, of a ghastly thing—of the gallows! Oh, mournful and terrible engine of horror and of crime—of agony and of death!

And now was I indeed wretched beyond the wretchedness of mere humanity. And a brute beast, whose fellow I had contemptuously destroyed—a brute beast to work out for me—for me, a man, fashioned in the image of the High God—so much of insufferable woe.

Alas! neither by day nor night knew I the blessing of rest any more. During the former the creature left me no moment alone, and in the latter I started hourly from dreams of unutterable fear, to find the hot breath of the thing upon my face, and its vast weight—an incarnate nightmare that I had no power to shake off—incumbent eternally upon my heart.

Beneath the pressure of torments such as these the feeble remnants of the good within me succumbed. Evil thoughts became my sole intimates—the darkest and most evil of thoughts. The moodiness of my usual temper increased to hatred of all things and of all mankind; while, from the sudden, frequent and ungovernable outbursts of a fury to which I now blindly abandoned myself, my uncomplaining wife, alas! was the most usual and the most patient of sufferers.

One day she accompanied me upon some household errand into the cellar of the old building, which our poverty compelled us to inhabit. The cat followed me down the steep stairs, and, nearly throwing me headlong, exasperated me to madness. Uplifting an axe, and forgetting, in my wrath, the childish dread which had hitherto stayed my hand, I aimed a blow at the animal which, of course, would have proved instantly fatal had it descended as I wished.

But this blow was arrested by the hand of my wife. Goaded, by the interference, into a rage more than demoniacal, I withdrew my arm from her grasp, and buried the ax in her brain. She fell dead upon the spot, without a groan.

This hideous murder accomplished, I set myself forthwith, and with entire deliberation, to the task of concealing the body. I knew that I could not remove it from the house, either by day or by night, without the risk of being observed by the neighbors. Many projects entered my mind.

At one period I thought of cutting the corpse into minute fragments and destroying them by fire. At another I resolved to dig a grave for it in the floor of the cellar. Again, I deliberated about casting it into the well in the yard—about packing it in a box, as if merchandise, with the usual arrangements, and so getting a porter to take it from the house. Finally I hit upon what I considered a far better expedient than either of these. I determined to wall it up in the cellar—as the monks of the middle ages are recorded to have walled up their victims.

For a purpose such as this the cellar was well adapted. Its walls were loosely constructed and had lately been plastered throughout with a rough plaster, which the dampness of the atmosphere had prevented from hardening. Moreover, in one of the walls was a projection, caused by a false chimney, or fireplace, that had been filled up, and made to resemble the rest of the cellar.

I made no doubt that I could readily displace the bricks at this point, insert the corpse, and wall the whole up as before, so that no eye could detect anything suspicious.

And in this calculation I was not deceived. By means of a crowbar I easily dislodged the bricks, and, having carefully deposited the body against the inner wall, I propped it in that position, while, with little trouble, I relaid the whole structure as it originally stood.

Having procured mortar, sand, and hair with every possible precaution, I prepared a plaster which could not be distinguished from the old, and with this I very carefully went over the new brickwork. When I had finished I felt satisfied that all was right. The wall did not present the slightest appearance of having been disturbed. The rubbish on the floor was picked up with the minutest care. I looked around triumphantly and said to myself, "Here, at least, then, my labor has not been in vain."

My next step was to look for the beast which had been the cause of so much wretchedness, for I had at length firmly resolved to put it to death. Had I been able to meet with it at the moment there could have been no doubt of its fate; but it appeared that the crafty animal had been alarmed at the violence of my previous anger and forebore to present itself in my present mood.

It is impossible to describe or to imagine the deep, the blissful sense of relief which the absence of the detested creature occasioned in my bosom. It did not make its appearance during the night—and thus, for one night at least since its introduction into the house, I soundly and tranquilly slept—aye, slept, even with the burden of murder upon my soul!

The second and the third day passed, and still my tormentor came not. Once again I breathed as a free man. The monster, in terror, had fled the premises forever! I should behold it no more! My happiness was supreme! The guilt of my dark deed disturbed me but little. Some few inquiries had been made, but these had been readily answered. Even a search had been instituted—but, of course, nothing was to be discovered. I looked upon my future felicity as secured.

Upon the fourth day of the assassination a party of the police came very unexpectedly into the house and proceeded again to make a rigorous investigation of the premises. Secure, however, in the inscrutability of my place of concealment, I felt no embarrassment whatever.

The officers bade me accompany them in their search. They left no nook or corner unexplored. At length, for the third or fourth time, they descended into the cellar. I quivered not in a muscle. My heart beat as calmly as that of one who slumbers in innocence. I walked the cellar from end to end. I folded my arms upon my bosom and roamed easily to and fro.

The police were thoroughly satisfied and prepared to depart. The glee at my heart was too strong to be restrained. I burned to say but one word, by way of triumph, and to render doubly sure their assurance of my guiltlessness.

"Gentlemen," I said at last, as the party ascended the steps, "I delight to have allayed your suspicions. I wish you all health and a little more courtesy. By the by, gentlemen, this—this is a very well constructed house." (In the rabid desire to say something easily I scarcely knew what I uttered at all.)

"I may say an excellently well constructed house. These walls—are you going, gentlemen?—these walls are solidly put together"; and here, through the mere frenzy of bravado, I rapped heavily, with a cane which I held in my hand, upon that very portion of the brickwork behind which stood the corpse of the wife of my bosom.

But may God shield and deliver me from the fangs of the Arch Fiend! No sooner had the reverberation of my blows sunk into silence than I was answered by a voice from within the tomb!—by a cry, at first muffled and broken, like the sobbing of a child, and then quickly swelling into one long, loud and continuous scream, utterly anomalous and inhuman—a howl!—a wailing shriek, half of horror and half of triumph, such as might have arisen only out of hell, conjointly from the throats of the damned in their agony and of the demons that exult in the damnation.

Of my own thoughts it is folly to speak. Swooning, I staggered to the opposite wall. For an instant the party upon the stairs remained motionless, through extremity of terror and of awe. In the next a dozen stout arms were toiling at the wall. It fell bodily. The corpse, already getting decayed and clotted with gore, stood erect before the eyes of the spectators.

Upon its head, with red, extended mouth and solitary eye of fire, sat the hideous beast whose craft had seduced me into murder, and whose informing voice had consigned me to the hangman. I had walled the monster up within the tomb!

Three

Peter

A Cat O'One Tail

Charles Morley

PETER, THE ADMIRABLE CAT WHOSE BRIEF HISTORY I AM ABOUT TO relate, appeared in the world on a terrible winter's night. A fierce snowstorm was raging, the sleet was driving at a terrific rate through the air, and the streets were banked up with snowdrifts. All traffic had been stopped, the roar of London was hushed, and everyone who had the merest pretence of a fireside sought it on this memorable occasion.

It was a wild night in the city, a wild night in the country, a wild night at sea, and certainly a most unpropitious night for the birth of a cat, an animal which is always associated with home and hearth. The fact remains that Peter was born on the night of one of the most terrible storms on record.

Our chairs were drawn up to the fire, the tea-things were on the table, and my mother was just about to try the strength of the brew, when Ann Tibbits, our faithful and well-tried maid-of-all-work, bounced into the room without knocking at the door. Her cap was all awry, her hair was dishevelled, and she gasped for breath as she addressed herself to my mother thus, in spasms:

"Please—ma'am—the cat has put her kittens—in—your—bonnet!"

Such a breach of discipline had never been known before in our prim household, where there was a place for everything, and everything had a place.

My mother pushed her spectacles onto her forehead, and, looking severely at Ann, said: "*Which* one, Ann? My summer bonnet, or—my winter bonnet?"

"The one with the fur lining, ma'am."

"And a most comfortable bonnet to live in, I'm sure!" replied my mother sarcastically, as much as to say that she wished all cats had such a choice under the circumstances. "Another cat would have chosen the one with the lace and the violets, out of sheer perverseness. But there—I *knew* I could depend on a cat which had been trained in *my* house."

My mother poured out a cup of tea, betraying no agitation as she dropped two lumps of sugar into the cup—her customary allowance—and helped herself to cream. In a minute or two, however, she took up her knitting, and I noticed that two stitches in succession were dropped, a sure sign that she was perturbed in spirit. Suddenly my mother turned her eyes to the fire.

"*How many*, Ann?" she continued, addressing our faithful servant, who still remained standing at the table awaiting her orders.

"Seven, ma'am."

"*Seven!*" cried my mother. "Seven—it's outrageous. Why, my bonnet wouldn't hold 'em!"

"Three in the bonnet, ma'am, and two in your new m-u-f-f!"

"My new muff!" cried my mother. "I *knew* you were keeping something back." And the stitches dropped fast and furious. "That's only *five*, Ann," she continued, looking up from her work. "Where are the other two? I insist upon knowing."

"In the Alaska tail boa, ma'am," responded Ann, timidly.

Slowly my mother's wrath evaporated, and her features settled down to their ordinary aspect of composure.

"Well," she said, "it might have been worse. She might have put them in my silk dress. But there—it is evident that something must be done. I'm a kind woman, I hope, but I'm not going to be responsible for seven young and tender kittens. Ann Tibbits, England expects every woman to do her duty!"

"*All?* asked Ann.

"*Four,*" replied my mother.

"Now?" asked Ann.

"The sooner the better," said my mother.

At this moment a sudden blast shook every window in the house, which seemed to be in momentary danger of a total collapse.

"Not fit to turn a dog out," murmured my mother. "Not fit to turn a dog out. Ugh! how cold it is, and here am I condemning to death four poor little kittens on a night like this—to snatch them away from their warm mother, my muff, and Alaska tail, and dip them in a bucket of ice-cold water. And yet they must go; but, Ann, I've an idea—WARM the water. They shall leave the world comfortably. They'll never know it."

The faithful, unemotional Ann carried out her instructions. Peter was one of the three kittens which were born in my mother's fur-lined bonnet, and the white marks on his body always remind me of the terrible snowstorm in the midst of which he sounded his first mew.

After several weeks the liberty which our cat Cordelia had taken with my mother's finery was forgotten, and the household had settled down into its usual humdrum routine. Tibbits had made the new arrivals a bed in the little box-room, and the doctor declared that Mrs. Cordelia was doing as well as could be expected.

Every morning we had asked the usual question: "How is Cordelia?" "Quite well, thank you." "And the kittens?" "Also quite well." In due course Ann brought the welcome news that the three kittens had opened their eyes, and the kid glove was at once detached from the knocker of the front door. It was on the morning after they had obtained their blessed sight that I was invited by Tibbits to go downstairs and take my choice.

I went down, but I could see nothing of the kittens; there was only Cordelia, with tail twisting, eyes aflame, and whiskers bristling, wheeling round and round a number of straw cases in which champagne had once been packed. Lo! one of the cases began to walk. The movement caught Cordelia's eye, and she knocked it over with her paw.

A fluffy, chubby kitten, consisting of a black body with a patch of white on it, was revealed. The little one so captivated my fancy that I put him in my pocket, and without more ado took him upstairs, and publicly announced my determination to claim him as my property.

"What shall we name it?" asked my mother.

"Fiz," said one, alluding to the empty champagne cases,—a suggestion which was at once overruled, as we were a temperate family and little given to sparkling liquids. "Pop" was also voted against, not only as being vulgar, but as going to the other extreme, and leading people to suppose that we were extensively addicted to ginger-ale.

"I think, my dears, as Peter was born on a—" My mother's speech was interrupted by an exultant "Cock-a-doodle-do."

"That horrid fowl again!" exclaimed my mother.

The cock in question was the property of a neighbor, and was a most annoying bird. Even my kitten was disturbed by the defiant note. "*M-e-w?*" said he, in a meek interrogative, as much as to say, "What *is* that dreadful noise?"

"Cock-a-doodle-do," cried the bird again.

"Mew," replied the kitten, this time with a note of anger in his voice. "COCK-A-DOODLE," screamed the bird, evidently in a violent temper. "Mew," said the kitten again, in a tone of remonstrance. The remaining syllable of his war-cry and the kitten's reply were cut short by my mother, who put her fingers to her ears, and said:

"And the cock crowed thrice. My dears, I have it!"

"What, mother?"

"We'll call him PETER," cried the family.

"Peter Gray?"

"Peter Simple?"

"Peter the Great?"

"No," replied my mother, with a humorous twinkle, "Peter the Apostle," pointing to the Family Bible, which was always kept on a little occasional table in a corner of the sitting-room. "And let Peter be a living warning against fibbing, my dears, whether on a small scale or a large one."

A bowl of water was then placed on the table and, having sprinkled a shower upon his devoted back, I as his proprietor, looking at him closely, cried:

"Arise, Peter; obey thy master."

In the middle of my exhortations, however, Cordelia jumped on the table, took little Peter by the scruff of his neck, and carried him back to the nursery.

The day came when I put Peter into the pocket of my overcoat and took him away to his new home. I had the greatest confidence in him, being a firm believer in the doctrine of heredity. His father I never knew, but his grandfather bore a great reputation for courage, as was indicated on his tombstone, the inscription on which ran as follows:

Here lies LEAR. Aged about 8 years. A Tom Cat killed in single combat with Tom the Templar whilst defending his hearth and home. England expects every cat to do his duty.

His mother Cordelia was of an affectionate nature, caring little for the chase, indifferent to birds (except sparrows), temperate in the matter of fish, timid of dogs, a kind mother, and had never been known to scratch a child. I believed then that there was every possibility of Peter's inheriting the admirable qualities of his relatives. The world into which he was introduced contained a large assortment of curios which I had bought in many a salesroom, such as bits of old oak, bits of armor, bits of china, bits of tapestry, and innumerable odds and ends which had taken my fancy.

Picture, then, Peter drinking his milk from a Crown Derby dish which I had placed in a corner between the toes of a gentleman skeleton whom Time had stained a tobacco brown. The Crown Derby dish and the skeleton were, like the rest of my furniture, "bargains." At this period of his life Peter resembled a series of irregular circles, such as a geometrician might have made in an absent moment: two round eyes, one round head, and one round body.

I regarded him much as a young mother would her first baby, for he was my first pet. I watched him lest he should get into danger; I conversed with him in a strange jargon, which I called cats' language; I played with him constantly, and introduced him to a black hole behind the skeleton's left heel, which was supposed to be the home of mice. He kept a close watch on the black hole, and one day, which is never to be forgotten, he caught his first mouse.

It was a very little one, but it clung to Peter's nose and made it bleed. Regardless of the pain, Peter marched up to me, tail in air, and laid the half-dead mouse at my feet, with a look in his eyes which said plainly enough, "Shades of Caesar! I claim a Triumph, master."

He returned to the black hole again, and mewed piteously for more. Peter was very green, as you will understand, but he soon discovered that mewing kept the mice away, and having taken the lesson to heart, preserved silence for the future. The mouse-hunts occupied but a small portion of Peter's time.

He was full of queer pranks, which youth and high spirits suggested to him. He took a delight in tumbling down the stairs; he hid himself in the mouth of a lion whose head was one of my chief treasures; he tilted against a dragon candlestick like a young St. George; he burnt his budding whiskers in an attempt to discover the source of the flame in the wick of the candle.

He became, too, a great connoisseur of vases, ornaments, and pictures, sitting before them and examining them for an hour at a time. He was also very much given to voyages of discovery, dark continents having a peculiar fascination for him. Even the lion's mouth had no terror for him. I once produced him from the interior of a brand-new top hat like a conjurer an omelette. Again, we were very much surprised at breakfast one morning to see Peter walk out of a rabbit-pie in which he had secreted himself.

I used to let my canary fly about the room, and Peter chased him. The canary flew to an old helmet on a shelf, and thus baffled Peter. The canary seemed to know this, for when Peter was in the room he always flew to the helmet and sang in peace. If he perched elsewhere there was a chase. The linnet's cage I placed on the windowsill in sunny weather, and Peter took great interest in him. He could not see the musician, but he heard the music, and tried every means he knew to discover its source.

At last he peeped through a little hole at the back of the cage, and when he saw the bird he was quite satisfied, and made no attempt to disturb it.

In the matter of eating and drinking Peter was inclined to vegetarianism, being fond of beet-root and cabbage, but he soon took to carnal habits, always liking his food to be divided into three portions, consisting of greens, potatoes, and meat. In addition to such food as we gave him he by no means despised any delicacies he could discover on his own account.

For instance he cleaned out a pot of glycerine. Having tilted the lid up, he pulled out the pins from a pincushion, but was saved in time; he was curious about a powder-box, and came mewing downstairs a Peter in white; he did not despise the birds out of a hat; he lost his temper when he saw his rival in the looking-glass, and was beside himself with rage when the glass swung round and he saw only a plain board.

His most curious experience was his first glimpse of the moon, which he saw from our bit of back garden. He was rooted to the ground with wonder at the amazing sight, and we called him in vain. The only reply was a melancholy, love-stricken mew which went to my heart.

So Peter rejoiced in the days of his youth, and there was no end to his frolics. But do not think for a moment that his education was neglected, especially in the invaluable matters of manners and deportment, both of which are so essential to advancement in life. I taught him to sit at table; to enter a room with grace, and to leave it with dignity.

Indeed, I spared no trouble, and Peter became as rigorous as a Chesterfield in the proper observance of all such matters. I can give you no better example of Peter's extensive knowledge of what was right and wrong in the ceremonial side of life than by telling you that when he felt an irrepressible sneeze forming he trotted out of the room and sneezed outside.

When Peter played, too, he played gently, and did not disturb his elders by obtrusive attentions. He never required to be told twice to do a thing. Once was enough for Peter. Then again in the matter of breakages he was as virtuous a kitten as ever lived. I had thirty precious blue china vases on my sideboard, and through this fragile maze Peter always wound in and out without moving a vase. His virtues in this respect were well known to my servants, who never accused Peter of breaking the milk-jug, or the cups and saucers, I can assure you. Like the best of human beings, he had his faults, but upon these it would be impertinent to touch more than lightly.

Peter was partial to Fridays, because Fridays were devoted to cleaning up. If you have ever watched someone washing the kitchen floor, you will have noticed that they complete one patch before proceeding with the next, as if they took pride in each patch, regarding it as a picture. It was Peter's delight to sit and watch this domestic operation; and no sooner was the woman's back turned toward a fresh portion of her territory than Peter ran all over the freshly washed patch and impressed it with the seal of his paws, just as an explorer would indicate a great annexation by a series of flags.

That was a mere frolic. It was about this time that I discovered Peter's power as a performing cat. I tied a hare's foot to a piece of string and dangled it before Peter's eyes. I hid the hare's foot in strange places. I flung it downstairs. I threw it upstairs. The hare's foot never failed to attract him. We used to roll on the floor together; we played hide-and-seek together. I noticed that he had a habit of lying on his back with his tail out, his head back, and his paws crossed. By degrees I taught him to assume this attitude at the word of command, so that when I said, "Die, Peter!" Peter turned on his back and became rigid until he received permission to live again.

I also taught him to talk in mews at the word of command. I hear some genial critic exclaim that this cannot be true. I decline to argue with any critic that ever lived, and repeat, fearlessly, and in measured terms, that Peter talked to *me*. Of course he would not drop into conversation with the first person who bade him "good-morning," but I assert again that Peter and I held many conversations together by means of the "mew," used with a score of inflections, often delicately shaded, each of which conveyed its meaning to me.

Peter took to reading, too, quite easily, and sat up with eye-glasses on his nose and a paper between his paws. It was, as you may well imagine, a red-letter day with me when Peter said his prayers for the first time; and I was better pleased when he put his little paws up and lifted his eyes up to the ceiling than with any other of his accomplishments, though they were more appreciated by unthinking friends. It was all very well to place a mouse at my feet and thus play to the gallery, but I felt that Peter's thirst for applause might be his ruin.

When the summer came, and the London pavements began to quake with heat, I determined to fly to the country. As delights are doubled when shared with those we care for, I determined to take Peter with me, so I packed him up in a specially constructed travelling saloon of his own, to wit, a flannel-lined basket containing all the necessary comforts for the journey, such as air-holes and feeding-bottles, and off we started in the highest of spirits.

Peter found a new world opened to him, and the thousand and one beauties of the country fascinated us both. We were the guests of a burly farmer, who lived in a queer old house, half timber and half brick, with low-ceilinged rooms. The general living-room was the capacious kitchen, which looked mighty picturesque. Oak panels ran half-way up to the ceiling; the pots and pans were ranged neatly in an open cupboard, pleasantly suggestive of good fare and plenty of it. There were flowers in red pots in the windows, and my bedroom was a picture of coolness and cleanliness.

Amid these pleasant surroundings Peter soon made himself very happy, and became a great friend of a cat called Jack, who took him under his charge and showed him the ways of the country. Jack was a favorite on the farm. He was certainly given to roving, and did not always "come home to tea." As a mouser he had few equals in the countryside, and one evening when we were telling stories by the fireside the farmer told me that Jack had despatched no less than four hundred mice from one hay-rick.

Jack was a disciple of Isaak Walton. He would crouch on a mossy knoll by the edge of the river, and sometimes was successful in capturing a small trout. The farmer was himself a great fisherman. Jack was a study while the preparations were in progress, and, all intent, would follow close at his master's heels. He would crouch among the rushes whilst the tackle was being adjusted, and anxiously scan the water as the fly drifted along the surface.

He took a keen delight in the sport, and when a fish was negotiating the bait he always purred loudly in anticipation of the feast in prospect. The trout landed and the line re-cast, he would seize his prey, and with stealthy gait slink off with his prize, leaving the old farmer to discover his loss when he might. Together, Jack and Peter roamed over the meadow lands, and the poultry-run was an object of great interest to them.

Together they fought the rats, and together they would lie in wait for the thrush and the blackbird,—I am happy to say in vain. The farmer told me that in his youth Jack once took up his residence in the hollow of an old oak, where he lived on the furred and feathered game. At last he returned home. For hours he wandered about his old home, fearful of discovery, now crouching amongst the flower-beds, and now flying in terror at the sound of the hall clock. At last he ventured into the kitchen, entering by the window and creeping to the kitchen hearth, where he dozed off to the music of the cricket, to be welcomed like another Prodigal Son.

Alas! these delights were cut short, for Peter and I were soon compelled to pack up our traps and proceed to the seaside for professional purposes. Peter was not fond of the sea. When I took him out yachting he was compelled to call for the steward; and one day when exploring the rocks at low water, gazing with rapture at his own charming face as it was reflected in the glassy surface of a deep pool, an inquiring young lobster nipped his tail, and the shore rang with piteous calls for help. Peter has never cared for the sea since then, and so deeply was the disaster impressed upon him that I have known him to reject a choice bit of meat which happened to have a few grains of salt on it. It wafted him back to the ocean, the lobster, and the steward. What powers of imagination were Peter's!

As these memoirs cover a period of seven or eight years, and as space is limited, my readers will kindly consent to take a seat on the convenient carpet of the magician, and be wafted gently to the next station on the road without further question. This is a pleasant byway in suburban

London, greatly frequented by organ-grinders, travelling bears, German bands, and peripatetic white mice. This road is always associated in my mind with the mysterious disappearance of Peter. We had often laughed at the odd old lady who lived two doors higher up, for the anxiety which she displayed when any of her pets were missing. It was our turn now.

This same old lady was very fond of her cats, and had nine of them at the time I am writing of. Every morning when the weather was warm, she and her cats would come out and unconsciously form a succession of tableaux for our amusement. A rug was spread out under the pear tree in the middle of the tiny lawn, a great basket-chair was placed in the middle of this rug, and, these preparations having been made, the old lady, who was very stout, and always wore a monster poke bonnet and a shapeless black silk dress, came out, followed by her nine cats, and took possession of the basket-chair.

A little maid then appeared with a tray, on which were nine little blue china saucers and a jug of milk. The nine little saucers were ranged in a semicircle, and filled with milk, whereupon the old lady cried out, "Who says breakfast, dearies? Who says breakfast—breakfast?" This invitation was immediately responded to by the nine cats. When they had done the old lady cried, "Who says washee, dearies? Washee, washee, washee?"

Whereupon the nine cats sat on their haunches and proceeded to make their toilettes. The requirements of cleanliness having been satisfied, and the nine basins having been taken away by the little maid, the old lady shouted out, "Who says play, dearies? Playee, playee, playee?" holding out her arms, and calling out, "Dido Dums, Dido Dums, come here, deary," when a fine Persian cat jumped on to her right shoulder. "Now Diddles Doddles, Diddles Doddles," and another Persian cat jumped on to her left shoulder. "Tootsy Wootsy," she called once more, and a black cat scrambled up to the crown of the poke bonnet.

And one by one they were summoned by some endearing diminutive, until the nine cats had taken possession of every possible coin of vantage which was offered by the old lady's capacious person. There they sat, waving their tails to and fro, evidently very pleased by their mistress's little attentions. Mrs. Mee was not very popular in the neighborhood, except with the milkman and the butcher. The cats'-meat-man, indeed, who supplied various families in our road, positively hated her—so I gathered from our servant,—and had been heard to say *sotto voce* in unguarded moments, "Ha! ha! I'll be revenged."

It was not unnatural, as the cats were fed on mutton cutlets and fresh milk, and cats' meat was at a discount. About three weeks before Peter disappeared, Mrs. Mee, in the short space of three or four days, had lost no less than five cats by a violent death, and five little graves had been dug, marked by five little tombstones, and the five dead cats had been laid in their last resting-places by the hands of the old lady herself.

A funeral is not generally amusing, but I could not restrain a smile when I saw my eccentric old neighbor follow the remains of her dead pets, which were reverently carried on the tea-tray by the little serving-maid, the old lady herself leading the way, ringing a muffled peal with the dinner-bell, the remaining cats bringing up the rear, pondering over the fate of their dead comrades.

It happened that three of these unfortunate victims had been found on my doorstep. I felt very angry with the old lady, who blamed me for the destruction of her pets, adducing the fact that they were found dying on my doorsteps as proof conclusive. One morning I received an anonymous postcard. Although it bore the Charing Cross postmark, I felt sure it came from the old lady. It read as follows:

"The Assyrian came down like a wolf on the fold."

This was the last straw, for I felt that as regards the old lady's cats I had behaved in a sympathetic and neighborly spirit. I remember this post-card because the same afternoon that it came, Peter disappeared and I began to fear that he had yielded to the temptation of a poisoned pig's foot which had been found in my garden stripped of its flesh.

This was a delicacy which Peter had never been able to resist, though why he should have preferred it to the choice foods that were daily piled upon his plate I cannot for the life of me say. We searched the neighborhood in vain, and at last I determined to advertise. Accordingly I addressed an advertisement to my favorite paper. It ran as follows:

"COME BACK, PETER. Lost, stolen, strayed, or poisoned, a white and black cat called Peter, who left his friends at—on Monday afternoon last. Round his neck he wore a blue ribbon with the word PETER embroidered upon it in red silk. Before retiring to rest he always says his prayers. Dead or alive, a reward of Two Pounds is offered to any one who will restore him to his mourning friends."

I little knew what I was bringing on my devoted head. I had been troubled enough before with dying cats, but now they were all alive. Cats were brought to me in baskets, in boxes, in arms; Manx cats and cats whose tails were missing for other than hereditary reasons; lame cats, blind cats, cats with one eye, and cats who squinted. Never before had I seen such an extraordinary collection. My whole time was now taken up in interviewing callers with cats.

If the boys were bad before, they were a thousand times worse now. Here is one example out of a score. He was a boy known as Pop, who carried the laundry baskets.

"'Ave yer found yer cat yet?"

"No, we haven't."

"Did yer say it was a yaller 'un?"

"No, I didn't."

"What did I say, Hop?" continued Pop, triumphantly turning to a one-legged friend who swept a crossing close by.

"Yer said, Pop, as it was a tortus," murmured the bashful Hop, who had sheltered himself behind Pop.

"A tortus, that's it. A tortus, and Hop and I's found it, sir. We've got it here."

"You're wrong. My cat's *not* a tortoise," I replied.

"Bless you, we know that, guv'nor. Just as if we didn't know Peter! Ah! Peter was a cat as wants a lot of replacin,' Peter does. But me and Hop's got a tortus as is a wunner, guv'nor. A heap better nor Peter. Poor old Peter! he's dead and gone. Be sure of that. This 'ere's a reg'lar bad road. A prize-winner, warn't 'e, Hoppy?" They held up the prize-winner, who was *not* a tortoise, and was mangy.

"Look here, my boys, you can take her away. Now, be off. Quick march!"

"Yer don't want it, guv'nor. Jest think agin. Why, 'ow will you get along without a cat? The mice is 'orrible in this 'ere road. Come, guv'nor, I'll tell you what I'll do. You shall 'ave a bargain," said Pop.

I insisted that the tortoise prize-winner should be taken away, and the next day I stopped the advertisement and resigned myself to despair. A week after Peter had disappeared I heard the voice of my friend Pop at the door. "I say, mister, I've some noose. Come along o' me. I think I've found 'im. Real. A blue ribbon round 'is neck and says 'is prayers. Put on yer 'at and foller, foller, foller me." Mr. Pop led the way along the road, and turned off to the right, and we walked up another road until we reached a large house which had been unoccupied for many months.

The drains were up, and two or three workmen were busy. Pop at once introduced me as "the gent as was lookin' for his cat." "Have you seen a cat with a blue ribbon round his neck?" I asked them, very dubious as to the honesty of Pop's intention. "Well, sich a cat *as* bin 'ere for some days," replied the workman to whom I had spoken. "He used to come when we were gettin' our bit of dinner. But we never know'd but wot it came from next door. You go upstairs to the first-floor front, and you'll see a sight."

On the top of the stairs was Peter, who knew me at once, and began to purr and rub himself against my legs in a most affectionate manner, as if to appease any outburst of wrath on my part. I felt too pleased to be angry, and followed Peter into the empty room, which was littered with paper and rubbish, and the remains of forty or fifty mice lay strewn about the floor.

Peter looked up to me as if to say: "Not a bad bag—eh, master?" In the corner of the room was a bit of sacking which Peter had used as a bed. Pop explained to me that he had heard the men talking about the funny cat that came and dined with them every day. This conversation induced him to search the house, with the happy result that Peter was restored to the bosom of his sorrowing family, and Pop gave up the laundry basket, and invested the reward in a small private business of his own.

Peter and I have had many homes in London and in the country. Together we have lived in flats, in hotels, in farm-houses, and in lodgings for single gentlemen. In lodgings for single gentlemen we had many strange experiences which would occupy too much time to relate, and I will therefore touch but lightly upon this period of Peter's career.

Peter, being a gentlemanly cat, never quarrelled with ladies, however hard they might be to please, and let them gird at him as they would. For did not that gracious animal, when Mrs. Nagsby was accusing him of stealing fowls, say—did he not arch his bonny back and purr against Mrs. Nagsby's ankles and endeavor to appease her?

In her softer moods she did sometimes relax, and even allowed Peter to sit by her side as she read the paper. Peter was held responsible for every article that was lost in Mrs. Nagsby's apartments, and the amount of money I paid to that good lady for breakage in the course of six months would have furnished a small cottage. Mrs. Nagsby was a widow, and the late lamented Nagsby had supported her by his performances on the euphonium. This instrument was kept in a case in Mrs. Nagsby's little room, which was on the ground-floor back, and looked on to a series of dingy walls.

Mrs. Nagsby used to polish up the euphonium every Saturday morning with a regularity which nothing prevented. Did it not speak volumes for her affection for the late lamented? On one of these Saturdays it happened that a German band stopped at the front door. Mrs. Nagsby could never resist the seductive power of brass music.

She rushed upstairs to the first-floor front to listen to the performance. Fate ordained it that Mrs. Nagsby should leave the precious euphonium on the floor in her haste to hear the band. Fate ordained it also that Peter should come downstairs at this particular moment and wend his way to Mrs. Nagsby's parlor. Fate also had ordained it that a mouse which lived in a hole behind Mrs. Nagsby's easy-chair should issue at this particular moment for a little bread-crumb expedition.

Mrs. Nagsby was a careful housekeeper, and finding no crumbs about, the mouse roamed into the silent highway presented by the orifice of the euphonium. It was natural enough that Peter should follow the mouse.

Unfortunately, Peter's progress was stopped, the girth of his body being too great to admit him; and my door being open, I at once rushed to the rescue, and found Peter with his head in the depths of the euphonium and making fierce struggles to vacate the position. Mrs. Nagsby came downstairs and entered her parlor just as I succeeded in extracting Peter from the musical instrument.

Fiercely was I reproached for Peter's escapade, and humbly did I make his apologies, little knowing the secret of the plight from which I had rescued him. Having soothed my landlady, she at length took up the euphonium and proceeded to apply her eye to the main orifice to see if Peter had damaged it, handling the euphonium in the manner of a telescope.

I was thinking of the reproaches in prospect, when I was startled by a loud shriek, to which the euphonium imparted a metallic vibration, and Mrs. Nagsby dropped the instrument on to the floor, the good lady herself following it with a thud. A wee mouse scuttled across her face, disappeared behind the easy chair, and doubtless rejoined his anxious family. Mrs. Nagsby recovered after her maid-of-all-work and I had burnt a few sheets of brown paper under her nostrils; but I had great difficulty in making the peace.

In vain I pointed out that the responsibility did not remain with me, or even with Peter. We agreed after some debate that it was the German band, which was never afterwards patronized by Mrs. Nagsby.

I got into further trouble with Mrs. Nagsby owing to a greyhound which I had bought at a sale. I had no character with him, for he had no character. If Mrs. Nagsby had killed him with the meat hatchet I would have held my peace, for never a day passed but King Arthur took his name in vain.

The first night I brought him home Mrs. Nagsby gave me permission as a great favor to chain him to the kitchen table. In the morning two of the table legs had been mangled, and that is our reason why I called him King Arthur, of the Round Table. The next night King Arthur was taken upstairs and attached to the leg of my wash-stand.

I was awakened out of my beauty sleep by a horrible clamor which caused me to think that the house had fallen in. I presently realized that King Arthur had mistaken the water-jug for a dragon. In any case it was smashed to bits, and the noise brought Mrs. Nagsby to my door in anger. I should be sorry to say what King Arthur cost me in hard cash for breakages and legs of mutton. Poor Peter! Thou wast a saint when compared with that fiend on four legs.

The *denouement* came at last, and it arose from King Arthur's fondness for the ladies. There was nothing remarkable in the appearance of the old lady who was Mrs. Nagsby's favorite lodger, who had held the rooms above mine for three years. But the lady had a most beautiful sealskin jacket, trimmed with tails of sable.

King Arthur had unluckily a feminine affection for furs, and I never dared to take him into any of the fashionable thoroughfares, as he had a way of following the ladies, not for their own dear sakes, but for the fur which they might happen to be wearing. Whether they were only tippets or dyed rabbit-skins, it did not matter to King Arthur.

Well, one unfortunate afternoon, I was leading my greyhound home. A few yards in front of us was Mrs. Nagsby's first-floor lady, taking the sun in all the glories of her sealskin jacket and sable tails. To my horror I dropped the chain in taking a match-box out of my pocket, and before I could take any steps to prevent him—*King Arthur was coursing Mrs. Nagsby's first-floor lodger at his highest rate of speed!!!*

King Arthur held on his course and literally took the old lady aback, and began to tear those choice sable tippets asunder. Nor was the base creature content to rest at the sable tippets. Before I reached his victim, his mouth was full of sealskin. Let me pass on, merely saying that King Arthur was shot that night in the mews at the back of Mrs. Nagsby's, a victim to his own indiscretions.

And now I come to the fatal catastrophe which finally drove me and Peter from the shelter of Mrs. Nagsby's roof. That lady had a set of false teeth which she was in the habit of depositing on her dressing-table when she went to bed. I had learned this from Sarah when that damsel was in a confidential mood.

Peter, I think I have told you, slept in my room. One very warm night Mrs. Nagsby left her door open, and her night light was burning as usual. I also slept with my door open, and Peter, being hot like the rest of us, left the room for a stroll, and visited Mrs. Nagsby's apartment.

Presently he came back with Mrs. Nagsby's teeth between his own—at least I suppose so, for I found them on the hearth-rug when I awoke. I was greatly amused, though a little puzzled to know how I could replace them. After some reflection I went down to breakfast, placed the trophy in a saucer, and showed it to Sarah, who screamed and traitorously ran up and informed her mistress. Mrs. Nagsby came down rampant, but of course speechless. I was thankful for this; but the violent woman, after sputtering spasmodically, caught sight of the missing article in the saucer, and, lost to all sense of shame, replaced it in position and poured forth a torrent of the most violent abuse.

Peter and I left.

Four

"Is Cats to be Trusted?"

W. Gordon Stables

"Is cats to be trusted?" was to have been the title of an essay from the pen of poor Artemus Ward. "Is cats to be trusted?" my starling has been taught to repeat, and often does so while running round the cat on the floor, examining her tail, opening up her paws with his beak, and occasionally making determined attempts to open up her nose also, and peep down her throat.

As far as she is concerned, the bird is I think perfectly safe; for although she often pats him with her gloved hand when he gets too insinuating, she never otherwise attempts to molest him. I fear in his essay Artemus meant to have had a few jokes at pussy's expense. My aim is a more serious one. A question like this, which to pussy is a most momentous one, affecting not only her comfort and happiness, but her standing as a social pet and her very existence itself, cannot be treated lightly in a work like the present.

My own opinion is, and always has been, that if cats are properly fed and cared for, they will do anything rather than steal. But not content with giving my own experience, which some might say was exceptional, I have placed pussy in court, as it were, and given her a long, fair, and impartial trial, summoning evidence *pro* and *con* from every part of Great Britain and Ireland.

The trial has lasted for months, and the Tichborne Case, as a Yankee would say, isn't a circumstance to it in regard to the number of witnesses examined. The judgment has been overwhelmingly in pussy's favour, and the verdict of the jury as follows:—

"*Cats are not as a rule thieves, but quite the reverse.*"

In every case investigated, where the theft was proved, it turned out that the cat was either starved, or illtreated, or spoiled. Moreover, the witnesses for the prosecution—in the minority—were, to use a homely phrase, a foggy lot, rude and illiterate, people with no definite ideas about their "h's," whose capitals were sown broadcast, who wrote "i Know," and spelt cat with a "k"; while those for the defence were in every way the reverse, both socially and orthographically; people with crests and monograms, who wrote on one side of the paper only, and all letters prepaid.

So Miss Puss I think may stand down: she leaves the court without a stain upon her character.

Now, while boldly asserting that cats are as a rule honest, I do not mean to say that all are so. There are rogues among cats as well as among men; but just as we find that the law often makes men thieves, so likewise will cats become thieves if badly treated. What can be more disgraceful than the habit that some people have of systematically starving their cats, under the mistaken notion that they will thus become better mousers; or the custom of many of putting their cats out all night, no matter how wet or cold the night should be. Such treatment of pussy is greatly to be condemned, and only tends to foster habits of uncleanliness, of thieving, and of prowling. By regular feeding, good housing, occasional judicious correction—when puss is found tripping—and kindness, you may make almost any cat honest.

Pussy does not soon forget having been corrected for a fault.

Black Tom, mentioned in a former chapter, never went back to Dan's hen-house again.

A Tom-cat, called Bruce, lived some years ago, at a farm-house near Dundee. This cat—honest in every other way—could never resist the temptation to steal the cream. All efforts to cure him of this habit were resorted to in vain. But one day, Bruce, much to his own satisfaction found himself shut up in the milk-house.

When all was quiet, Bruce came from his corner and had a look round. What a grand and imposing array of basins of milk and tubs-full of cream! One of the latter stood on a table beneath the window, the edge of the tub being on a level with the sill. It was the largest tub in the room; and blessing his luck, up jumped Bruce and began to lick.

It was so delicious, and Bruce closed his eyes to get the full flavour of it. Just then, however, some noise outside startled him,—he knew he was sinning, and was consequently nervous,—and in turning round, he missed his feet, and fell heels over head into the tub. Although half-choked, so soon as he came up, Bruce struck out boldly for the shore, but the sides of the vessel were too slippery even for a cat to hold on to; besides, the weight of the cream clogged his movements.

He would fain not have screamed, but death stared him in the face, and the idea of dying in a tub of milk, as he had seen mice die, was awful; so he opened his mouth and gave vent to a smothered yell. That yell, loud-resounding through the house, brought "ben" the good-wife, and Bruce's life was saved at the expense of about three pints of cream; but never more did that cat go near the milk-house. He was a reformed cat from that day; a burning and a shining light to all the cats in the country-side.

I know a cat—a Tom, as usual—who always sits on his master's counter, surrounded by provisions of all sorts, but he was never known to steal. This cat has a penchant for pickled herrings; and although he might easily help himself by day or night, he always prefers asking his master for one.

This he accomplishes in the usual cat fashion, by running towards the barrel and mewing up in his master's face; and of course this appeal is never made in vain.

Cats are remarkably fond of fish. The other day, a bonnie fishwife was standing on the pavement with her creel on her back. Suddenly she was heard to scream aloud. "For the love o' the Lord, sir," she cried to a bystander, "tell me what's that on my back."

The party addressed looked about, just in time to see a pussy disappearing round a corner, with a large fish in its mouth. That was what the newspapers would call an impudent theft, and it was certainly a clever one.

If not properly trained and cared for, pussy comes to look upon stealing as a virtue; and no wonder, for she must think it hard to starve in the midst of plenty, and in her master's house. Besides, there is always two ways of viewing a matter.

Out on the coast of Africa, I have often gone on shore—for the fun of the thing—with a party of other officers, to assist in replenishing our larder by the addition of a few fat fowls, a sucking grunter, or a kid of the goats. I rather think we stole them; but we called these little trips, "cutting-out expeditions"; still we swore "*pon honour*," and wore our swords none the less clankingly on a Sunday morning; nor would it have been safe for any one to have hinted that we were dishonest.

Just so with poor pussy. She is often tempted by hunger to make a little reprisal. It is vulgar to accuse her of stealing the steak, nailing a fish, or boning a cold chicken, "cutting-out," is the proper term. It is a feline virtue, from the path of which she must be seduced in early kitten-hood, and by good treatment. But poor pussy is often made the scape-goat for the sins of others.

"Mary, bring up those cold pigeons."

"O ma'am! how *ever* shall I tell you? That thief of a cat—"

"The cat must be drowned," says her mistress.

"Oh, no, ma'am! Poor thing! no, ma'am."

It wouldn't exactly suit Mary's book to have pussy drowned. It would seriously interfere with those nice little suppers she is in the habit of having with Matilda Jane.

"Sarah, we'll have the remains of that cold lamb for supper."

"Oh! dear me, ma'am; I forgot to tell you, the cat has eaten every bit of it. Can open the pantry-door, just like you or I, ma'am."

I should think it could; the cat in this case being an enormous blue Tom tabby, with a stripe round one forearm, and a belt about his waist, and X 99 on the collar of his coat.

The following is the story of a real feline Jack Sheppard, I have no excuse to offer for this cat; I can only say that if he was a thief, he was a *swell at it*.

In a sweet little village not far from the famous old town of bonnie Dundee, lived, and I believe still lives, Peter McFarlane, a shoemaker, and his wife Tibbie; two as decent old bodies as you would see in all broad Scotland. They were honest and industrious, and, as a rule, agreed, or as the folks say, they both "said one way," except when Peter took a dram, when, it must be confessed, the ashes did at times find their way up the chimney along with the smoke. They had no family but one,—a cat. A fine gentlemanly fellow he was too; dressed in the blackest of fur, and faultless to a degree, barring that he was the biggest thief ever known in the village, or whole country-side.

Everyone complained of Tom; and, as he got older, his delinquencies were ever on the increase. Allowing thieving to be a virtue among cats of his class, Tom was a saint, and ripe for glory long ago. The butcher, do what he liked, could not save his kidneys,—it was remarkable that Tom never touched the sausages,—he was always content with kidneys, although if none were to be had, to pussy's honour be it said, he did not despise a lump of steak or even a nice lamb chop.

Tom was a regular customer at the fish-monger's; his weakness here being for Loch Fyne herrings,—they were handy; but he delighted also in the centre cut of a salmon, and in half-pound sea-trout. It has even been said that Tom did not share his custom equally among the shop-keepers, spending too much of his time at the fish-monger's counter; but, as his biographer, I must defend his name from any such allegation. Although it must be admitted he never paid ready-money, still he was never too proud to carry away his purchase.

Tom used to enter the poor people's houses about dinner-time, watch his chance, and purloin the meat from under their very noses. Once he lifted the lid from a broth-pot, and decamped with the boiling chicken. This cat was never known to drink water when he could find a milk-pan; nor milk, either, if the cream-jug was at all handy. He was even accused of having sucked the cows; and when hard pressed with hunger, he did not despise a piece of cheese or a tallow candle from the grocers round the corner. He never troubled himself catching mice,—chickens came handier; and tame pigeons he found were more satisfying than sparrows. Tom could break in or out of any place, climb anything, and jump—the neighbours all said—"the d——l's height"; I don't know how tall that gentleman is at Dundee, but he must be over twenty feet, for Tom could do that easily, and alight on his pumps. At long-last the cat became so notorious, and the outcry against him so loud and universal, that the shoemaker and Tibbie, yielding to the entreaties of the villagers, resolved to have him drowned.

On a cold winter's night, then, honest Peter and three of the neighbours might have been seen—had there been light enough to see them—trudging along towards the pier, with the unhappy but virtuous Tom in a sack. Arrived at the place of execution, a consultation was held as to how the job should be done.

There wasn't a stone to be had, and Peter said he wasn't going to lose his sack; it was bad enough to lose the cat; so it was resolved to take Tom out and swing him clear off into the water. More easily said than done. Tom was no sooner out of the bag, than by a successful application of tooth and nail, he wriggled himself free, and in a moment more was lost in the darkness. Peter scratched his head, the neighbours scratched their three heads, and they all felt funny and foolish. They determined however not to make laughing-stocks of themselves, so they returned to Peter's house with the joyful intelligence, that Tom was a cat of the past.

Here were the fishwife and the milkwife, and the grocer and his wife, and the butcher—who hadn't a wife, all assembled to hear the good news; and it was unanimously resolved to celebrate the event by making a night of it; and, although the people of Dundee and round-about are generally glad of any excuse to make a night of it, still it must be admitted that the present occasion urgently called for "cakes and whuskey."

So the fishwife brought salmon, the milkwife brought milk, the butcher brought steak, and the grocer whiskey galore; Tibbie with her best new mutch did the cooking, and they all sat down to eat and to drink and be merry. No Indian villagers, just released from the dominion of a man-eating tiger, could have felt jollier than did those good folks at the thoughts of thieving Tom's demise.

"May the deil gang wi' him," was one of the toasts to Tom's memory.

"And a' the ill-weather," was another.

"If there be," said the fishwife, "an ill-place for the souls o' cats, that black beast 'll hae a hot neuk in't."

"Ay, but," said the grocer,—a godly man and an elder of the Free Church,—"speak nae ill o' the dead, Eppie, but pass the whuskey, and I'll gie ye a bit sang." He sung the death of Heather Jock, which was by no means inappropriate.

"And so the nicht drave on wi' sangs and clatter," and the fingers of old Peter's eight-day clock were creeping slowly toward "the wee short hour ayont the twal," when,—

"Well, neighbours," says Peter, the hypocrite, "we're a' glad the cat has gane we a' his weight o' crime on his sinfu' shou'ders. Let us eat that last pound o' steak, finish the bottle, and gang to bed."

"There is many a slip 'twixt the cup and the lip"; and scarcely had Peter done speaking, when the door opened, apparently of its own accord. The cold night-wind blew in with a ghostly sough, and the candles were extinguished. But lo! on the table, in their very midst, and dimly seen by the smouldering firelight, stood Tom himself, with back erect and gleaming eyes. Never was such kicking and screaming heard anywhere. The fishwife fainted, and the milkwife fainted, and the godly grocer and his wife fainted, and the butcher—who hadn't a wife at all, fell down on top of the others, for company's sake. But Peter and the three guilty neighbours stood in a corner—dumb. When order was at length restored, and the candles re-lit, the old shoemaker told his true version of the story, and was very properly forgiven.

But where was Tom? Tom was gone, and *so was the beef steak*! And from that day to this, never again was Tom heard of in that sweet little village near bonnie Dundee.

That cat *was* a thief.

The Case for Cats

Charles H. Ross

"I DO NOT LOVE A CAT," SAYS A POPULAR AUTHOR, OFTEN QUOTED; "HIS disposition is mean and suspicious. A friendship of years is canceled in a moment by an accidental tread on the tail. He spits, twirls his tail of malignity, and shuns you, turning back as he goes off a staring vindictive face full of horrid oaths and unforgiveness, seeming to say, "Perdition catch you! I hate you for ever."

But the Dog is my delight. Tread on his tail, he expresses for a moment the uneasiness of his feelings, but in a moment the complaint is ended: he runs round you, jumps up against you, seems to declare his sorrow for complaining, as it was not intentionally done,—nay, to make himself the aggressor, and begs, by whinings and lickings, that the master will think of it no more.

No sentiments could be more popular with some gentlemen. In the same way there are those who would like to beat their wives, and for them to come and kiss the hand that struck them in all humility. It is not only when hurt by accident that the dog comes whining round its master.

The lashed hound crawls back and licks the boot that kicked him, and so makes friends again. Pussy will not do that though. If you want to be friendly with a cat on Tuesday, you must not kick him on Monday. You must not fondle him one moment and illtreat him the next, or he will be shy of your advances. This really human way of behaving makes Pussy unpopular.

FIVE

I am afraid that if it were to occur to one of our legislators to tax the Cats, the feline slaughter would be fearful. Everyone is fond of dogs, and yet Mr. Edmund Yates, travelling by water to Greenwich last June, said that the journey was pleasingly diversified by practical and nasal demonstrations of the efficient working of the Dog-tax.

"No fewer than 292 bodies of departed canines, in various stages of decomposition, were floating off Greenwich during the space of seven days in the previous month, seventy-eight of which were found jammed in the chains and landing-stages of the 'Dreadnought' hospital ship, thereby enhancing the salubrity of that celebrated hothouse for sick seamen." And I cannot venture to repeat the incredible stories of the numbers said to have been taken from the Regent's Canal.

There are some persons who profess to have a great repugnance to Cats. King Henry III. of France, a poor, weak, dissipated creature, was one of these. According to Conrad Gesner, men have been known to lose their strength, perspire violently, and even faint at the sight of a cat. Others are said to have gone even further than this, for some have fainted at a cat's picture, or when they have been in a room where such a picture was concealed, or when the picture was as far off as the next room. It was supposed that this sensitiveness might be cured by medicine. Let us hope that these gentlemen were all properly physicked. I myself have often heard men express similar sentiments of aversion to the feline race; and sometimes young ladies have done so in my hearing. In both cases I have little doubt but that the weakness is easily overcome. As for a hidden and unheard Cat's presence affecting a person's nerves, I beg to state my conviction that such a story is utterly ridiculous; and I was vastly entertained by the following narrative, written by a lady for a Magazine for Boys, and given as a truth. Such a valuable fact in natural history should not be allowed to perish; she calls it, A TALE OF MY GRANDMOTHER.

My maternal grandmother had so strong an aversion to Cats that it seemed to endow her with an additional sense. You may, perhaps, have heard people use the phrase, that they were "frightened out of their seven senses," without troubling yourselves to wonder how they came to have more than *five*. But the Druids of old used to include sympathy and antipathy in the number, a belief which has, no doubt, left its trace in the

44

above popular and otherwise unmeaning expression; and this extra sense of antipathy my grandmother certainly exhibited as regarding Cats.

When she was a young and pretty little bride, dinner parties and routs, as is usual on such occasions, were given in her honour. In those days, now about eighty years ago, people usually dined early in the afternoon, and you may imagine somewhere in Yorkshire, a large company assembled for a grand dinner by daylight. With all due decorum and old-fashioned stately politeness, the ladies in rustling silks, stately hoops, and nodding plumes, are led to their seats by their respective cavaliers, in bright coloured coats with large gilt buttons.

With dignified bows and profound curtsies, they take their places, the bride, of course, at her host's right hand. The bustle subsides, the servants remove the covers, the carving-knives are brandished by experienced hands, and the host having made the first incision in a goodly sirloin or haunch, turns to enquire how his fair guest wishes to be helped.

To his surprise, he beholds her pretty face flushed and uneasy, while she lifts the snowy damask and looks beneath the table.

"What is the matter, my dear madam? Have you lost something?"

"No, sir, nothing, thank you;—it is the *Cat*," replied the timid bride, with a slight shudder, as she pronounced the word.

"The Cat?" echoed the gentleman, with a puzzled smile; "but, my dear Mrs. H——, we have no Cat!"

"Indeed! that is very odd, for there is certainly a Cat in the room."

"Did you see it then?"

"No, sir, no: I did not *see* it, but I *know* it is in the room."

"Do you fancy you heard one then?"

"No, sir."

"What is the matter, my dear?" now enquires the lady of the house, from the end of the long table; "the dinner will be quite cold while you are talking to your fair neighbour so busily."

"Mrs. H——says there is a Cat in the room, my love; but we have no Cat, have we?"

"No, certainly!" replied the lady tartly. "Do carve the haunch, Mr.——."

The footman held the plate nearer, a due portion of the savoury meat was placed upon it.

"To Mrs. H——," said the host, and turned to look again at his fair neighbour; but her uneasiness and confusion were greater than ever. Her brow was crimson—every eye was turned towards her, and she looked ready to cry.

"I will leave the room, if you will allow me, sir, for I *know* that there is a Cat in the room."

"But, my dear madam——"

"I am quite sure there is, sir; I *feel* it—I would rather go."

"John, Thomas, Joseph, *can* there be a Cat in the room?" demanded the embarrassed host of the servants.

"Quite impossible, sir;—have not seen such a hanimal about the place since I comed, any way."

"Well, look under the table, at any rate; the lady says she *feels* it; look in every corner of the room, and let us try to convince her."

"My dear, my dear!" remonstrated the annoyed bridegroom from a distant part of the table; "what trouble you are giving."

"Indeed, I would rather leave the room," said the little bride, slipping from her chair. But, meanwhile, the servants ostentatiously bustled in their unwilling search for what they believed to be a phantom fancy of the young lady's brain; when, lo! one of the footmen took hold of a half-closed window-shutter, and from the aperture behind out sprang a large cat into the midst of the astonished circle, eliciting cries and exclamations from others than the finely organised bride, who clasped her hands rigidly, and gasped with pallid lips.

Such facts as this are curious, certainly, and remain a puzzle to philosophers.

This habit of hiding itself in secret places is one of the most unpleasant characteristics of the Cat. I know many instances of it—especially of a night alarm when we were children, ending in a strange cat being found in a clothes bag.

Here, indeed, we have truth several degrees stranger than fiction; but this is not the only wonderful story the authoress has to tell. I will give you some others very slightly abridged.

"A year or two ago, a man in the south of Ireland severely chastised his cat for some misdemeanour, immediately after which the animal stole away, and was seen no more.

"A few days subsequently, as this man was starting to go from home, the Cat met and stood before him in a narrow path, with rather a wicked aspect. Its owner slashed his handkerchief at her to frighten her out of the way, but the Cat, undismayed, sprang at the hand, and held it with so ferocious a grip, that it was impossible to make it open its jaws, and the creature's body had actually to be cut from the head, and the jaws afterwards to be severed, before the mangled hand could be extricated. The man died from the injuries."

The jaws of a Cat are comparatively strong, and worked by powerful muscles; it has thirty-four teeth, but they are for the most part very tiny teeth, like pin's points. What, I wonder, were the dimensions of this ferocious animal with the iron jaws; and how many courageous souls were engaged in its destruction. If this story is, however, rather hard to swallow, the next is not less so. Says our authoress:—

"I also know an Irish gentleman, who being an only son without any playmates, was allowed, when he was a child, to have a whole family of Cats sleeping in the bed with him every night.

"One day he had beaten the father of the family for some offence, and when he was asleep at night, the revengeful beast seized him by the throat, and would probably have killed him had not instant help been at hand. "The Cat sprang from the window, and was never more seen." (Probably went away in a flash of blue fire.)

What do you think of these very strange stories? If they surprise you, however, what will you say to this one? "Dr. C——, an Italian gentleman still living in Florence (the initial is just a little unsatisfactory), who knew at least one of the parties, related to the authoress the following singular story. A certain country priest in Tuscany, who lived quite alone with his servants, naturally attached himself, in the want of better society, to a fine he-cat, which sat by his stove in winter, and always ate from his plate.

One day a brother priest was the good man's guest, and, in the rare enjoyment of genial conversation, the Cat was neglected; resenting this, he attempted to help himself from his master's plate, instead of waiting for the special morsels which were usually placed on the margin for his use, and was requited with a sharp rap on the head for the liberty.

This excited the animal's indignation still more, and springing from the table with an angry cry, he darted to the other side of the room. The two priests thought no more of the Cat until the cloth was about to be removed; when the master of the house prepared a plateful of scraps for his forward favourite, and called him by name to come and enjoy his share of the feast. No joyful Cat obeyed the familiar call: his master observed him looking sulkily from the recess of the window, and rose, holding out the plate, and calling to him in a caressing voice.

As he did not approach, however, the old gentleman put the platter aside, saying he might please himself, and sulk instead of dine, if he preferred it; and then resumed his conversation with his friend. A little later the old gentleman showed symptoms of drowsiness, so his visitor begged that he would not be on ceremony with him, but lie down and take the nap which he knew he was accustomed to indulge in after dinner, and he in the meantime would stroll in the garden for an hour. This was agreed to. The host stretched himself on a couch, and threw his handkerchief over his face to protect him from the summer flies, while the guest stepped through a French window which opened on a terrace and shrubbery.

An hour or somewhat more had passed when he returned, and found his friend still recumbent: he did not at first think of disturbing him, but after a few minutes, considering that he had slept very long, he looked more observantly towards the couch, and was struck by the perfect immobility of the figure, and with something peculiar in the position of the head over which the handkerchief lay disordered. Approaching nearer he saw that it was stained with blood, and hastily removing it, saw, to his unutterable horror, that his poor friend's throat was gashed across, and that life was already extinct.

He started back, shocked and dismayed, and for a few moments remained gazing on the dreadful spectacle almost paralysed. Then came the speculation who could have done so cruel a deed? An old man murdered sleeping—a good man, beloved by his parishioners and scarcely known beyond the narrow circle of his rural home. It was his duty to investigate the mystery, so he composed his countenance as well as he was able, and going to the door of the room, called for a servant.

The man who had waited at table presently appeared, rubbing his eyes, for he, too, had been asleep.

"Tell me who has been into this room while I was in the garden."

"Nobody, your reverence; no one ever disturbs the master during his siesta."

He then asked the servant where he had been, and was told in the ante-room. He next enquired whether any person had been in or out of the house, or if he had heard any movement or voice in the room, and also how many fellow-servants the man had. He was told that he had heard no noise or voices, and that he had two fellow-servants—the cook and a little boy. His reverence demanded that they should be brought in, that he might question them.

They came, and were cross-questioned as closely as possible, but they declared that they had not been in that part of the house all day long, and that nobody could possibly get into the house without their knowledge, unless it was through the garden. The priest had been walking all the time in view of the house, and he felt convinced that the murderer could not have passed in or out on that side without his knowledge.

"Listen to me; some person has been into that room since dinner, and your master is cruelly murdered."

"Murdered!" cried the three domestics in tones of terror and amazement; "did your reverence say 'murdered'?"

"He lies where I left him, but his throat is gashed from ear to ear—he is dead. My poor old friend!"

"Dead! the poor master dead, murdered in his own house."

They wrung their hands, tore their hair, and wept aloud.

"Silence! I command you; and consider that every one of us standing here is liable to the suspicion of complicity in this foul deed; so look to it. Giuseppe was asleep."

"But I sleep very lightly, your reverence."

"Come in and see your master," said the priest solemnly.

They crept in, white with fear and stepping noiselessly. They gazed on the shocking spectacle transfixed with horror. Then a cry of "Who can have done it?" burst from all lips.

"Who, indeed?" repeated the cook.

The priest desired Giuseppe to look round the premises, and count the plate, and ascertain if there had been a robbery, or if any one was concealed about the house. The man returned without throwing any new light upon the mystery; but, in his absence, while surveying the room more carefully than he had previously done, the priest's eye met those of the Cat glowing like lurid flames, as he sat crouching in the shade near a curtain. The orbs had a fierce malignant expression, which startled him, and at once recalled to his recollection the angry and sullen demeanour of the creature during dinner.

"Could it possibly be the Cat that killed him?" demanded of the cook the awe-struck priest.

"Who knows?" replied he; "the beast was surly to others, but always seemed to love him fondly; and then the wound seems as though it were made with a weapon."

Six

The Cat

Andrew Barton Paterson

MOST PEOPLE THINK THAT THE CAT IS AN UNINTELLIGENT ANIMAL, fond of ease, and caring little for anything but mice and milk. But a cat has really more character than most human beings, and gets a great deal more satisfaction out of life. Of all the animal kingdom, the cat has the most many-sided character.

He—or she—is an athlete, a musician, an acrobat, a Lothario, a grim fighter, a sport of the first water. All day long the cat loafs about the house, takes things easy, sleeps by the fire, and allows himself to be pestered by the attentions of our womenfolk and annoyed by our children. To pass the time away he sometimes watches a mouse-hole for an hour or two—just to keep himself from dying of ennui; and people get the idea that this sort of thing is all that life holds for the cat. But watch him as the shades of evening fall, and you see the cat as he really is.

When the family sits down to tea, the cat usually puts in an appearance to get his share, and purrs noisily, and rubs himself against the legs of the family; and all the time he is thinking of a fight or a love-affair that is coming off that evening. If there is a guest at table the cat is particularly civil to him, because the guest is likely to have the best of what is going. Sometimes, instead of recognizing this civility with something to eat, the guest stoops down and strokes the cat, and says, "Poor pussy! Poor pussy!"

The cat soon tires of that; he puts up his claw and quietly but firmly rakes the guest in the leg.

"Ow!" says the guest, "the cat stuck his claws into me!" The delighted family remarks, "Isn't it sweet of him? Isn't he intelligent? He wants you to give him something to eat."

The guest dares not do what he would like to do—kick the cat through the window—so, with tears of rage and pain in his eyes, he affects to be very much amused, and sorts out a bit of fish from his plate and hands it down. The cat gingerly receives it, with a look in his eyes that says: "Another time, my friend, you won't be so dull of comprehension," and purrs maliciously as he retires to a safe distance from the guest's boot before eating it. A cat isn't a fool—not by a long way.

When the family has finished tea, and gathers round the fire to enjoy the hours of indigestion, the cat slouches casually out of the room and disappears. Life, true life, now begins for him.

He saunters down his own backyard, springs to the top of the fence with one easy bound, drops lightly down on the other side, trots across the right-of-way to a vacant allotment, and skips to the roof of an empty shed. As he goes, he throws off the effeminacy of civilization; his gait becomes lithe and pantherlike; he looks quickly and keenly from side to side, and moves noiselessly, for he has so many enemies—dogs, cabmen with whips, and small boys with stones.

Arrived on the top of the shed, the cat arches his back, rakes his claws once or twice through the soft bark of the old roof, wheels round and stretches himself a few times; just to see that every muscle is in full working order; then, dropping his head nearly to his paws, he sends across a league of backyards his call to his kindred—a call to love, or war, or sport.

Before long they come, gliding, graceful shadows, approaching circuitously, and halting occasionally to reconnoiter—tortoiseshell, tabby, and black, all domestic cats, but all transformed for the nonce into their natural state. No longer are they the hypocritical, meek creatures who an hour ago were cadging for fish and milk. They are now ruffling, swaggering blades with a Gascon sense of dignity. Their fights are grim and determined, and a cat will be clawed to ribbons before he will yield.

Even young lady cats have this inestimable superiority over human beings, that they can work off jealousy, hatred, and malice in a sprawling, yelling combat on a flat roof. All cats fight, and all keep themselves more or less in training while they are young. Your cat may be the acknowledged lightweight champion of his district—a Griffo of the feline ring!

Just think how much more he gets out of his life than you do out of yours—what a hurricane of fighting and lovemaking his life is—and blush for yourself. You have had one little love affair, and never had a good, all-out fight in your life!

And the sport they have, too! As they get older and retire from the ring, they go in for sport more systematically; the suburban backyards, that are to us but dullness indescribable, are to them hunting-grounds and trysting-places where they may have more gallant adventure than ever had King Arthur's knights or Robin Hood's merry men.

Grimalkin decides to kill a canary in a neighboring verandah.

Consider the fascination of it—the stealthy reconnaissance from the top of the fence; the care to avoid waking the house-dog, the noiseless approach and the hurried dash, and the fierce clawing at the fluttering bird till its mangled body is dragged through the bars of the cage; the exultant retreat with the spoil; the growling over the feast that follows. Not the least entertaining part of it is the demure satisfaction of arriving home in time for breakfast and hearing the house-mistress say: "Tom must be sick; he seems to have no appetite."

It is always leveled as a reproach against cats that they are more fond of their home than of the people in it. Naturally, the cat doesn't like to leave his country, the land where all his friends are, and where he knows every landmark. Exiled in a strange land, he would have to learn a new geography, to exploit another tribe of dogs, to fight and make love to an entirely new nation of cats. Life isn't long enough for that sort of thing.

So, when the family moves, the cat, if allowed, will stay at the old house and attach himself to the new tenants. He will give them the privilege of boarding him while he enjoys life in his own way. He is not going to sacrifice his whole career for the doubtful reward which fidelity to his old master or mistress might bring.

SEVEN

The Greedy Cat

G. W. Dasent

ONCE ON A TIME THERE WAS A MAN WHO HAD A CAT, AND SHE WAS SO awfully big, and such a beast, he couldn't keep her any longer. So she was to go down to the river with a stone round her neck, but before she started she was to have a meal of meat.

So he set before her a bowl of porridge and a little trough of fat. That she crammed into her and ran off and jumped through the window. Outside stood the goodman by the barn door, threshing.

"Good day, goodman," said the cat.

"Good day, pussy," said the goodman.

"Have you had any food to-day?"

"Oh, I've had a little, but I'm fasting," said the cat. "It was only a bowl of porridge and a trough of fat—and, now I think of it, I'll take you too,"

And so she took the goodman and gobbled him up.

When she had done that, she went into the byre, and there sat the goody milking.

"Good day, goody," said the cat.

"Good day, pussy," said the goody. "Are you here, and have you eaten up your food yet?"

"Oh, I've eaten a little to-day, but I'm fasting," said pussy. "It was only a bowl of porridge, and a trough of fat, and the goodman—and, now I think of it, I'll take you too."

And so she took the goody and gobbled her up.

55

"Good day, you cow at the manger," said the cat to Daisy the cow.

"Good day, pussy," said the bell-cow. "Have you had any food to-day?"

"Oh, I've had a little, but I'm fasting," said the cat. "I've only had a bowl of porridge, and a trough of fat, and the goodman, and the goody—and, now I think of it, I'll take you too,"

And so she took the cow and gobbled her up.

Then off she set up into the home-field, and there stood a man picking up leaves.

"Good day, you leaf-picker in the field," said the cat.

"Good day, pussy. Have you had anything to eat to-day?" said the leaf-picker.

"Oh, I've had a little, but I'm fasting," said the cat. "It was only a bowl of porridge, and a trough of fat, and the goodman and the goody, and Daisy the cow—and, now I think of it, I'll take you too."

So she took the leaf-picker and gobbled him up.

Then she came to a heap of stones, and there stood a stoat.

"Good day, Mr. Stoat of Stoneheap," said the cat.

"Good day, Mrs. Pussy. Have you had anything to eat to-day?"

"Oh, I've had a little, but I'm fasting," said the cat. "It was only a bowl of porridge, and a trough of fat, and the goodman, and the goody, and the cow, and the leaf-picker—and, now I think of it, I'll take you too."

So she took the stoat and gobbled him up.

When she had gone a bit farther, she came to a hazel-brake, and there sat a squirrel gathering nuts.

"Good day, Sir Squirrel of the Brake," said the cat.

"Good day, Mrs. Pussy. Have you had anything to eat to-day?"

"Oh, I've had a little, but I'm fasting," said the cat. "It was only a bowl of porridge, and a trough of fat, and the goodman, and the goody, and the cow, and the leaf-picker, and the stoat—and, now I think of it, I'll take you too."

So she took the squirrel and gobbled him up.

When she had gone a little farther, she saw Reynard the Fox, who was prowling about by the woodside.

"Good day, Reynard Slyboots," said the cat.

"Good day, Mrs. Pussy. Have you had anything to eat to-day?"

"Oh, I've had a little, but I'm fasting," said the cat. "It was only a bowl of porridge, and a trough of fat, and the goodman, and the goody, and the cow, and the leaf-picker, and the stoat, and the squirrel—and, now I think of it, I'll take you too."

So she took Reynard and gobbled him up.

When she had gone a while farther, she met Long Ears the Hare.

"Good day, Mr. Hopper the Hare," said the cat.

"Good day, Mrs. Pussy. Have you had anything to eat to-day?"

"Oh, I've had a little, but I'm fasting," said the cat. "It was only a bowl of porridge, and a trough of fat, and the goodman, and the goody, and the cow, and the leaf-picker, and the stoat, and the squirrel, and the fox—and, now I think of it, I'll take you too."

So she took the hare and gobbled him up.

When she had gone a bit farther, she met a wolf.

"Good day, Greedy Greylegs," said the cat.

"Good day, Mrs. Pussy. Have you had anything to eat to-day?"

"Oh, I've had a little, but I'm fasting," said the cat. "It was only a bowl of porridge, and a trough of fat, and the goodman, and the goody, and the cow, and the leaf-picker, and the stoat, and the squirrel, and the fox and the hare—and, now I think of it, I may as well take you too."

She took and gobbled up Greylegs too.

So she went on into the wood, and when she had gone far and farther than far, o'er hill and dale, she met a bear-cub.

"Good day, you bare-breeched Bear," said the cat.

"Good day, Mrs. Pussy," said the bear-cub. "Have you had anything to eat to-day?"

"Oh, I've had a little, but I'm fasting," said the cat. "It was only a bowl of porridge, and a trough of fat, and the goodman, and the goody, and the cow, and the leaf-picker, and the stoat, and the squirrel, and the fox, and the hare, and the wolf—and, now I think of it, I may as well take you too."

And so she took the bear-cub and gobbled him up.

When the cat had gone a bit farther, she met a she-bear, who was tearing away at a stump till the splinters flew, so angry was she at having lost her cub.

"Good day, Mrs. Bruin," said the cat.

"Good day, Mrs. Pussy. "Have ave you had anything to eat to-day?"

"Oh, I've had a little, but I'm fasting," said the cat. "It was only a bowl of porridge, and a trough of fat, and the goodman, and the goody, and the cow, and the leaf-picker, and the stoat, and the squirrel, and the fox, and the hare, and the wolf, and the bear-cub—and, now I think of it, I'll take you too."

And so she took Mrs. Bruin and gobbled her up too.

When the cat got still farther on, she met Baron Bruin himself.

"Good day, you Baron Bruin," said the cat.

"Good day, Mrs. Pussy," said Bruin. "Have you had anything to eat to-day?"

"Oh, I've had a little, but I'm fasting," said the cat. "It was only a bowl of porridge, and a trough of fat, and the goodman, and the goody, and the cow, and the leaf-picker, and the stoat, and the squirrel, and the fox, and the hare, and the wolf, and the bear-cub, and the she-bear—and, now I think of it, I'll take you too."

And so she took Bruin and ate him up too.

So the cat went on and on, and farther than far, till she came to the abodes of men again, and there she met a bridal train on the road.

"Good day, you bridal train on the king's highway," said she.

"Good day, Mrs. Pussy; have you had anything to eat to-day?"

"Oh, I've had a little, but I'm fasting," said the cat. "It was only a bowl of porridge, and a trough of fat, and the goodman, and the goody, and the cow, and the leaf-picker, and the stoat, and the squirrel, and the fox, and the hare, and the wolf, and the bear-cub, and the she-bear, and the he-bear—and, now I think of it, I'll take you too."

And so she rushed at them, and gobbled up both the bride and bridegroom, and the whole train, with the cook and the fiddler, and the horses, and all.

When she had gone still farther, she came to a church, and there she met a funeral.

"Good day, you funeral train," said she.

"Good day, Mrs. Pussy; have you had anything to eat to-day?"

"Oh, I've had a little, but I'm fasting," said the cat. "It was only a bowl of porridge, and a trough of fat, and the goodman, and the goody, and the cow, and the leaf-picker, and the stoat, and the squirrel, and the fox, and the hare, and the wolf, and the bear-cub, and the she-bear, and the he-bear, and the bride and bridegroom and the whole train—and, now, I don't mind if I take you too."

And so she fell on the funeral train and gobbled up both the body and the bearers.

Now when the cat had got the body in her, she was taken up to the sky, and when she had gone a long, long way, she met the moon.

"Good day, Mrs. Moon," said the cat.

"Good day, Mrs. Pussy. Have you had anything to eat to-day?"

"Oh, I've had a little, but I'm fasting," said the cat. "It was only a bowl of porridge, and a trough of fat, and the goodman, and the goody, and the cow, and the leaf-picker, and the stoat, and the squirrel, and the fox, and the hare, and the wolf, and the bear-cub, and the she-bear, and the he-bear, and the bride and bridegroom and the whole train, and the funeral train—and, now I think of it, I don't mind if I take you too," and so she seized hold of the moon, and gobbled her up, both new and full.

So the cat went a long way still, and then she met the sun.

"Good day, you Sun in heaven."

"Good day, Mrs. Pussy," said the sun. "Have you had anything to eat to-day?"

"Oh, I've had a little, but I'm fasting," said the cat. "It was only a bowl of porridge, and a trough of fat, and the goodman, and the goody, and the cow, and the leaf-picker, and the stoat, and the squirrel, and the fox, and the hare, and the wolf, and the bear-cub, and the she-bear, and the he-bear, and the bride and bridegroom, and the whole train, and the funeral train, and the moon—and, now I think of it, I don't mind if I take you too."

And so she rushed at the sun in heaven and gobbled him up.

So the cat went far and farther than far, till she came to a bridge, and on it she met a big Billygoat.

"Good day, Billygoat on Broad-bridge," said the cat.

"Good day, Mrs. Pussy. Have you had anything to eat to-day?" said the Billygoat.

"Oh, I've had a little, but I'm fasting. "I've only had a bowl of porridge, and a trough of fat, and the goodman, and the goody in the byre, and Daisy the cow at the manger, and the leaf-picker in the home-field, and Mr. Stoat of Stoneheap, and Sir Squirrel of the Brake, and Reynard Slyboots, and Mr. Hopper the Hare, and Greedy Greylegs the Wolf, and Bare-breech the Bear-cub, and Mrs. Bruin, and Baron Bruin, and a Bridal train on the king's highway, and a Funeral at the church, and Lady Moon in the sky, and Lord Sun in heaven, and, now I think of it, I'll take you too."

"That we'll fight about," said the Billygoat, and butted at the cat till she fell right over the bridge into the river, and there she burst.

So they all crept out one after the other, and went about their business, and were just as good as ever, all that the cat had gobbled up.

The Goodman of the house, and the Goody in the byre, and Daisy the cow at the manger, and the Leaf-picker in the home-field, and Mr. Stoat of Stoneheap, and Sir Squirrel of the Brake, and Reynard Slyboots, and Mr. Hopper the Hare, and Greedy Greylegs the Wolf, and Bare-breech the Bear-cub, and Mrs. Bruin, and Baron Bruin, and the Bridal train on the highway, and the Funeral train at the church, and Lady Moon in the Sky, and Lord Sun in heaven.

The Gray Cat

Arthur Christopher Benson

THE KNIGHT SIR JAMES LEIGH LIVED IN A REMOTE VALLEY OF THE Welsh Hills. The manor house, of rough grey stone, with thick walls and mullioned windows, stood on a rising ground; at its foot ran a little river, through great boulders. There were woods all about; but above the woods, the bare green hills ran smoothly up, so high, that in the winter the sun only peeped above the ridge for an hour or two; beyond the house, the valley wound away into the heart of the hills, and at the end a black peak looked over.

The place was very sparsely inhabited; within a close of ancient yew trees stood a little stone church, and a small parsonage smothered in ivy, where an old priest, a cousin of the knight, lived. There were but three farms in the valley, and a rough track led over the hills, little used, except by drovers. At the top of the pass stood a stone cross; and from this point you could see the dark scarred face of the peak to the left, streaked with snow, which did not melt until the summer was far advanced.

Sir James was a silent sad man, in ill-health; he spoke little and bore his troubles bitterly; he was much impoverished, through his own early carelessness, and now so feeble in body that he had small hope of repairing the fortune he had lost. His wife was a wise and loving woman, who, though she found it hard to live happily in so lonely a place with a sickly husband, met her sorrows with a cheerful face, visited her poorer neighbors, and was like a ray of sunlight in the gloomy valley.

They had one son, a boy Roderick, now about fifteen; he was a bright and eager child, who was happy enough, taking his life as he found it—and indeed he had known no other. He was taught a little by the priest; but he had no other schooling, for Sir James would spend no money except when he was obliged to do so. Roderick had no playmates, but he never found the time to be heavy; he was fond of long solitary rambles on the hills, being light of foot and strong.

One day he had gone out to fish in the stream, but it was bright and still, and he could catch nothing; so at last he laid his rod aside in a hollow place beneath the bank, and wandered without any certain aim along the stream. Higher and higher he went, till he found, looking about him, that he was as high as the pass; and then it came into his mind to track the stream to its source.

The Manor was now out of sight, and there was nothing round him but the high green hills, with here and there a sheep feeding. Once a kite came out and circled slowly in the sun, pouncing like a plummet far down the glen; and still Roderick went onward till he saw that he was at the top of the lower hills, and that the only thing higher than him was the peak itself.

He saw now that the stream ran out of a still black pool some way in front of him, that lay under the very shadow of the dark precipice, and was fed by the snows that melted from the face. It was surrounded by rocks that lay piled in confusion.

But the whole place wore an air that was more than desolate; the peak itself had a cruel look, and there was an intent silence, which was only broken, as he gazed, by the sound of rocks falling loudly from the face of the hill and thundering down. The sun warned him that he had gone far enough; and he determined to go homewards, half pleased at his discovery, and half relieved to quit so lonely and grim a spot.

That evening, when he sat with his father and mother at their simple meal, he began to say where he had been. His father heard him with little attention, but when Roderick described the dark pool and the sharp front of the peak, he asked him abruptly how near he had gone to the pool.

Roderick said that he had seen it from a distance, and then Sir James said somewhat sharply that he must not wander so far, and that he was not to go near that place again. Roderick was surprised at this, for his father as a rule interfered little with what he did; but he did not ask his father the reason, for there was something peevish, even harsh, in his tone.

But afterwards, when he went out with his mother, leaving the knight to his own gloomy thoughts, as his will and custom was, his mother said with some urgency, "Roderick, promise me not to go to the pool again; it has an evil name, and is better left to itself."

Roderick was eager to know the story of the place, but his mother would not tell him—only she would have him promise; so he promised, but complained that he would rather have had a reason given for his promise; but his mother, smiling and holding his hand, said that it should be enough for him to please her by doing her will. So Roderick gave his promise again, but was not satisfied.

The next day Roderick was walking in the valley and met one of the farmers, a young good-humored man, who had always been friendly with the boy, and had often been to fish with him; Roderick walked beside him, and told him that he had followed the stream nearly to the pool, when the young farmer, with some seriousness, asked him how near he had been to the water.

Roderick was surprised at the same question that his father had asked him being asked again, and told him that he had but seen it from a hill-top near, adding, "But what is amiss with the place, for my father and mother have made me promise not to go there again?"

The young farmer said nothing for a moment, but seemed to reflect; then he said that there were stories about the place, stories that perhaps it was foolish to believe, but he went on to say that it was better to be on the safe side in all things, and that the place had an evil fame. Then Roderick with childish eagerness asked him what the stories were; and little by little the farmer told him.

He said that something dwelt near or in the pool, it was not known what, that had an enmity to the life of man; that twice since he was a boy a strange thing had happened there; a young shepherd had come by his death at the pool, and was found lying in the water, strangely battered; that, he said, was long before Roderick was born.

Then he added, "You remember old Richard the shepherd?"

"What!" said Roderick, "the old strange man that used to go about muttering to himself, that the boys threw stones at?"

"Yes," said the farmer, "the very same. Well, he was not always so—I remember him a strong and cheerful man; but once when the sheep had got lost in the hills, he would go to the pool because he thought he heard them calling there, though we prayed him not to go. He came back, indeed, bringing no sheep, but an altered and broken man, as he was thenceforth and as you knew him. He had seen something by the pool, he could not say what, and had had a sore strife to get away."

"But what sort of a thing is this?" said Roderick. "Is it a beast or a man, or what?"

"Neither," said the farmer very gravely. "You have heard them read in the church of the evil spirits who dwelt with men, and entered their bodies, and it was sore work even for the Lord Christ to cast them forth. I think it is one of these who has wandered thither; they say he goes not far from the pool, for he cannot abide the cross on the pass, and the church bell gives him pains."

And then the farmer looked at Roderick and said, "You know that they ring the bell all night on the feast of All Souls?"

"Yes," said Roderick, "I have heard it ring."

"Well, on that night alone," said the farmer, "they say that spirits have power upon men, and come abroad to do them hurt; and so they ring the bell, which the spirits cannot listen to—but, young master, it is ill to talk of these things, and Christian men should not even think of them. But as I said, though Satan has but little power over the baptized soul, yet even so, says the priest, he can enter in, if the soul be willing to admit him—and so I say, avoid the place! It may be that these are silly stories to affright folk, but it is ill to touch pitch, and no good can be got by going to the pool, and perhaps evil. And now I think I have told you enough and more than enough."

For Roderick was looking at him pale and with wide open eyes.

Is it strange that from that day the thing that Roderick most desired was to see the pool and what dwelt there? I think not; when hearts are young and before trouble has laid its heavy hand upon them, the hard and cruel things of life, wounds, blows, agonies, terrors, seen only in the mirrors of another spirit, are but as a curious and lively spectacle that feeds the mind with wonder.

The stories to which Roderick had listened in church of men that were haunted by demons seemed to him but as dim and distant experiences on which he would fain look; and the fainter the thought of his promise grew, the stronger grew his desire to see for himself.

In the month of June, when the heart is light, and the smell of the woods is fresh and sharp, Roderick's father and mother were called to go on a journey, to see an ancient friend who was thought to be dying.

The night before they set off Roderick had a strange dream; it seemed to him that he wandered over bare hillsides, and came at last to the pool; the peak rose sharp and clear, and the water was very black and still; while he gazed upon it, it seemed to be troubled; the water began to spin round and round, and bubbling waves rose and broke on the surface. Suddenly a hand emerged from the water, and then a head, bright and unwetted, as though the water had no power to touch it.

Roderick saw that it was a man of youthful aspect and commanding mien; he waded out to the shore and stood for a moment looking round him; then he beckoned Roderick to approach, looking at him kindly, and spoke to him gently, saying that he had waited for him long. They walked together to the crag, and then, in some way that Roderick could not clearly see, the man opened a door into the mountain, and Roderick saw a glimmering passage within. The air came out laden with a rich and heavy fragrance, and there was a faint sound of distant music in the hill. The man turned and looked upon Roderick as though inviting him to enter; but Roderick shook his head and refused, saying that he was not ready; at which the man stepped inside with a smile, half of pity, and the door was shut.

Then Roderick woke with a start and wished that he had been bold enough to go within the door; the light came in serenely through the window, and he heard the faint piping of awakening birds in the dewy trees. He could not sleep, and presently dressed himself and went down.

Soon the household was awake, for the knight was to start betimes; Roderick sat at the early meal with his father and mother. His father was cumbered with the thought of the troublesome journey, and asked many questions about the baggage.

So Roderick said little, but felt his mother's eyes dwell on his face with love. Soon after they rode away. Roderick stood at the door to see them go, and there was so eager and bright a look in his face that his mother was somehow troubled, and almost called him to her to make him repeat his promise, but she feared that he would feel that she did not trust him, and therefore put the thought aside; and so they rode away, his mother waving her hand till they turned the corner by the wood and were out of sight.

Then Roderick began to consider how he would spend the day, with a half-formed design in his mind; when suddenly the temptation to visit the pool came upon him with a force that he had neither strength nor inclination to resist.

So he took his rod, which might seem to be an excuse, and set off rapidly up the stream. He was surprised to find how swiftly the hills rose all about him, and how easily he went. Very soon he came to the top— and there lay the pool in front of him, within the shadow of the peak, that rose behind it very clear and sharp.

He hesitated no longer, but ran lightly down the slope, and next moment he was on the brink of the pool. It lay before him very bright and pure, like a jewel of sapphire, the water being of a deep azure blue; he went all round it. There was no sign of life in the water; at the end nearest the cliff he found a little cool runnel of water that bubbled into the pool from the cliffs. No grass grew round about it, and he could see the stones sloping down and becoming more beautiful the deeper they lay, from the pure tint of the water.

He looked all around him; the moorland quivered in the bright hot air, and he could see far away the hills lie like a map, with blue mountains on the horizon, and small green valleys where men dwelt.

He sat down by the pool, and he had a thought of bathing in the water; but his courage did not rise to this, because he felt still as though something sat in the depths that would not show itself, but might come forth and drag him down; so he sat at last by the pool, and presently he fell asleep.

When he woke he felt somewhat chilly; the shadow of the peak had come round, and fell on the water; the place was still as calm as ever, but looking upon the pool he had an obscure sense as though he were being watched by an unclosing eye. He was thirsting with the heat, so he drew up, in his closed hands, some of the water, which was very cool and sweet; and his drowsiness came upon him, and again he slept.

When next he woke it was with a sense of delicious ease, and the thought that someone who loved him was near him stroking his hand. He looked up, and there close to his side sat very quietly what gave him a shock of surprise. It was a great gray cat, with soft abundant fur, which turned its yellow eyes upon him lazily, purred, and licked his hand.

He caressed the cat, which arched its back and seemed pleased to be with him, and presently leapt upon his knee. The soft warmth of the fur against his hands, and the welcoming caresses of this fearless wild creature pleased him greatly, and he sat long in quiet thought, taking care not to disturb the cat, which, whenever he took his hand away, rubbed against him as though to show that it was pleased at his touch.

But at last he thought that he must go homewards, for the day began to turn to the west. So he put the cat off his knee and began to walk to the top of the pass, as it was quicker to follow the road. For awhile the cat accompanied him, sometimes rubbing against his leg and sometimes walking in front, but looking round from time to time as though to consult his pleasure.

Roderick began to hope that it would accompany him home, but at a certain place the cat stopped, and would go no farther. Roderick lifted it up, but it leapt from him as if displeased, and at last he left it reluctantly. In a moment he came within sight of the cross in the hilltop, so that he saw the road was near. Often he looked round and saw the great cat regarding him as though it were sorry to be left; till at last he could see it no more.

He went home well pleased, his head full of happy thoughts. He had gone half expecting to see some dreadful thing, but had found instead a creature who seemed to love him.

The next day he went again, and this time he found the cat sitting by the pool; as soon as it saw him, it ran to him with a glad and yearning cry, as though it had feared he would not return; to-day it seemed brighter and larger to look upon; and he was pleased that when he returned by the stream it followed him much farther, leaping lightly from stone to stone; but at a certain place, where the valley began to turn eastward, just before the little church came in sight, it sat down as before and took its leave of him.

The third day he began to go up the valley again; but while he rested in a little wood that came down to the stream, to his surprise and delight the cat sprang out of a bush, and seemed more than ever glad of his presence. While he sat fondling it, he heard the sound of footsteps coming up the path; but the cat heard the sound too, and as he rose to see who was coming, the cat sprang lightly into a tree beside him and was hidden from his sight.

It was the old priest on his way to an upland farm, who spoke fondly to Roderick, and asked him of his father and mother. Roderick told him that they were to return that night, and said that it was too bright to remain indoors and yet too bright to fish; the priest agreed, and after a little more talk rose to go, and as his manner was, holding Roderick by the hand, he blessed him, saying that he was growing a tall boy.

When he was gone—and Roderick was ashamed to find how eager he was that the priest should go—he called low to the cat to come back; but the cat came not, and though Roderick searched the tree into which it had sprung, he could find no sign of it, and supposed that it had crept into the wood.

That evening the travelers returned, the knight seeming cheerful, because the vexatious journey was over; but Roderick was half ashamed to think that his mind had been so full of his new plaything that he was hardly glad to see his parents return.

Presently his mother said, "You look very bright and happy, dear child," and Roderick, knowing that he spoke falsely, said that he was glad to see them again; his mother smiled and asked him what he had been doing, and he said that he had wandered on the hills, for it was too bright to fish. His mother looked at him for a moment, and he knew in his heart that she wondered if he had kept his promise, but he thought

of his secret, and looked at her so straight and full that she asked him no
further questions.

The next day he woke feeling sad, because he knew that there would
be no chance to go to the pool. He went to and fro with his mother, for
she had many little duties to attend to.

At last she said, "What are you thinking of, Roderick? You seem to
have little to say to me."

She said it laughingly, and Roderick was ashamed, but said that he
was only thinking; and so bestirred himself to talk. But late in the day he
went a little alone through the wood, and reaching the end of it, looked
up to the hill, kissing his hand toward the pool as a greeting to his friend;
and as he turned, the cat came swiftly and lovingly out of the wood to
him; and he caught it up in his arms and clasped it close, where it lay as
if contented.

Then he thought that he would carry it to the house, and say nothing
as to where he had found it. But hardly had he moved a step when the cat
leapt from him and stood as though angry. And it came into Roderick's
mind that the cat was his secret friend, and that their friendship must
somehow be unknown; but he loved it even the better for that.

In the weeks that followed, the knight was ill and the lady much at
home; from time to time Roderick saw the cat. He could never tell when
it would visit him. It came and went unexpectedly, and always in some
lonely and secret place. But gradually Roderick began to care for nothing
else; his fishing and his riding were forgotten, and he began to plan how
he might be alone, so that the cat would come to him.

He began to lose his spirits and to be dull without it, and to hate the
hours when he could not see it; and all the time it grew or seemed to
grow stronger and sleeker; his mother soon began to notice that he was
not well. He became thin and listless, but his eyes were large and bright;
she asked him more than once if he were well, but he only laughed. Once
indeed he had a fright; he had been asleep under a hawthorn in the glen
on a hot July day, and waking saw the cat close to him, watching him
intently with yellow eyes, as though it were about to spring upon him; but
seeing him awake, it came wheedling and fondling him as often before;
but he could not forget the look in its eyes, and felt grave and sad.

Then he began to be troubled with dreams; the man whom he had seen in his former dream rising from the pool was often with him— sometimes he led him to pleasant places; but one dream he had, that he was bathing in the pool, and caught his foot between the rocks and could not draw it out. Then he heard a rushing sound and looking round saw that a great stream of water was plunging heavily into the pool, so that it rose every moment, and was soon up to his chin.

Then he saw in his dream that the man sat on the edge of the pool and looked at him with a cold smile, but did not offer to help; till at last when the water touched his lips, the man rose and held up his hand; and the stream ceased to run, and presently his foot came out of the rock easily, and he swam ashore but saw no one.

Then it came to the autumn, and the days grew colder and shorter, and he could not be so much abroad. He felt, too, less and less disposed to stir out, and it now began to be on his mind that he had broken his promise to his mother. For a week he saw nothing of the cat, though he longed to see it. But one night, as he went to bed, when he had put out his light, he saw that the moon was very bright; and he opened the window and looked out, and saw the gleaming stream and the grey valley. He was turning away when he heard a light sound of the scratching of claws, and presently the cat sprang upon the windowsill and entered the room.

It was now cold and he got into bed, and the cat sprang upon his pillow. Roderick was so glad that the cat had returned that while he caressed it he talked to it in low tones. Suddenly came a step at the door, and a light beneath it, and his mother with a candle entered the room. She stood for a moment looking, and Roderick became aware that the cat was gone. Then his mother came near, thinking that he was asleep, and he sat up.

She said to him, "Dear child, I heard you speaking, and wondered whether you were in a dream," and she looked at him with an anxious gaze.

And he said, "Was I speaking, mother? I was asleep and must have spoken in a dream."

Then she said, "Roderick, you are not old enough yet to sleep so uneasily—is all well, dear child?"

Roderick, hating to deceive his mother, said, "How should not all be well?"

So she kissed him and went quietly away, but Roderick heard her sighing.

Then it came at last to All Souls' Day. Roderick, going to his bed that night, had a strange dizziness and cried out, and found the room swim round him. Then he got up into his bed, for he thought that he must be ill, and soon fell asleep; and in his sleep he dreamed a dreadful dream.

He thought that he lay on the hills beside the pool; and yet he was out of the body, for he could see himself lying there. The pool was very dark, and a cold wind ruffled the waves. And again the water was troubled, and the man stepped out; but behind him came another man, like a hunchback, very swarthy of face, with long thin arms, that looked both strong and evil.

Then it seemed as if the first man pointed to Roderick where he lay and said, "You can take him hence, for he is mine now, and I have need of him."

Then he added, "Who could have thought it would be so easy?" and then he smiled very bitterly. And the hunchback went toward himself, and he tried to cry out in warning, and straining woke. In the chilly dawn he saw the cat sit in his room, but very different from what it had been. It was gaunt and famished, and the fur was all marred. Its yellow eyes gleamed horribly, and Roderick saw that it hated him, he knew not why. Such fear came upon him that he screamed out, and as he screamed the cat rose as if furious, twitching its tail and opening its mouth. He heard steps without, and screamed again, and his mother came in haste into the room, and the cat was gone in a moment, and Roderick held out his hands to his mother, and she soothed and quieted him, and presently with many sobs he told her all the story.

She did not reproach him, nor say a word of his disobedience, the fear was too urgent upon her. She tried to think for a little that it was the sight of some real creature lingering in a mind that was wrought upon by illness, but those were not the days when men preferred to call the strange afflictions of body and spirit, the sad scars that stain the fair works of God, by reasonable names.

She did not doubt that by some dreadful hap her own child had somehow crept within the circle of darkness, and she only thought of how to help and rescue him; that he was sorry and that he did not wholly consent was her hope.

So she merely kissed and quieted him, and then she told him that she would return anon and he must rest quietly. But he would not let her leave him, so she stood in the door and called a servant softly. Sir James was long abed, for he had been in ill-health that day, and she gave word that someone must be found at once and go to call the priest, saying that Roderick was ill and she was uneasy.

Then she came back to the bed, and holding Roderick's hand she said, that he must try to sleep. Roderick said to her, "Mother, say that you forgive me."

To which she only replied, "Dear child, do I not love you better than all the world? Do not think of me now, only ask help of God."

So she sat with his hand in both of her own, and presently he fell asleep, but she saw that he was troubled in his dreams, for he groaned and cried out often, and now through the window she heard the soft tolling of the bell of the church, and she knew that a contest must be fought out that night over the child.

After a sore passage of misery, and a bitter questioning as to why one so young and innocent should thus be bound with evil bonds, she found strength to leave the matter in the Father's hands, and to pray with an eager hopefulness.

But the time passed heavily and still the priest did not arrive, and the ghostly terror was so sore on the child that she could bear it no longer and awakened him. And he told her in broken words of the terrible things that had oppressed him. Sore fightings and struggles, and a voice in his ear that it was too late, and that he had yielded himself to the evil.

And at last there came a quiet footfall on the stair, and the old priest himself entered the room, looking anxious, yet calm, and seeming to bring a holy peace with him.

Then she bade the priest sit down; and so the two sat by the bedside, with the solitary lamp burning in the chamber; and she would have had Roderick tell the tale, but he covered his face with his hands and could not. So she told the tale herself to the priest, saying, "Correct me, Roderick, if I am wrong"; and once or twice the boy corrected her, and added a few words to make the story plain, and then they sat awhile in silence, while the terrified looks of the mother and her son dwelt on the old priest's strongly lined face; yet they found comfort in the smile with which he met them.

At length he said, "Yes, dear lady and dear Roderick, the case is plain enough—the child has yielded himself to some evil power, but not too far, I think.

And now must we meet the foe with all our might. I will abide here with the boy; and, dear lady, you were better in your own chamber, for we know not what will pass. If there were need I would call you."

Then the lady said, "I will do as you direct me, Father, but I would fain stay."

Then he said, "Nay, but there are things on which a Christian should not look, lest they should daunt his faith—so go, dear lady, and help us with your prayers."

Then she said, "I will be below; and if you beat your foot thrice upon the floor, I will come. Roderick, I shall be close at hand; only be strong, and all shall be well." Then she went softly away.

Then the priest said to Roderick, "And now, dear son, confess your sin and let me shrive you."

So Roderick made confession, and the priest blessed him: but while he blessed him there came the angry crying of a cat from somewhere in the room, so that Roderick shuddered in his bed. Then the priest drew from his robe a little holy book, and with a reverence laid it under Roderick's hand.

And he himself took his book of prayers and said, "Sleep now, dear son, fear not."

So Roderick closed his eyes, and being very weary slept. And the old priest in a low whisper said the blessed psalms. And it came near to midnight; and the place that the priest read was, *Thou shalt not be afraid for any terror by night, nor for the arrow that flieth by day; for the pestilence that walketh in darkness, nor for the sickness that destroyeth in the noonday.*

Suddenly there ran as it were a shiver through his bones, and he knew that the time was come. He looked at Roderick, who slept wearily on his bed, and it seemed to him as though suddenly a small and shadowy thing, like a bird, leapt from the boy's mouth and on to the bed; it was like a wren, only white, with dusky spots upon it; and the priest held his breath, for now he knew that the soul was out of the body, and that unless it could return uninjured into the limbs of the child, nothing could avail the boy.

Then he said quietly in his heart to God that if He so willed He should take the boy's life, if only his soul could be saved.

Then the priest was aware of a strange and horrible thing. There sprang softly on to the bed the form of the great gray cat, very lean and angry, which stood there, as though ready to spring upon the bird, which hopped hither and thither, as though careless of what might be. The priest cast a glance upon the boy, who lay rigid and pale, his eyes shut, and hardly seeming to breathe, as though dead and prepared for burial.

Then the priest signed the cross and said "*In Nomine*"; and as the holy words fell on the air, the cat looked fiercely at the bird, but seemed to shrink into itself; and then it slipped away.

Then the priest's fear was that the bird might stray further outside of his care; and yet he dared not try and wake the boy, for he knew that this was death, if the soul was thrust apart from the body, and if he broke the unseen chain that bound them; so he waited and prayed.

And the bird hopped upon the floor; and then presently the priest saw the cat draw near again, and in a stealthy way; and now the priest himself was feeling weary of the strain, for he seemed to be wrestling in spirit with something that was strong and strongly armed. But he signed the cross again and said faintly "*In Nomine*"; and the cat again withdrew.

Then a dreadful drowsiness fell upon the priest, and he thought that he must sleep. Something heavy, leaden-handed, and powerful seemed to be busy in his brain. Meanwhile the bird hopped upon the windowsill and stood as if preparing its wings for a flight. Then the priest beat with his foot upon the floor, for he could no longer battle.

In a moment the lady glided in, and seemed as though scared to find the scene of so fierce an encounter so still and quiet. She would have spoken, but the priest signed her to be silent, and pointed to the boy and to the bird; and then she partly understood. They stood in silence, but the priest's brain grew more numb, though he was aware of a creeping blackness that seemed to overshadow the bird, in the midst of which glared two bright eyes.

With a sudden effort he signed the cross, and said "*In Nomine*" again, and at the same moment the lady held out her hand; and the priest sank down on the floor; but he saw the bird raise its wings for a flight, and just as the dark thing rose, and, as it were, struck open-mouthed, the bird sailed softly through the air, alighted on the lady's hand, and then with a light flutter of wings on to the bed and to the boy's face, and was seen no more.

At the same moment the bells stopped in the church and left a sweet silence. The black form shrank and slipped aside, and seemed to fall on the ground; and outside there was a shrill and bitter cry which echoed horribly on the air; and the boy opened his eyes, and smiled; and his mother fell on his neck and kissed him.

Then the priest said, "Give God the glory!" and blessed them and was gone so softly that they knew not when he went; for he had other work to do. Then mother and son had great joy together.

But the priest walked swiftly and sternly through the wood, and to the church; and he dipped a vessel in the stoup of holy water, turning his eyes aside, and wrapped it in a veil of linen. Then he took a lantern in his hand, and with a grave and fixed look on his face he walked sadly up the valley, putting one foot before another, like a man who forced himself to go unwilling.

There were strange sounds on the hillside, the crying of sad birds, and the beating of wings, and sometimes a hollow groaning seemed to come down the stream. The priest took no heed, but went on heavily till he reached the stone cross, where the wind whistled dry in the grass. Then he struck off across the moorland. Presently he came to a rise in the ground; and here, though it was dark, he seemed to see a blacker darkness in the air, where the peak lay.

But beneath the peak he saw a strange sight; for the pool shone with a faint white light, that showed the rocks about it. The priest never turned his head, but walked thither, with his head bent, repeating words to himself, but hardly knowing what he said.

He came to the brink, and there he saw a dreadful sight. In the water writhed large and luminous worms, that came sometimes up to the surface, as though to breathe, and sank again. The priest knew well enough that it was a device of Satan's to frighten him. So he delayed not; but setting the lantern down on the ground, he stood. In a moment the lantern was obscured as by the rush of bat-like wings. But the priest took the veil off the vessel; and holding it up in the air, he let the water fall in the pool, saying softly, "Lord, let them be bound!"

But when the holy water touched the lake, there was a strange sight; for the bright worms quivered and fell to the depth of the pool; and a shiver passed over the surface, and the light went out like a flickering lamp. Then there came a foul yelling from the stones; and with a roar like thunder, rocks fell crashing from the face of the peak; and then all was still.

Then the priest sat down and covered his face with his hands, for he was sore spent; but he rose at length, and with grievous pain made his slow way down the valley and reached the parsonage house at last.

Roderick lay long between life and death; and youth and a quiet mind prevailed.

Long years have passed since that day. All those that I have spoken of are dust. But in the window of the old church hangs a picture in glass which shows Christ standing, with one lying at his feet from whom he had cast out a devil; and on a scroll are the words, *DE ABYSSIS · TER-RAE · ITERUM · REDUXISTI · ME*, the which may be written in English, *Yea, and broughtest me from the deep of the earth again.*

NINE

The Home Life of a Holy Cat

Arthur Weigall

ONE SUMMER DURING A HEAT WAVE, WHEN THE TEMPERATURE IN THE shade of my veranda in Luxor was 125 degrees Fahrenheit, I went down to cooler Lower Egypt to pay a visit to an English friend of mine stationed at Zagazig, the native city which stands beside the ruins of ancient Bubastis.

He was about to leave Egypt and asked me whether I would like to have his cat, a dignified, mystical-minded, long-legged, small-headed, green-eyed female, whose orange-yellow hair, marked with grayish black stripes in tabby pattern, was so short that she gave the impression of being naked—an impression, however, which did not in any way detract from her air of virginal chastity.

Her name was Basta, and though recent ancestors had lived wild amongst the ruins, she was so obviously a descendant of holy cats of ancient times, who were incarnations of the goddess Basta, that I thought it only right to accept the offer and take her to Luxor to live with me. To be the expert in charge of Egyptian antiquities and not have an ancient Egyptian cat to give an air of mystery to my headquarters had, indeed, always seemed to me to be somewhat wanting in showmanship on my part.

Thus it came about that, on my departure, I drove off to the railroad station with the usually dignified Basta bumping around and uttering unearthly howls inside a cardboard hatbox, in the side of which I had

77

cut a small round hole for ventilation. The people in the streets and on the station platform seemed to be under the impression that the noises were digestive and that I was in dire need of a doctor; and it was a great relief to my embarrassment when the hot and panting train steamed in Zagazig.

Fortunately, I found myself alone in the compartment, and the hatbox at my side had begun to cause me less anxiety, when suddenly Basta was seized with a sort of religious frenzy. The box rocked about, and presently out through the airhole came a long, snakelike paw which pushed itself outward with such frantic force that the sides of the hole gave way, and out burst the entire sandy, sacred head.

She then began to choke, for the cardboard was pressing tightly around her neck; and to save her from strangulation I was obliged to tear the aperture open, whereupon she wriggled out, leaped in divine frenzy up the side of the carriage and prostrated herself on the network of the baggage-rack, where her hysteria caused her to lose all control of her internal arrangements if and I say modestly that she was overcome with nausea, I shall be telling but a part of the dreadful tale.

The rest of the journey was like a bad dream; but at the Cairo terminus, where I had to change into the night express for Luxor, I got the help of a native policeman who secured a large laundry basket from the sleeping-car department. And after a prolonged struggle, during which the train was shunted into a distant siding, we imprisoned the struggling Basta again.

The perspiring policeman and I then carried the basket at a run along the tracks back to the station in the sweltering heat of the late afternoon, and I just managed to catch my train; but during the second part of my journey Basta traveled in the baggage-van whence, in the hot and silent night, whenever we were at a standstill, her appalling incantations came drifting to my ears.

I opened the basket in an unfurnished spare room in my house, and like a flash Basta was up the bare wall and onto the curtain pole above the window. There she remained all day, in a sort of hypnotic trance; but at sunset the saucer of milk and plate of fish which I had provided for her at last enticed her down, and in the end she reconciled herself to her new surroundings and indicated by her behavior that she was willing to accept my house as her earthly temple.

With Pedro, my pariah dog, there was not the slightest trouble; he had no strong feelings about cats, and she on her part graciously deigned to acknowledge his status—as, I believe, is generally the case in native households. She sometimes condescended to visit my horse and donkey in their stalls; and for Laura, my camel, she quickly developed a real regard, often sleeping for hours in her stable.

I was not worried as to how she would treat the chickens and pigeons, because her former owner in Zagazig had insisted upon her respecting his hen coop and pigeon cote; but I was a little anxious about the ducks, for she had not previously known any, and in ancient times her ancestors used to be trained to hunt wild geese and ducks and were fed with pâté de foie gras, or whatever it was called then, on holy days and anniversaries.

In a corner of the garden I had made a miniature duck pond which was sunk rather deeply in the ground and down to which I had cut a narrow, steeply sloping passage, or gangway. During the day, after the ducks had been up and down this slope several times, the surface used to become wet and slippery, and the ducks, having waddled down the first few inches, were forced to toboggan down the rest of it on their tails, with their two feet sticking out in front of them and their heads well up.

Basta was always fascinated by this slide and by the splash at the bottom and used to sit and watch it for hours, which made me think at first that she would one day spring at one of them; but she never did. Field mice, and water rats down by the Nile, were her only prey; and in connection with the former I may mention a curious occurrence.

One hot night I was sitting smoking my pipe on the veranda when my attention was attracted by two mice which had crept into the patch of brilliant moonlight before my feet and were boldly nibbling some crumbs left over from a cracker thrown to Pedro earlier in the evening. I watched them silently for a while and did not notice that Basta had seen them and was preparing to spring, nor did I observe a large white owl sitting aloft amongst the overhanging roses and also preparing to pounce.

Suddenly, and precisely at the same moment, the owl shot down on the mice from above and Basta leaped at them from beside me. There was a scuffle; fur and feathers flew; I fell out of my chair; and then the owl made off screeching in one direction and the cat dashed away on the other; while the mice, practically clinging to each other, remained for a moment or two too terrified to move.

During the early days of her residence in Luxor, Basta often used to go down to the edge of the Nile to fish with her paw; but she never caught anything, and in the end she got a fright and gave it up. I was sitting by the river watching her tying to catch one of the little shoal of small fish which were sunning themselves in the shallow water when there came swimming into view a twelve- or fourteen-inch fish which I recognized (by its whiskers and the absence of a dorsal fin) as the electric catfish, pretty common in the Nile—a strange creature able to give you an electric shock like hitting your funny bone.

These fish obtain their food in a curious way: they hang around any shoal of small fry engaged in feeding, and then glide quietly into their midst and throw out this electric shock, whereupon the little fellows are all sick to their stomachs, and the big fellow gets their disgorged dinners.

I was just waiting to see this happen with my own eyes—for it had always seemed a bit farfetched—when Basta made a dart at the intruder with her paw and got a shock. She uttered a yowl as though somebody had trodden on her and leaped high in the air; and never again did she put a foot near the water. She was content after that with our daily offering of a fish brought from the market and fried for her like a burnt sacrifice.

Basta had a most unearthly voice, and when she was feeling emotional would let out a wail which at first was like the crying of a phantom baby and then became the tuneless song of a lunatic, and finally developed into the blood-curdling howl of a soul in torment. And when she spat, the percussion was like that of a spring-gun.

There were some wild cats or, rather, domestic cats who, like Basta's own forebears, had taken to a wild life, living in a grove of trees beside the river just beyond my garden wall; and it was generally the proximity of one of these which started her off; but sometimes the outburst was caused by her own unfathomable thoughts as she went her mysterious ways in the darkness of the night.

I think she must have been clairvoyant, for she often seemed to be seeing things not visible to me. Sometimes, perhaps when she was cleaning fish or mouse from her face, she would pause with one foot off the ground and stare in front of her, and then back away with bristling hair or go forward with friendly mewing noises; and sometimes she would leap off a chair or sofa, her tail lashing and her green eyes dilated. But it may have been worms.

Once I saw her standing absolutely rigid and tense on the lawn, staring at the rising moon; and then all of a sudden she did a sort of dance such as cats do sometimes when they are playing with other cats. But there was no other cat and, anyway, Basta never played; she never forgot that she was a holy cat.

Her chaste hauteur was so great that she would not move out of the way when people were walking about, and many a time her demoniacal shriek and perhaps a crash of breaking glass informed the household that somebody had tripped over her. It was astonishing, however, how quickly she recovered her dignity and how well she maintained the pretence that whatever happened to her was at her own celestial wish and was not our doing.

If I called her she would pretend not to hear, but would come a few moments later when it could appear that she had thought of doing so first; and if I lifted her off a chair she would jump back up on it and then descend with dignity as though of her own free will. But in this, of course, she was more like a woman than a divinity.

The Egyptian cat is a domesticated species of the African wildcat, and no doubt its strange behavior and its weird voice were the cause of it being regarded as sacred in ancient times; but, although the old gods and their worship have been forgotten these many centuries, the traditional sanctity of the race has survived.

Modern Egyptians think it unlucky to hurt a cat and, in the native quarters of Cairo and other cities, hundreds of cats are daily fed at the expense of benevolent citizens. They say that they do this because cats are so useful to mankind in killing off mice and other pests; but actually it is an unrecognized survival of the old beliefs.

In the days of the Pharaohs, when a cat died the men of the household shaved off their eyebrows and sat around wailing and rocking themselves to and fro in simulated anguish. The body was embalmed and buried with solemn rites in the local cats' cemetery, or was sent down to Bubastis to rest in the shadow of the temple of their patron goddess.

I myself have dug up hundreds of mummified cats; and once, when I had a couple dozen of the best specimens standing on my veranda waiting to be dispatched to the Cairo Museum, Basta was most excited about it, and walked around sniffing at them all day. They certainly smelled awful.

On my lawn there was a square slab of stone which had once been the top of an altar dedicated to the sun god, but was now used as a sort of low garden table; and sometimes when she had caught a mouse she used to deposit the chewed corpse upon this slab—nobody could think why, unless, as I always told people, she was really making an offering to the sun. It was most mysterious of her; but it led once to a very unfortunate episode.

A famous French antiquarian, who was paying a polite call, was sitting with me beside this sacred stone, drinking afternoon tea and eating fresh dates, when Basta appeared on the scene with a small dead mouse in her mouth, which in her usual way she deposited upon the slab—only on this occasion she laid it on my guest's plate, which was standing on the slab.

We were talking at the moment and did not see her do this and, anyhow, the Frenchman was as blind as a bat; and, of course, as luck would have it, he immediately picked up the wet, mole-colored mouse instead of a ripe brown date, and the thing has almost gone into his mouth before he saw what it was and, with a yell, flung it into the air.

It fell into his upturned sun helmet which was lying on the grass beside him; but he did not see where it had gone and, jumping angrily to his feet in the momentary belief that I had played a schoolboy joke on him, he snatched up his helmet and was in the act of putting it on his head when the mouse tumbled out onto the front of his shirt and slipped down inside his buttoned jacket.

At this he went more or less mad, danced about, shook himself, and finally trod on Basta, who completed his frenzy by uttering a fiendish howl and digging her claws into his leg. The dead mouse, I am glad to say, fell onto the grass during the dance without it passing through his roomy trousers, as I had feared it might; and Basta, recovering her dignity, picked it up and walked off with it.

It is a remarkable fact that, during the five or six years she spent with me, she showed no desire to be anything but a spinster all her life, and when I arranged a marriage for her she displayed such dignified but violent antipathy towards the bridegroom that the match was a failure. In the end, however, she fell in love with one of the wild cats who lived among the trees beyond my wall, and nothing could prevent her from going off to visit him from time to time, generally at dead of night.

He did not care a hoot about her sanctity, and she was feminine enough to enjoy the novelty of being roughly treated. I never actually saw him, for he did not venture into the garden, but I used to hear him knocking her about the outside garden gates; and when she came home, scratched and bitten and muttering something about holy cats, it was plain that she was desperately happy. She licked her wounds, indeed, with deep voluptuous satisfaction.

A dreadful change came over her. She lost her precious dignity and was restless and inclined to be savage; her digestion played embarrassing tricks on her; and once she mortally offended Laura by clawing her nose. There was a new glint in her green eyes as she watched the ducks sliding into the pond; the pigeons interested her for the first time; and for the first time, too, she ate the mice she had caught.

Then she began to disappear for a whole day or night at a time, and once when I went in search of her among the trees outside and found her sharpening her claws on a branch above my head, she put her ears back and hissed at me until I could see halfway down her pink throat. I tried by every method to keep her at home when she came back, but it was all in vain, and at last she left me forever.

Weeks afterwards I caught sight of her once again among the trees, and it was evident that she was soon to become a mother. She gave me a friendly mew this time; but she would not let me touch her; and presently she slipped away into the undergrowth. I never knew what became of her.

TEN

The Cats of Ulthar

H. P. Lovecraft

IT IS SAID THAT IN ULTHAR, WHICH LIES BEYOND THE RIVER SKAI, NO man may kill a cat; and this I can verily believe as I gaze upon him who sitteth purring before the fire. For the cat is cryptic, and close to strange things which men cannot see. He is the soul of antique Aegyptus, and bearer of tales from forgotten cities in Meroe and Ophir. He is the kin of the jungle's lords, and heir to the secrets of hoary and sinister Africa. The Sphinx is his cousin, and he speaks her language; but he is more ancient than the Sphinx, and remembers that which she hath forgotten.

In Ulthar, before ever the burgesses forbade the killing of cats, there dwelt an old cotter and his wife who delighted to trap and slay the cats of their neighbors. Why they did this I know not; save that many hate the voice of the cat in the night, and take it ill that cats should run stealthily about yards and gardens at twilight. But whatever the reason, this old man and woman took pleasure in trapping and slaying every cat which came near to their hovel; and from some of the sounds heard after dark, many villagers fancied that the manner of slaying was exceedingly peculiar. But the villagers did not discuss such things with the old man and his wife; because of the habitual expression on the withered faces of the two, and because their cottage was so small and so darkly hidden under spreading oaks at the back of a neglected yard. In truth, much as the owners of cats hated these odd folk, they feared them more; and instead of berating them as brutal assassins, merely took care that no cherished pet or mouser should stray toward the remote hovel under the dark trees. When through some unavoidable oversight a cat was missed, and sounds heard after dark, the loser would lament impotently; or console himself by thanking Fate that it was not one of his children who had thus vanished. For the people of Ulthar were simple, and knew not whence it is all cats first came.

One day a caravan of strange wanderers from the South entered the narrow, cobbled streets of Ulthar. Dark wanderers they were, and unlike the other roving folk who passed through the village twice every year. In the market-place they told fortunes for silver, and bought gay beads from the merchants. What was the land of these wanderers none could tell; but it was seen that they were given to strange prayers, and that they had painted on the sides of their wagons strange figures with human bodies and the heads of cats, hawks, rams, and lions. And the leader of the caravan wore a headdress with two horns and a curious disk betwixt the horns.

There was in this singular caravan a little boy with no father or mother, but only a tiny black kitten to cherish. The plague had not been kind to him, yet had left him this small furry thing to mitigate his sorrow; and when one is very young, one can find great relief in the lively antics of a black kitten. So the boy whom the dark people called Menes smiled more often than he wept as he sat playing with his graceful kitten on the steps of an oddly painted wagon.

On the third morning of the wanderers' stay in Ulthar, Menes could not find his kitten; and as he sobbed aloud in the market-place certain villagers told him of the old man and his wife, and of sounds heard in the night. And when he heard these things his sobbing gave place to meditation, and finally to prayer. He stretched out his arms toward the sun and prayed in a tongue no villager could understand; though indeed the villagers did not try very hard to understand, since their attention was mostly taken up by the sky and the odd shapes the clouds were assuming. It was very peculiar, but as the little boy uttered his petition there seemed to form overhead the shadowy, nebulous figures of exotic things; of hybrid creatures crowned with horn-flanked disks. Nature is full of such illusions to impress the imaginative.

That night the wanderers left Ulthar, and were never seen again. And the householders were troubled when they noticed that in all the village there was not a cat to be found. From each hearth the familiar cat had vanished; cats large and small, black, grey, striped, yellow, and white. Old Kranon, the burgomaster, swore that the dark folk had taken the cats away in revenge for the killing of Menes's kitten; and cursed the caravan and the little boy. But Nith, the lean notary, declared that the old cotter and his wife were more likely persons to suspect; for their hatred of cats was notorious and increasingly bold. Still, no one durst complain to the sinister couple; even when little Atal, the innkeeper's son, vowed that he had at twilight seen all the cats of Ulthar in that accursed yard under the trees, pacing very slowly and solemnly in a circle around the cottage, two abreast, as if in performance of some unheard-of rite of beasts. The villagers did not know how much to believe from so small a boy; and though they feared that the evil pair had charmed the cats to their death, they preferred not to chide the old cotter till they met him outside his dark and repellent yard.

So Ulthar went to sleep in vain anger, and when the people awakened at dawn—behold! every cat was back at his accustomed hearth! Large and small, black, grey, striped, yellow, and white, none was missing. Very sleek and fat did the cats appear, and sonorous with purring content. The citizens talked with one another of the affair, and marveled not a little. Old Kranon again insisted that it was the dark folk who had taken them, since cats did not return alive from the cottage of the ancient man and his wife. But all agreed on one thing: that the refusal of all the cats to eat their portions of meat or drink their saucers of milk was exceedingly curious. And for two whole days the sleek, lazy cats of Ulthar would touch no food, but only doze by the fire or in the sun.

It was fully a week before the villagers noticed that no lights were appearing at dusk in the windows of the cottage under the trees. Then the lean Nith remarked that no one had seen the old man or his wife since the night the cats were away. In another week the burgomaster decided to overcome his fears and call at the strangely silent dwelling as a matter of duty, though in so doing he was careful to take with him Shang the blacksmith and Thul the cutter of stone as witnesses. And when they had broken down the frail door they found only this: two cleanly picked human skeletons on the earthen floor, and a number of singular beetles crawling in the shadowy corners.

There was subsequently much talk among the burgesses of Ulthar. Zath, the coroner, disputed at length with Nith, the lean notary; and Kranon and Shang and Thul were overwhelmed with questions. Even little Atal, the innkeeper's son, was closely questioned and given a sweet-meat as reward. They talked of the old cotter and his wife, of the caravan of dark wanderers, of small Menes and his black kitten, of the prayer of Menes and of the sky during that prayer, of the doings of the cats on the night the caravan left, and of what was later found in the cottage under the dark trees in the repellent yard.

And in the end the burgesses passed that remarkable law which is told of by traders in Hatheg and discussed by travelers in Nir; namely, that in Ulthar no man may kill a cat.

ELEVEN

The Empty Sleeve

Algernon Blackwood

I

The Gilmer brothers were a couple of fussy and pernickety old bachelors of a rather retiring, not to say timid, disposition. There was gray in the pointed beard of John, the elder, and if any hair had remained to William it would also certainly have been of the same shade. They had private means. Their main interest in life was the collection of violins, for which they had the instinctive flair of true connoisseurs. Neither John nor William, however, could play a single note. They could only pluck the open strings. The production of tone, so necessary before the purchase was done vicariously for them by another.

The only objection they had to the big building in which they occupied the roomy top floor was that Morgan, liftman and caretaker, insisted on wearing a billycock with his uniform after six o'clock in the evening, with a result disastrous to the beauty of the universe. For "Mr. Morgan," as they called him between themselves, had a round and pasty face on the top of a round and conical body. In view, however, of the man's other rare qualities—including his devotion to themselves—this objection was not serious.

He had another peculiarity that amused them. On being found fault with, explained nothing, but merely repeated the words of the complaint.

"Water in the bath wasn't really hot this morning, Morgan!"

"Water in the bath not reely 'ot, wasn't it, sir?"

Or, from William, who was something of a faddist:

"My jar of sour milk came up late yesterday, Morgan."

"Your jar of sour milk come up late, sir, yesterday?"

Since, however, the statement of a complaint invariably resulted in its remedy, the brothers had learned to look for no further explanation. Next morning the bath was hot, the sour milk was "brortup" punctually. The uniform and billycock hat, though, remained an eyesore and source of oppression.

On this particular night John Gilmer, the elder, returning from a Masonic rehearsal, stepped into the lift and found Mr. Morgan with his hand ready on the iron rope.

"Fog's very thick outside," said Mr. John pleasantly; and the lift was a third of the way up before Morgan had completed his customary repetition: "Fog very thick outside, yes, sir." And Gilmer then asked casually if his brother were alone, and received the reply that Mr. Hyman had called and had not yet gone away.

Now this Mr. Hyman was a Hebrew, and, like themselves, a connoisseur in violins, but, unlike themselves, who only kept their specimens to look at, he was a skillful and exquisite player. He was the only person they ever permitted to handle their pedigree instruments, to take them from the glass cases where they reposed in silent splendor, and to draw the sound out of their wondrous painted hearts of golden varnish. The brothers loathed to see his fingers touch them, yet loved to hear their singing voices in the room, for the latter confirmed their sound judgment as collectors, and made them certain their money had been well spent. Hyman, however, made no attempt to conceal his contempt and hatred for the mere collectors. The atmosphere of the room fairly pulsed with these opposing forces of silent emotion when Hyman played and the Gilmers, alternately writhing and admiring, listened. The occasions, however, were not frequent. The Hebrew only came by invitation, and both brothers made a point of being in. It was a very formal proceeding—something of a sacred rite almost.

John Gilmer, therefore, was considerably surprised by the information Morgan had supplied. For one thing, Hyman, he had understood, was away on the Continent.

"Still in there, you say?" he repeated, after a moment's reflection.

"Still in there, Mr. John, sir." Then, concealing his surprise from the liftman, he fell back upon his usual mild habit of complaining about the billycock hat and the uniform.

"You really should try and remember, Morgan," he said, though kindly. "That hat does not go well with that uniform!"

Morgan's pasty countenance betrayed no vestige of expression.

"At don't go well with the yewniform, sir," he repeated, hanging up the disreputable bowler and replacing it with a gold-braided cap from the peg. "No, sir, it don't, do it?" he added cryptically, smiling at the transformation thus effected.

And the lift then halted with an abrupt jerk at the top floor. By somebody's carelessness the landing was in darkness, and, to make things worse, Morgan, clumsily pulling the iron rope, happened to knock the billycock from its peg so that his sleeve, as he stooped to catch it, struck the switch and plunged the scene in a moment's complete obscurity.

And it was then, in the act of stepping out before the light was turned on again, that John Gilmer stumbled against something that shot along the landing past the open door. First he thought it must be a child, then a man, then—an animal. Its movement was rapid yet stealthy. Starting backwards instinctively to allow it room to pass, Gilmer collided in the darkness with Morgan, and Morgan incontinently screamed. There was a moment of stupid confusion. The heavy framework of the lift shook a little, as though something had stepped into it and then as quickly jumped out again. A rushing sound followed that resembled footsteps, yet at the same time was more like gliding—someone in soft slippers or stockinged feet, greatly hurrying. Then came silence again. Morgan sprang to the landing and turned up the electric light. Mr. Gilmer, at the same moment, did likewise to the switch in the lift. Light flooded the scene. Nothing was visible.

"Dog or cat, or something, I suppose, wasn't it?" exclaimed Gilmer, following the man out and looking round with bewildered amazement upon a deserted landing. He knew quite well, even while he spoke, that the words were foolish.

"Dog or cat, yes, sir, or—something," echoed Morgan, his eyes narrowed to pin-points, then growing large, but his face stolid.

"The light should have been on," Mr. Gilmer spoke with a touch of severity. The little occurrence had curiously disturbed his equanimity. He felt annoyed, upset, uneasy.

For a perceptible pause the liftman made no reply, and his employer, looking up, saw that, besides being flustered, he was white about the jaws. His voice, when he spoke, was without its normal assurance. This time he did not merely repeat. He explained.

"The light was on, sir, when last I come up!" he said, with emphasis, obviously speaking the truth. "Only a moment ago," he added.

Mr. Gilmer, for some reason, felt disinclined to press for explanations. He decided to ignore the matter.

Then the lift plunged down again into the depths like a diving-bell into water; and John Gilmer, pausing a moment first to reflect, let himself in softly with his latchkey, and, after hanging up hat and coat in the hall, entered the big sitting room he and his brother shared in common.

The December fog that covered London like a dirty blanket had penetrated, he saw, into the room. The objects in it were half shrouded in the familiar yellowish haze.

II

In his dressing-gown and slippers, William Gilmer, almost invisible in his armchair by the gas-stove across the room, spoke at once. Through the thick atmosphere his face gleamed, showing an extinguished pipe hanging from his lips. His tone of voice conveyed emotion, an emotion he sought to suppress, of a quality, however, not easy to define.

"Hyman's been here," he announced abruptly. "You must have met him. He's this very instant gone out."

It was quite easy to see that something had happened, for "scenes" leave disturbance behind them in the atmosphere. But John made no immediate reference to this. He replied that he had seen no one—which was strictly true—and his brother thereupon, sitting bolt upright in the chair, turned quickly and faced him. His skin, in the foggy air, seemed paler than before.

"That's odd," he said nervously.

"What's odd?" asked John.

"That you didn't see—anything. You ought to have run into one another on the doorstep." His eyes went peering about the room. He was distinctly ill at ease. "You're positive you saw no one? Did Morgan take him down before you came? Did Morgan see him?" He asked several questions at once.

"On the contrary, Morgan told me he was still here with you. Hyman probably walked down, and didn't take the lift at all," he replied. "That accounts for neither of us seeing him." He decided to say nothing about the occurrence in the lift, for his brother's nerves, he saw plainly, were on edge.

William then stood up out of his chair, and the skin of his face changed its hue, for whereas a moment ago it was merely pale, it had now altered to a tint that lay somewhere between white and a livid gray. The man was fighting internal terror. For a moment these two brothers of middle age looked each other straight in the eye. Then John spoke:

"What's wrong, Billy?" he asked quietly. "Something's upset you. What brought Hyman in this way—unexpectedly? I thought he was still in Germany."

The brothers, affectionate and sympathetic, understood one another perfectly. They had no secrets. Yet for several minutes the younger one made no reply. It seemed difficult to choose his words apparently.

"Hyman played, I suppose—on the fiddles?" John helped him, wondering uneasily what was coming. He did not care much for the individual in question, though his talent was of such great use to them.

The other nodded in the affirmative, then plunged into rapid speech, talking under his breath as though he feared someone might overhear. Glancing over his shoulder down the foggy room, he drew his brother close.

"Hyman came," he began, "unexpectedly. He hadn't written, and I hadn't asked him. You hadn't either, I suppose?"

John shook his head.

"When I came in from the dining-room I found him in the passage. The servant was taking away the dishes, and he had let himself in while the front door was ajar. Pretty cool, wasn't it?"

"He's an original," said John, shrugging his shoulders. "And you welcomed him?" he asked.

"I asked him in, of course. He explained he had something glorious for me to hear. Silenski had played it in the afternoon, and he had bought the music since. But Silenski's 'Strad' hadn't the power—it's thin on the upper strings, you remember, unequal, patchy—and he said no instrument in the world could do it justice but our 'Joseph'—the small Guarnerius, you know, which he swears is the most perfect in the world."

"And what was it? Did he play it?" asked John, growing more uneasy as he grew more interested. With relief he glanced round and saw the matchless little instrument lying there safe and sound in its glass case near the door.

"He played it—divinely: Zigeuner Lullaby, a fine, passionate, rushing bit of inspiration, oddly misnamed 'lullaby.' And, fancy the fellow had memorized it already! He walked about the room on tiptoe while he played it, complaining of the light—"

"Complaining of the light?"

"Said the thing was crepuscular, and needed dusk for its full effect. I turned the lights out one by one, till finally there was only the glow of the gas logs. He insisted. You know that way he has with him? And then he got over me in another matter: insisted on using some special strings he had brought with him, and put them on, too, himself—thicker than the A and E we use."

For though neither Gilmer could produce a note, it was their pride that they kept their precious instruments in perfect condition for playing, choosing the exact thickness and quality of strings that suited the temperament of each violin; and the little Guarnerius in question always "sang" best, they held, with thin strings.

"Infernal insolence," exclaimed the listening brother, wondering what was coming next. "Played it well, though, didn't he, this Lullaby thing?" he added, seeing that William hesitated. As he spoke he went nearer, sitting down close beside him in a leather chair.

"Magnificent! Pure fire of genius!" was the reply with enthusiasm, the voice at the same time dropping lower. "Staccato like a silver hammer; harmonics like flutes, clear, soft, ringing; and the tone—well, the G string was a baritone, and the upper registers creamy and mellow as a boy's voice. John," he added, "that Guarnerius is the very pick of the period and"—again he hesitated—"Hyman loves it. He'd give his soul to have it."

The more John heard, the more uncomfortable it made him. He had always disliked this gifted Hebrew, for in his secret heart he knew that he had always feared and distrusted him. Sometimes he had felt half afraid of him; the man's very forcible personality was too insistent to be pleasant. His type was of the dark and sinister kind, and he possessed a violent will that rarely failed of accomplishing its desire.

"Wish I'd heard the fellow play," he said at length, ignoring his brother's last remark, and going on to speak of the most matter-of-fact details he could think of. "Did he use the Dodd bow, or the Tourte? That Dodd I picked up last month, you know, is the most perfectly balanced I have ever—"

He stopped abruptly, for William had suddenly got upon his feet and was standing there, searching the room with his eyes. A chill ran down John's spine as he watched him.

"What is it, Billy?" he asked sharply. "Hear anything?"

William continued to peer about him through the thick air.

"Oh, nothing, probably," he said, an odd catch in his voice; "only—I keep feeling as if there was somebody listening. Do you think, perhaps"—he glanced over his shoulder—"there is someone at the door? I wish—I wish you'd have a look, John."

John obeyed, though without great eagerness. Crossing the room slowly, he opened the door, then switched on the light. The passage leading past the bathroom towards the bedrooms beyond was empty. The coats hung motionless from their pegs.

"No one, of course," he said, as he closed the door and came back to the stove. He left the light burning in the passage. It was curious the way both brothers had this impression that they were not alone, though only one of them spoke of it.

"Used the Dodd or the Tourte, Billy—which?" continued John in the most natural voice he could assume.

But at that very same instant the water started to his eyes. His brother, he saw, was close upon the thing he really had to tell. But he had stuck fast.

III

By a great effort John Gilmer composed himself and remained in his chair. With detailed elaboration he lit a cigarette, staring hard at his brother over the flaring match while he did so. There he sat in his dressing-gown and slippers by the fireplace, eyes downcast, fingers playing idly with the red tassel. The electric light cast heavy shadows across the face. In a flash then, since emotion may sometimes express itself in attitude even better than in speech, the elder brother understood that Billy was about to tell him an unutterable thing.

By instinct he moved over to his side so that the same view of the room confronted him.

"Out with it, old man," he said, with an effort to be natural. "Tell me what you saw."

Billy shuffled slowly round and the two sat side by side, facing the fog-draped chamber.

"It was like this," he began softly, "only I was standing instead of sitting, looking over to that door as you and I do now. Hyman moved to and fro in the faint glow of the gas logs against the far wall, playing the 'crepuscular' thing in his most inspired sort of way, so that the music seemed to issue from himself rather than from the shining bit of wood under his chin, when—I noticed something coming over me that was"— he hesitated, searching for words—"that wasn't all due to the music," he finished abruptly.

"His personality put a bit of hypnotism on you, eh?"

William shrugged his shoulders.

"The air was thickish with fog and the light was dim, cast upwards upon him from the stove," he continued. "I admit all that. But there wasn't light enough to throw shadows, you see, and—"

"Hyman looked queer?" the other helped him quickly.

96

Billy nodded his head without turning.

"Changed there before my very eyes"—he whispered it—"turned animal—"

"Animal?" John felt his hair rising.

"That's the only way I can put it. His face and hands and body turned otherwise than usual. I lost the sound of his feet. When the bow-hand or the fingers on the strings passed into the light, they were"—he uttered a soft, shuddering little laugh—"furry, oddly divided, the fingers massed together. And he paced stealthily. I thought every instant the fiddle would drop with a crash and he would spring at me across the room."

"My dear chap—"

"He moved with those big, lithe, striding steps one sees"—John held his breath in the little pause, listening keenly—"one sees those big brutes make in the cages when their desire is aflame for food or escape, or—or fierce passionate desire for anything they want with their whole nature—"

"The big felines!" John whistled softly.

"And every minute getting nearer and nearer to the door, as though he meant to make a sudden rush for it and get out."

"With the violin! Of course you stopped him?"

"In the end. But for a long time, I swear to you, I found it difficult to know what to do, even to move. I couldn't get my voice for words of any kind; it was like a spell."

"It was a spell," suggested John firmly.

"Then, as he moved, still playing," continued the other, "he seemed to grow smaller; to shrink down below the line of the gas. I thought I should lose sight of him altogether. I turned the light up suddenly. There he was over by the door—crouching."

"Playing on his knees, you mean?"

William closed his eyes in an effort to visualize it again.

"Crouching," he repeated, at length, "close to the floor. At least, I think so. It all happened so quickly, and I felt so bewildered, it was hard to see straight. But at first I could have sworn he was half his natural size. I called to him, I think I swore at him—I forget exactly, but I know he straightened up at once and stood before me down there in the light"— he pointed across the room to the door—"eyes gleaming, face white as chalk, perspiring like midsummer, and gradually filling out, straightening up, whatever you like to call it, to his natural size and appearance again. It was the most horrid thing I've ever seen."

"As an—animal, you saw him still?"

"No; human again. Only much smaller."

"What did he say?"

Billy reflected a moment.

"Nothing that I can remember," he replied. "You see, it was all over in a few seconds. In the full light, I felt so foolish, and nonplused at first. To see him normal again baffled me. And, before I could collect myself, he had let himself out into the passage, and I heard the front door slam. A minute later—the same second almost, it seemed—you came in. I only remember grabbing the violin and getting it back safely under the glass case. The strings were still vibrating."

The account was over. John asked no further questions. Nor did he say a single word about the lift, Morgan, or the extinguished light on the landing. There fell a longish silence between the two men; and then, while they helped themselves to a generous supply of whisky-and-soda before going to bed, John looked up and spoke:

"If you agree, Billy," he said quietly, "I think I might write and suggest to Hyman that we shall no longer have need for his services."

And Billy, acquiescing, added a sentence that expressed something of the singular dread lying but half-concealed in the atmosphere of the room, if not in their minds as well:

"Putting it, however, in a way that need not offend him."

"Of course. There's no need to be rude, is there?"

Accordingly, next morning the letter was written; and John, saying nothing to his brother, took it round himself by hand to the Hebrew's rooms near Euston. The answer he dreaded was forthcoming:

"Mr. Hyman's still away abroad," he was told. "But we're forwarding letters; yes. Or I can give you his address if you'll prefer it." The letter went, therefore, to the number in Konigstrasse, Munich, thus obtained.

Then, on his way back from the insurance company where he went to increase the sum that protected the small Guarnerius from loss by fire, accident, or theft, John Gilmer called at the offices of certain musical agents and ascertained that Silenski, the violinist, was performing at the time in Munich. It was only some days later, though, by diligent inquiry, he made certain that at a concert on a certain date the famous virtuoso had played a Zigeuner Lullaby of his own composition—the very date, it turned out, on which he himself had been to the Masonic rehearsal at Mark Masons' Hall.

John, however, said nothing of these discoveries to his brother William.

TWELVE

The Watchers

Bram Stoker

MY DEAR DAUGHTER:

I want you to take this letter as an instruction—absolute and impera-
tive, and admitting of no deviation whatever—in case anything untoward
or unexpected by you or by others should happen to me. If I should be
suddenly and mysteriously stricken down—either by sickness, accident or
attack—you must follow these directions implicitly. If I am not already
in my bedroom when you are made cognizant of my state, I am to be
brought there as quickly as possible. Even should I be dead, my body is
to be brought there. Thenceforth, until I am either conscious and able
to give instructions on my own account, or buried, I am never to be left
alone—not for a single instant. From nightfall to sunrise at least two
persons must remain in the room. It will be well that a trained nurse be in
the room from time to time, and will note any symptoms, either permanent or changing, which may strike her. My solicitors, Marvin & Jewkes,
of 27B Lincoln's Inn, have full instructions in case of my death; and Mr.
Marvin has himself undertaken to see personally my wishes carried out. I
should advise you, my dear Daughter, seeing that you have no relative to
apply to, to get some friend whom you can trust to either remain within
the house where instant communication can be made, or to come nightly
to aid in the watching, or to be within call. Such friend may be either
male or female; but, whichever it may be, there should be added one other
watcher or attendant at hand of the opposite sex. Understand, that it is

of the very essence of my wish that there should be, awake and exercising themselves to my purposes, both masculine and feminine intelligences. Once more, my dear Margaret, let me impress on you the need for observation and just reasoning to conclusions, howsoever strange. If I am taken ill or injured, this will be no ordinary occasion; and I wish to warn you, so that your guarding may be complete.

Nothing in my room—I speak of the curios—must be removed or displaced in any way, or for any cause whatever. I have a special reason and a special purpose in the placing of each; so that any moving of them would thwart my plans.

Should you want money or counsel in anything, Mr. Marvin will carry out your wishes; to the which he has my full instructions.

ABEL TRELAWNY

. . . That night we were not yet regularly organized for watching, so that the early part of the evening showed an unevenly balanced guard. Nurse Kennedy, who had been on duty all day, was lying down, as she had arranged to come on again by twelve o'clock. Doctor Winchester, who was dining in the house, remained in the room until dinner was announced; and went back at once when it was over. During dinner Mrs. Grant remained in the room, and with her Sergeant Daw, who wished to complete a minute examination which he had undertaken of everything in the room and near it. At nine o'clock Miss Trelawny and I went in to relieve the Doctor. She had lain down for a few hours in the afternoon so as to be refreshed for her work at night. She told me that she had determined that for this night at least she would sit up and watch. I did not try to dissuade her, for I knew that her mind was made up. Then and there I made up my mind that I would watch with her—unless, of course, I should see that she really did not wish it. I said nothing of my intentions for the present. We came in on tiptoe, so silently that the Doctor, who was bending over the bed, did not hear us, and seemed a little startled when suddenly looking up he saw our eyes upon him. I felt that the mystery of the whole thing was getting on his nerves, as it had already got on the nerves of some others of us. He was, I fancied, a little annoyed with himself for having been so startled, and at once began to talk in a hurried manner as though to get over our idea of his embarrassment:

"I am really and absolutely at my wits' end to find any fit cause for this stupor. I have made again as accurate an examination as I know how, and I am satisfied that there is no injury to the brain, that is, no external injury. Indeed, all his vital organs seem unimpaired. I have given him, as you know, food several times and it has manifestly done him good. His breathing is strong and regular, and his pulse is slower and stronger than it was this morning. I cannot find evidence of any known drug, and his unconsciousness does not resemble any of the many cases of hypnotic sleep which I saw in the Charcot Hospital in Paris. And as to these wounds"—he laid his finger gently on the bandaged wrist which lay outside the coverlet as he spoke—"I do not know what to make of them. They might have been made by a carding-machine; but that supposition is untenable. It is within the bounds of possibility that they might have been made by a wild animal if it had taken care to sharpen its claws. That too is, I take it, impossible. By the way, have you any strange pets here in the house; anything of an exceptional kind, such as a tiger-cat or anything out of the common?" Miss Trelawny smiled a sad smile which made my heart ache, as she made answer:

"Oh no! Father does not like animals about the house, unless they are dead and mummied." This was said with a touch of bitterness—or jealousy, I could hardly tell which. "Even my poor kitten was only allowed in the house on sufferance; and though he is the dearest and best-conducted cat in the world, he is now on a sort of parole, and is not allowed into this room."

As she was speaking a faint rattling of the door handle was heard. Instantly Miss Trelawny's face brightened. She sprang up and went over to the door, saying as she went:

"There he is! That is my Silvio. He stands on his hind legs and rattles the door handle when he wants to come into a room." She opened the door, speaking to the cat as though he were a baby: "Did him want his movver? Come then; but he must stay with her!" She lifted the cat, and came back with him in her arms. He was certainly a magnificent animal. A chinchilla grey Persian with long silky hair; a really lordly animal with a haughty bearing despite his gentleness; and with great paws which spread out as he placed them on the ground. Whilst she was fondling him, he suddenly gave a wriggle like an eel and slipped out of her arms. He ran across the room and stood opposite a low table on which stood the mummy of an animal, and began to mew and snarl. Miss Trelawny was after him in an instant and lifted him in her arms, kicking and struggling and wriggling to get away; but not biting or scratching, for evidently he loved his beautiful mistress. He ceased to make a noise the moment he was in her arms; in a whisper she admonished him:

"O you naughty Silvio! You have broken your parole that mother gave for you. Now, say goodnight to the gentlemen, and come away to mother's room!" As she was speaking she held out the cat's paw to me to shake. As I did so I could not but admire its size and beauty. "Why," said I, "his paw seems like a little boxing-glove full of claws." She smiled:

"So it ought to. Don't you notice that my Silvio has seven toes, see!" she opened the paw; and surely enough there were seven separate claws, each of them sheathed in a delicate, fine, shell-like case. As I gently stroked the foot the claws emerged and one of them accidentally—there was no anger now and the cat was purring—stuck into my hand. Instinctively I said as I drew back:

"Why, his claws are like razors!"

Doctor Winchester had come close to us and was bending over looking at the cat's claws; as I spoke he said in a quick, sharp way:

"Eh!" I could hear the quick intake of his breath. While I was stroking the now quiescent cat, the Doctor went to the table and tore off a piece of blotting-paper from the writing-pad and came back. He laid the paper on his palm and, with a simple "pardon me!" to Miss Trelawny, placed the cat's paw on it and pressed it down with his other hand. The haughty cat seemed to resent somewhat the familiarity, and tried to draw its foot away. This was plainly what the Doctor wanted, for in the act the cat opened the sheaths of its claws and made several reefs in the soft paper. Then Miss Trelawny took her pet away. She returned in a couple of minutes; as she came in she said:

"It is most odd about that mummy! When Silvio came into the room first—indeed I took him in as a kitten to show to Father—he went on just the same way. He jumped up on the table, and tried to scratch and bite the mummy. That was what made Father so angry, and brought the decree of banishment on poor Silvio. Only his parole, given through me, kept him in the house."

Whilst she had been gone, Doctor Winchester had taken the bandage from her father's wrist. The wound was now quite clear, as the separate cuts showed out in fierce red lines. The Doctor folded the blotting-paper across the line of punctures made by the cat's claws, and held it down close to the wound. As he did so, he looked up triumphantly and beckoned us over to him.

The cuts in the paper corresponded with the wounds in the wrist! No explanation was needed, as he said:

"It would have been better if master Silvio had not broken his parole!"

We were all silent for a little while. Suddenly Miss Trelawny said:

"But Silvio was not in here last night!"

"Are you sure? Could you prove that if necessary?" She hesitated before replying:

"I am certain of it; but I fear it would be difficult to prove. Silvio sleeps in a basket in my room. I certainly put him to bed last night; I remember distinctly laying his little blanket over him, and tucking him in. This morning I took him out of the basket myself. I certainly never noticed him in here; though, of course, that would not mean much, for I was too concerned about poor father, and too much occupied with him, to notice even Silvio."

The Doctor shook his head as he said with a certain sadness:

"Well, at any rate it is no use trying to prove anything now. Any cat in the world would have cleaned blood-marks—did any exist—from his paws in a hundredth part of the time that has elapsed."

Again we were all silent; and again the silence was broken by Miss Trelawny:

"But now that I think of it, it could not have been poor Silvio that injured Father. My door was shut when I first heard the sound; and Father's was shut when I listened at it. When I went in, the injury had been done; so that it must have been before Silvio could possibly have got in." This reasoning commended itself, especially to me as a barrister, for it was proof to satisfy a jury. It gave me a distinct pleasure to have Silvio acquitted of the crime—possibly because he was Miss Trelawny's cat and was loved by her. Happy cat! Silvio's mistress was manifestly pleased as I said:

"Verdict, 'not guilty!'" Doctor Winchester after a pause observed:

"My apologies to master Silvio on this occasion; but I am still puzzled to know why he is so keen against that mummy. Is he the same toward the other mummies in the house? There are, I suppose, a lot of them. I saw three in the hall as I came in."

"There are lots of them," she answered. "I sometimes don't know whether I am in a private house or the British Museum. But Silvio never concerns himself about any of them except that particular one. I suppose it must be because it is of an animal, not a man or a woman."

"Perhaps it is of a cat!" said the Doctor as he started up and went across the room to look at the mummy more closely. "Yes," he went on, "it is the mummy of a cat; and a very fine one, too. If it hadn't been a special favorite of some very special person it would never have received so much honor. See! A painted case and obsidian eyes—just like a human mummy. It is an extraordinary thing, that knowledge of kind to kind. Here is a dead cat—that is all; it is perhaps four or five thousand years old—and another cat of another breed, in what is practically another world, is ready to fly at it, just as it would if it were not dead. I should like to experiment a bit about that cat if you don't mind, Miss Trelawny." She hesitated before replying:

"Of course, do anything you may think necessary or wise; but I hope it will not be anything to hurt or worry my poor Silvio." The Doctor smiled as he answered:

"Oh, Silvio would be all right: it is the other one that my sympathies would be reserved for."

"How do you mean?"

"Master Silvio will do the attacking; the other one will do the suffering."

"Suffering?" There was a note of pain in her voice. The Doctor smiled more broadly:

THE WATCHERS

"Oh, please make your mind easy as to that. The other won't suffer as we understand it; except perhaps in his structure and outfit."

"What on earth do you mean?"

"Simply this, my dear young lady, that the antagonist will be a mummy cat like this one. There are, I take it, plenty of them to be had in Museum Street. I shall get one and place it here instead of that one—you won't think that a temporary exchange will violate your Father's instructions, I hope. We shall then find out, to begin with, whether Silvio objects to all mummy cats, or only to this one in particular."

"I don't know," she said doubtfully. "Father's instructions seem very uncompromising." Then after a pause she went on: "But of course under the circumstances anything that is to be ultimately for his good must be done. I suppose there can't be anything very particular about the mummy of a cat."

Doctor Winchester said nothing. He sat rigid, with so grave a look on his face that his extra gravity passed on to me; and in its enlightening perturbation I began to realize more than I had yet done the strangeness of the case in which I was now so deeply concerned. When once this thought had begun there was no end to it. Indeed it grew, and blossomed, and reproduced itself in a thousand different ways. The room and all in it gave grounds for strange thoughts. There were so many ancient relics that unconsciously one was taken back to strange lands and strange times. There were so many mummies or mummy objects, round which there seemed to cling for ever the penetrating odors of bitumen, and spices and gums—"Nard and Circassia's balmy smells"—that one was unable to forget the past. Of course, there was but little light in the room, and that carefully shaded; so that there was no glare anywhere. None of that direct light which can manifest itself as a power or an entity, and so make for companionship. The room was a large one, and lofty in proportion to its size. In its vastness was place for a multitude of things not often found in a bedchamber. In far corners of the room were shadows of uncanny shape. More than once as I thought, the multitudinous presence of the dead and the past took such hold on me that I caught myself looking round fearfully as though some strange personality or influence was present. Even the manifest presence of Doctor Winchester and Miss Trelawny

107

could not altogether comfort or satisfy me at such moments. It was with a distinct sense of relief that I saw a new personality in the room in the shape of Nurse Kennedy. There was no doubt that that business-like, self-reliant, capable young woman added an element of security to such wild imaginings as my own. She had a quality of common sense that seemed to pervade everything around her, as though it were some kind of emanation. Up to that moment I had been building fancies around the sick man; so that finally all about him, including myself, had become involved in them, or enmeshed, or saturated, or . . . But now that she had come, he relapsed into his proper perspective as a patient; the room was a sick-room, and the shadows lost their fearsome quality. The only thing which it could not altogether abrogate was the strange Egyptian smell. You may put a mummy in a glass case and hermetically seal it so that no corroding air can get within; but all the same it will exhale its odor. One might think that four or five thousand years would exhaust the olfactory qualities of anything; but experience teaches us that these smells remain, and that their secrets are unknown to us. Today they are as much mysteries as they were when the embalmers put the body in the bath of natron . . .

All at once I sat up. I had become lost in an absorbing reverie. The Egyptian smell had seemed to get on my nerves—on my memory—on my very will.

At that moment I had a thought which was like an inspiration. If I was influenced in such a manner by the smell, might it not be that the sick man, who lived half his life or more in the atmosphere, had gradually and by slow but sure process taken into his system something which had permeated him to such degree that it had a new power derived from quantity—or strength—or . . .

I was becoming lost again in a reverie. This would not do. I must take such precaution that I could remain awake, or free from such entrancing thought. I had had but half a night's sleep last night; and this night I must remain awake. Without stating my intention, for I feared that I might add to the trouble and uneasiness of Miss Trelawny, I went downstairs and out of the house. I soon found a chemist's shop, and came away with a respirator. When I got back, it was ten o'clock; the Doctor was going for the night. The Nurse came with him to the door of the sick-room, taking her last instructions. Miss Trelawny sat still beside the bed. Sergeant Daw, who had entered as the Doctor went out, was some little distance off.

When Nurse Kennedy joined us, we arranged that she should sit up till two o'clock, when Miss Trelawny would relieve her. Thus, in accordance with Mr. Trelawny's instructions, there would always be a man and a woman in the room; and each one of us would overlap, so that at no time would a new set of watchers come on duty without someone to tell of what—if anything—had occurred. I lay down on a sofa in my own room, having arranged that one of the servants should call me a little before twelve. In a few moments I was asleep.

When I was waked, it took me several seconds to get back my thoughts so as to recognize my own identity and surroundings. The short sleep had, however, done me good, and I could look on things around me in a more practical light than I had been able to do earlier in the evening. I bathed my face, and thus refreshed went into the sick-room. I moved very softly. The Nurse was sitting by the bed, quiet and alert; the Detective sat in an arm-chair across the room in deep shadow. He did not move when I crossed, until I got close to him, when he said in a dull whisper:

"It is all right; I have not been asleep!" An unnecessary thing to say, I thought—it always is, unless it be untrue in spirit. When I told him that his watch was over; that he might go to bed till I should call him at six o'clock, he seemed relieved and went with alacrity. At the door he turned and, coming back to me, said in a whisper:

"I sleep lightly and I shall have my pistols with me. I won't feel so heavy-headed when I get out of this mummy smell."

He too, then, had shared my experience of drowsiness!

I asked the Nurse if she wanted anything. I noticed that she had a vinaigrette in her lap. Doubtless she, too, had felt some of the influence which had so affected me. She said that she had all she required, but that if she should want anything she would at once let me know. I wished to keep her from noticing my respirator, so I went to the chair in the shadow where her back was toward me. Here I quietly put it on, and made myself comfortable.

For what seemed a long time, I sat and thought and thought. It was a wild medley of thoughts, as might have been expected from the experiences of the previous day and night. Again I found myself thinking of the Egyptian smell; and I remember that I felt a delicious satisfaction that I did not experience it as I had done. The respirator was doing its work.

It must have been that the passing of this disturbing thought made for repose of mind, which is the corollary of bodily rest, for, though I really cannot remember being asleep or waking from it, I saw a vision—I dreamed a dream, I scarcely know which.

I was still in the room, seated in the chair. I had on my respirator and knew that I breathed freely. The Nurse sat in her chair with her back toward me. She sat quite still. The sick man lay as still as the dead. It was rather like the picture of a scene than the reality; all were still and silent; and the stillness and silence were continuous. Outside, in the distance I could hear the sounds of a city, the occasional roll of wheels, the shout of a reveler, the far-away echo of whistles and the rumbling of trains. The light was very, very low; the reflection of it under the green-shaded lamp was a dim relief to the darkness, rather than light. The green silk fringe of the lamp had merely the color of an emerald seen in the moonlight. The room, for all its darkness, was full of shadows. It seemed in my whirling thoughts as though all the real things had become shadows—shadows which moved, for they passed the dim outline of the high windows. Shadows which had sentience. I even thought there was sound, a faint sound as of the mew of a cat—the rustle of drapery and a metallic clink as of metal faintly touching metal. I sat as one entranced. At last I felt, as in nightmare, that this was sleep, and that in the passing of its portals all my will had gone.

All at once my senses were full awake. A shriek rang in my ears. The room was filled suddenly with a blaze of light. There was the sound of pistol shots—one, two; and a haze of white smoke in the room. When my waking eyes regained their power, I could have shrieked with horror myself at what I saw before me.

The Cat of the Cane-Brake

Frederick Stuart Greene

Sally! O-oh, Sally! I'm a-goin' now." Jim Gantt pushed back the limp brim of his rusty felt hat and turned colorless eyes toward the cabin.

A young woman came from around the corner of the house. From each hand dangled a bunch of squawking chickens. She did not speak until she had reached the wagon.

"Now, Jim, you ain't a-goin' to let them fellers down in Andalushy git you inter no blind tiger, air you?" The question came in a hopeless drawl; hopeless, too, her look into the man's sallow face.

"I ain't tetched a drop in more'n three months, has I?" Jim's answer was in a sullen key.

"No, Jim, you bin doin' right well lately."

She tossed the chickens into the wagon, thoughtless of the hurt to their tied and twisted legs. "They're worth two bits apiece. That comes to two dollars, Jim. Don't you take a nickel less'n that."

Jim gave a listless pull at the cotton rope that served as reins.

"Git up thar, mule!" he called, and the wagon creaked off on wobbling wheels down the hot, dusty road.

The woman looked scornfully at the man's humped-over back for a full minute, turned and walked to the house, a hard smile at her mouth.

Sally Gantt gave no heed to her drab surroundings as she crossed the short stretch from road to cabin. All her twenty-two years had been spent in this far end of Alabama, where one dreary, unkempt clearing in the pine-woods is as dismal as the next.

Comparisons which might add their fuel to her smoldering discontent were spared her. Yet, unconsciously, this bare, grassless country, with its flat miles of monotonous pine forests, its flatter miles of rank cane-brake, served to distil gall, poisoning all her thoughts.

The double cabin of Jim Gantt, its two rooms separated by a "dog-trot"—an open porch cut through the center of the structure—was counted a thing of luxury by his scattered neighbors. Gantt had built it four years before, when he took up the land as his homestead, and Sally for his wife.

The labor of building this cabin had apparently drained his stock of energy to the dregs. Beyond the necessary toil of planting a small patch of corn, a smaller one of sweet potatoes, and fishing in the sluggish waters of Pigeon Creek, he now did nothing. Sally tended the chickens, their one source of money, and gave intermittent attention to the half-dozen razor-back hogs, which, with the scrubby mule, comprises their toll of live-stock.

As the woman mounted the hewn log that answered as a step to the dog-trot, she stopped to listen. From the kitchen came a faint noise; a sound of crunching. Sally went on silent feet to the door. On the table, littered with unwashed dishes, a cat was gnawing at a fish head—a gaunt beast, its lean flanks covered with wiry fur except where ragged scars left exposed the bare hide. Its strong jaws crushed through the thick skull-bone of the fish as if it were an empty bird's egg.

Sally sprang to the stove and seized a pine knot.

"Dog-gone your yaller hide!" she screamed. "Git out of hyar!"

The cat wheeled with a start and faced the woman, its evil eyes glittering.

"Git, you yaller devil!" the woman screamed again.

The cat sprang sidewise to the floor. Sally sent the jagged piece of wood spinning through the air. It crashed against the far wall, missing the beast by an inch. The animal arched its huge body and held its ground.

"You varmint, I'll git you this time!" Sally stooped for another piece of wood. The cat darted through the door ahead of the flying missile.

"I'll kill you yit!" Sally shouted after it. "An' he kain't hinder me neither!"

She sat down heavily and wiped the sweat from her forehead.

It was several minutes before the woman rose from the chair and crossed the dog-trot to the sleeping-room. Throwing her faded sunbonnet into a corner, she loosened her hair and began to brush it.

Sally Gantt was neither pretty nor handsome. But in a country peopled solely by pinewoods crackers, her black hair and eyes, clear skin and white teeth, made her stand out. She was a woman, and young. To a man, also young, who for two years had seen no face unpainted with the sallow hue of chills and fever, no eyes except faded blue ones framed by white, straggling lashes, no sound teeth, and the unsound ones stained always by the snuff stick, she might easily appear alluring.

With feminine deftness Sally re-coiled her hair. She took from a wooden peg a blue calico dress, its printed pattern as yet unbleached by the fierce suns. It gave to her slender figure some touch of grace. From beneath the bed she drew a pair of heavy brogans; a shoe fashioned, doubtless, to match the listless nature of the people who most use them, slipping on or off without hindrance from lace or buckle. As a final touch, she fastened about her head a piece of blue ribbon, the band of cheap silk making the flash in her black eyes the brighter.

Sally left the house and started across the rubbish-littered yard. A short distance from the cabin she stopped to look about her.

"I'm dog-tired of it all," she said fiercely. "I hates the house. I hates the whole place, an' more'n all I hates Jim."

She turned, scowling, and walked between the rows of growing corn that reached to the edge of the clearing. Here began the pinewoods, the one saving touch nature has given to this land. Beneath the grateful shade she hastened her steps. The trees stood in endless disordered ranks, rising straight and bare of branch until high aloft their spreading tops caught the sunlight.

A quarter of a mile brought her to the lowland. She went down the slight decline and stepped within the cane-brake. Here gloom closed about her. The thickly growing cane reached to twice her height. Above the cane the cypress spread its branches, draped with the sad gray moss of the South.

No sun's ray struggled through the rank foliage to lighten the sodden earth beneath. Sally picked her way slowly through the swamp, peering cautiously beyond each fallen log before venturing a further step. Crawfish scuttled backward from her path to slip down the mud chimneys of their homes.

The black earth and decaying plants filled the hot, still air with noisome odors. Thousands of hidden insects sounded through the dank stretches their grating calls. Slimy water oozed from beneath the heavy soles of her brogans, green and purple bubbles were left in each footprint, bubbles with iridescent oily skins.

As she went around a sharp turn she was caught up and lifted clear from the ground in the arms of a young man—a boy of twenty or therabout.

"Oh, Bob, you scairt me—you certainly air rough!" Without words he kissed her again and again.

"Now, Bob, you quit! Ain't you had enough?"

"Could I ever have enough? Oh, Sally, I love you so!" The words trembled from the boy.

"You certainly ain't like none of 'em 'round hyar, Bob." There was some pride in Sally's drawling voice. "I never seed none of the men folks act with gals like you does."

"There's no other girl like you to make them." Then, holding her from him, he went on fiercely: "You don't let any of them try it, do you?"

Sally smiled up into his glowing eyes.

"You knows I don't. They'd be afeard of Jim."

The blood rushed to the boy's cheeks, his arms dropped to his side; he stood sobered.

"Sally, we can't go on this way any longer. That's why I asked you to come to the river to-day."

"What's a-goin' to stop us?" A frightened look crossed the woman's face.

"I'm going away."

She made a quick step toward him.

"You ain't lost your job on the new railroad?"

"No. Come down to the boat where we can talk this over."

He helped her down the bank of the creek to a flat-bottomed skiff, and seated her in the stern with a touch of courtesy before taking the cross seat facing her.

"No, I haven't lost my job," he began earnestly, "but my section of the road is about finished. They'll move me to another residency farther up the line in about a week."

She sat silent a moment, her black eyes wide with question. He searched them for some sign of sorrow.

"What kin I do after you air gone?"

There was a hopeless note in her voice; it pleased the boy.

"That's the point: instead of letting them move me, I'm going to move myself." He paused that she might get the full meaning of his coming words.

"I'm going away from here to-night, and I'm going to take you with me."

"No, no! I dasn't!" She shrank before his steady gaze.

He moved swiftly across to her. Throwing his arms around her, he poured out his words.

"Yes! You will! You must! You love me, don't you?"

Sally nodded in helpless assent.

"Better than anything in this world?"

Again Sally nodded.

"Then listen. To-night at twelve you come to the river. I'll be waiting for you at the edge of the swamp. We'll row down to Brewton. We can easily catch the six-twenty to Mobile, and, once there, we'll begin to live," he finished grandly.

"But I can't! Air you crazy? How kin I git away an' Jim right in the house?"

"I've thought of all that; you just let him see this." He drew a bottle from beneath the seat. "You know what he'll do to this; it's the strongest corn whisky I could find."

"Oh, Bob! I'm a-scairt to."

"Don't you love me?" His young eyes looked reproach.

Sally threw both arms about the boy's neck and drew his head down to her lips. Then she pushed him from her.

"Bob, is it so what the men-folks all say, that the railroad gives you a hundred dollars every month?"

He laughed. "Yes, you dear girl, and more. I get a hundred and a quarter, and I've been getting it for two years in this God-forsaken country, and nothing to spend it on. I've got over a thousand dollars saved up."

The woman's eyes widened. She kissed the boy on the mouth.

"They 'lows as how you're the smartest engineer on the road."

The boy's head was held high.

Sally made some mental calculations before she spoke again.

"Oh, Bob, I jes' cain't. I'm a-scairt to."

He caught her to him. A man of longer experience might have noted the sham in her reluctance.

"My darling, what are you afraid of?" he cried.

"What air we a-goin' to do after we gits to Mobile?"

"Oh, I've thought of everything. They're building a new line down in Texas. We'll go there. I'll get another job as resident engineer. I have my profession," he ended proudly.

"You might git tired, and want to git shed of me Bob."

He smothered her words under fierce kisses. His young heart beat at bursting pressure. In bright colours he pictured the glory of Mobile, New Orleans, and all the world that lay before them to love each other in.

When Sally left the boat she had promised to come. Where the pine-trees meet the cane-brake he would be waiting for her, at midnight.

At the top of the bank she turned to wave.

"Wait! Wait!" called the boy. He rushed up the slope.

"Quit, Bob, you're hurtin' me." She tore herself from his arms and hastened back along the slimy path. When she reached the pinewood she paused.

"More'n a thousand dollars!" she murmured, and a slow, satisfied smile crossed her shrewd face.

The sun, now directly over the tops of the trees, shot its scorching rays through the foliage. They struck the earth in vertical shafts, heating it to the burning point. Not a breath stirred the glistening pine-needles on the towering branches. It was one of those noon-times which, in the moisture-charged air of southern Alabama, makes life a steaming hell to all living things save reptiles and lovers.

Reaching the cabin, Sally went first to the kitchen room. She opened a cupboard and, taking the cork from the bottle, placed the whisky on the top shelf and closed the wooden door.

She crossed the dog-trot to the sleeping-room; a spitting snarl greeted her entrance. In the center of the bed crouched the yellow cat, its eyes gleaming, every muscle over its bony frame drawn taut, ready for the spring. The woman, startled, drew back. The cat moved on stiff legs nearer. Unflinchingly they glared into each other's eyes.

"Git out of hyar afore I kill yer! You yaller devil!" Sally's voice rang hard as steel.

The cat stood poised at the edge of the bed, its glistening teeth showing in its wide mouth. Without an instant's shift of her defiant stare, Sally wrenched a shoe from her foot. The animal with spread claws sprang straight for the woman's throat. The cat and the heavy brogan crashed together in mid-air. Together they fell to the floor; the cat landed lightly, silently, and bounded through the open door.

Sally fell back against the log wall of the cabin, feeling the skin at her throat with trembling fingers. . . .

"Jim! Oh-h, Jim!" Sally called from the cabin. "Come on in, yer supper's ready."

"He ain't took nothin' to drink to-day," she thought. "It's nigh three months now, he'll be 'most crazy."

The man took a few sticks of wood from the ground, and came on dragging feet through the gloom. As Sally watched his listless approach she felt in full force the oppressive melancholy of her dismal surroundings. Awakened by the boy's enthusiastic plans, imagination stirred within her. In the distance a girdled pine stood clear-cut against the horizon.

Its bark peeled and fallen left the dead, naked trunk the color of dried bones. Near the stunted top one bare limb stretched out. Unnoticed a thousand times before, to the woman it looked tonight a ghostly gibbet against the black sky.

Sally shuddered and went into the lighted kitchen.

"I jes' kilt a rattler down by the wood-pile." Jim threw down his load and drew a splint-bottomed chair to the table.

"Ground-rattler, Jim?"

"Naw, sir-ee! A hell-bendin' big diamondback."

"Did you hurt the skin?" Sally asked quickly.

"Naw. I chopped his neck clean, short to the haid. An' I done it so durn quick his fangs is a-stickin' out yit, I reckon."

"Did he strike at you?"

"Yes, sir-ee, an' the pizen came out of his mouth jes' like a fog."

"Ah, you're foolin' me!"

"No, I ain't neither. I've heard tell of it, bit I never seed it afore. The ground was kinda black whar he lit, an' jes' as I brought the axe down on him, thar I seed a little puff like, same as white steam, in front of his mouth."

"How big was he, Jim?"

"'Leven rattle an' a button."

"Did you skin him?"

"Naw, it was too durn dark, but I hung him high up, so's the hawgs won't git at him. His skin 'll fotch ol' bits down at Andalushy."

"Ax 'em six, Jim, them big ones gittin' kinda skeerce."

Jim finished his supper in silence; the killing of the snake had provided more conversation than was usual during three meals among pinewoods people.

As Sally was clearing away the dishes, the yellow cat came through the door. Slinking close to the wall, it avoided the woman, and sprang upon the knees of its master. Jim grinned into the eyes of the beast and began stroking its coarse hair. The cat set up a grating purr.

Sally looked at the two for a moment in silence.

"Jim, you gotta kill that cat."

Jim's grin widened, showing his tobacco-stained teeth.

"Jim, I'm a-tellin' you, you gotta kill that cat."

"An' I'm a-tellin' you I won't."

"Jim, it sprung at me to-day, an' would have hurt me somethin' turrible if I hadn't hit it over the haid with my shoe."

"Well, you must 'a' done somethin' to make him. You leave him alone an' he won't pester you."

The woman hesitated; she looked at the man as yet undecided; after a moment she spoke again.

"Jim Gantt, I'm axin' you for the las' time, which does you think more'n of, me or that snarlin' varmint?"

"He don't snarl at me so much as you does," the man answered doggedly. "Anyway, I ain't a-goin' to kill him; an' you gotta leave him alone, too. You jes' min yer own business an' go tote the mattress out on the trot. It's too durn hot to sleep in the house."

The woman passed behind him to the cupboard, reached up, opened wide the wooden door, and went out of the room.

Jim stroked the cat, its grating purr growing louder in the stillness.

A minute passed.

Into the dull eyes of the man a glitter came, and grew. Slowly he lifted his head. Farther and farther his chin drew up until the cords beneath the red skin of his neck stood out in ridges. The nostrils of his bony nose quivered, he sniffed the hot air like a dog straining to catch a distant scent. His tongue protruded and moved from side to side across his lips.

Standing in the darkness without, the woman smiled grimly.

Abruptly the man rose. The forgotten cat fell, twisted in the air, and lighted on its feet. Jim wheeled and strode to the cupboard. As his hand closed about the bottle, the gleam in his eyes became burning flames. He jerked the bottle from the shelf, threw his head far back. The fiery liquor ran down his throat. He returned to his seat; the cat rubbed its ribbed flank against his leg, he stooped and lifted it to the table. Waving the bottle in front of the yellow beast he laughed:

"Here's to yer—an' to'ad yer!" and swallowed half a tumblerful of the colorless liquid.

Sally dragged the shuck mattress to the dog-trot. Fully dressed, she lay waiting for midnight.

An hour went by before Jim shivered the empty bottle against the log wall of the kitchen. Pressing both hands hard upon the table, he heaved himself to his feet, upsetting the candle in the effort. He leered at the flame and slapped his bare palm down on it. The hot, melted wax oozed up, unheeded, between his fingers. Clinging to the tabletop, he turned himself toward the open door, steadied his swaying body for an instant, then lurched forward. His shoulder crashed against the doorpost, his body spun halfway round.

The man fell flat upon his back, missing the mattress by a yard. The back of his head struck hard on the rough boards of the porch floor. He lay motionless, his feet sticking straight up on the doorsill.

The yellow cat sprang lightly over the fallen body and went out into the night . . .

Wide-eyed, the woman lay, watching. After moments of tense listening the sound of faint breathing came to her from the prone figure. Sally frowned. "He's too no 'count to git kilt," she said aloud, and turned on her side. She judged, from the stars, it was not yet eleven.

Drowsiness came; she fell into uneasy slumber.

Out in the night the yellow cat was prowling. It stopped near the wood-pine. With extended paw, it touched lightly something that lay on the ground. Its long teeth fastened upon it. The cat slunk off toward the house. Without sound it sprang to the floor of the dog-trot. Stealthily, its body crouched low, it started to cross through the open way. As it passed the woman she muttered and struck out in her sleep. The cat flattened to the floor. Near the moving arm, the thing it carried fell from its teeth. The beast scurried out across the opening.

The night marched on to the sound of a million voices calling shrilly through the gloom.

The woman awoke. The stars glowed pale from a cloudy midnight sky. She reached out her right hand, palm down, to raise herself from the bed, throwing her full weight upon it. Two needlepoints pierced her wrist. A smothered cry was wrung from her lips. She reached with her left hand to pluck at the hurt place. It touched something cold, something hard and clammy, some dead thing. She jerked back the hand. A scream shivered through the still air. Pains becoming instantly acute, unbearable, darted through her arm. Again she tried to pull away the torturing needle points. Her quivering hand groped aimlessly in the darkness. She could not force herself, a second time, to touch the dead, clinging thing at her wrist. Screaming, she dragged herself to the man.

"Jim, I'm hurt, help me! Help me!"

The man did not move.

"Jim, wake up! Help me!" she wailed uselessly to the inert man.

The terrifying pain spurted from wrist to shoulder. With her clenched left hand she beat against the man's upturned face.

"You drunken fool, help me! Take this thing away!"

The man lay torpid beneath her pounding fist . . .

Along the path to Pigeon Creek, where the pinewoods run into the cane-brake, a boy waited; waited until the eastern sky grew from black to gray. Then with cautious tread he began to move, his face turned toward the cabin.

As he neared the clearing the gray in the east changed to red. He left the woods and entered the field of corn. His footfalls made no sound on the earth between the furrows.

At the cabin he drew close against the wall and listened. A man's heavy breathing reached his straining ears. Slowly he moved toward the opening in the middle of the house. Above the breathing he heard a grating noise; between the deep-drawn breaths and the grating, another sound came to him; a harsh, rhythmic scratching.

The edge of the sun rose abruptly above the flat earth, sending light within the opening.

The boy thrust his head around the angle. A yellow cat was sitting at the foot of the mattress. From its throat grating purrs came in regular measure; between each purr the beast's spread claws clutched and released the stiff ticking.

Beyond lay the man.

Between the cat and the man, stretched across the shuck bed, was the woman; her glassy eyes staring up into the grinning face of the cat. From her shoulder, reaching out toward the boy, was a livid, turgid thing; a hand and arm, puffed beyond all human shape. From the swollen wrist, its poisoned fangs sunk deep into an artery, hung the mangled head of a snake.

The swaying corn blades whipped against the boy's white face as he fled between the rows.

The Brazilian Cat

Arthur Conan Doyle

IT IS HARD LUCK ON A YOUNG FELLOW TO HAVE EXPENSIVE TASTES, great expectations, aristocratic connections, but no actual money in his pocket, and no profession by which he may earn any. The fact was that my father, a good, sanguine, easygoing man, had such confidence in the wealth and benevolence of his bachelor elder brother, Lord Southerton, that he took it for granted that I, his only son, would never be called upon to earn a living for myself. He imagined that if there were not a vacancy for me on the great Southerton Estates, at least there would be found some post in that diplomatic service which still remains the special preserve of our privileged classes. He died too early to realize how false his calculations had been. Neither my uncle nor the State took the slightest notice of me, or showed any interest in my career. An occasional brace of pheasants, or basket of hares, was all that ever reached me to remind me that I was heir to Otwell House and one of the richest estates in the country. In the meantime, I found myself a bachelor and man about town, living in a suite of apartments in Grosvenor Mansions, with no occupation save that of pigeon shooting and polo playing at Hurlingham. Month by month I realized that it was more and more difficult to get the brokers to renew my bills, or to cash any further post-obits upon an unentailed property. Ruin lay right across my path, and every day I saw it clearer, nearer, and more absolutely unavoidable.

What made me feel my own poverty the more was that, apart from the great wealth of Lord Southerton, all my other relations were fairly well-to-do. The nearest of these was Everard King, my father's nephew and my own first cousin, who had spent an adventurous life in Brazil, and had now returned to this country to settle down on his fortune. We never knew how he made his money, but he appeared to have plenty of it, for he bought the estate of Greylands, near Clipton-on-the-Marsh, in Suffolk. For the first year of his residence in England he took no more notice of me than my miserly uncle; but at last one summer morning, to my very great relief and joy, I received a letter asking me to come down that very day and spend a short visit at Greylands Court. I was expecting a rather long visit to Bankruptcy Court at the time, and this interruption seemed almost providential. If I could only get on terms with this unknown relative of mine, I might pull through yet. For the family credit he could not let me go entirely to the wall. I ordered my valet to pack my valise, and I set off the same evening for Clipton-on-the-Marsh.

After changing at Ipswich, a little local train deposited me at a small, deserted station lying amidst a rolling grassy country, with a sluggish and winding river curving in and out amid the valleys, between high, silted banks, which showed that we were within reach of the tide. No carriage was awaiting me (I found afterwards that my telegram had been delayed), so I hired a dogcart at the local inn. The driver, an excellent fellow, was full of my relative's praises, and I learned from him that Mr. Everard King was already a name to conjure with in that part of the county. He had entertained the schoolchildren, he had thrown his grounds open to visitors, he had subscribed to charities—in short, his benevolence had been so universal that my driver could only account for it on the supposition that he had parliamentary ambitions.

My attention was drawn away from my driver's panegyric by the appearance of a very beautiful bird which settled on a telegraph-post beside the road. At first I thought that it was a jay, but it was larger, with a brighter plumage. The driver accounted for its presence at once by saying that it belonged to the very man whom we were about to visit. It seems that the acclimatization of foreign creatures was one of his hobbies, and that he had brought with him from Brazil a number of birds and beasts which he was endeavoring to rear in England. When once we had passed the gates of Greylands Park we had ample evidence of this taste of his. Some small spotted deer, a curious wild pig known, I believe, as a peccary, a gorgeously feathered oriole, some sort of armadillo, and a singular lumbering in-toed beast like a very fat badger, were among the creatures which I observed as we drove along the winding avenue.

Mr. Everard King, my unknown cousin, was standing in person upon the steps of his house, for he had seen us in the distance, and guessed that it was I. His appearance was very homely and benevolent, short and stout, forty-five years old, perhaps, with a round, good-humored face, burned brown with the tropical sun, and shot with a thousand wrinkles. He wore white linen clothes, in true planter style, with a cigar between his lips, and a large Panama hat upon the back of his head. It was such a figure as one associates with a verandahed bungalow, and it looked curiously out of place in front of this broad, stone English mansion, with its solid wings and its Palladio pillars before the doorway.

"My dear!" he cried, glancing over his shoulder; "My dear, here is our guest! Welcome, welcome to Greylands! I am delighted to make your acquaintance, Cousin Marshall, and I take it as a great compliment that you should honor this sleepy little country place with your presence."

Nothing could be more hearty than his manner, and he set me at my ease in an instant. But it needed all his cordiality to atone for the frigidity and even rudeness of his wife, a tall, haggard woman, who came forward at his summons. She was, I believe, of Brazilian extraction, though she spoke excellent English, and I excused her manners on the score of her ignorance of our customs. She did not attempt to conceal, however, either then or afterwards, that I was no very welcome visitor at Greylands Court. Her actual words were, as a rule, courteous, but she was the possessor of a pair of particularly expressive dark eyes, and I read in them very clearly from the first that she heartily wished me back in London once more.

However, my debts were too pressing and my designs upon my wealthy relative were too vital for me to allow them to be upset by the ill-temper of his wife, so I disregarded her coldness and reciprocated the extreme cordiality of his welcome. No pains had been spared by him to make me comfortable. My room was a charming one. He implored me to tell him anything which could add to my happiness. It was on the tip of my tongue to inform him that a blank cheque would materially help towards that end, but I felt that it might be premature in the present state of our acquaintance. The dinner was excellent, and as we sat together afterwards over his Havanas and coffee, which later he told me was specially prepared upon his own plantation, it seemed to me that all my driver's eulogies were justified, and that I had never met a more large-hearted and hospitable man.

But, in spite of his cheery good nature, he was a man with a strong will and a fiery temper of his own. Of this I had an example upon the following morning. The curious aversion which Mrs. Everard King had conceived toward me was so strong, that her manner at breakfast was almost offensive. But her meaning became unmistakable when her husband had quitted the room.

"The best train in the day is at twelve-fifteen," said she.

"But I was not thinking of going today," I answered, frankly—perhaps even defiantly, for I was determined not to be driven out by this woman.

"Oh, if it rests with you—" said she, and stopped with a most insolent expression in her eyes.

"I am sure," I answered, "that Mr. Everard King would tell me if I were outstaying my welcome."

"What's this? What's this?" said a voice, and there he was in the room. He had overheard my last words, and a glance at our faces had told him the rest. In an instant his chubby, cheery face set into an expression of absolute ferocity.

"Might I trouble you to walk outside, Marshall?" said he. (I may mention that my own name is Marshall King.)

He closed the door behind me, and then, for an instant, I heard him talking in a low voice of concentrated passion to his wife. This gross breach of hospitality had evidently hit upon his tenderest point. I am no eavesdropper, so I walked out on to the lawn. Presently I heard a hurried step behind me, and there was the lady, her face pale with excitement, and her eyes red with tears.

"My husband has asked me to apologize to you, Mr. Marshall King," said she, standing with downcast eyes before me.

"Please do not say another word, Mrs. King."

Her dark eyes suddenly blazed out at me. "You fool!" she hissed, with frantic vehemence, and turning on her heel swept back to the house.

The insult was so outrageous, so insufferable, that I could only stand staring after her in bewilderment. I was still there when my host joined me. He was his cheery, chubby self once more.

"I hope that my wife has apologized for her foolish remarks," said he.

"Oh, yes—yes, certainly!"

He put his hand through my arm and walked with me up and down the lawn.

"You must not take it seriously," said he. "It would grieve me inexpressibly if you curtailed your visit by one hour. The fact is—there is no reason why there should be any concealment between relatives—that my poor dear wife is incredibly jealous. She hates that anyone—male or female—should for an instant come between us. Her ideal is a desert island and an eternal tête-à-tête. That gives you the clue to her actions, which are, I confess, upon this particular point, not very far removed from mania. Tell me that you will think no more of it."

"No, no; certainly not."

"Then light this cigar and come round with me and see my little menagerie."

The whole afternoon was occupied by this inspection, which included all the birds, beasts, and even reptiles which he had imported. Some were free, some in cages, a few actually in the house. He spoke with enthusiasm of his successes and his failures, his births and his deaths, and he would cry out in his delight, like a schoolboy, when, as we walked, some gaudy bird would flutter up from the grass, or some curious beast slink into the cover.

Finally he led me down a corridor which extended from one wing of the house. At the end of this there was a heavy door with a sliding shutter in it, and beside it there projected from the wall an iron handle attached to a wheel and a drum. A line of stout bars extended across the passage.

"I am about to show you the jewel of my collection," said he. "There is only one other specimen in Europe, now that the Rotterdam cub is dead. It is a Brazilian cat."

"But how does that differ from any other cat?"

"You will soon see that," said he, laughing. "Will you kindly draw that shutter and look through?"

I did so, and found that I was gazing into a large, empty room, with stone flags, and small, barred windows upon the farther wall. In the centre of this room, lying in the middle of a golden patch of sunlight, there was stretched a huge creature, as large as a tiger, but as black and sleek as ebony. It was simply a very enormous and very well-kept black cat, and it cuddled up and basked in that yellow pool of light exactly as a cat would do. It was so graceful, so sinewy, and so gently and smoothly diabolical, that I could not take my eyes from the opening.

"Isn't he splendid?" said my host, enthusiastically.

"Glorious! I never saw such a noble creature."

"Some people call it a black puma, but really it is not a puma at all. That fellow is nearly eleven feet from tail to tip. Four years ago he was a little ball of back fluff, with two yellow eyes staring out of it. He was sold to me as a newborn cub up in the wild country at the head-waters of the Rio Negro. They speared his mother to death after she had killed a dozen of them."

"They are ferocious, then?"

"The most absolutely treacherous and bloodthirsty creatures upon earth. You talk about a Brazilian cat to an up-country Indian, and see him get the jumps. They prefer humans to game. This fellow has never tasted living blood yet, but when he does he will be a terror. At present he won't stand anyone but me in his den. Even Baldwin, the groom, dare not go near him. As to me, I am his mother and father in one."

As he spoke he suddenly, to my astonishment, opened the door and slipped in, closing it instantly behind him. At the sound of his voice the huge, lithe creature rose, yawned and rubbed its round, black head affectionately against his side, while he patted and fondled it.

"Now, Tommy, into your cage!" said he.

The monstrous cat walked over to one side of the room and coiled itself up under a grating. Everard King came out, and taking the iron handle which I have mentioned, he began to turn it. As he did so the line of bars in the corridor began to pass through a slot in the wall and closed up the front of this grating, so as to make an effective cage. When it was in position he opened the door once more and invited me into the room, which was heavy with the pungent, musty smell peculiar to the great carnivora.

"That's how we work it," said he. "We give him the run of the room for exercise, and then at night we put him in his cage. You can let him out by turning the handle from the passage, or you can, as you have seen, coop him up in the same way. No, no, you should not do that!"

I had put my hand between the bars to pat the glossy, heaving flank. He pulled it back, with a serious face.

"I assure you that he is not safe. Don't imagine that because I can take liberties with him anyone else can. He is very exclusive in his friends—aren't you, Tommy? Ah, he hears his lunch coming to him! Don't you, boy?"

A step sounded in the stone-flagged passage, and the creature had sprung to his feet, and was pacing up and down the narrow cage, his yellow eyes gleaming, and his scarlet tongue rippling and quivering over the white line of his jagged teeth. A groom entered with a coarse joint upon a tray, and thrust it through the bars to him. He pounced lightly upon it, carried it off to the corner, and there, holding it between his paws, tore and wrenched at it, raising his bloody muzzle every now and then to look at us. It was a malignant and yet fascinating sight.

"You can't wonder that I am fond of him, can you?" said my host, as we left the room, "especially when you consider that I have had the rearing of him. It was no joke bringing him over from the centre of South America; but here he is safe and sound—and, as I have said, far the most perfect specimen in Europe. The people at the Zoo are dying to have him, but I really can't part with him. Now, I think that I have inflicted my hobby upon you long enough, so we cannot do better than follow Tommy's example, and go to our lunch."

My South American relative was so engrossed by his grounds and their curious occupants, that I hardly gave him credit at first for having any interests outside them. That he had some, and pressing ones, was soon borne in upon me by the number of telegrams which he received. They arrived at all hours, and were always opened by him with the utmost eagerness and anxiety upon his face. Sometimes I imagined that it must be the Turf, and sometimes the Stock Exchange, but certainly he had some very urgent business going forwards which was not transacted upon the Downs of Suffolk. During the six days of my visit he had never fewer than three or four telegrams a day, and sometimes as many as seven or eight.

I had occupied these six days so well, that by the end of them I had succeeded in getting upon the most cordial terms with my cousin. Every night we had sat up late in the billiard-room, he telling me the most extraordinary stories of his adventures in America—stories so desperate and reckless, that I could hardly associate them with the brown, little, chubby man before me. In return, I ventured upon some of my own reminiscences of London life, which interested him so much, that he vowed he would come up to Grosvenor Mansions and stay with me. He was anxious to see the faster side of city life, and certainly, though I say it, he could not have chosen a more competent guide. It was not until the last day of my visit that I ventured to approach that which was on my mind. I told him frankly about my pecuniary difficulties and my impending ruin, and I asked his advice—though I hoped for something more solid. He listened attentively, puffing hard at his cigar.

"But surely," said he, "you are the heir of our relative, Lord Southerton?"

"I have every reason to believe so, but he would never make me any allowance."

"No, no, I have heard of his miserly ways. My poor Marshall, your position has been a very hard one. By the way, have you heard any news of Lord Southerton's health lately?"

"He has always been in a critical condition ever since my childhood."

"Exactly—a creaking hinge, if ever there was one. Your inheritance may be a long way off. Dear me, how awkwardly situated you are!"

"I had some hopes, sir, that you, knowing all the facts, might be inclined to advance—"

"Don't say another word, my dear boy," he cried, with the utmost cordiality; "we shall talk it over tonight, and I give you my word that whatever is in my power shall be done."

I was not sorry that my visit was drawing to a close, for it is unpleasant to feel that there is one person in the house who eagerly desires your departure. Mrs. King's sallow face and forbidding eyes had become more and more hateful to me. She was no longer actively rude—her fear of her husband prevented her—but she pushed her insane jealousy to the extent of ignoring me, never addressing me, and in every way making my stay at Greylands as uncomfortable as she could. So offensive was her manner during that last day, that I should certainly have left had it not been for that interview with my host in the evening which would, I hoped, retrieve my broken fortunes.

It was very late when it occurred, for my relative, who had been receiving even more telegrams than usual during the day, went off to his study after dinner, and only emerged when the household had retired to bed. I heard him go round locking the doors, as custom was of a night, and finally he joined me in the billiard-room. His stout figure was wrapped in a dressing-gown, and he wore a pair of red Turkish slippers without any heels. Settling down into an armchair, he brewed himself a glass of grog, in which I could not help noticing that the whisky considerably predominated over the water.

"My word!" said he, "what a night!"

It was, indeed. The wind was howling and screaming round the house, and the latticed windows rattled and shook as if they were coming in. The glow of the yellow lamps and the flavor of our cigars seemed the brighter and more fragrant for the contrast.

"Now, my boy," said my host, "we have the house and the night to ourselves. Let me have an idea of how your affairs stand, and I will see what can be done to set them in order. I wish to hear every detail."

Thus encouraged, I entered into a long exposition, in which all my tradesmen and creditors from my landlord to my valet, figured in turn. I had notes in my pocketbook, and I marshaled my facts, and gave, I flatter myself, a very businesslike statement of my own un-businesslike ways and lamentable position. I was depressed, however, to notice that my companion's eyes were vacant and his attention elsewhere. When he did occasionally throw out a remark it was so entirely perfunctory and pointless, that I was sure he had not in the least followed my remarks. Every now and then he roused himself and put on some show of interest, asking me to repeat or to explain more fully, but it was always to sink once more into the same brown study. At last he rose and threw the end of his cigar into the grate.

"I'll tell you what, my boy," said he. "I never had a head for figures, so you will excuse me. You must jot it all down upon paper, and let me have a note of the amount. I'll understand it when I see it in black and white."

The proposal was encouraging. I promised to do so.

"And now it's time we were in bed. By Jove, there's one o'clock striking in the hall."

The tingling of the chiming clock broke through the deep roar of the gale. The wind was sweeping past with the rush of a great river.

"I must see my cat before I go to bed," said my host. "A high wind excites him. Will you come?"

"Certainly," said I.

"Then tread softly and don't speak, for everyone is asleep."

We passed quietly down the lamp-lit Persian-rugged hall, and through the door at the farther end. All was dark in the stone corridor, but a stable lantern hung on a hook, and my host took it down and lit it. There was no grating visible in the passage, so I knew that the beast was in its cage.

"Come in!" said my relative, and opened the door.

A deep growling as we entered showed that the storm had really excited the creature. In the flickering light of the lantern, we saw it, a huge black mass coiled in the corner of its den and throwing a squat, uncouth shadow upon the whitewashed wall. Its tail switched angrily among the straw.

"Poor Tommy is not in the best of tempers," said Everard King, holding up the lantern and looking in at him. "What a black devil he looks, doesn't he? I must give him a little supper to put him in a better humor. Would you mind holding the lantern for a moment?"

I took it from his hand and he stepped to the door.

"His larder is just outside here," said he. "You will excuse me for an instant won't you?" He passed out, and the door shut with a sharp metallic click behind him.

That hard crisp sound made my heart stand still. A sudden wave of terror passed over me. A vague perception of some monstrous treachery turned me cold. I sprang to the door, but there was no handle upon the inner side.

"Here!" I cried. "Let me out!"

"All right! Don't make a row!" said my host from the passage. "You've got the light all right."

"Yes, but I don't care about being locked in alone like this."

"Don't you?" I heard his hearty, chuckling laugh. "You won't be alone long."

"Let me out, sir!" I repeated angrily. "I tell you I don't allow practical jokes of this sort."

"Practical is the word," said he, with another hateful chuckle. And then suddenly I heard, amidst the roar of the storm, the creak and whine of the winch-handle turning and the rattle of the grating as it passed through the slot. Great God, he was letting loose the Brazilian cat!

In the light of the lantern I saw the bars sliding slowly before me. Already there was an opening a foot wide at the farther end. With a scream I seized the last bar with my hands and pulled with the strength of a madman. I was a madman with rage and horror. For a minute or more I held the thing motionless. I knew that he was straining with all his force upon the handle, and that the leverage was sure to overcome me. I gave inch by inch, my feet sliding along the stones, and all the time I begged and prayed this inhuman monster to save me from this horrible death. I conjured him by his kinship. I reminded him that I was his guest; I begged to know what harm I had ever done him. His only answers were the tugs and jerks upon the handle, each of which, in spite of all my struggles, pulled another bar through the opening. Clinging and clutching, I was dragged across the whole front of the cage, until at last, with aching wrists and lacerated fingers, I gave up the hopeless struggle. The grating clanged back as I released it, and an instant later I heard the shuffle of the Turkish slippers in the passage, and the slam of the distant door. Then everything was silent.

The creature had never moved during this time. He lay still in the corner, and his tail had ceased switching. This apparition of a man adhering to his bars and dragged screaming across him had apparently filled him with amazement. I saw his great eyes staring steadily at me. I had dropped the lantern when I seized the bars, but it still burned upon the floor, and I made a movement to grasp it, with some idea that its light might protect me. But the instant I moved, the beast gave a deep and menacing growl. I stopped and stood still, quivering with fear in every limb. The cat (if one may call so fearful a creature by so homely a name) was not more than ten feet from me. The eyes glimmered like two disks of phosphorus in the darkness. They appalled and yet fascinated me. I could not take my own eyes from them. Nature plays strange tricks with us at such moments of intensity, and those glimmering lights waxed and waned with a steady rise and fall. Sometimes they seemed to be tiny points of extreme brilliancy—little electric sparks in the black obscurity—then they would widen and widen until all that corner of the room was filled with their shifting and sinister light. And then suddenly they went out altogether.

The beast had closed its eyes. I do not know whether there may be any truth in the old idea of the dominance of the human gaze, or whether the huge cat was simply drowsy, but the fact remains that, far from showing any symptom of attacking me, it simply rested its sleek, black head upon its huge forepaws and seemed to sleep. I stood, fearing to move lest I should rouse it into malignant life once more. But at least I was able to think clearly now that the baleful eyes were off me. Here I was shut up for the night with the ferocious beast. My own instincts, to say nothing of the words of the plausible villain who laid this trap for me, warned me that the animal was as savage as its master. How could I stave it off until morning? The door was hopeless, and so were the narrow, barred windows. There was no shelter anywhere in the bare, stone- flagged room. To cry for assistance was absurd. I knew that this den was an outhouse, and that the corridor which connected it with the house was at least a hundred feet long. Besides, with the gale thundering outside, my cries were not likely to be heard. I had only my own courage and my own wits to trust to.

And then, with a fresh wave of horror, my eyes fell upon the lantern. The candle had burned low, and was already beginning to gutter. In ten minutes it would be out. I had only ten minutes then in which to do something, for I felt that if I were once left in the dark with that fearful beast I should be incapable of action. The very thought of it paralyzed me. I cast my despairing eyes round this chamber of death, and they rested upon one spot which seemed to promise I will not say safety, but less immediate and imminent danger than the open floor.

I have said that the cage had a top as well as a front, and this top was left standing when the front was wound through the slot in the wall. It consisted of bars at a few inches' interval, with stout wire netting between, and it rested upon a strong stanchion at each end. It stood now as a great barred canopy over the crouching figure in the corner. The space between this iron shelf and the roof may have been from two or three feet. If I could only get up there, squeezed in between bars and ceiling, I should have only one vulnerable side. I should be safe from below, from behind, and from each side. Only on the open face of it could I be attacked. There, it is true, I had no protection whatever; but at least, I should be out of the brute's path when he began to pace about his den. He would have to come out of his way to reach me. It was now or never, for if once the light were out it would be impossible. With a gulp in my throat I sprang up, seized the iron edge of the top, and swung myself panting on to it. I writhed in face downwards, and found myself looking straight into the terrible eyes and yawning jaws of the cat. Its fetid breath came up into my face like the steam from some foul pot.

It appeared, however, to be rather curious than angry. With a sleek ripple of its long, black back it rose, stretched itself, and then rearing itself on its hind legs, with one forepaw against the wall, it raised the other, and drew its claws across the wire meshes beneath me. One sharp, white hook tore through my trousers—for I may mention that I was still in evening dress—and dug a furrow in my knee. It was not meant as an attack, but rather as an experiment, for upon my giving a sharp cry of pain he dropped down again, and springing lightly into the room, he began walking swiftly round it, looking up every now and again in my direction. For my part I shuffled backwards until I lay with my back against the wall, screwing myself into the smallest space possible. The farther I got the more difficult it was for him to attack me.

He seemed more excited now that he had begun to move about, and he ran swiftly and noiselessly round and round the den, passing continually underneath the iron couch upon which I lay. It was wonderful to see so great a bulk passing like a shadow, with hardly the softest thudding of velvety pads. The candle was burning low—so low that I could hardly see the creature. And then, with a last flare and splutter it went out altogether. I was alone with the cat in the dark!

It helps one to face a danger when one knows that one has done all that possibly can be done. There is nothing for it then but to quietly await the result. In this case, there was no chance of safety anywhere except the precise spot where I was. I stretched myself out, therefore, and lay silently, almost breathlessly, hoping that the beast might forget my presence if I did nothing to remind him. I reckoned that it must already be two o'clock. At four it would be full dawn. I had not more than two hours to wait for daylight.

Outside, the storm was still raging, and the rain lashed continually against the little windows. Inside, the poisonous and fetid air was overpowering. I could neither hear nor see the cat. I tried to think about other things—but only one had power enough to draw my mind from my terrible position. That was the contemplation of my cousin's villainy, his unparalleled hypocrisy, his malignant hatred of me. Beneath that cheerful face there lurked the spirit of a mediaeval assassin. And as I thought of it I saw more clearly how cunningly the thing had been arranged. He had apparently gone to bed with the others. No doubt he had his witness to prove it. Then, unknown to them, he had slipped down, had lured me into his den and abandoned me. His story would be so simple. He had left me to finish my cigar in the billiard-room. I had gone down on my own account to have a last look at the cat. I had entered the room without observing that the cage was opened, and I had been caught. How could such a crime be brought home to him? Suspicion, perhaps—but proof, never!

How slowly those dreadful two hours went by! Once I heard a low, rasping sound, which I took to be the creature licking its own fur. Several times those greenish eyes gleamed at me through the darkness, but never in a fixed stare, and my hopes grew stronger that my presence had been forgotten or ignored. At last the least faint glimmer of light came through the windows—I first dimly saw them as two grey squares upon the black wall, then grey turned to white, and I could see my terrible companion once more. And he, alas, could see me!

It was evident to me at once that he was in a much more dangerous and aggressive mood than when I had seen him last. The cold of the morning had irritated him, and he was hungry as well. With a continual growl he paced swiftly up and down the side of the room which was farthest from my refuge, his whiskers bristling angrily, and his tail switching and lashing. As he turned at the corners his savage eyes always looked upwards at me with a dreadful menace. I knew then that he meant to kill me. Yet I found myself even at that moment admiring the sinuous grace of the devilish thing, its long, undulating, rippling movements, the gloss of its beautiful flanks, the vivid, palpitating scarlet of the glistening tongue which hung from the jet-black muzzle. And all the time that deep, threatening growl was rising and rising in an unbroken crescendo. I knew that the crisis was at hand.

It was a miserable hour to meet such a death—so cold, so comfortless, shivering in my light dress clothes upon this gridiron of torment upon which I was stretched. I tried to brace myself to it, to raise my soul above it, and at the same time, with the lucidity which comes to a perfectly desperate man, I cast round for some possible means of escape. One thing was clear to me. If that front of the cage was only back in its position once more, I could find a sure refuge behind it. Could I possibly pull it back? I hardly dared to move for fear of bringing the creature upon me. Slowly, very slowly, I put my hand forward until it grasped the edge of the front, the final bar which protruded through the wall. To my surprise it came quite easily to my jerk. Of course the difficulty of drawing it out arose from the fact that I was clinging to it. I pulled again, and three inches of it came through. It ran apparently on wheels. I pulled again . . . and then the cat sprang!

It was so quick, so sudden, that I never saw it happen. I simply heard the savage snarl, and in an instant afterwards the blazing yellow eyes, the flattened black head with its red tongue and flashing teeth, were within reach of me. The impact of the creature shook the bars upon which I lay, until I thought (as far as I could think of anything at such a moment) that they were coming down. The cat swayed there for an instant, the head and front paws quite close to me, the hind paws clawing to find a grip upon the edge of the grating. I heard the claws rasping as they clung to the wire-netting, and the breath of the beast made me sick. But its bound had been miscalculated. It could not retain its position. Slowly, grinning with rage, and scratching madly at the bars, it swung backwards and dropped heavily upon the floor. With a growl it instantly faced round to me and crouched for another spring.

I knew that the next few moments would decide my fate. The creature had learned by experience. It would not miscalculate again. I must act promptly, fearlessly, if I were to have a chance for life. In an instant I had formed my plan. Pulling off my dress-coat, I threw it down over the head of the beast. At the same moment I dropped over the edge, seized the end of the front grating, and pulled it frantically out of the wall.

It came more easily than I could have expected. I rushed across the room, bearing it with me; but, as I rushed, the accident of my position put me upon the outer side. Had it been the other way, I might have come off scathless. As it was, there was a moment's pause as I stopped it and tried to pass in through the opening which I had left. That moment was enough to give time to the creature to toss off the coat with which I had blinded him and to spring upon me. I hurled myself through the gap and pulled the rails to behind me, but he seized my leg before I could entirely withdraw it. One stroke of that huge paw tore off my calf as a shaving of wood curls off before a plane. The next moment, bleeding and fainting, I was lying among the foul straw with a line of friendly bars between me and the creature which ramped so frantically against them.

Too wounded to move, and too faint to be conscious of fear, I could only lie, more dead than alive, and watch it. It pressed its broad, black chest against the bars and angled for me with its crooked paws as I have seen a kitten do before a mousetrap. It ripped my clothes, but, stretch as it would, it could not quite reach me. I have heard of the curious numbing effect produced by wounds from the great carnivora, and now I was destined to experience it, for I had lost all sense of personality, and was as interested in the cat's failure or success as if it were some game which I was watching. And then gradually my mind drifted away into strange vague dreams, always with that black face and red tongue coming back into them, and so I lost myself in the nirvana of delirium, the blessed relief of those who are too sorely tried.

Tracing the course of events afterwards, I conclude that I must have been insensible for about two hours. What roused me to consciousness once more was that sharp metallic click which had been the precursor of my terrible experience. It was the shooting back of the spring lock. Then, before my senses were clear enough to entirely apprehend what they saw, I was aware of the round, benevolent face of my cousin peering in through the open door. What he saw evidently amazed him. There was the cat crouching on the floor. I was stretched upon my back in my shirtsleeves within the cage, my trousers torn to ribbons and a great pool of blood all round me. I can see his amazed face now, with the morning sunlight upon it. He peered at me, and peered again. Then he closed the door behind him, and advanced to the cage to see if I were really dead.

I cannot undertake to say what happened. I was not in a fit state to witness or to chronicle such events. I can only say that I was suddenly conscious that his face was away from me—that he was looking towards the animal.

"Good old Tommy!" he cried. "Good old Tommy!"

Then he came near the bars, with his back still towards me.

"Down, you stupid beast!" he roared. "Down, sir! Don't you know your master?"

Suddenly even in my bemuddled brain a remembrance came of those words of his when he had said that the taste of blood would turn the cat into a fiend. My blood had done it, but he was to pay the price.

"Get away!" he screamed. "Get away, you devil! Baldwin! Baldwin! Oh, my God!"

And then I heard him fall, and rise, and fall again, with a sound like the ripping of sacking. His screams grew fainter until they were lost in the worrying snarl. And then, after I thought that he was dead, I saw, as in a nightmare, a blinded, tattered, blood-soaked figure running wildly round the room—and that was the last glimpse which I had of him before I fainted once again.

I was many months in my recovery—in fact, I cannot say that I have ever recovered, for to the end of my days I shall carry a stick as a sign of my night with the Brazilian cat. Baldwin, the groom, and the other servants could not tell what had occurred, when, drawn by the death-cries of their master, they found me behind the bars, and his remains—or what they afterwards discovered to be his remains—in the clutch of the creature which he had reared. They stalled him off with hot irons, and afterwards shot him through the loophole of the door before they could finally extricate me. I was carried to my bedroom, and there, under the roof of my would-be murderer, I remained between life and death for several weeks. They had sent for a surgeon from Clipton and a nurse from London, and in a month I was able to be carried to the station, and so conveyed back once more to Grosvenor Mansions.

I have one remembrance of that illness, which might have been part of the ever-changing panorama conjured up by a delirious brain were it not so definitely fixed in my memory. One night, when the nurse was absent, the door of my chamber opened, and a tall woman in blackest mourning slipped into the room. She came across to me, and as she bent her sallow face I saw by the faint gleam of the night-light that it was the Brazilian woman whom my cousin had married. She stared intently into my face, and her expression was more kindly than I had ever seen it.

"Are you conscious?" she asked.

I feebly nodded—for I was still very weak.

"Well; then, I only wished to say to you that you have yourself to blame. Did I not do all I could for you? From the beginning I tried to drive you from the house. By every means, short of betraying my husband, I tried to save you from him. I knew that he had a reason for bringing you here. I knew that he would never let you get away again. No one knew him as I knew him, who had suffered from him so often. I did not dare to tell you all this. He would have killed me. But I did my best for you. As things have turned out, you have been the best friend that I have ever had. You have set me free, and I fancied that nothing but death would do that. I am sorry if you are hurt, but I cannot reproach myself. I told you that you were a fool—and a fool you have been." She crept out of the room, the bitter, singular woman, and I was never destined to see her again. With what remained from her husband's property she went back to her native land, and I have heard that she afterwards took the veil at Pernambuco.

It was not until I had been back in London for some time that the doctors pronounced me to be well enough to do business. It was not a very welcome permission to me, for I feared that it would be the signal for an inrush of creditors; but it was Summers, my lawyer, who first took advantage of it.

"I am very glad to see that your lordship is so much better," said he. "I have been waiting a long time to offer my congratulations."

"What do you mean, Summers? This is no time for joking."

"I mean what I say," he answered. "You have been Lord Southerton for the last six weeks, but we feared that it would retard your recovery if you were to learn it."

Lord Southerton! One of the richest peers in England! I could not believe my ears. And then suddenly I thought of the time which had elapsed, and how it coincided with my injuries.

"Then Lord Southerton must have died about the same time that I was hurt?"

"His death occurred upon that very day." Summers looked hard at me as I spoke, and I am convinced—for he was a very shrewd fellow—that he had guessed the true state of the case. He paused for a moment as if awaiting a confidence from me, but I could not see what was to be gained by exposing such a family scandal.

"Yes, a very curious coincidence," he continued, with the same knowing look. "Of course, you are aware that your cousin Everard King was the next heir to the estates. Now, if it had been you instead of him who had been torn to pieces by this tiger, or whatever it was, then of course he would have been Lord Southerton at the present moment."

"No doubt," said I.

"And he took such an interest in it," said Summers. "I happen to know that the late Lord Southerton's valet was in his pay, and that he used to have telegrams from him every few hours to tell him how he was getting on. That would be about the time when you were down there. Was it not strange that he should wish to be so well informed, since he knew that he was not the direct heir?"

"Very strange," said I. "And now, Summers, if you will bring me my bills and a new cheque-book, we will begin to get things into order."

The White Cat

W. W. Jacobs

THE TRAVELER STOOD LOOKING FROM THE TAPROOM WINDOW OF THE Cauliflower at the falling rain. The village street below was empty, and everything was quiet with the exception of the garrulous old man smoking with much enjoyment on the settle behind him.

"It'll do a power o' good," said the ancient, craning his neck round the edge of the settle and turning a bleared eye on the window. "I ain't like some folk; I never did mind a drop o' rain."

The traveler grunted and, returning to the settle opposite the old man, fell to lazily stroking a cat which had strolled in, attracted by the warmth of the small fire which smoldered in the grate.

"He's a good mouser," said the old man, "but I expect that Smith the landlord would sell 'im to anybody for arf a crown; but we 'ad a cat in Claybury once that you couldn't ha' bought for a hundred golden sovereigns."

The traveler continued to caress the cat.

"A white cat, with one yaller eye and one blue one," continued the old man. "It sounds queer, but it's as true as I sit 'ere wishing that I 'ad another mug o' ale as good as the last you gave me."

The traveler, with a start that upset the cat's nerves, finished his own mug, and then ordered both to be refilled. He stirred the fire into a blaze, and, lighting his pipe and putting one foot on to the hob, prepared to listen.

"It used to belong to old man Clark, young Joe Clark's uncle," said the ancient, smacking his lips delicately over the ale and extending a tremulous claw to the tobacco-pouch pushed towards him; "and he was never tired of showing it off to people. He used to call it 'is blue-eyed darling, and the fuss 'e made o' that cat was sinful.

"Young Joe Clark couldn't bear it, but being down in 'is uncle's will for five cottages and a bit o' land bringing in about forty pounds a year, he 'ad to 'ide his feelings and pretend as he loved it. He used to take it little drops o' cream and tit-bits o' meat, and old Clark was so pleased that 'e promised 'im that he should 'ave the cat along with all the other property when 'e was dead.

"Young Joe said he couldn't thank 'im enough, and the old man, who 'ad been ailing a long time, made 'im come up every day to teach 'im 'ow to take care of it arter he was gone. He taught Joe 'ow to cook its meat and then chop it up fine; 'ow it liked a clean saucer every time for its milk; and 'ow he wasn't to make a noise when it was asleep.

"'Take care your children don't worry it, Joe,' he ses one day, very sharp. 'One o' your boys was pulling its tail this morning, and I want you to clump his 'ead for 'im.'

"'Which one was it?' ses Joe.

"'The slobbery-nosed one,' ses old Clark.

"'I'll give 'im a clout as soon as I get 'ome,' ses Joe, who was very fond of 'is children.

"'Go and fetch 'im and do it 'ere,' ses the old man; 'that'll teach 'im to love animals.'

"Joe went off 'ome to fetch the boy, and arter his mother 'ad washed his face, and wiped his nose, an' put a clean pinneyfore on 'im, he took 'im to 'is uncle's and clouted his 'ead for 'im. Arter that Joe and 'is wife 'ad words all night long, and next morning old Clark, coming in from the garden, was just in time to see 'im kick the cat right acrost the kitchen.

"He could 'ardly speak for a minute, and when 'e could Joe see plain wot a fool he'd been. Fust of all 'e called Joe every name he could think of—which took 'im a long time—and then he ordered 'im out of 'is house.

"'You shall 'ave my money wen your betters have done with it,' he ses, 'and not afore. That's all you've done for yourself.'

"Joe Clark didn't know wot he meant at the time, but when old Clark died three months arterwards 'e found out. His uncle 'ad made a new will and left everything to old George Barstow for as long as the cat lived, providing that he took care of it. When the cat was dead the property was to go to Joe.

"The cat was only two years old at the time, and George Barstow, who was arf crazy with joy, said it shouldn't be 'is fault if it didn't live another twenty years.

"The funny thing was the quiet way Joe Clark took it. He didn't seem to be at all cut up about it, and when Henery Walker said it was a shame, 'e said he didn't mind, and that George Barstow was an old man, and he was quite welcome to 'ave the property as long as the cat lived.

"'It must come to me by the time I'm an old man,' he ses, 'ard that's all I care about.'

"Henery Walker went off, and as 'e passed the cottage where old Clark used to live, and which George Barstow 'ad moved into, 'e spoke to the old man over the palings and told 'im wot Joe Clark 'ad said. George Barstow only grunted and went on stooping and prying over 'is front garden.

"'Bin and lost something?' ses Henery Walker, watching 'im.

"'No; I'm finding,' ses George Barstow, very fierce, and picking up something. 'That's the fifth bit o' powdered liver I've found in my garden this morning.'

"Henery Walker went off whistling, and the opinion he'd 'ad o' Joe Clark began to improve. He spoke to Joe about it that arternoon, and Joe said that if 'e ever accused 'im o' such a thing again he'd knock 'is 'ead off. He said that he 'oped the cat 'ud live to be a hundred, and that 'e'd no more think of giving it poisoned meat than Henery Walker would of paying for 'is drink so long as 'e could get anybody else to do it for 'im.

"They 'ad bets up at this 'ere Cauliflower public-'ouse that evening as to 'ow long that cat 'ud live. Nobody gave it more than a month, and Bill Chambers sat and thought o' so many ways o' killing it on the sly that it was wunnerful to hear 'im.

"George Barstow took fright when he 'eard of them, and the care 'e took o' that cat was wunnerful to behold. Arf its time it was shut up in the back bedroom, and the other arf George Barstow was fussing arter it till that cat got to hate 'im like pison. Instead o' giving up work as he'd thought to do, 'e told Henery Walker that 'e'd never worked so 'ard in his life.

"'Wot about fresh air and exercise for it?' ses Henery.

"'Wot about Joe Clark?' ses George Barstow. 'I'm tied 'and and foot. I dursent leave the house for a moment. I ain't been to the Cauliflower since I've 'ad it, and three times I got out o' bed last night to see if it was safe.'

"'Mark my words,' ses Henery Walker; 'if that cat don't 'ave exercise, you'll lose it.'

"'I shall lose it if it does 'ave exercise,' ses George Barstow, 'that I know.'

"He sat down thinking arter Henery Walker 'ad gone, and then he 'ad a little collar and chain made for it, and took it out for a walk. Pretty nearly every dog in Claybury went with 'em, and the cat was in such a state o' mind afore they got 'ome he couldn't do anything with it. It 'ad a fit as soon as they got indoors, and George Barstow, who 'ad read about children's fits in the almanac, gave it a warm bath. It brought it round immediate, and then it began to tear round the room and up and down-stairs till George Barstow was afraid to go near it.

"It was so bad that evening, sneezing, that George Barstow sent for Bill Chambers, who'd got a good name for doctoring animals, and asked 'im to give it something. Bill said he'd got some powders at 'ome that would cure it at once, and he went and fetched 'em and mixed one up with a bit o' butter.

"'That's the way to give a cat medicine,' he ses; 'smear it with the butter and then it'll lick it off, powder and all.'

"He was just going to rub it on the cat when George Barstow caught 'old of 'is arm and stopped 'im.

"'How do I know it ain't pison?' he ses. 'You're a friend o' Joe Clark's, and for all I know he may ha' paid you to pison it.'

"'I wouldn't do such a thing,' ses Bill. 'You ought to know me better than that.'

"'All right,' ses George Barstow; 'you eat it then, and I'll give you two shillings in stead o' one. You can easy mix some more.'

"'Not me,' ses Bill Chambers, making a face.

"'Well, three shillings, then,' ses George Barstow, getting more and more suspicious like; 'four shillings—five shillings.'

"Bill Chambers shook his 'ead, and George Barstow, more and more certain that he 'ad caught 'im trying to kill 'is cat and that 'e wouldn't eat the stuff, rose 'im up to ten shillings.

"Bill looked at the butter and then 'e looked at the ten shillings on the table, and at last he shut 'is eyes and gulped it down and put the money in 'is pocket.

"'You see, I 'ave to be careful, Bill,' ses George Barstow, rather upset.

"Bill Chambers didn't answer 'im. He sat there as white as a sheet, and making such extraordinary faces that George was arf afraid of 'im.

"Anything wrong, Bill?' he ses at last.

"Bill sat staring at 'im, and then all of a sudden he clapped 'is 'and-kerchief to 'is mouth and, getting up from his chair, opened the door and rushed out. George Barstow thought at fust that he 'ad eaten pison for the sake o' the ten shillings, but when 'e remembered that Bill Chambers 'ad got the most delikit stummick in Claybury he altered 'is mind.

"The cat was better next morning, but George Barstow had 'ad such a fright about it 'e wouldn't let it go out of 'is sight, and Joe Clark began to think that 'e would 'ave to wait longer for that property than 'e had thought, arter all. To 'ear 'im talk anybody'd ha' thought that 'e loved that cat. We didn't pay much attention to it up at the Cauliflower 'ere, except maybe to wink at 'im—a thing he couldn't a bear—but at 'ome, o' course, his young 'uns thought as everything he said was Gospel; and one day, coming 'ome from work, as he was passing George Barstow's he was paid out for his deceitfulness.

"'I've wronged you, Joe Clark,' ses George Barstow, coming to the door, 'and I'm sorry for it.'

"'Oh!' ses Joe, staring.

"'Give that to your little Jimmy,' ses George Barstow, giving 'im a shilling. 'I've give ''im one, but I thought arterwards it wasn't enough.'

"'What for?' ses Joe, staring at 'im agin.

"'For bringing my cat 'ome,' ses George Barstow. "'Ow it got out I can't think, but I lost it for three hours, and I'd about given it up when your little Jimmy brought it to me in 'is arms. He's a fine little chap and 'e does you credit.'

"Joe Clark tried to speak, but he couldn't get a word out, and Henery Walker, wot 'ad just come up and 'eard wot passed, took hold of 'is arm and helped 'im home. He walked like a man in a dream, but arf-way he stopped and cut a stick from the hedge to take 'ome to little Jimmy. He said the boy 'ad been asking him for a stick for some time, but up till then 'e'd always forgotten it.

"At the end o' the fust year that cat was still alive, to everybody's surprise; but George Barstow took such care of it 'e never let it out of 'is sight. Every time 'e went out he took it with 'im in a hamper, and, to prevent its being poisoned, he paid Isaac Sawyer, who 'ad the biggest family in Claybury, sixpence a week to let one of 'is boys taste its milk before it had it.

"The second year it was ill twice, but the horse-doctor that George Barstow got for it said that it was as 'ard as nails, and with care it might live to be twenty. He said that it wanted more fresh air and exercise; but when he 'eard 'ow George Barstow come by it he said that p'r'aps it would live longer indoors arter all.

"At last one day, when George Barstow 'ad been living on the fat o' the land for nearly three years, that cat got out agin. George 'ad raised the front-room winder two or three inches to throw something outside, and, afore he knew wot was 'appening, the cat was out-side and going up the road about twenty miles an hour.

"George Barstow went arter it, but he might as well ha' tried to catch the wind. The cat was arf wild with joy at getting out agin, and he couldn't get within arf a mile of it.

"He stayed out all day without food or drink, follering it about until it came on dark, and then, o' course, he lost sight of it, and, hoping against 'ope that it would come home for its food, he went 'ome and waited for it. He sat up all night dozing in a chair in the front room with the door left open, but it was all no use; and arter thinking for a long time wot was best to do, he went out and told some o' the folks it was lost and offered a reward of five pounds for it.

"You never saw such a hunt then in all your life. Nearly every man, woman, and child in Claybury left their work or school and went to try and earn that five pounds. By the arternoon George Barstow made it ten pounds provided the cat was brought 'ome safe and sound, and people as was too old to walk stood at their cottage doors to snap it up as it came by.

"Joe Clark was hunting for it 'igh and low, and so was 'is wife and the boys. In fact, I b'lieve that everybody in Claybury excepting the parson and Bob Pretty was trying to get that ten pounds.

"O' course, we could understand the parson—'is pride wouldn't let 'im; but a low, poaching, thieving rascal like Bob Pretty turning up 'is nose at ten pounds was more than we could make out. Even on the second day, when George Barstow made it ten pounds down and a shilling a week for a year besides, he didn't offer to stir; all he did was to try and make fun o' them as was looking for it.

"'Have you looked everywhere you can think of for it, Bill?' he ses to Bill Chambers. 'Yes, I 'ave,' ses Bill.

"'Well, then, you want to look everywhere else,' ses Bob Pretty. 'I know where I should look if I wanted to find it.'

"'Why don't you find it, then?' ses Bill.

"''Cos I don't want to make mischief,' ses Bob Pretty. 'I don't want to be unneighborly to Joe Clark by interfering at all.'

"'Not for all that money?' ses Bill.

"'Not for fifty pounds,' ses Bob Pretty; 'you ought to know me better than that, Bill Chambers.'

"'It's my belief that you know more about where that cat is than you ought to,' ses Joe Gubbins.

"'You go on looking for it, Joe,' ses Bob Pretty, grinning; 'it's good exercise for you, and you've only lost two days' work.'

"'I'll give you arf a crown if you let me search your 'ouse, Bob,' ses Bill Chambers, looking at 'im very 'ard.

"'I couldn't do it at the price, Bill,' ses Bob Pretty, shaking his 'ead. 'I'm a pore man, but I'm very partikler who I 'ave come into my 'ouse.'

"O' course, everybody left off looking at once when they heard about Bob—not that they believed that he'd be such a fool as to keep the cat in his 'ouse; and that evening, as soon as it was dark, Joe Clark went round to see 'im.

"'Don't tell me as that cat's found, Joe,' ses Bob Pretty, as Joe opened the door.

"'Not as I've 'eard of,' said Joe, stepping inside. 'I wanted to speak to you about it; the sooner it's found the better I shall be pleased.'

"'It does you credit, Joe Clark,' ses Bob Pretty.

"'It's my belief that it's dead,' ses Joe, looking at 'im very 'ard; 'but I want to make sure afore taking over the property.'

"Bob Pretty looked at 'im and then he gave a little cough. 'Oh, you want it to be found dead,' he ses. "'Now, I wonder whether that cat's worth most dead or alive?'

"Joe Clark coughed then. 'Dead, I should think,' he ses at last. 'George Barstow's just 'ad bills printed offering fifteen pounds for it,' ses Bob Pretty.

"'I'll give that or more when I come into the property,' ses Joe Clark.

"'There's nothing like ready-money, though, is there?' ses Bob.

"'I'll promise it to you in writing, Bob,' ses Joe, trembling.

"'There's some things that don't look well in writing, Joe,' says Bob Pretty, considering; 'besides, why should you promise it to me?'

"'O' course, I meant if you found it,' ses Joe.

"'Well, I'll do my best, Joe,' ses Bob Pretty; 'and none of us can do no more than that, can they?'

"They sat talking and argufying over it for over an hour, and twice Bob Pretty got up and said 'e was going to see whether George Barstow wouldn't offer more. By the time they parted they was as thick as thieves, and next morning Bob Pretty was wearing Joe Clark's watch and chain, and Mrs. Pretty was up at Joe's 'ouse to see whether there was any of 'is furniture as she 'ad a fancy for.

"She didn't seem to be able to make up 'er mind at fust between a chest o' drawers that 'ad belonged to Joe's mother and a grand-father clock. She walked from one to the other for about ten minutes, and then Bob, who 'ad come in to 'elp her, told 'er to 'ave both.

"'You're quite welcome,' he ses';ain't she, Joe?'

"Joe Clark said 'Yes,' and arter he 'ad helped them carry 'em 'ome the Prettys went back and took the best bedstead to pieces, cos Bob said as it was easier to carry that way. Mrs. Clark 'ad to go and sit down at the bottom o' the garden with the neck of 'er dress undone to give herself air, but when she saw the little Prettys each walking 'ome with one of 'er best chairs on their 'eads she got and walked up and down like a mad thing.

"'I'm sure I don't know where we are to put it all,' ses Bob Pretty to Joe Gubbins, wot was looking on with other folks, 'but Joe Clark is that generous he won't 'ear of our leaving anything.'

"'Has 'e gorn mad?' ses Bill Chambers, staring at 'im.

"'Not as I knows on,' ses Bob Pretty. 'It's 'is good-'artedness, that's all. He feels sure that that cat's dead, and that he'll 'ave George Barstow's cottage and furniture. I told 'im he'd better wait till he'd made sure, but 'e wouldn't.'

"Before they'd finished, the Prettys 'ad picked that 'ouse as clean as a bone, and Joe Clark 'ad to go and get clean straw for his wife and children to sleep on; not that Mrs. Clark 'ad any sleep that night, nor Joe neither.

"Henery Walker was the fust to see what it really meant, and he went rushing off as fast as 'e could run to tell George Barstow. George couldn't believe 'im at fust, but when 'e did he swore that if a 'air of that cat's head was harmed 'e'd 'ave the law o' Bob Pretty, and arter Henery Walker 'ad gone 'e walked round to tell 'im so.

"'You're not yourself, George Barstow, else you wouldn't try and take away my character like that,' ses Bob Pretty.

"'Wot did Joe Clark give you all them things for?' ses George, pointing to the furniture.

"'Took a fancy to me, I s'pose,' ses Bob. 'People do sometimes. There's something about me at times that makes 'em like me.'

"'He gave 'em to you to kill my cat,' ses George Barstow. 'It's plain enough for any-body to see.'

"Bob Pretty smiled. 'I expect it'll turn up safe and sound one o' these days,' he ses, 'and then you'll come round and beg my pardon. P'r'aps—.'

"'P'r'aps wot?' ses George Barstow, arter waiting a bit.

"'P'r'aps somebody 'as got it and is keeping it till you've drawed the fifteen pounds out o' the bank,' ses Bob, looking at 'im very hard.

"'I've taken it out o' the bank,' ses George, starting; 'if that cat's alive, Bob, and you've got it, there's the fifteen pounds the moment you 'and it over.'

"'Wot d'ye mean—me got it?' ses Bob Pretty. 'You be careful o' my character.'

'I mean if you know where it is,' ses George Barstow trembling all over.

"'I don't say I couldn't find it, if that's wot you mean,' ses Bob. 'I can gin'rally find things when I want to.'

"'You find me that cat, alive and well, and the money's yours, Bob,' ses George, 'ardly able to speak, now that 'e fancied the cat was still alive.

"Bob Pretty shook his 'ead. 'No; that won't do,' he ses. 'S'pose I did 'ave the luck to find that pore animal, you'd say I'd had it all the time and refuse to pay.'

"'I swear I wouldn't, Bob,' ses George Barstow, jumping up.

"'Best thing you can do if you want me to try and find that cat,' says Bob Pretty, 'is to give me the fifteen pounds now, and I'll go and look for it at once. I can't trust you, George Barstow.'

"'And I can't trust you,' ses George Barstow.

"'Very good,' ses Bob, getting up; 'there's no 'arm done. P'r'aps Joe Clark 'll find the cat is dead and p'r'aps you'll find it's alive. It's all one to me.'

"George Barstow walked off 'ome, but he was in such a state o' mind 'e didn't know wot to do. Bob Pretty turning up 'is nose at fifteen pounds like that made 'im think that Joe Clark 'ad promised to pay 'im more if the cat was dead; and at last, arter worrying about it for a couple o' hours, 'e came up to this 'ere Cauliflower and offered Bob the fifteen pounds.

"'Wot's this for?' ses Bob.

"'For finding my cat,' ses George.

"'Look here,' ses Bob, handing it back, 'I've 'ad enough o' your insults; I don't know where your cat is.'

"'I mean for trying to find it, Bob,' ses George Barstow.

"'Oh, well, I don't mind that,' ses Bob, taking it. 'I'm a 'ard-working man, and I've got to be paid for my time; it's on'y fair to my wife and children. I'll start now.'

"He finished up 'is beer, and while the other chaps was telling George Barstow wot a fool he was Joe Clark slipped out arter Bob Pretty and began to call 'im all the names he could think of.

"'Don't you worry,' ses Bob; 'the cat ain't found yet.'

"'Is it dead?' ses Joe Clark, 'ardly able to speak.

"''Ow should I know?' ses Bob; 'that's wot I've got to try and find out. That's wot you gave me your furniture for, and wot George Barstow gave me the fifteen pounds for, ain't it? Now, don't you stop me now, 'cos I'm goin' to begin looking.'

"He started looking there and then, and for the next two or three days George Barstow and Joe Clark see 'im walking up and down with his 'ands in 'is pockets looking over garden fences and calling 'Puss.' He asked everybody 'e see whether they 'ad seen a white cat with one blue eye and one yaller one, and every time 'e came into the Cauliflower he put his 'ead over the bar and called 'Puss,' 'cos, as 'e said, it was as likely to be there as anywhere else.

"It was about a week after the cat 'ad disappeared that George Barstow was standing at 'is door talking to Joe Clark, who was saying the cat must be dead and 'e wanted 'is property, when he sees a man coming up the road carrying a basket stop and speak to Bill Chambers. Just as 'e got near them an awful 'miaow' come from the basket and George Barstow and Joe Clark started as if they'd been shot.

"'He's found it?' shouts Bill Chambers, pointing to the man.

"'It's been living with me over at Ling for a week pretty nearly,' ses the man. 'I tried to drive it away several times, not knowing that there was fifteen pounds offered for it.'

"George Barstow tried to take 'old of the basket.

"'I want that fifteen pounds fust,' ses the man.

"'That's on'y right and fair, George,' ses Bob Pretty, who 'ad just come up. 'You've got all the luck, mate. We've been hunting 'igh and low for that cat for a week.'

"Then George Barstow tried to explain to the man and call Bob Pretty names at the same time; but it was all no good. The man said it 'ad nothing to do with 'im wot he 'ad paid to Bob Pretty; and at last they fetched Policeman White over from Cudford, and George Barstow signed a paper to pay five shillings a week till the reward was paid.

"George Barstow 'ad the cat for five years arter that, but he never let it get away agin. They got to like each other in time and died within a fortnight of each other, so that Joe Clark got 'is property arter all."

SIXTEEN

Who Was to Blame?

Anton Chekhov

As my uncle Pyotr Demyanitch, a lean, bilious collegiate coun-
cilor, exceedingly like a stale smoked fish with a stick through it, was
getting ready to go to the high school, where he taught Latin, he noticed
that the corner of his grammar was nibbled by mice.

"I say, Praskovya," he said, going into the kitchen and addressing the
cook, "how is it we have got mice here? Upon my word! yesterday my top
hat was nibbled, to-day they have disfigured my Latin grammar. . . . At
this rate they will soon begin eating my clothes!"

"What can I do? I did not bring them in!" answered Praskovya.

"We must do something! You had better get a cat, hadn't you?"

"I've got a cat, but what good is it?"

And Praskovya pointed to the corner where a white kitten, thin as a
match, lay curled up asleep beside a broom.

"Why is it no good?" asked Pyotr Demyanitch.

"It's young yet, and foolish. It's not two months old yet."

"H'm. . . . Then it must be trained. It had much better be learning
instead of lying there."

Saying this, Pyotr Demyanitch sighed with a careworn air and went
out of the kitchen. The kitten raised his head, looked lazily after him, and
shut his eyes again.

The kitten lay awake thinking. Of what? Unacquainted with real
life, having no store of accumulated impressions, his mental processes

could only be instinctive, and he could but picture life in accordance with the conceptions that he had inherited, together with his flesh and blood, from his ancestors, the tigers (vide Darwin). His thoughts were of the nature of daydreams. His feline imagination pictured something like the Arabian desert, over which flitted shadows closely resembling Praskovya, the stove, the broom. In the midst of the shadows there suddenly appeared a saucer of milk; the saucer began to grow paws, it began moving and displayed a tendency to run; the kitten made a bound, and with a thrill of blood-thirsty sensuality thrust his claws into it.

When the saucer had vanished into obscurity a piece of meat appeared, dropped by Praskovya; the meat ran away with a cowardly squeak, but the kitten made a bound and got his claws into it. . . . Everything that rose before the imagination of the young dreamer had for its starting-point leaps, claws, and teeth. . . . The soul of another is darkness, and a cat's soul more than most, but how near the visions just described are to the truth may be seen from the following fact: under the influence of his day-dreams the kitten suddenly leaped up, looked with flashing eyes at Praskovya, ruffled up his coat, and making one bound, thrust his claws into the cook's skirt. Obviously he was born a mouse catcher, a worthy son of his bloodthirsty ancestors. Fate had destined him to be the terror of cellars, storerooms and cornbins, and had it not been for education . . . we will not anticipate, however.

On his way home from the high school, Pyotr Demyanitch went into a general shop and bought a mousetrap for fifteen kopecks. At dinner he fixed a little bit of his rissole on the hook, and set the trap under the sofa, where there were heaps of the pupils' old exercise-books, which Praskovya used for various domestic purposes. At six o'clock in the evening, when the worthy Latin master was sitting at the table correcting his pupils' exercises, there was a sudden "klop!" so loud that my uncle started and dropped his pen. He went at once to the sofa and took out the trap. A neat little mouse, the size of a thimble, was sniffing the wires and trembling with fear.

"Aha," muttered Pyotr Demyanitch, and he looked at the mouse malignantly, as though he were about to give him a bad mark. "You are cau—aught, wretch! Wait a bit! I'll teach you to eat my grammar!"

Having gloated over his victim, Pyotr Demyanitch put the mouse-trap on the floor and called:

"Praskovya, there's a mouse caught! Bring the kitten here!"

"I'm coming," responded Praskovya, and a minute later she came in with the descendant of tigers in her arms.

"Capital!" said Pyotr Demyanitch, rubbing his hands. "We will give him a lesson. . . . Put him down opposite the mouse-trap . . . that's it. . . . Let him sniff it and look at it. . . . That's it. . . . "

The kitten looked wonderingly at my uncle, at his arm-chair, sniffed the mouse-trap in bewilderment, then, frightened probably by the glaring lamplight and the attention directed to him, made a dash and ran in terror to the door.

"Stop!" shouted my uncle, seizing him by the tail, "stop, you rascal! He's afraid of a mouse, the idiot! Look! It's a mouse! Look! Well? Look, I tell you!"

Pyotr Demyanitch took the kitten by the scruff of the neck and pushed him with his nose against the mouse-trap.

"Look, you carrion! Take him and hold him, Praskovya. . . . Hold him opposite the door of the trap. . . . When I let the mouse out, you let him go instantly. . . . Do you hear? . . . Instantly let go! Now!"

My uncle assumed a mysterious expression and lifted the door of the trap. . . . The mouse came out irresolutely, sniffed the air, and flew like an arrow under the sofa. . . . The kitten on being released darted under the table with his tail in the air.

"It has got away! got away!" cried Pyotr Demyanitch, looking ferocious. "Where is he, the scoundrel? Under the table? You wait . . . "

My uncle dragged the kitten from under the table and shook him in the air.

"Wretched little beast," he muttered, smacking him on the ear. "Take that, take that! Will you shirk it next time? Wr-r-r-etch . . . "

Next day Praskovya heard again the summons.

"Praskovya, there is a mouse caught! Bring the kitten here!"

After the outrage of the previous day the kitten had taken refuge under the stove and had not come out all night. When Praskovya pulled him out and, carrying him by the scruff of the neck into the study, set him down before the mousetrap, he trembled all over and mewed piteously.

"Come, let him feel at home first," Pyotr Demyanitch commanded. "Let him look and sniff. Look and learn! Stop, plague take you!" he shouted, noticing that the kitten was backing away from the mousetrap. "I'll thrash you! Hold him by the ear! That's it. . . . Well now, set him down before the trap . . ."

My uncle slowly lifted the door of the trap . . . the mouse whisked under the very nose of the kitten, flung itself against Praskovya's hand and fled under the cupboard; the kitten, feeling himself free, took a desperate bound and retreated under the sofa.

"He's let another mouse go!" bawled Pyotr Demyanitch. "Do you call that a cat? Nasty little beast! Thrash him! thrash him by the mousetrap!"

When the third mouse had been caught, the kitten shivered all over at the sight of the mousetrap and its inmate, and scratched Praskovya's hand. . . . After the fourth mouse my uncle flew into a rage, kicked the kitten, and said:

"Take the nasty thing away! Get rid of it! Chuck it away! It's no earthly use!"

A year passed, the thin, frail kitten had turned into a solid and sagacious tomcat. One day he was on his way by the back yards to an amatory interview. He had just reached his destination when he suddenly heard a rustle, and thereupon caught sight of a mouse which ran from a water-trough towards a stable; my hero's hair stood on end, he arched his back, hissed, and trembling all over, took to ignominious flight.

Alas! sometimes I feel myself in the ludicrous position of the flying cat. Like the kitten, I had in my day the honor of being taught Latin by my uncle. Now, whenever I chance to see some work of classical antiquity, instead of being moved to eager enthusiasm, I begin recalling, *ut consecutivum*, the irregular verbs, the sallow grey face of my uncle, the ablative absolute. . . . I turn pale, my hair stands up on my head, and, like the cat, I take to ignominious flight.

SEVENTEEN

Plato

The Story of a Cat

A. S. Downs

ONE DAY LAST SUMMER A LARGE HANDSOME BLACK CAT WALKED gravely up one side of Main Street, crossed, and went halfway down the other. He stopped at a house called The Den, went up the piazza steps, and paused by an open window.

A lady sitting inside saw and spoke to him; but without taking any notice, he put his paws on the sill, looked around the room as if wondering if it would suit him, and finally gazed into her face.

After thinking a minute he went in, and from that hour took his place as an important member of the family. Civil to all, he gives his love only to the lady whom he first saw; and it is odd to see, as he lies by the fire, how he listens to all conversation, but raises his head only when she speaks, and drops it again when she has finished, with a pleased air.

No other person in the house is so wise, for he alone never makes a mistake. The hours he selects for his exercise are the sunniest; the carpets he lies upon the softest, and he knows the moment he enters the room whether his friend will let him lie in her lap, or whether because of her best gown she will have none of him. No one at The Den can tell how he came to be called Plato. It is a fact that he answers to the name, and when asked if so known before he came there, smiles wisely. "What matters it," the smile says, "how I was called, or where I came from, since I am Plato, and am here?"

He dislikes noise, and entirely disapproves sweeping. A broom and dustpan fill him with anxiety, and he seeks the soft cushions of the big lounge; but when these in their turn are beaten and tossed about, he retreats to the study-table. However, as soon as he learned that once a week his favorite room was turned into chaos, he sought another refuge, and refuses to get up that day until noon.

Many were the speculations as to Plato's Christmas present. All were satisfied with a rattan basket just large enough for him to lie in, with a light open canopy, cushions of cardinal chintz, and a cardinal satin bow to which was fastened a lovely card.

It was set down before Plato, and although it is probable it was the first he had ever seen, he showed neither surprise nor curiosity, but looked at it loftily as if such a retreat should have been given him long ago, for could not any discerning person see he was accustomed to luxury? He stepped in carefully and curled himself gracefully upon the soft cushions, the glowing tints of which were very becoming to his sable beauty.

It was soon seen that Plato was very fond of his basket, and was unwilling to share it in the smallest degree. When little Bessie put her doll in, "just to see if cardinal was becoming to her," he looked so stern and walked so fiercely toward them that dolly's heart sank within her, and Bessie said, "Please excuse us, Plato." If balls and toys were carelessly dropped there he would push them out without delay, and if visitors took up the basket to examine it, he would fix his eyes upon them, thinking, "O yes, you would pick pockets or steal the spoons if I did not watch you."

As his conduct can never be predicted, great was the curiosity when one cold afternoon he was noticed walking up the avenue while a miserable yellow kitten dragged herself after him. She was so thin you could count her bones, and she had been so pulled and kicked that there seemed to be nothing of her but length and—dirt.

When Lord Plato chooses, he enters the front doors, but as he waits no man's pleasure, unless it pleases him first, he has a way of getting in on his own account. Upon one of the shed doors is an old-fashioned latch, which by jumping he can reach and lift with his paw. Having opened the door, he pushed his poor yellow straggler in and followed himself. She laid down at once on the floor, and Plato began washing her with his rough tongue, while the lookers-on assisted his hospitality by bringing a saucer of milk. While she ate, Plato rested, looking as pleased as if he were her mother at her enjoyment. The luncheon finished, the washing was resumed, and as the waif was now able to help, she soon looked more respectable. But Plato had not finished his work of mercy. He looked at the door leading to the parlor, then at her; and finally bent down tenderly to her little torn ears, as if whispering, but she would not move. Perhaps in all her wretched life she had never been so comfortable, and believed in letting well enough alone. Reason and persuasion alike useless, Plato concluded to try force and, taking her by the back of the neck, carried her through the house and dropped her close to his dainty cherished basket.

Then he appeared a little uncertain what to do. The basket was nice and warm; he was tired and cold; it had been a present to him; the street wanderer was dirty still; and the rug would be a softer bed than she had ever known. Were these his thoughts, and was it selfishness he conquered when at last he lifted the shivering homeless creature into his own beautiful nest?

EIGHTEEN

A Talk with Mark Twain's Cat, the Owner Being Invisible

New York Times, April 9, 1905

Mark Twain had lost his cat. Consumed with an attack of wan-derlust, Bambino had fled from home and roamed for a day and a half. The humorist had offered a reward of $5. Then his secretary, Miss Lyon, had met Bambino on University Place and haled him home.

It was all in the papers.

Failing to understand why it shouldn't be in the papers some more, a woman from the *Times* had called at the Clemens mansion, 21 Fifth Avenue.

A man with china blue eyes and a white waistcoat opened the door for her. He opened it just half way.

Upon her request to see Mr. Clemens, he gave a start of surprise, frowned, and said:

"Mr. Clemens is asleep."

It was then 1:30 in the afternoon.

"When can I see him?" asked the woman.

"I will find out," said the servant, and shut the door upon her while he did so.

By and by he reopened it.

"He may see you," he told her, "if you come back at 5 o'clock."

It was a beautiful sunshiny day, but the woman went home, stayed indoors to rest up for this interview, and at 5 o'clock again sauntered toward the Clemens mansion.

The same man appeared. He wore the same waistcoat. He had, likewise, the same blue eyes.

"Mr. Clemens is not in now," he said, "but his secretary might see you."

"Very well," responded the woman, and stood outside the shut door once more while he searched for the secretary.

As she gazed upon Fifth Avenue, gay in the sunshine with automobiles and carriages and people enjoying themselves, she wondered vaguely if thieves were in the habit of infesting the Clemens mansion; if that was the reason they were so particular about the door.

Then it opened cautiously and the servant said:

"You may come in."

Precious privilege. The woman went in and stood in the hall as if she were a book agent. There were chairs, but she was afraid to sit down.

Presently the secretary, a nice little woman with brown eyes and old-fashioned sleeves, came down the stairs and asked her what she wanted.

"I want to see Mr. Clemens about the cat," replied the woman.

"Mr. Clemens never sees anybody—I mean any newspaper people. Besides, he is not at home."

"Then," said the woman, "may I see the cat?"

"Yes," nodded the secretary, "you may see the cat," and she ran lightly up the long stairway and came down soon with Bambino in her arms, a beautiful black silent cat with long velvety fur and luminous eyes that looked very intelligently into the face of the woman.

The secretary and the woman then sat down on a bench in the hall, and talked about the cat. The cat listened but said nothing.

"We were terribly distressed about him," cooed the secretary. "He is a great pet with Mr. Clemens. He is a year old. It is the first time he has ever run away. He lies curled up on Mr. Clemens's bed all day long."

"Does Mr. Clemens breakfast at five o'clock tea and dine on the following day?" asked the woman.

"Oh, no. He does all his writing before he gets up. That's why he gets up at 5 o'clock. Bambino always stays with him while he writes."

"I should consider it a great privilege," smiled the woman, "to breathe the same atmosphere with Mr. Clemens for about three minutes. Don't you think if I came back at 7 you might arrange it?"

"I will try," promised the secretary, kindly.

At 7, therefore, the woman toiled up the dark red steps and rang the bell. The man with the white waistcoat opened the door, disclosed one eye and the half of his face, said abruptly, "Mr. Clemens doesn't wish to see you," and slammed the door.

The woman walked slowly down the red steps and looked up Fifth Avenue, wondering whether she would walk home or take a car.

Fifth Avenue was very beautiful.

Purplish in the dusk, it was gemmed with softly gleaming opalescent electric balls of light.

It was, moreover, admirably bare of people.

She concluded to walk home.

She was about to start forward when she became aware of a furry gentle something rubbing against her skirts.

She looked down, and there was Bambino, purring at her, looking up at her out of his luminous cat eyes.

The man at the door had shut him out, too!

She took him in both hands and lifted him up. He nestled against her shoulder.

"I don't like to prejudice you against the people you have to live with, Bambino," she said. "It seems they will make you live with them. But they weren't so nice. Were they? They might have told me at the start he wouldn't see me. They needn't have made me lose all the sunshine of to-day. You can't bring back a day and you can't bring back sunshine.

"You wouldn't have treated me like that, would you?"

Bambino purred musically in his earnest assurance that he would not.

"I suppose you heard it all," she went on, "and you sympathized with me. You are awfully tired yourself. I can see that. If you were a Parisian cat we'd call it ennui, that expresses it better, but we'll let it go at tired. You are. Aren't you? Or you wouldn't have run off."

Bambino sighed wearily and half closed his eyes.

"It's a pretty rarefied atmosphere, I imagine, for a cat," she reasoned. "I don't blame you for wanting to get out with the common cats and whoop it up a little. Any self respecting cat would rather run himself in a gutter or walk the back fence than sit cooped up the livelong day with a humorist. You can't tell me anything about that. It's a deadly thing to see people grind out fun. I used to know a comic artist. I had to sit by and watch him try to match his jokes to pictures!"

She clasped Bambino closer and caught her breath in a sigh.

"I don't blame you one bit for running off," she reiterated. "I can imagine what you must have suffered. Shall we walk along a little on this beautiful street that's so wide and empty now of people?" she asked politely. "I get as tired as you do sometimes of people, Bambino. They are not always so nice. There are a lot of times that I like cats better."

Bambino curled himself up in her arms and laid an affectionate paw on her wrist by way of rewarding her.

She walked on, fondling him.

"I've the greatest notion," she confided presently, "to run off with you and paralyze them. It would serve them right. How would you like, Bambino, to come and live with me in my studio?"

Bambino raised his head and purred loudly against her cheek to show how well he would like it.

"Now, I want to tell you exactly how it will be. I want to be perfectly fair with you. If you come with me you must come with your eyes open. Maybe you won't have half as soft a bed to lie on, but you won't have to lie on it all day long. I'll promise you that. In the first place, it masquerades as a couch full of pillows in the daytime, and in the second place I've got to get out and hustle if I want to eat. Not that I mind hustling. I wouldn't stay in bed all day long out of the sunshine if I could. And you mayn't have as much to eat either, but if you get too hungry there are the gold-fish—and the canary wouldn't make half a bad meal. I am pretty fond of both, but I am reckless to-night somehow. You'll be welcome to them."

Bambino licked his chops preparatorily.

"There are a good many little things you are apt to miss. The studio isn't as big as a house by any means, but you'll have all out doors to roam in. I'll trust to your coming home of nights because you'll like it there," she concluded confidently.

"And you'll be rid of the man at the door for good and all. Tell me, now, doesn't he step on your tail and 'sic' the mice on you when they are all away?"

Bambino groaned slightly, but he was otherwise noncommittal.

"I knew he did. He looks capable of anything. He's not as wise as he looks, though. He may not know it, but I push the pen for the tallest newspaper building in the city, the tallest in the world, I think. I'll take you up to the top of that building of mine, and let you climb the flag pole. Then if there should happen to be another cat on the Flatiron Building there'd be some music, wouldn't there, for the rest of the city? And they couldn't throw that flatiron at you anyway, could they? Want to go?"

Bambino put both paws around her neck, and purred an eloquent assent.

"You talk less than anybody I ever interviewed," remarked the woman, "but I think I know what you mean."

She pressed his affectionate black paws against her neck and hurried up the avenue, looking back over her shoulder to see that nobody followed.

She almost ran until she got to the bridge over the yawning chasm near Sixteenth Street. Then she stopped.

Bambino looked anxiously up to see what was the matter.

But turned deliberately around.

Bambino gave a long-drawn sigh. He looked appealingly up at her out of his luminous eyes.

"I reckon I won't steal you, Bambino," she concluded, sadly. "I'd like to, but it wouldn't be fair.

"In the morning he'd be sorry. Maybe he couldn't work without you there, looking at him out of your beautiful eyes. You don't have to hear him dictate, too, do you Bambino? If I thought that! *** But no. There is a limit. He's had his troubles, too, you know. He's bound to be a little lenient. The goose hasn't always hung so high for him. Of course you don't remember it, but he had an awful time establishing himself as the great American humorist. Couldn't get a single publisher to believe it.

Had to publish his *Innocents Abroad* himself. Just said to the American public, 'Now, you've got to take this. It's humor,' and made them take it. Held their noses. That was a long time ago. Couldn't do it to-day. Not with *Innocents Abroad*. The American public is getting too well educated. Who ever reads *Innocents Abroad* now? Not the rising generation. You ask any boy of to-day what is the funniest book, and see if he doesn't say *Alice in Wonderland*?

"Still, for an old back date book, that wasn't half bad. He has never written anything better. It must give him the heartache to see it laid on the shelf. I suppose you must hear these things discussed, but not this side of them, perhaps. No. Naturally no. They don't make you read their books, they can't, but you must have to hear about them. *** Life is hard! But I must take you back. We mustn't do anything at all to hurt his feelings."

Bambino was fairly limp with disappointment. He had set his heart on the top of the *Times* building flagpole. He had almost tasted the canary, to say nothing of the goldfish. He hadn't the heart to purr any longer. His paws fell from the woman's neck. She had to carry him like that, all four feet hanging lifeless, his head drooping.

"And there's another thing, Bambino," she continued, as they went along. "I don't want anything I said about his having to establish himself as a humorist to disillusion you or make you more dissatisfied than you are. All humorists are like that. They have to establish themselves. Why, wasn't I in London when Nat Goodwin produced his *Cowboy and the Lady* at Daly's? Couldn't I hear people he had planted all over the audience that first night explaining that he was a humorist, and the play was intended to be funny? Certainly. But it didn't work that well. Those English people are more determined than we are. They wouldn't stand for it. He had to take the play off.

"Your master happened to catch us when we were young and innocent. He deserves a lot of credit for bamboozling us. You ought to admire him for it. I do."

They were nearly home by now. Bambino managed to emit another purr. It was like a whimper.

"Don't you cry, Bambino," she soothed. "We all have our troubles. You must be a brave cat and bear up under yours," and she tiptoed up the red steps and set him at the door where they could find him when they missed him.

He sat there, a crumpled, black, discouraged ball, his eyes following her hungrily.

She ran back to him.

"Bear up under it the best you can, Bambino," she implored; "but if it gets so you can't stand it again, you know where to find a friend."

There was a sound of approaching footsteps in the hall.

She pressed her lips to Bambino's ear, whispered her address to him, and fled.

NINETEEN

The Cat and the King

Ambrose Bierce

A CAT WAS LOOKING AT A KING, AS PERMITTED BY PROVERB.

"Well," said the monarch, observing her inspection of the royal person, "how do you like me?"

"I can imagine a King," said the Cat, "whom I should like better."

"For example?"

"The King of the Mice."

The sovereign was so pleased with the wit of the reply that he gave her permission to scratch his Prime Minister's eyes out.

Twenty

How a Cat Played Robinson Crusoe

Charles G. D. Roberts

THE ISLAND WAS A MERE SANDBANK OFF THE LOW, FLAT COAST. NOT A tree broke its bleak levels—not even a shrub. But the long, gritty stalks of the marsh grass clothed it everywhere above tide-mark; and a tiny rivulet of sweet water, flowing from a spring at its centre, drew a ribbon of inland herbage and tenderer green across the harsh and sombre yellow grey of the grass. Few would have chosen the island as a place to live, yet at its seaward end, where the changing tides were never still, stood a spacious, one-storied, wide-verandaed cottage, with a low shed behind it. The virtue of this lone plot of sand was coolness. When the neighbor mainland would be sweltering day and night alike under a breathless heat, out here on the island there was always a cool wind blowing. Therefore a wise city dweller had appropriated the sea waif and built his summer home thereon, where the tonic airs might bring back the rose to the pale cheeks of his children.

The family came to the island toward the end of June. In the first week of September they went away, leaving every door and window of house and shed securely shuttered, bolted or barred against the winter's storms. A roomy boat, rowed by two fishermen, carried them across the half mile of racing tides that separated them from the mainland. The elders of the household were not sorry to get back to the world of men, after two months of mere wind, and sun, and waves, and waving grass tops. But the children went with tear-stained faces. They were leaving

173

behind them their favorite pet, the accustomed comrade of their migrations, a handsome, moon-faced cat, striped like a tiger. The animal had mysteriously disappeared two days before, vanishing from the face of the island without leaving a trace behind. The only reasonable explanation seemed to be that she had been snapped up by a passing eagle. The cat, meanwhile, was a fast prisoner at the other end of the island, hidden beneath a broken barrel and some hundred-weight of drifted sand.

The old barrel, with the staves battered out of one side, had stood, half buried, on the crest of a sand ridge raised by a long prevailing wind. Under its lee the cat had found a sheltered hollow, full of sun, where she had been wont to lie curled up for hours at a time, basking and sleeping. Meanwhile the sand had been steadily piling itself higher and higher behind the unstable barrier. At last it had piled too high; and suddenly, before a stronger gust, the barrel had come toppling over beneath a mass of sand, burying the sleeping cat out of sight and light. But at the same time the sound half of the barrel had formed a safe roof to her prison, and she was neither crushed nor smothered. When the children in their anxious search all over the island chanced upon the mound of fine, white sand they gave it but one careless look. They could not hear the faint cries that came, at intervals, from the close darkness within. So they went away sorrowfully, little dreaming that their friend was imprisoned almost beneath their feet.

For three days the prisoner kept up her appeals for help. On the third day the wind changed and presently blew up a gale. In a few hours it had uncovered the barrel. At one corner a tiny spot of light appeared.

Eagerly the cat stuck her paw through the hole. When she withdrew it again the hole was much enlarged. She took the hint and fell to scratching. At first her efforts were rather aimless; but presently, whether by good luck or quick sagacity, she learned to make her scratching more effective. The opening rapidly enlarged, and at last she was able to squeeze her way out.

The wind was tearing madly across the island, filled with flying sand. The seas hurled themselves trampling up the beach, with the uproar of a bombardment. The grasses lay bowed flat in long quivering ranks. Over the turmoil the sun stared down from a deep, unclouded blue. The cat, when first she met the full force of the gale, was fairly blown off her feet. As soon as she could recover herself she crouched low and darted into the grasses for shelter. But there was little shelter there, the long stalks being held down almost level. Through their lashed lines, however, she sped straight before the gale, making for the cottage at the other end of the island, where she would find, as she fondly imagined, not only food and shelter but also loving comfort to make her forget her terrors.

Still and desolate in the bright sunshine and the tearing wind, the house frightened her. She could not understand the tight-closed shutters, the blind, unresponsive doors that would no longer open to her anxious appeal. The wind swept her savagely across the naked veranda. Climbing with difficulty to the dining-room windowsill, where so often she had been let in, she clung there a few moments and yowled heartbrokenly. Then, in a sudden panic, she jumped down and ran to the shed. That, too, was closed. Never before had she seen the shed doors closed, and she could not understand it. Cautiously she crept around the foundations— but those had been built honestly: there was no such thing as getting in that way. On every side it was nothing but a blank, forbidding face that the old familiar house confronted her with.

The cat had always been so coddled and pampered by the children that she had had no need to forage for herself; but, fortunately for her, she had learned to hunt the marsh mice and grass sparrows for amusement. So now, being ravenous from her long fast under the sand, she slunk mournfully away from the deserted house and crept along under the lee of a sand ridge to a little grassy hollow which she knew. Here the gale caught only the tops of the grasses; and here, in the warmth and comparative calm, the furry little marsh folk, mice and shrews, were going about their business undisturbed.

The cat, quick and stealthy, soon caught one and eased her hunger. She caught several. And then, making her way back to the house, she spent hours in heartsick prowling, around it and around, sniffing and peering, yowling piteously on the threshold and windowsill; and every now and then being blown ignominiously across the smooth, naked expanse of the veranda floor. At last, hopelessly discouraged, she curled herself up beneath the children's window and went to sleep.

In spite of her loneliness and grief the life of the island prisoner during the next two or three weeks was by no means one of hardship. Besides her abundant food of birds and mice she quickly learned to catch tiny fish in the mouth of the rivulet, where salt water and fresh water met. It was an exciting game, and she became expert at dashing the grey tom-cod and blue-and-silver sand-lance far up the slope with a sweep of her armed paw. But when the equinoctial storms roared down upon the island, with furious rain, and low, black clouds torn to shreds, then life became more difficult for her. Game all took to cover, where it was hard to find. It was difficult to get around in the drenched and lashing grass; and, moreover, she loathed wet. Most of the time she went hungry, sitting sullen and desolate under the lee of the house, glaring out defiantly at the rush and battling tumult of the waves.

The storm lasted nearly ten days before it blew itself clean out. On the eighth day the abandoned wreck of a small Nova Scotia schooner drove ashore, battered out of all likeness to a ship. But hulk as it was it had passengers of a sort. A horde of rats got through the surf and scurried into the hiding of the grass roots. They promptly made themselves at home, burrowing under the grass and beneath old, half-buried timbers, and carrying panic into the ranks of the mice and shrews.

When the storm was over the cat had a decided surprise in her first long hunting expedition. Something had rustled the grass heavily and she trailed it, expecting a particularly large, fat marsh mouse. When she pounced and alighted upon an immense old ship's rat, many-voyaged and many-battled, she got badly bitten. Such an experience had never before fallen to her lot. At first she felt so injured that she was on the point of backing out and running away. Then her latent pugnacity awoke, and the fire of far-off ancestors. She flung herself into the fight with a rage that took no accounting of the wounds she got; and the struggle was soon over. Her wounds, faithfully licked, quickly healed themselves in that clean and tonic air; and after that, having learned how to handle such big game, she no more got bitten.

During the first full moon after her abandonment—the first week in October—the island was visited by still weather with sharp night frosts. The cat discovered then that it was most exciting to hunt by night and do her sleeping in the daytime. She found that now, under the strange whiteness of the moon, all her game was astir—except the birds, which had fled to the mainland during the storm, gathering for the southward flight. The blanched grasses, she found, were now everywhere a-rustle; and everywhere dim little shapes went darting with thin squeaks across ghostly-white sands. Also she made the acquaintance of a new bird, which she regarded at first uneasily and then with vengeful wrath. This was the brown marsh owl, which came over from the mainland to do some autumn mouse hunting. There were two pairs of these big, downy-winged, round-eyed hunters, and they did not know there was a cat on the island.

The cat, spying one of them as it swooped soundlessly hither and thither over the silvered grass tops, crouched with flattened ears. With its wide spread of wing it looked bigger than herself; and the great round face, with hooked beak and wild, staring eyes, appeared extremely formidable. However, she was no coward; and presently, though not without reasonable caution, she went about her hunting. Suddenly the owl caught a partial glimpse of her in the grass—probably of her ears or head. He swooped; and at the same instant she sprang upward to meet the assault, spitting and growling harshly and striking with unsheathed claws. With a frantic flapping of his great wings the owl checked himself and drew back into the air, just escaping the clutch of those indignant claws. After that the marsh owls were careful to give her a wide berth. They realized that the black-striped animal with the quick spring and the clutching claws was not to be interfered with. They perceived that she was some relation to that ferocious prowler, the lynx.

In spite of all this hunting, however, the furry life of the marsh grass was so teeming, so inexhaustible, that the depredations of cat, rats and owls were powerless to make more than a passing impression upon it. So the hunting and the merry-making went on side by side under the indifferent moon.

As the winter deepened—with bursts of sharp cold and changing winds that forced the cat to be continually changing her refuge—she grew more and more unhappy. She felt her homelessness keenly. Nowhere on the whole island could she find a nook where she might feel secure from both wind and rain. As for the old barrel, the first cause of her misfortunes, there was no help in that. The winds had long ago turned it completely over, open to the sky, then drifted it full of sand and reburied it. And in any case the cat would have been afraid to go near it again. So it came about that she alone of all the island dwellers had no shelter to turn to when the real winter arrived, with snows that smothered the grass tops out of sight, and frosts that lined the shore with grinding ice cakes. The rats had their holes under the buried fragments of wreckage; the mice and shrews had their deep, warm tunnels; the owls had nests in hollow trees far away in the forests of the mainland. But the cat, shivering and frightened, could do nothing but crouch against the blind walls of the unrelenting house and let the snow whirl itself and pile itself about her.

And now, in her misery, she found her food cut off. The mice ran secure in their hidden runways, where the grass roots on each side of them gave them easy and abundant provender. The rats, too, were out of sight—digging burrows themselves in the soft snow in the hope of intercepting some of the tunnels of the mice, and now and then snapping up an unwary passer-by. The ice fringe, crumbling and heaving under the ruthless tide, put an end to her fishing. She would have tried to capture one of the formidable owls in her hunger, but the owls no longer came to the island. They would return, no doubt, later in the season when the snow had hardened and the mice had begun to come out and play on the surface.

But for the present they were following an easier chase in the deeps of the upland forest.

When the snow stopped falling and the sun came out again there fell such keen cold as the cat had never felt before. The day, as it chanced, was Christmas; and if the cat had had any idea as to the calendar she would certainly have marked the day in her memory as it was an eventful one for her. Starving as she was she could not sleep, but kept ceaselessly on the prowl. This was fortunate, for had she gone to sleep without any more shelter than the wall of the house she would never have wakened again. In her restlessness she wandered to the farther side of the island where, in a somewhat sheltered and sunny recess of the shore facing the mainland, she found a patch of bare sand, free of ice cakes and just uncovered by the tide. Opening upon this recess were the tiny entrances to several of the mouse tunnels.

Close beside one of these holds in the snow the cat crouched, quiveringly intent. For ten minutes or more she waited, never so much as twitching a whisker. At last a mouse thrust out its little pointed head. Not daring to give it time to change its mind or take alarm, she pounced. The mouse, glimpsing the doom ere it fell, doubled back upon itself in the narrow runway. Hardly realizing what she did in her desperation the cat plunged head and shoulders into the snow, reaching blindly after the vanished prize. By great good luck she caught it.

It was her first meal in four bitter days. The children had always tried to share with her their Christmas cheer and enthusiasm, and had usually succeeded in interesting her by an agreeable lavishness in the matter of cream; but never before had she found a Christmas feast so good.

Now she had learned a lesson. Being naturally clever and her wits sharpened by her fierce necessities, she had grasped the idea that it was possible to follow her prey a little way into the snow. She had not realized that the snow was so penetrable. She had quite wiped out the door of this particular runway; so she went and crouched beside a similar one, but here she had to wait a long time before an adventurous mouse came to peer out. But this time she showed that she had grasped her lesson. It was straight at the side of the entrance that she pounced, where instinct told her that the body of the mouse would be.

One outstretched paw thus cut off the quarry's retreat. Her tactics were completely successful; and as her head went plunging into the fluffy whiteness she felt the prize between her paws.

Her hunger now fairly appeased, she found herself immensely excited over this new fashion of hunting. Often before had she waited at mouse holes, but never had she found it possible to break down the walls and invade the holes themselves. It was a thrilling idea. As she crept toward another hole a mouse scurried swiftly up the sand and darted into it. The cat, too late to catch him before he disappeared, tried to follow him. Scratching clumsily but hopefully she succeeded in forcing the full length of her body into the snow. She found no sign of the fugitive, which was by this time racing in safety down some dim transverse tunnel. Her eyes, mouth, whiskers and fur full of the powdery white particles, she backed out, much disappointed. But in that moment she had realized that it was much warmer in there beneath the snow than out in the stinging air. It was a second and vitally important lesson; and though she was probably unconscious of having learned it she instinctively put the new lore into practice a little while later.

Having succeeded in catching yet another mouse for which her appetite made no immediate demand, she carried it back to the house and laid it down in tribute on the veranda steps while she meowed and stared hopefully at the desolate, snow-draped door. Getting no response she carried the mouse down with her to the hollow behind the drift which had been caused by the bulging front of the bay-window on the end of the house. Here she curled herself up forlornly, thinking to have a wink of sleep.

But the still cold was too searching. She looked at the sloping wall of snow beside her and cautiously thrust her paw into it. It was very soft and light. It seemed to offer practically no resistance. She pawed away in an awkward fashion till she had scooped out a sort of tiny cave. Gently she pushed herself into it, pressing back the snow on every side till she had room to turn around.

Then turn around she did several times, as dogs do in getting their beds arranged to their liking. In this process she not only packed down the snow beneath her, but she also rounded out for herself a snug chamber with a comparatively narrow doorway. From this snowy retreat she gazed forth with a solemn air of possession; then she went to sleep with a sense of comfort, of 'homeyness,' such as she had never before felt since the disappearance of her friends.

Having thus conquered misfortune and won herself the freedom of the winter wild, her life though strenuous was no longer one of any terrible hardship. With patience at the mouse holes she could catch enough to eat; and in her snowy den she slept warm and secure. In a little while, when a crust had formed over the surface, the mice took to coming out at night and holding revels on the snow. Then the owls, too, came back; and the cat, having tried to catch one, got sharply bitten and clawed before she realized the propriety of letting it go. After this experience she decided that owls, on the whole, were meant to be let alone. But for all that she found it fine hunting, out there on the bleak, unfenced, white reaches of the snow.

Thus, mistress of the situation, she found the winter slipping by without further serious trials. Only once, toward the end of January, did Fate send her another bad quarter of an hour. On the heels of a peculiarly bitter cold snap a huge white owl from the Arctic Barrens came one night to the island. The cat, taking observations from the corner of the veranda, caught sight of him. One look was enough to assure her that this was a very different kind of visitor from the brown marsh owls. She slipped inconspicuously down into her burrow; and until the great white owl went away, some twenty-four hours later, she kept herself discreetly out of sight.

When spring came back to the island, with the nightly shrill chorus of fluting frogs in the shallow, sedgy pools and the young grass alive with nesting birds, the prisoner's life became almost luxurious in its easy abundance. But now she was once more homeless, since her snug den had vanished with the snow. This did not much matter to her, however, for the weather grew warmer and more tranquil day by day; and moreover, she herself, in being forced back upon her instincts, had learned to be as contented as a tramp. Nevertheless, with all her capacity for learning and adapting herself she had not forgotten anything. So when, one day in June, a crowded boat came over from the mainland, and children's voices, clamouring across the grass tops, broke the desolate silence of the island, the cat heard and sprang up out of her sleep on the veranda steps.

For one second she stood, listening intently. Then, almost as a dog would have done, and as few of her supercilious tribe ever condescend to do, she went racing across to the landing place—to be snatched up into the arms of four happy children at once, and to have her fine fur ruffled to a state which it would cost her an hour's assiduous toilet to put in order.

The Yellow Terror

W. L. Alden

Speaking of cats," said Captain Foster, "I'm free to say that I don't like 'em. I don't care to be looked down on by any person, whether he be man or cat. I know I ain't the President of the United States, nor yet a millionaire, nor yet the Boss of New York, but all the same I calculate that I'm a man, and entitled to be treated as such. Now, I never knew a cat yet that didn't look down on me, same as cats do on everybody. A cat considers that men are just dirt under his or her paws, as the case may be. I can't see what it is that makes a cat believe that he is so everlastingly superior to all the men that have ever lived, but there's no denying the fact that such is his belief, and he acts according. There was a Professor here one day, lecturing on all sorts of animals, and I asked him if he could explain this aggravating conduct of cats. He said that it was because cats used to be gods, thousands of years ago in the land of Egypt; but I didn't believe him. Egypt is a Scripture country, and consequently we ought not to believe anything about it that we don't read in the Bible. Show me anywhere in the Bible that Egyptian cats are mentioned as having practised as gods, and I'll believe it. Till you show it to me, I'll take the liberty of disbelieving any worldly statement that Professors or anybody else may make about Egypt.

"The most notorious cat I ever met was old Captain Smedley's Yellow Terror. His real legal name was just plain Tom: but being yellow, and being a holy terror in many respects, it got to be the fashion among his acquaintances to call him 'The Yellow Terror.' He was a tremendous big cat, and he had been with Captain Smedley for five years before I saw him.

"Smedley was one of the best men I ever knew. I'll admit that he was a middling hard man on his sailors, so that his ship got the reputation of being a slaughter-house, which it didn't really deserve. And there is no denying that he was a very religious man, which was another thing which made him unpopular with the men. I'm a religious man myself, even when I'm at sea, but I never held with serving out religion to a crew, and making them swallow it with belaying pins. That's what old Smedley used to do. He was in command of the barque *Medford*, out of Boston, when I knew him.

I mean the city of Boston in Massachusetts, and not the little town that folks over in England call Boston: and I must say that I can't see why they should copy the names of our cities, no matter how celebrated they may be. Well! The *Medford* used to sail from Boston to London with grain, where she discharged her cargo and loaded again for China. On the outward passage we used to stop at Madeira, and the Cape, and generally Bangkok, and so on to Canton, where we filled up with tea, and then sailed for home direct.

"Now thishyer Yellow Terror had been on the ship's books for upwards of five years when I first met him. Smedley had him regularly shipped, and signed his name to the ship articles, and held a pen in his paw while he made a cross. . . . You see, in those days the underwriters wouldn't let a ship go to sea without a cat, so as to keep the rats from getting at the cargo. I don't know what a land cat may do, but there ain't a seafaring cat that would look at a rat. What with the steward, and the cook and the men forrard, being always ready to give the ship's cat a bite, the cat is generally full from kelson to deck, and wouldn't take the trouble to speak to a rat, unless one was to bite her tail. But, then, underwriters never know anything about what goes on at sea, and it's a shame that a sailorman should be compelled to give in to their ideas. The Yellow Terror had the general idea that the *Medford* was his private yacht, and that all hands were there to wait on him. And Smedley sort of confirmed him in that idea, by treating him with more respect than he treated his owners, when he was ashore. I don't blame the cat, and after I got to know what sort of a person the cat really was, I can't say as I blamed Smedley to any great extent.

"Tom, which I think I told you was the cat's real name, was far and away the best fighter of all cats in Europe, Asia, Africa, and America. Whenever we sighted land he would get himself up in his best fur, spending hours brushing and polishing it, and biting his claws so as to make sure that they were as sharp as they could be made. As soon as the ship was made fast to the quay, or anchored in the harbour, the Yellow Terror went ashore to look for trouble. He always got it too, though he had such a reputation as a fighter, that whenever he showed himself, every cat that recognised him broke for cover. Why, the gatekeeper at the London Docks—I mean the one at the Shadwell entrance—told me that he always knew when the *Medford* was warping into dock, by the stream of cats that went out of the gate, as if a pack of hounds were after them. You see that as soon as the *Medford* was reported, and word passed among the cats belonging to the ships in dock that the Yellow Terror had arrived, they judged that it was time for them to go ashore, and stop till the *Medford* should sail. Whitechapel used to be regularly overflowed with cats, and the newspapers used to have letters from scientific chaps trying to account for what they called the wave of cats that had spread over East London.

"I remember that once we laid alongside of a Russian brig, down in the basin by Old Gravel Lane. There was a tremendous big black cat sitting on the poop, and as soon as he caught sight of our Tom, he sung out to him, remarking that he was able and ready to wipe the deck up with him at any time. We all understood that the Russian was a new arrival who hadn't ever heard of the Yellow Terror, and we knew that he was, as the good book says, rushing on his fate. Tom was sitting on the rail near the mizzen rigging when the Russian made his remarks, and he didn't seem to hear them. But presently we saw him going slowly aloft till he reached our crossjack yard. He laid out on the yard arm till he was near enough to jump on to the mainyard of the Russian, and the first thing that the Russian cat knew Tom landed square on his back. The fight didn't last more than one round, and at the end of that, the remains of the Russian cat sneaked behind a water cask, and the Yellow Terror came back by the way of the crossjack yard and went on fur brushing, as if nothing had happened.

"When Tom went ashore in a foreign port he generally stopped ashore till we sailed. A few hours before we cast off hawsers, Tom would come aboard. He always knew when we were going to sail, and he never once got left. I remember one time when we were just getting up anchor in Cape Town harbour, and we all reckoned that this time we should have to sail without Tom, he having evidently stopped ashore just a little too long. But presently alongside comes a boat, with Tom lying back at full length in the sternsheets, for all the world like a drunken sailor who has been delaying the ship, and is proud of it. The boatman said that Tom had come down to the pier and jumped into his boat, knowing that the man would row him off to the ship, and calculating that Smedley would be glad to pay the damage. It's my belief that if Tom hadn't found a boat-man, he would have chartered the government launch. He had the cheek to do that or anything else.

"Fighting was really Tom's only vice; and it could hardly be called a vice, seeing as he always licked the other cat, and hardly ever came out of a fight with a torn ear or a black eye. Smedley always said that Tom was religious. I used to think that was rubbish; but after I had been with Tom for a couple of voyages I began to believe what Smedley said about him. Every Sunday when the weather permitted, Smedley used to hold service on the quarter-deck. He was a Methodist, and when it came to ladling out Scripture, or singing a hymn, he could give odds to almost any preacher. All hands, except the man at the wheel, and the lookout, were required to attend service on Sunday morning, which naturally caused considerable grumbling, as the watch below considered they had a right to sleep in peace, instead of being dragged aft for service.

But they had to knock under, and what they considered even worse, they had to sing, for the old man kept a bright lookout while the singing was going on, and if he caught any man malingering and not doing his full part of the singing he would have a few words to say to that man with a belaying pin, or a rope's end, after the service was over.

"Now Tom never failed to attend service, and to do his level best to help. He would sit somewhere near the old man and pay attention to what was going on better than I've seen some folks do in first-class churches ashore. When the men sang, Tom would start in and let out a yell here and there, which showed that he meant well even if he had never been to a singing-school, and didn't exactly understand singing according to Gunter. First along, I thought that it was all an accident that the cat came to service, and I calculated that his yelling during the singing meant that he didn't like it. But after a while I had to admit that Tom enjoyed the Sunday service as much as the Captain himself, and I agreed with Smedley that the cat was a thoroughgoing Methodist.

"Now after I'd been with Smedley for about six years, he got married all of a sudden. I didn't blame him, for in the first place it wasn't any of my business; and, in the next place, I hold that a ship's captain ought to have a wife, and the underwriters would be a sight wiser if they insisted that all captains should be married, instead of insisting that all ships should carry cats. You see that if a ship's captain has a wife, he is naturally anxious to get back to her, and have his best clothes mended, and his food cooked to suit him. Consequently he wants to make good passages and he don't want to run the risk of drowning himself, or of getting into trouble with his owners, and losing his berth. You'll find, if you look into it, that married captains live longer, and get on better than unmarried men, as it stands to reason that they ought to do.

"But it happened that the woman Smedley married was an Agonostic, which is a sort of person that doesn't believe in anything, except the multiplication table, and such-like human vanities. She didn't lose any time in getting Smedley round to her way of thinking, and instead of being the religious man he used to be, he chucked the whole thing, and used to argue with me by the hour at a time, to prove that religion was a waste of time, and that he hadn't any soul, and had never been created, but had just descended from a family of seafaring monkeys. It made me sick to hear a respectable sailorman talking such rubbish, but of course, seeing as he was my commanding officer, I had to be careful about contradicting him. I wouldn't ever yield an inch to his arguments, and I told him as respectfully as I could, that he was making the biggest mistake of his life. 'Why, look at the cat,' I used to say, 'he's got sense enough to be religious, and if you was to tell him that he was descended from a monkey, he'd consider himself insulted.' But it wasn't any use. Smedley was full of his new agonyostical theories, and the more I disagreed with him, the more set he was in his way.

"Of course he knocked off holding Sunday morning services; and the men ought to have been delighted, considering how they used to grumble at having to come aft and sing hymns, when they wanted to be below. But there is no accounting for sailors. They were actually disappointed when Sunday came and there wasn't any service. They said that we should have an unlucky voyage, and that the old man, now that he had got a rich wife, didn't consider sailors good enough to come aft on the quarter-deck, and take a hand in singing. Smedley didn't care for their opinion, but he was some considerable worried about the Yellow Terror.

Tom missed the Sunday morning service, and he said so as plain as he could. Every Sunday, for three or four weeks, he came on deck, and took his usual seat near the captain, and waited for the service to begin. When he found out that there was no use in waiting for it, he showed that he disapproved of Smedley's conduct in the strongest way. He gave up being intimate with the old man, and once when Smedley tried to pat him, and be friendly, he swore at him, and bit him on the leg—not in an angry way, you understand, but just to show his disapproval of Smedley's irreligious conduct.

"When we got to London, Tom never once went ashore, and he hadn't a single fight. He seemed to have lost all interest in worldly things. He'd sit on the poop in a melancholy sort of way, never minding how his fur looked, and never so much as answering if a strange cat sang out to him.

After we left London he kept below most of the time, and finally, about the time that we were crossing the line, he took to his bed, as you might say, and got to be as thin and weak as if he had been living in the forecastle of a lime-juicer. And he was that melancholy that you couldn't get him to take an interest in anything. Smedley got to be so anxious about him that he read up in his medical book to try and find out what was the matter with him; and finally made up his mind that the cat had a first-class disease with a big name something like spinal menagerie.

That was some little satisfaction to Smedley, but it didn't benefit the cat any; for nothing that Smedley could do would induce Tom to take medicine. He wouldn't so much as sniff at salts, and when Smedley tried to poultice his neck, he considered himself insulted, and roused up enough to take a piece out of the old man's ear.

"About that time we touched at Funchal, and Smedley sent ashore to lay in another tom-cat, thinking that perhaps a fight would brace Tom up a little. But when the new cat was put down alongside of Tom, and swore at him in the most impudent sort of way, Tom just turned over on his other side, and pretended to go asleep. After that we all felt that the Yellow Terror was done for. Smedley sent the new cat ashore again, and told me that Tom was booked for the other world, and that there wouldn't be any more luck for us on that voyage.

"I went down to see the cat, and though he was thin and weak, I couldn't see any signs of serious disease about him. So I says to Smedley that I didn't believe the cat was sick at all.

"'Then what's the matter with him?' says the old man. 'You saw yourself that he wouldn't fight, and when he's got to that point I consider that he is about done with this world and its joys and sorrows.'

"'His nose is all right,' said I. 'When I felt it just now it was as cool as a teetotaller's.'

"'That does look as if he hadn't any fever to speak of,' says Smedley, 'and the book says that if you've got spinal menagerie you're bound to have a fever.'

"'The trouble with Tom,' says I, 'is mental: that's what it is. He's got something on his mind that is wearing him out.'

"'What can he have on his mind?' says the captain. 'He's got everything to suit him aboard this ship. If he was a millionaire he couldn't be better fixed. He won all his fights while we were in Boston, and hasn't had a fight since, which shows that he can't be low-spirited on account of a licking. No, sir! You'll find that Tom's mind is all right.'

"'Then what gives him such a mournful look out of his eyes?' says I. 'When you spoke to him this morning he looked at you as if he was on the point of crying over your misfortunes—that is to say, if you've got any. Come to think of it, Tom begun to go into thishyer decline just after you were married. Perhaps that's what's the matter with him.'

"But there was no convincing Smedley that Tom's trouble was mental, and he was so sure that the cat was going to die, that he got to be about as low-spirited as Tom himself. 'I begin to wish,' says Smedley to me one morning, 'that I was a Methodist again, and believed in a hereafter. It does seem kind of hard that a first-class cat-fighter like Tom shouldn't have a chance when he dies. He was a good religious cat if ever there was one, and I'd like to think that he was going to a better world.'

"Just then an idea struck me. 'Captain Smedley,' says I, 'you remember how Tom enjoyed the meetings that we used to have aboard here on Sunday mornings!'

"'He did so,' said Smedley. 'I never saw a person who took more pleasure in his Sunday privileges than Tom did.'

"'Captain Smedley,' says I, putting my hand on the old man's sleeve. 'All that's the matter with Tom is seeing you deserting the religion that you was brought up in, and turning agonyostical, or whatever you call it. I call it turning plain infidel. Tom's mourning about your soul, and he's miserable because you don't have any more Sunday morning meetings. I told you the trouble was mental, and now you know it is.'

"'Mebbe you're right,' says Smedley, taking what I'd said in a peaceable way, instead of flying into a rage, as I expected he would. "To tell you the truth, I ain't so well satisfied in my own mind as I used to be, and I was thinking last night, when I started in to say 'Now I lay me'—just from habit you know—that if I'd stuck to the Methodist persuasion I should be a blamed sight happier than I am now."

"'Tomorrow's Sunday,' says I, 'and if I was you, Captain, I should have the bell rung for service, same as you used to do, and bring Tom up on deck, and let him have the comfort of hearing the rippingest hymns you can lay your hand to. It can't hurt you, and it may do him a heap of good. Anyway, it's worth trying, if you really want the Yellow Terror to get well.'

"'I don't mind saying,' says Smedley, 'that I'd do almost anything to save his life. He's been with me now going on for seven years, and we've never had a hard word. If a Sunday morning meeting will be any comfort to him, he shall have it. Mebbe if it doesn't cure him, it may sort of smooth his hatchway to the tomb.'

"Now the very next day was Sunday, and at six the Captain had the bell rung for service, and the men were told to lay aft. The bell hadn't fairly stopped ringing, when Tom comes up the companion way, one step at a time, looking as if he was on his way to his own funeral. He came up to his usual place alongside of the capstan, and lay down on his side at the old man's feet, and sort of looked up at him with what anybody would have said was a grateful look.

I could see that Smedley was feeling pretty serious. He understood what the cat wanted to say, and when he started in to give out a hymn, his voice sort of choked. It was a ripping good hymn, with a regular hurricane chorus, and the men sung it for all they were worth, hoping that it would meet Tom's views. He was too weak to join in with any of his old-time yells, but he sort of flopped the deck with his tail, and you could see he was enjoying it down to the ground.

"Well, the service went on just as it used to do in old times, and Smedley sort of warmed up as it went along, and by and by he'd got the regular old Methodist glow on his face. When it was all through, and the men had gone forrard again, Smedley stooped down, and picked up Tom, and kissed him, and the cat nestled up in the old man's neck and licked his chin. Smedley carried Tom down into the saloon, and sung out to the steward to bring some fresh meat. The cat turned to and ate as good a dinner as he'd ever eaten in his best days, and after he was through, he went into Smedley's own cabin, and curled up in the old man's bunk, and went to sleep purring fit to take the deck off. From that day Tom improved steadily, and by the time we got to Cape Town he was well enough to go ashore, though he was still considerable weak.

I went ashore at the same time, and kept an eye on Tom, to see what he would do. I saw him pick out a small measly-looking cat, that couldn't have stood up to a full-grown mouse, and lick him in less than a minute. Then I knew that Tom was all right again, and I admired his judgment in picking out a small cat that was suited to his weak condition. By the time that we got to Canton, Tom was as well in body and mind as he had ever been; and when we sailed, he came aboard with two inches of his tail missing, and his starboard ear carried away, but he had the air of having licked all creation, which I don't doubt he had done, that is to say, so far as all creation could be found in Canton.

"I never heard any more of Smedley's agonyostical nonsense. He went back to the Methodists again, and he always said that Tom had been the blessed means of showing him the error of his ways. I heard that when he got back to Boston, he gave Mrs. Smedley notice that he expected her to go to the Methodist meeting with him every Sunday, and that if she didn't, he should consider that it was a breach of wedding articles, and equivalent to mutiny. I don't know how she took it, or what the consequences were, for I left the *Medford* just then, and took command of a barque that traded between Boston and the West Indies. And I never heard of the Yellow Terror after that voyage, though I often thought of him, and always held that for a cat he was the ablest cat, afloat or ashore, that any man ever met."

TWENTY-TWO

Midshipman, the Cat

John Coleman Adams

This is a true story about a real cat who, for aught I know, is still alive and following the sea for a living. I hope to be excused if I use the pronouns "who" and "he" instead of "which" and "it," in speaking of this particular cat; because although I know very well that the grammars all tell us that "he" and "who" apply to persons, while "it" and "which" apply to things, yet this cat of mine always seemed to us who knew him to be so much like a human being that I find it unsatisfactory to speak of him in any other way. There are some animals of whom you prefer to say "he," just as there are persons whom you sometimes feel like calling "it."

The way we met this cat was after this fashion: It was back somewhere in the seventies, and a party of us were cruising east from Boston in the little schooner-yacht *Eyvor*. We had dropped into Marblehead for a day and a night, and some of the boys had gone ashore in the tender. As they landed on the wharf, they found a group of small boys running sticks into a woodpile, evidently on a hunt for something inside.

"What have you in there?" asked one of the yachtsmen.

"Nothin' but a cat," said the boys.

"Well, what are you doing to him?"

"Oh, pokin' him up! When he comes out we'll rock him," was the answer, in good Marblehead dialect.

"Well, don't do it anymore. What's the use of tormenting a poor cat? Why don't you take somebody of your size?"

The boys slowly moved off, a little ashamed and a little afraid of the big yachtsman who spoke; and when they were well out of sight the yachtsmen went on, too, and thought no more about the cat they had befriended. But when they had wandered about the tangled streets of the town for a little while, and paid the visits which all good yachtsmen pay, to the grocery and the post office and the apothecary's soda fountain, they returned to the wharf and found their boat. And behold, there in the stern sheets sat the little gray-and-white cat of the woodpile! He had crawled out of his retreat and made straight for the boat of his champions. He seemed in no wise disturbed or disposed to move when they jumped on board, nor did he show anything but pleasure when they stroked and patted him. But when one of the boys started to put him ashore, the plucky little fellow showed his claws; and no sooner was he set on his feet at the edge of the wharf than he turned about and jumped straight back into the boat.

"He wants to go yachting," said one of the party, whom we called "The Bos'n."

"Ye might as wal take the cat," said a grizzly old fisherman standing on the wharf. "He doesn't belong to anybody, and ef he stays here the boys'll worry him t'death."

"Let's take him aboard," said the yachtsmen. "It's good luck to have a cat on board ship."

Whether it was good luck to the ship or not, it was very clear that pussy saw it meant good luck to him, and curled himself down in the bottom of the boat, with a look that meant business. Evidently he had thought the matter all over and made up his mind that this was the sort of people he wanted to live with; and, being a Marblehead cat, it made no difference to him whether they lived afloat or ashore; he was going where they went, whether they wanted him or not. He had heard the conversation from his place in the woodpile, and had decided to show his gratitude by going to sea with these protectors of his. By casting in his lot with theirs he was paying them the highest compliment of which a cat is capable. It would have been the height of impoliteness not to recognize his distinguished appreciation. So he was allowed to remain in the boat, and was taken off to the yacht.

Upon his arrival there, a council was held, and it was unanimously decided that the cat should be received as a member of the crew; and as we were a company of amateur sailors, sailing our own boat, each man having his particular duties, it was decided that the cat should be appointed midshipman, and should be named after his position.

So he was at once and ever after known as "Middy." Everybody took a great interest in him, and he took an impartial interest in everybody—though there were two people on board to whom he made himself particularly agreeable. One was the quiet, kindly professor, the captain of the *Eyvor*; the other was Charlie, our cook and only hired hand. Middy, you see, had a seaman's true instinct as to the official persons with whom it was his interest to stand well.

It was surprising to see how quickly Middy made himself at home. He acted as if he had always been at sea. He was never seasick, no matter how rough it was or how uncomfortable any of the rest of us were. He roamed wherever he wanted to, all over the boat.

At mealtimes he came to the table with the rest, sat up on a valise, and lapped his milk and took what bits of food were given him, as if he had eaten that way all his life. When the sails were hoisted it was his especial joke to jump upon the main gaff and be hoisted with it; and once he stayed on his perch till the sail was at the masthead. One of us had to go aloft and bring him down.

When we had come to anchor and everything was snug for the night, he would come on deck and scamper out on the main boom, and race from there to the bowsprit end as fast as he could gallop, then climb, monkey-fashion, halfway up the masts, and drop back to the deck or dive down into the cabin and run riot among the berths.

One day, as we were jogging along, under a pleasant southwest wind, and everybody was lounging and dozing after dinner, we heard the Bos'n call out, "Stop that, you fellows!" and a moment after, "I tell you, quit! Or I'll come up and make you!"

We opened our lazy eyes to see what was the matter, and there sat the Bos'n, down in the cabin, close to the companionway, the tassel of his knitted cap coming nearly up to the combings of the hatch; and on the deck outside sat Middy, digging his claws into the tempting yarn, and occasionally going deep enough to scratch the Bos'n's scalp.

When night came and we were all settled down in bed, it was Middy's almost invariable custom to go the rounds of all the berths, to see if we were properly tucked in, and to end his inspection by jumping into the captain's bed, treading himself a comfortable nest there among the blankets, and curling himself down to sleep. It was his own idea to select the captain's berth as the only proper place in which to turn in.

But the most interesting trait in Middy's character did not appear until he had been a week or so on board. Then he gave us a surprise. It was when we were lying in Camden Harbor. Everybody was going ashore to take a tramp among the hills, and Charlie, the cook, was coming too, to row the boat back to the yacht.

Middy discovered that he was somehow "getting left." Being a prompt and very decided cat, it did not take him long to make up his mind what to do. He ran to the low rail of the yacht, put his forepaws on it, and gave us a long, anxious look. Then as the boat was shoved off he raised his voice in a plaintive mew. We waved him a good-bye, chaffed him pleasantly, and told him to mind the anchor, and have dinner ready when we got back.

That was too much for his temper. As quick as a flash he had dived overboard, and was swimming like a water spaniel, after the dinghy!

That was the strangest thing we had ever seen in all our lives! We were quite used to elephants that could play at seesaw, and horses that could fire cannon, to learned pigs and to educated dogs; but a cat that of his own accord would take to the water like a full-blooded Newfoundland was a little beyond anything we had ever heard of.

Of course the boat was stopped, and Middy was taken aboard drenched and shivering, but perfectly happy to be once more with the crew. He had been ignored and slighted; but he had insisted on his rights, and as soon as they were recognized he was quite contented.

Of course, after that we were quite prepared for anything that Middy might do. And yet he always managed to surprise us by his bold and independent behavior. Perhaps his most brilliant performance was a visit he paid a few days after his swim in Camden Harbor.

We were lying becalmed in a lull of the wind off the entrance to Southwest Harbor. Near us, perhaps a cable's-length away, lay another small yacht, a schooner hailing from Lynn. As we drifted along on the tide, we noticed that Middy was growing very restless; and presently we found him running along the rail and looking eagerly toward the other yacht.

What did he see—or smell—over there which interested him? It could not be the dinner, for they were not then cooking. Did he recognize any of his old chums from Marblehead? Perhaps there were some cat friends of his on the other craft. Ah, that was it! There they were on the deck, playing and frisking together—two kittens! Middy had spied them, and was longing to take a nearer look. He ran up and down the deck, mewing and snuffing the air. He stood up on his favorite position when on lookout, with his forepaws on the rail. Then, before we realized what he was doing, he had plunged overboard again, and was making for the other boat as fast as he could swim! He had attracted the attention of her company, and no sooner did he come up alongside than they prepared to welcome him. A fender was lowered, and when Middy saw it he swam toward it, caught it with his forepaws, clambered along it to the gunwale, and in a twinkling was over the side and on the deck scraping acquaintance with the strange kittens.

How they received him I hardly know, for by that time our boat was alongside to claim the runaway. And we were quite of the mind of the skipper of the *Winnie L.*, who said, as he handed our bold midshipman over the side, "Well, that beats all my going a-fishing!"

Only a day or two later Middy was very disobedient when we were washing decks one morning. He trotted about in the wet till his feet were drenched, and then retired to dry them on the white spreads of the berths below.

That was quite too much for the captain's patience. Middy was summoned aft, and, after a sound rating, was hustled into the dinghy which was moored astern, and shoved off to the full length of her painter. The punishment was a severe one for Middy, who could bear anything better than exile from his beloved shipmates. So of course he began to exercise his ingenious little brain to see how he could escape. Well under the overhang of the yacht he spied, just about four inches out of water, a little shoulder of the rudder.

That was enough for him. He did not stop to think whether he would be any better off there. It was a part of the yacht, and that was home. So overboard he went, swam for the rudder, scrambled on to it, and began howling piteously to be taken on deck again; and, being a spoiled and much-indulged cat, he was soon rescued from his uncomfortable roosting place and restored to favor.

I suppose I shall tax your powers of belief if I tell you many more of Middy's doings. But truly he was a strange cat, and you may as well be patient, for you will not soon hear of his equal. The captain was much given to rifle practice, and used to love to go ashore and shoot at a mark. On one of his trips he allowed Middy to accompany him, for the simple reason, I suppose, that Middy decided to go, and got on board the dinghy when the captain did.

Once ashore, the marksman selected a fine large rock as a rest for his rifle, and opened fire upon his target. At the first shot or two Middy seemed a little surprised, but showed no disposition to run away. After the first few rounds, however, he seemed to have made up his mind that since the captain was making all that racket it must be entirely right and proper, and nothing about which a cat need bother his head in the least. So, as if to show how entirely he confided in the captain's judgment and good intentions, that imperturbable cat calmly lay down, curled up, and went to sleep in the shade of the rock over which the captain's rifle was blazing and cracking about once in two minutes. If anybody was ever acquainted with a cooler or more self-possessed cat I should be pleased to hear the particulars.

I wish that this chronicle could be confined to nothing but our shipmate's feats of daring and nerve. But, unfortunately, he was not always blameless in his conduct. When he got hungry he was apt to forget his position as midshipman, and to behave just like any cat with an empty stomach. Or perhaps he may have done just what any hungry midshipman does under the circumstances; I do not quite know what a midshipman does under all circumstances and so I cannot say. But here is one of this cat midshipman's exploits. One afternoon, on our way home, we were working along with a head wind and sea toward Wood Island, a haven for many of the small yachts between Portland and the Shoals. The wind was light and we were a little late in making port. But as we were all agreed that it would be pleasanter to postpone our dinner till we were at anchor, the cook was told to keep things warm and wait till we were inside the port before he set the table.

Now, his main dish that day was to be a fine piece of baked fish; and, unfortunately, it was nearly done when we gave orders to hold back the dinner. So he had closed the drafts of his little stove, left the door of the oven open, and turned into his bunk for a quiet doze—a thing which every good sailor does on all possible occasions; for a seafaring life is very uncertain in the matter of sleep, and one never quite knows when he will lose some, nor how much he will lose. So it is well to lay in a good stock of it whenever you can.

It seems that Middy was on watch, and when he saw Charlie fast asleep he undertook to secure a little early dinner for himself. He evidently reasoned with himself that it was very uncertain when we should have dinner and he'd better get his while he could. He quietly slipped down to the stove, walked coolly up to the oven, and began to help himself to baked haddock.

He must have missed his aim or made some mistake in his management of the business, and, by some lucky chance for the rest of us, waked the cook. For, the first we knew, Middy came flying up the cabin companionway, followed by a volley of shoes and spoons and pieces of coal, while we could hear Charlie, who was rather given to unseemly language when he was excited, using the strongest words in his dictionary about "that thief of a cat!"

"What's the matter?" we all shouted at once.

"Matter enough, sir!" growled Charlie. "That little cat's eaten up half the fish! It's a chance if you get any dinner tonight, sir."

You may be very sure that Middy got a sound wigging for that trick, but I am afraid the captain forgot to deprive him of his rations as he threatened. He was much too kindhearted.

The very next evening Middy startled us again by a most remarkable display of coolness and courage. After a weary thrash to windward all day, under a provokingly light breeze, we found ourselves under the lee of the little promontory at Cape Neddick, where we cast anchor for the night. Our supply of water had run very low, and so, just after sunset, two of the party rowed ashore in the tender to replenish our water keg, and by special permission Middy went with them.

It took some time to find a well, and by the time the jugs were filled it had grown quite dark. In launching the boat for the return to the yacht, by some ill luck a breaker caught her and threw her back upon the beach. There she capsized and spilled out the boys, together with their precious cargo. In the confusion of the moment, and the hurry of setting matters to rights, Middy was entirely forgotten, and when the boat again was launched, nobody thought to look for the cat. This time everything went well, and in a few minutes the yacht was sighted through the dusk.

Then somebody happened to think of Middy! He was nowhere to be seen. Neither man remembered anything about him after the capsize. There was consternation in the hearts of those unlucky wights. To lose Middy was almost like losing one of the crew.

But it was too late and too dark to go back and risk another landing on the beach. There was nothing to be done but to leave poor Middy to his fate, or at least to wait until morning before searching for him.

But just as the prow of the boat bumped against the fender on the yacht's quarter, out from under the stern sheets came a wet, bedraggled, shivering cat, who leaped on board the yacht and hurried below into the warm cabin. In that moist adventure in the surf, Middy had taken care of himself, rescued himself from a watery grave, got on board the boat as soon as she was ready, and sheltered himself in the warmest corner. All this he had done without the least outcry, and without asking any help whatever. His self-reliance and courage were extraordinary.

Well, the pleasant month of cruising drew to a close, and it became a question what should be done with Middy. We could not think of turning him adrift in the cold world, although we had no fears but that so bright and plucky a cat would make a living anywhere. But we wanted to watch over his fortunes, and perhaps take him on the next cruise with us when he should have become a more settled and dignified Thomas. Finally, it was decided that he should be boarded for the winter with an artist, Miss Susan H——, a friend of one of our party. She wanted a studio cat, and would be particularly pleased to receive so accomplished and traveled a character as Middy.

So when the yacht was moored to the little wharf at Annisquam, where she always ended her cruises, and we were packed and ready for our journey to Boston, Middy was tucked into a basket and taken to the train. He bore the confinement with the same good sense which had marked all his life with us, though I think his feelings were hurt at the lack of confidence we showed in him. And, in truth, we were a little ashamed of it ourselves, and when once we were on the cars somebody suggested that he be released from his prison just to see how he would behave. We might have known he would do himself credit. For when he had looked over his surroundings, peeped above the back of the seat at the passengers, taken a good look at the conductor, and counted the rest of the party to see that none of us was missing, Middy snuggled down upon the seat, laid his head upon the captain's knee, and slept all the way to Boston.

That was the last time I ever saw Middy. He was taken to his new boarding place in Boylston Street, where he lived very pleasantly for a few months, and made many friends by his pleasing manners and unruffled temper. But I suppose he found it a little dull in Boston. He was not quite at home in his aesthetic surroundings. I have always believed he sighed for the freedom of a sailor's life. He loved to sit by the open window when the wind was east, and seemed to be dreaming of faraway scenes. One day he disappeared. No trace of him was ever found. A great many things may have happened to him. But I never could get rid of the feeling that he went down to the wharves and the ships and the sailors, trying to find his old friends, looking everywhere for the stanch little *Eyvor*; and, not finding her, I am convinced that he shipped on some East Indiaman and is now a sailor cat on the high seas.

The Philanthropist and the Happy Cat

Saki (H. H. Munro)

Jocantha Bessbury was in the mood to be serenely and graciously happy. Her world was a pleasant place, and it was wearing one of its pleasantest aspects. Gregory had managed to get home for a hurried lunch and a smoke afterwards in the little snuggery; the lunch had been a good one, and there was just time to do justice to the coffee and cigarettes. Both were excellent in their way, and Gregory was, in his way, an excellent husband. Jocantha rather suspected herself of making him a very charming wife, and more than suspected herself of having a first-rate dressmaker.

"I don't suppose a more thoroughly contented personality is to be found in all Chelsea," observed Jocantha in allusion to herself; "except perhaps Attab," she continued, glancing toward the large tabby-marked cat that lay in considerable ease in a corner of the divan. "He lies there, purring and dreaming, shifting his limbs now and then in an ecstasy of cushioned comfort. He seems the incarnation of everything soft and silky and velvety, without a sharp edge in his composition, a dreamer whose philosophy is sleep and let sleep; and then, as evening draws on, he goes out into the garden with a red glint in his eyes and slays a drowsy sparrow."

"As every pair of sparrows hatches out ten or more young ones in the year, while their food supply remains stationary, it is just as well that the Attabs of the community should have that idea of how to pass an amusing afternoon," said Gregory. Having delivered himself of this sage comment he lit another cigarette, bade Jocantha a playfully affectionate good-bye, and departed into the outer world.

"Remember, dinner's a wee bit earlier to-night, as we're going to the Haymarket," she called after him.

Left to herself, Jocantha continued the process of looking at her life with placid, introspective eyes. If she had not everything she wanted in this world, at least she was very well pleased with what she had got. She was very well pleased, for instance, with the snuggery, which contrived somehow to be cozy and dainty and expensive all at once. The porcelain was rare and beautiful, the Chinese enamels took on wonderful tints in the firelight, the rugs and hangings led the eye through sumptuous harmonies of coloring. It was a room in which one might have suitably entertained an ambassador or an archbishop, but it was also a room in which one could cut out pictures for a scrapbook without feeling that one was scandalizing the deities of the place with one's litter. And as with the snuggery, so with the rest of the house, and as with the house, so with the other departments of Jocantha's life; she really had good reason for being one of the most contented women in Chelsea.

From being in a mood of simmering satisfaction with her lot she passed to the phase of being generously commiserating for those thousands around her whose lives and circumstances were dull, cheap, pleasureless, and empty.

Work girls, shop assistants and so forth, the class that have neither the happy-go-lucky freedom of the poor nor the leisured freedom of the rich, came specially within the range of her sympathy. It was sad to think that there were young people who, after a long day's work, had to sit alone in chill, dreary bedrooms because they could not afford the price of a cup of coffee and a sandwich in a restaurant, still less a shilling for a theatre gallery.

Jocantha's mind was still dwelling on this theme when she started forth on an afternoon campaign of desultory shopping; it would be rather a comforting thing, she told herself, if she could do something, on the spur of the moment, to bring a gleam of pleasure and interest into the life of even one or two wistful-hearted, empty-pocketed workers; it would add a good deal to her sense of enjoyment at the theatre that night. She would get two upper circle tickets for a popular play, make her way into some cheap teashop, and present the tickets to the first couple of interesting work girls with whom she could casually drop into conversation.

She could explain matters by saying that she was unable to use the tickets herself and did not want them to be wasted, and, on the other hand, did not want the trouble of sending them back. On further reflection she decided that it might be better to get only one ticket and give it to some lonely-looking girl sitting eating her frugal meal by herself; the girl might scrape acquaintance with her next-seat neighbor at the theatre and lay the foundations of a lasting friendship.

With the Fairy Godmother impulse strong upon her, Jocantha marched into a ticket agency and selected with immense care an upper circle seat for the "Yellow Peacock," a play that was attracting a considerable amount of discussion and criticism.

Then she went forth in search of a teashop and philanthropic adventure, at about the same time that Attab sauntered into the garden with a mind attuned to sparrow stalking. In a corner of an A.B.C. shop she found an unoccupied table, whereat she promptly installed herself, impelled by the fact that at the next table was sitting a young girl, rather plain of feature, with tired, listless eyes, and a general air of uncomplaining forlornness.

Her dress was of poor material, but aimed at being in the fashion, her hair was pretty, and her complexion bad; she was finishing a modest meal of tea and scone, and she was not very different in her way from thousands of other girls who were finishing, or beginning, or continuing their teas in London teashops at that exact moment. The odds were enormously in favor of the supposition that she had never seen the "Yellow Peacock": obviously she supplied excellent material for Jocantha's first experiment in haphazard benefaction.

Jocantha ordered some tea and a muffin, and then turned a friendly scrutiny on her neighbor with a view to catching her eye. At that precise moment the girl's face lit up with sudden pleasure, her eyes sparkled, a flush came into her cheeks, and she looked almost pretty. A young man, whom she greeted with an affectionate "Hullo, Bertie," came up to her table and took his seat in a chair facing her. Jocantha looked hard at the newcomer; he was in appearance a few years younger than herself, very much better looking than Gregory, rather better looking, in fact, than any of the young men of her set. She guessed him to be a well-mannered young clerk in some wholesale warehouse, existing and amusing himself as best he might on a tiny salary, and commanding a holiday of about two weeks in the year.

He was aware, of course, of his good looks, but with the shy self-consciousness of the Anglo-Saxon, not the blatant complacency of the Latin. He was obviously on terms of friendly intimacy with the girl he was talking to, probably they were drifting towards a formal engagement. Jocantha pictured the boy's home, in a rather narrow circle, with a tiresome mother who always wanted to know how and where he spent his evenings. He would exchange that humdrum thralldom in due course for a home of his own, dominated by a chronic scarcity of pounds, shillings, and pence, and a dearth of most of the things that made life attractive or comfortable. Jocantha felt extremely sorry for him. She wondered if he had seen the "Yellow Peacock": the odds were enormously in favor of the supposition that he had not. The girl had finished her tea and would shortly be going back to her work; when the boy was alone it would be quite easy for Jocantha to say: "My husband has made other arrangements for me this evening; would you care to make use of this ticket, which would otherwise be wasted?"

Then she could come there again one afternoon for tea, and, if she saw him, ask him how he liked the play. If he was a nice boy and improved on acquaintance he could be given more theatre tickets, and perhaps asked to come one Sunday to tea at Chelsea. Jocantha made up her mind that he would improve on acquaintance, and that Gregory would like him, and that the Fairy Godmother business would prove far more entertaining than she had originally anticipated. The boy was distinctly presentable; he knew how to brush his hair, which was possibly an imitative faculty; he knew what color of tie suited him, which might be intuition; he was exactly the type that Jocantha admired, which of course was accident. Altogether she was rather pleased when the girl looked at the clock and bade a friendly but hurried farewell to her companion.

Bertie nodded "good-bye," gulped down a mouthful of tea, and then produced from his overcoat pocket a paper-covered book, bearing the title *Sepoy and Sahib, a Tale of the Great Mutiny.*

The laws of teashop etiquette forbid that you should offer theatre tickets to a stranger without having first caught the stranger's eye. It is even better if you can ask to have a sugar basin passed to you, having previously concealed the fact that you have a large and well-filled sugar basin on your own table; this is not difficult to manage, as the printed menu is generally nearly as large as the table, and can be made to stand on end. Jocantha set to work hopefully; she had a long and rather high-pitched discussion with the waitress concerning alleged defects in an altogether blameless muffin, she made loud and plaintive inquiries about the tube service to some impossibly remote suburb, she talked with brilliant insincerity to the teashop kitten, and as a last resort she upset a milk-jug and swore at it daintily. Altogether she attracted a good deal of attention, but never for a moment did she attract the attention of the boy with the beautifully brushed hair, who was some thousands of miles away in the baking plains of Hindostan, amid deserted bungalows, seething bazaars, and riotous barrack squares, listening to the throbbing of tom-toms and the distant rattle of musketry.

Jocantha went back to her house in Chelsea, which struck her for the first time as looking dull and over-furnished. She had a resentful conviction that Gregory would be uninteresting at dinner, and that the play would be stupid after dinner. On the whole her frame of mind showed a marked divergence from the purring complacency of Attab, who was again curled up in his corner of the divan with a great peace radiating from every curve of his body.

But then he had killed his sparrow.

TWENTY-FOUR

My Cat

Michel de Montaigne

WHEN MY CAT AND I ENTERTAIN EACH OTHER WITH MUTUAL ANTICS, as playing with a garter, who knows but that I make more sport for her than she makes for me? Shall I conclude her to be simple that has her time to begin or to refuse to play, as freely as I have mine. Nay, who knows but that it a defect of not my understanding her language (for doubtless cats can talk and reason with one another) that we agree no better; and who knows but that she pities me for being no wiser than to play with her; and laughs, and censures my folly in making sport for her, when we two play together.

TWENTY-FIVE

Calvin

A Study of Character

Charles Dudley Warner

Calvin is dead. His life, long to him, but short for the rest of us, was not marked by startling adventures, but his character was so uncommon and his qualities were so worthy of imitation, that I have been asked by those who personally knew him to set down my recollections of his career.

His origin and ancestry were shrouded in mystery; even his age was a matter of pure conjecture. Although he was of the Maltese race, I have reason to suppose that he was American by birth as he certainly was in sympathy. Calvin was given to me eight years ago by Mrs. Stowe, but she knew nothing of his age or origin. He walked into her house one day out of the great unknown and became at once at home, as if he had been always a friend of the family. He appeared to have artistic and literary tastes, and it was as if he had inquired at the door, if that was the residence of the author of *Uncle Tom's Cabin*, and, upon being assured that it was, had decided to dwell there. This is, of course, fanciful, for his antecedents were wholly unknown, but in his time he could hardly have been in any household where he would not have heard *Uncle Tom's Cabin* talked about. When he came to Mrs. Stowe, he was as large as he ever was, and apparently as old as he ever became. Yet there was in him no appearance of age; he was in the happy maturity of all his powers, and you would rather have said that in that maturity he had found the secret of perpetual youth. And it was as difficult to believe that he would ever be aged as it was to imagine that he had ever been in immature youth.

There was in him a mysterious perpetuity.

After some years, when Mrs. Stowe made her winter home in Florida, Calvin came to live with us. From the first moment, he fell into the ways of the house and assumed a recognized position in the family,—I say recognized, because after he became known he was always inquired for by visitors, and in the letters to the other members of the family he always received a message. Although the least obtrusive of beings, his individuality always made itself felt.

His personal appearance had much to do with this, for he was of royal mold, and had an air of high breeding. He was large, but he had nothing of the fat grossness of the celebrated Angora family; though powerful, he was exquisitely proportioned, and as graceful in every movement as a young leopard. When he stood up to open a door—he opened all the doors with old-fashioned latches—he was portentously tall, and when stretched on the rug before the fire he seemed too long for this world—as indeed he was. His coat was the finest and softest I have ever seen, a shade of quiet Maltese; and from his throat downward, underneath, to the white tips of his feet, he wore the whitest and most delicate ermine; and no person was ever more fastidiously neat. In his finely formed head you saw something of his aristocratic character; the ears were small and cleanly cut, there was a tinge of pink in the nostrils, his face was handsome and the expression of his countenance exceedingly intelligent—I should call it even a sweet expression if the term were not inconsistent with his look of alertness and sagacity.

It is difficult to convey a just idea of his gayety in connection with his dignity and gravity, which his name expressed. As we know nothing of his family, of course it will be understood that Calvin was his Christian name. He had times of relaxation into utter playfulness, delighting in a ball of yarn, catching sportively at stray ribbons when his mistress was at her toilet, and pursuing his own tail, with hilarity, for lack of anything better. He could amuse himself by the hour, and he did not care for children; perhaps something in his past was present to his memory. He had absolutely no bad habits, and his disposition was perfect. I never saw him exactly angry, though I have seen his tail grow to an enormous size when a strange cat appeared upon his lawn. He disliked cats, evidently regarding them as feline and treacherous, and he had no association with them. Occasionally there would be heard a night concert in the shrubbery. Calvin would ask to have the door opened, and then you would hear a rush and a "pestzt," and the concert would explode, and Calvin would quietly come in and resume his seat on the hearth. There was no trace of anger in his manner, but he wouldn't have any of that about the house. He had the rare virtue of magnanimity. Although he had fixed notions about his own rights, and extraordinary persistency in getting them, he never showed temper at a repulse; he simply and firmly persisted till he had what he wanted. His diet was one point; his idea was that of the scholars about dictionaries,—to "get the best." He knew as well as any one what was in the house, and would refuse beef if turkey was to be had; and if there were oysters, he would wait over the turkey to see if the oysters would not be forthcoming. And yet he was not a gross gourmand; he would eat bread if he saw me eating it, and thought he was not being imposed on. His habits of feeding, also, were refined; he never used a knife, and he would put up his hand and draw the fork down to his mouth as gracefully as a grown person. Unless necessity compelled, he would not eat in the kitchen, but insisted upon his meals in the dining-room, and would wait patiently, unless a stranger were present; and then he was sure to importune the visitor, hoping that the latter was ignorant of the rule of the house, and would give him something. They used to say that he preferred as his table-cloth on the floor a certain well-known church journal; but this was said by an Episcopalian. So far as I know, he had no religious prejudices, except that he did not like the association with Romanists. He tolerated the servants, because they belonged to the house, and would sometimes linger by the kitchen stove; but the moment visitors came in he arose, opened the door, and marched into the drawing-room. Yet he enjoyed the company of his equals, and never withdrew, no matter how many callers—whom he recognized as of his society,—might come into the drawing-room. Calvin was fond of company, but he wanted to choose it; and I have no doubt that his was an aristocratic fastidiousness, rather than one of faith. It is so with most people.

The intelligence of Calvin was something phenomenal, in his rank of life. He established a method of communicating his wants, and even some of his sentiments; and he could help himself in many things. There was a furnace register in a retired room, where he used to go when he wished to be alone, that he always opened when he desired more heat; but never shut it, any more than he shut the door after himself. He could do almost everything but speak; and you would declare sometimes that you could see a pathetic longing to do that in his intelligent face. I have no desire to overdraw his qualities, but if there was one thing in him more noticeable than another, it was his fondness for nature. He could content himself for hours at a low window, looking into the ravine and at the great trees, noting the smallest stir there; he delighted, above all things, to accompany me walking about the garden, hearing the birds, getting the smell of the fresh earth, and rejoicing in the sunshine. He followed me and gamboled like a dog, rolling over on the turf and exhibiting his delight in a hundred ways. If I worked, he sat and watched me, or looked off over the bank, and kept his ear open to the twitter in the cherry-trees. When it stormed, he was sure to sit at the window, keenly watching the rain or the snow, glancing up and down at its falling; and a winter tempest always delighted him. I think he was genuinely fond of birds, but, so far as I know, he usually confined himself to one a day; he never killed, as some sportsmen do, for the sake of killing, but only as civilized people do,—from necessity. He was intimate with the flying-squirrels who dwell in the chestnut-trees,—too intimate, for almost every day in the summer he would bring in one, until he nearly discouraged them.

He was, indeed, a superb hunter, and would have been a devastating one, if his bump of destructiveness had not been offset by a bump of moderation. There was very little of the brutality of the lower animals about him; I don't think he enjoyed rats for themselves, but he knew his business, and for the first few months of his residence with us he waged an awful campaign against the horde, and after that his simple presence was sufficient to deter them from coming on the premises. Mice amused him, but he usually considered them too small game to be taken seriously;

I have seen him play for an hour with a mouse, and then let him go with a royal condescension. In this whole matter of "getting a living," Calvin was a great contrast to the rapacity of the age in which he lived.

I hesitate a little to speak of his capacity for friendship and the affectionateness of his nature, for I know from his own reserve that he would not care to have it much talked about. We understood each other perfectly, but we never made any fuss about it; when I spoke his name and snapped my fingers, he came to me; when I returned home at night, he was pretty sure to be waiting for me near the gate, and would rise and saunter along the walk, as if his being there were purely accidental,—so shy was he commonly of showing feeling; and when I opened the door he never rushed in, like a cat, but loitered, and lounged, as if he had had no intention of going in, but would condescend to. And yet, the fact was, he knew dinner was ready, and he was bound to be there.

He kept the run of dinner-time. It happened sometimes, during our absence in the summer, that dinner would be early, and Calvin, walking about the grounds, missed it and came in late. But he never made a mistake the second day. There was one thing he never did,—he never rushed through an open doorway. He never forgot his dignity. If he had asked to have the door opened, and was eager to go out, he always went deliberately; I can see him now, standing on the sill, looking about at the sky as if he was thinking whether it were worth while to take an umbrella, until he was near having his tail shut in.

His friendship was rather constant than demonstrative. When we returned from an absence of nearly two years, Calvin welcomed us with evident pleasure, but showed his satisfaction rather by tranquil happiness than by fuming about. He had the faculty of making us glad to get home. It was his constancy that was so attractive. He liked companionship, but he wouldn't be petted, or fussed over, or sit in anyone's lap a moment; he always extricated himself from such familiarity with dignity and with no show of temper. If there was any petting to be done, however, he chose to do it. Often he would sit looking at me, and then, moved by a delicate affection, come and pull at my coat and sleeve until he could touch my face with his nose, and then go away contented. He had a habit of coming to my study in the morning, sitting quietly by my side or on the table for hours, watching the pen run over the paper, occasionally swinging his tail round for a blotter, and then going to sleep among the papers by the inkstand. Or, more rarely, he would watch the writing from a perch on my shoulder. Writing always interested him, and, until he understood it, he wanted to hold the pen.

He always held himself in a kind of reserve with his friend, as if he had said, "Let us respect our personality, and not make a 'mess' of friendship." He saw, with Emerson, the risk of degrading it to trivial conveniency. "Why insist on rash personal relations with your friend?" "Leave this touching and clawing." Yet I would not give an unfair notion of his aloofness, his fine sense of the sacredness of the me and the not-me. And, at the risk of not being believed, I will relate an incident, which was often repeated. Calvin had the practice of passing a portion of the night in the contemplation of its beauties, and would come into our chamber over the roof of the conservatory through the open window, summer and winter, and go to sleep on the foot of my bed. He would do this always exactly in this way; he never was content to stay in the chamber if we compelled him to go upstairs and through the door. He had the obstinacy of General Grant. But this is by the way. In the morning, he performed his toilet and went down to breakfast with the rest of the family.

Now, when the mistress was absent from home, and at no other time, Calvin would come in the morning, when the bell rang, to the head of the bed, put up his feet and look into my face, follow me about when I rose, "assist" at the dressing, and in many purring ways show his fondness, as if he had plainly said, "I know that she has gone away, but I am here."

Such was Calvin in rare moments.

He had his limitations. Whatever passion he had for nature, he had no conception of art. There was sent to him once a fine and very expressive cat's head in bronze, by Frémiet. I placed it on the floor. He regarded it intently, approached it cautiously and crouchingly, touched it with his nose, perceived the fraud, turned away abruptly, and never would notice it afterward. On the whole, his life was not only a successful one, but a happy one. He never had but one fear, so far as I know: he had a mortal and a reasonable terror of plumbers. He would never stay in the house when they were here. No coaxing could quiet him. Of course he didn't share our fear about their charges, but he must have had some dreadful experience with them in that portion of his life which is unknown to us. A plumber was to him the devil, and I have no doubt that, in his scheme, plumbers were foreordained to do him mischief.

In speaking of his worth, it has never occurred to me to estimate Calvin by the worldly standard. I know that it is customary now, when anyone dies, to ask how much he was worth, and that no obituary in the newspapers is considered complete without such an estimate. The plumbers in our house were one day overheard to say that, "They say that she says that he says that he wouldn't take a hundred dollars for him." It is unnecessary to say that I never made such a remark, and that, so far as Calvin was concerned, there was no purchase in money.

As I look back upon it, Calvin's life seems to me a fortunate one, for it was natural and unforced. He ate when he was hungry, slept when he was sleepy, and enjoyed existence to the very tips of his toes and the end of his expressive and slow-moving tail. He delighted to roam about the garden, and stroll among the trees, and to lie on the green grass and luxuriate in all the sweet influences of summer. You could never accuse him of idleness, and yet he knew the secret of repose. The poet who wrote so prettily of him that his little life was rounded with a sleep, understated his felicity; it was rounded with a good many.

His conscience never seemed to interfere with his slumbers. In fact, he had good habits and a contented mind. I can see him now walk in at the study door, sit down by my chair, bring his tail artistically about his feet, and look up at me with unspeakable happiness in his handsome face. I often thought that he felt the dumb limitation which denied him the power of language. But since he was denied speech, he scorned the inarticulate mouthings of the lower animals.

The vulgar mewing and yowling of the cat species was beneath him; he sometimes uttered a sort of articulate and well-bred ejaculation, when he wished to call attention to something that he considered remarkable, or to some want of his, but he never went whining about. He would sit for hours at a closed window, when he desired to enter, without a murmur, and when it was opened he never admitted that he had been impatient by "bolting" in. Though speech he had not, and the unpleasant kind of utterance given to his race he would not use, he had a mighty power of purr to express his measureless content with congenial society.

There was in him a musical organ with stops of varied power and expression, upon which I have no doubt he could have performed Sebastian Bach's celebrated cat's-fugue.

Whether Calvin died of old age, or was carried off by one of the diseases incident to youth, it is impossible to say; for his departure was as quiet as his advent was mysterious. I only know that he appeared to us in this world in his perfect stature and beauty, and that after a time, like Lohengrin, he withdrew. In his illness, there was nothing more to be regretted than in all his blameless life. I suppose there never was an illness that had more of dignity, and sweetness, and resignation in it.

It came on gradually, in a kind of listlessness and want of appetite. An alarming symptom was his preference for the warmth of a furnace-register to the lively sparkle of the open wood-fire. Whatever pain he suffered, he bore it in silence, and seemed only anxious not to obtrude his malady. We tempted him with the delicacies of the season, but it soon became impossible for him to eat, and for two weeks he ate or drank scarcely anything.

Sometimes he made an effort to take something, but it was evident that he made the effort to please us. The neighbors—and I am convinced that the advice of neighbors is never good for anything—suggested catnip. He wouldn't even smell it. We had the attendance of an amateur practitioner of medicine, whose real office was the cure of souls, but nothing touched his case. He took what was offered, but it was with the air of one to whom the time for pellets was passed. He sat or lay day after day almost motionless, never once making a display of those vulgar convulsions or contortions of pain which are so disagreeable to society.

His favorite place was on the brightest spot of a Smyrna rug by the conservatory, where the sunlight fell and he could hear the fountain play. If we went to him and exhibited our interest in his condition, he always purred in recognition of our sympathy. And when I spoke his name, he looked up with an expression that said, "I understand it, old fellow, but it's no use." He was to all who came to visit him a model of calmness and patience in affliction.

I was absent from home at the last, but heard by daily postal-card of his failing condition; and never again saw him alive. One sunny morning, he rose from his rug, went into the conservatory (he was very thin then), walked around it deliberately, looking at all the plants he knew, and then went to the bay window in the dining-room, and stood a long time looking out upon the little field, now brown and sere, and toward the garden, where perhaps the happiest hours of his life had been spent. It was a last look. He turned and walked away, laid himself down upon the bright spot in the rug, and quietly died.

It is not too much to say that a little shock went through the neighborhood when it was known that Calvin was dead, so marked was his individuality; and his friends, one after another, came in to see him.

There was no sentimental nonsense about his obsequies; it was felt that any parade would have been distasteful to him. John, who acted as undertaker, prepared a candle-box for him, and I believe assumed a professional decorum; but there may have been the usual levity underneath, for I heard that he remarked in the kitchen that it was the "dryest wake he ever attended." Everybody, however, felt a fondness for Calvin, and regarded him with a certain respect. Between him and Bertha there existed a great friendship, and she apprehended his nature; she used to say that sometimes she was afraid of him, he looked at her so intelligently; she was never certain that he was what he appeared to be.

When I returned, they had laid Calvin on a table in an upper chamber by an open window. It was February. He reposed in a candle-box, lined about the edge with evergreen, and at his head stood a little wine-glass with flowers. He lay with his head tucked down in his arms,—a favorite position of his before the fire,—as if asleep in the comfort of his soft and exquisite fur. It was the involuntary exclamation of those who saw him, "How natural he looks!" As for myself, I said nothing. John buried him under the twin hawthorn-trees,—one white and the other pink,—in a spot where Calvin was fond of lying and listening to the hum of summer insects and the twitter of birds.

Perhaps I have failed to make appear the individuality of character that was so evident to those who knew him. At any rate, I have set down nothing concerning him but the literal truth. He was always a mystery.

I did not know whence he came; I do not know whither he has gone. I would not weave one spray of falsehood in the wreath I lay upon his grave.

The Cat That Walked by Himself

Rudyard Kipling

HEAR AND ATTEND AND LISTEN; FOR THIS BEFELL AND BEHAPPENED
and became and was, O my Best Beloved, when the Tame animals were
wild. The Dog was wild, and the Horse was wild, and the Cow was wild,
and the Sheep was wild, and the Pig was wild—as wild as wild could
be—and they walked in the Wet Wild Woods by their wild lones. But
the wildest of all the wild animals was the Cat. He walked by himself,
and all places were alike to him.

Of course the Man was wild too. He was dreadfully wild. He didn't
even begin to be tame till he met the Woman, and she told him that
she did not like living in his wild ways. She picked out a nice dry Cave,
instead of a heap of wet leaves, to lie down in; and she strewed clean sand
on the floor; and she lit a nice fire of wood at the back of the Cave; and
she hung a dried wild-horse skin, tail-down, across the opening of the
Cave; and she said, "Wipe youra feet, dear, when you come in, and now
we'll keep house."

That night, Best Beloved, they ate wild sheep roasted on the hot
stones, and flavoured with wild garlic and wild pepper; and wild duck
stuffed with wild rice and wild fenugreek and wild coriander; and
marrow-bones of wild oxen; and wild cherries, and wild grenadillas. Then
the Man went to sleep in front of the fire ever so happy; but the Woman
sat up, combing her hair. She took the bone of the shoulder of mutton—
the big fat blade-bone—and she looked at the wonderful marks on it, and

she threw more wood on the fire, and she made a Magic. She made the First Singing Magic in the world.

Out in the Wet Wild Woods all the wild animals gathered together where they could see the light of the fire a long way off, and they wondered what it meant.

Then Wild Horse stamped with his wild foot and said, "O my Friends and O my Enemies, why have the Man and the Woman made that great light in that great Cave, and what harm will it do us?"

Wild Dog lifted up his wild nose and smelled the smell of roast mutton, and said, "I will go up and see and look, and say; for I think it is good. Cat, come with me."

"Nenni!" said the Cat. "I am the Cat who walks by himself, and all places are alike to me. I will not come."

"Then we can never be friends again," said Wild Dog, and he trotted off to the Cave. But when he had gone a little way the Cat said to himself, "All places are alike to me. Why should I not go too and see and look and come away at my own liking." So he slipped after Wild Dog softly, very softly, and hid himself where he could hear everything.

When Wild Dog reached the mouth of the Cave he lifted up the dried horse-skin with his nose and sniffed the beautiful smell of the roast mutton, and the Woman, looking at the blade-bone, heard him, and laughed, and said, "Here comes the first. Wild Thing out of the Wild Woods, what do you want?"

Wild Dog said, "O my Enemy and Wife of my Enemy, what is this that smells so good in the Wild Woods?"

Then the Woman picked up a roasted mutton-bone and threw it to Wild Dog, and said, "Wild Thing out of the Wild Woods, taste and try." Wild Dog gnawed the bone, and it was more delicious than anything he had ever tasted, and he said, "O my Enemy and Wife of my Enemy, give me another."

The Woman said, "Wild Thing out of the Wild Woods, help my Man to hunt through the day and guard this Cave at night, and I will give you as many roast bones as you need."

"Ah!" said the Cat, listening. "This is a very wise Woman, but she is not so wise as I am."

Wild Dog crawled into the Cave and laid his head on the Woman's lap, and said, "O my Friend and Wife of my Friend, I will help Your Man to hunt through the day, and at night I will guard your Cave."

"Ah!" said the Cat, listening. "That is a very foolish Dog." And he went back through the Wet Wild Woods waving his wild tail, and walking by his wild lone. But he never told anybody.

When the Man waked up he said, "What is Wild Dog doing here?" And the Woman said, "His name is not Wild Dog any more, but the First Friend, because he will be our friend for always and always and always. Take him with you when you go hunting."

Next night the Woman cut great green armfuls of fresh grass from the water-meadows, and dried it before the fire, so that it smelt like new-mown hay, and she sat at the mouth of the Cave and plaited a halter out of horse-hide, and she looked at the shoulder of mutton-bone—at the big broad blade-bone—and she made a Magic. She made the Second Singing Magic in the world.

Out in the Wild Woods all the wild animals wondered what had happened to Wild Dog, and at last Wild Horse stamped with his foot and said, "I will go and see and say why Wild Dog has not returned. Cat, come with me."

"Nenni!" said the Cat. "I am the Cat who walks by himself, and all places are alike to me. I will not come." But all the same he followed Wild Horse softly, very softly, and hid himself where he could hear everything.

When the Woman heard Wild Horse tripping and stumbling on his long mane, she laughed and said, "Here comes the second. Wild Thing out of the Wild Woods what do you want?"

Wild Horse said, "O my Enemy and Wife of my Enemy, where is Wild Dog?"

The Woman laughed, and picked up the blade-bone and looked at it, and said, "Wild Thing out of the Wild Woods, you did not come here for Wild Dog, but for the sake of this good grass."

And Wild Horse, tripping and stumbling on his long mane, said, "That is true; give it me to eat."

The Woman said, "Wild Thing out of the Wild Woods, bend your wild head and wear what I give you, and you shall eat the wonderful grass three times a day."

"Ah," said the Cat, listening, "this is a clever Woman, but she is not so clever as I am." Wild Horse bent his wild head, and the Woman slipped the plaited hide halter over it, and Wild Horse breathed on the Woman's feet and said, "O my Mistress, and Wife of my Master, I will be your servant for the sake of the wonderful grass."

"Ah," said the Cat, listening, "that is a very foolish Horse." And he went back through the Wet Wild Woods, waving his wild tail and walking by his wild lone. But he never told anybody.

When the Man and the Dog came back from hunting, the Man said, "What is Wild Horse doing here?" And the Woman said, "His name is not Wild Horse any more, but the First Servant, because he will carry us from place to place for always and always and always. Ride on his back when you go hunting."

Next day, holding her wild head high that her wild horns should not catch in the wild trees, Wild Cow came up to the Cave, and the Cat followed, and hid himself just the same as before; and everything happened just the same as before; and the Cat said the same things as before, and when Wild Cow had promised to give her milk to the Woman every day in exchange for the wonderful grass, the Cat went back through the Wet Wild Woods waving his wild tail and walking by his wild lone, just the same as before. But he never told anybody. And when the Man and the Horse and the Dog came home from hunting and asked the same questions same as before, the Woman said, "Her name is not Wild Cow any more, but the Giver of Good Food. She will give us the warm white milk for always and always and always, and I will take care of her while you and the First Friend and the First Servant go hunting."

Next day the Cat waited to see if any other Wild thing would go up to the Cave, but no one moved in the Wet Wild Woods, so the Cat walked there by himself; and he saw the Woman milking the Cow, and he saw the light of the fire in the Cave, and he smelt the smell of the warm white milk.

Cat said, "O my Enemy and Wife of my Enemy, where did Wild Cow go?"

The Woman laughed and said, "Wild Thing out of the Wild Woods, go back to the Woods again, for I have braided up my hair, and I have put away the magic blade-bone, and we have no more need of either friends or servants in our Cave."

Cat said, "I am not a friend, and I am not a servant. I am the Cat who walks by himself, and I wish to come into your cave."

Woman said, "Then why did you not come with First Friend on the first night?"

Cat grew very angry and said, "Has Wild Dog told tales of me?"

Then the Woman laughed and said, "You are the Cat who walks by himself, and all places are alike to you. You are neither a friend nor a servant. You have said it yourself. Go away and walk by yourself in all places alike."

Then Cat pretended to be sorry and said, "Must I never come into the Cave? Must I never sit by the warm fire? Must I never drink the warm white milk? You are very wise and very beautiful. You should not be cruel even to a Cat."

Woman said, "I knew I was wise, but I did not know I was beautiful. So I will make a bargain with you. If ever I say one word in your praise you may come into the Cave."

"And if you say two words in my praise?" said the Cat.

"I never shall," said the Woman, "but if I say two words in your praise, you may sit by the fire in the Cave."

"And if you say three words?" said the Cat.

"I never shall," said the Woman, "but if I say three words in your praise, you may drink the warm white milk three times a day for always and always and always.'

Then the Cat arched his back and said, "Now let the Curtain at the mouth of the Cave, and the Fire at the back of the Cave, and the Milk-pots that stand beside the Fire, remember what my Enemy and the Wife of my Enemy has said." And he went away through the Wet Wild Woods waving his wild tail and walking by his wild lone.

That night when the Man and the Horse and the Dog came home from hunting, the Woman did not tell them of the bargain that she had made with the Cat, because she was afraid that they might not like it.

Cat went far and far away and hid himself in the Wet Wild Woods by his wild lone for a long time till the Woman forgot all about him. Only the Bat—the little upside-down Bat—that hung inside the Cave, knew where Cat hid; and every evening Bat would fly to Cat with news of what was happening.

One evening Bat said, "There is a Baby in the Cave. He is new and pink and fat and small, and the Woman is very fond of him."

"Ah," said the Cat, listening, "but what is the Baby fond of?"

"He is fond of things that are soft and tickle," said the Bat. "He is fond of warm things to hold in his arms when he goes to sleep. He is fond of being played with. He is fond of all those things."

"Ah," said the Cat, listening, "then my time has come."

Next night Cat walked through the Wet Wild Woods and hid very near the Cave till morning-time, and Man and Dog and Horse went hunting. The Woman was busy cooking that morning, and the Baby cried and interrupted. So she carried him outside the Cave and gave him a handful of pebbles to play with. But still the Baby cried.

Then the Cat put out his paddy paw and patted the Baby on the cheek, and it cooed; and the Cat rubbed against its fat knees and tickled it under its fat chin with his tail. And the Baby laughed; and the Woman heard him and smiled.

Then the Bat—the little upside-down bat—that hung in the mouth of the Cave said, "O my Hostess and Wife of my Host and Mother of my Host's Son, a Wild Thing from the Wild Woods is most beautifully playing with your Baby."

"A blessing on that Wild Thing whoever he may be," said the Woman, straightening her back, "for I was a busy woman this morning and he has done me a service."

That very minute and second, Best Beloved, the dried horse-skin Curtain that was stretched tail-down at the mouth of the Cave fell down—whoosh!—because it remembered the bargain she had made with the Cat, and when the Woman went to pick it up—lo and behold!—the Cat was sitting quite comfy inside the Cave.

"O my Enemy and Wife of my Enemy and Mother of my Enemy," said the Cat, "it is I: for you have spoken a word in my praise, and now I can sit within the Cave for always and always and always. But still I am the Cat who walks by himself, and all places are alike to me."

The Woman was very angry, and shut her lips tight and took up her spinning-wheel and began to spin. But the Baby cried because the Cat had gone away, and the Woman could not hush it, for it struggled and kicked and grew black in the face.

"O my Enemy and Wife of my Enemy and Mother of my Enemy," said the Cat, "take a strand of the wire that you are spinning and tie it to your spinning-whorl and drag it along the floor, and I will show you a magic that shall make your Baby laugh as loudly as he is now crying."

"I will do so," said the Woman, "because I am at my wits' end; but I will not thank you for it."

She tied the thread to the little clay spindle whorl and drew it across the floor, and the Cat ran after it and patted it with his paws and rolled head over heels, and tossed it backward over his shoulder and chased it between his hind-legs and pretended to lose it, and pounced down upon it again, till the Baby laughed as loudly as it had been crying, and scrambled after the Cat and frolicked all over the Cave till it grew tired and settled down to sleep with the Cat in its arms.

"Now," said the Cat, "I will sing the Baby a song that shall keep him asleep for an hour. And he began to purr, loud and low, low and loud, till the Baby fell fast asleep. The Woman smiled as she looked down upon the two of them and said, "That was wonderfully done. No question but you are very clever, O Cat."

That very minute and second, Best Beloved, the smoke of the fire at the back of the Cave came down in clouds from the roof—puff!— because it remembered the bargain she had made with the Cat, and when it had cleared away—lo and behold!—the Cat was sitting quite comfy close to the fire.

"O my Enemy and Wife of my Enemy and Mother of My Enemy," said the Cat, "it is I, for you have spoken a second word in my praise, and now I can sit by the warm fire at the back of the Cave for always and always and always. But still I am the Cat who walks by himself, and all places are alike to me."

Then the Woman was very very angry, and let down her hair and put more wood on the fire and brought out the broad blade-bone of the shoulder of mutton and began to make a Magic that should prevent her from saying a third word in praise of the Cat. It was not a Singing Magic, Best Beloved, it was a Still Magic; and by and by the Cave grew so still that a little wee-wee mouse crept out of a corner and ran across the floor.

"O my Enemy and Wife of my Enemy and Mother of my Enemy," said the Cat, "is that little mouse part of your magic?"

"Ouh! Chee! No indeed!" said the Woman, and she dropped the blade-bone and jumped upon the footstool in front of the fire and braided up her hair very quick for fear that the mouse should run up it.

"Ah," said the Cat, watching, "then the mouse will do me no harm if I eat it?"

"No," said the Woman, braiding up her hair, "eat it quickly and I will ever be grateful to you."

Cat made one jump and caught the little mouse, and the Woman said, "A hundred thanks. Even the First Friend is not quick enough to catch little mice as you have done. You must be very wise."

That very moment and second, O Best Beloved, the Milk-pot that stood by the fire cracked in two pieces—ffft—because it remembered the bargain she had made with the Cat, and when the Woman jumped down from the footstool—lo and behold!—the Cat was lapping up the warm white milk that lay in one of the broken pieces.

"O my Enemy and Wife of my Enemy and Mother of my Enemy, said the Cat, "it is I; for you have spoken three words in my praise, and now I can drink the warm white milk three times a day for always and always and always. But still I am the Cat who walks by himself, and all places are alike to me."

Then the Woman laughed and set the Cat a bowl of the warm white milk and said, "O Cat, you are as clever as a man, but remember that your bargain was not made with the Man or the Dog, and I do not know what they will do when they come home."

"What is that to me?" said the Cat. "If I have my place in the Cave by the fire and my warm white milk three times a day I do not care what the Man or the Dog can do."

That evening when the Man and the Dog came into the Cave, the Woman told them all the story of the bargain while the Cat sat by the fire and smiled. Then the Man said, "Yes, but he has not made a bargain with me or with all proper Men after me." Then he took off his two leather boots and he took up his little stone axe (that makes three) and he fetched a piece of wood and a hatchet (that is five altogether), and he set them out in a row and he said, "Now we will make our bargain. If you do not catch mice when you are in the Cave for always and always and always, I will throw these five things at you whenever I see you, and so shall all proper Men do after me."

"Ah," said the Woman, listening, "this is a very clever Cat, but he is not so clever as my Man."

The Cat counted the five things (and they looked very knobby) and he said, "I will catch mice when I am in the Cave for always and always and always; but still I am the Cat who walks by himself, and all places are alike to me."

"Not when I am near," said the Man. "If you had not said that last I would have put all these things away for always and always and always; but I am now going to throw my two boots and my little stone axe (that makes three) at you whenever I meet you. And so shall all proper Men do after me!"

Then the Dog said, "Wait a minute. He has not made a bargain with me or with all proper Dogs after me." And he showed his teeth and said, "If you are not kind to the Baby while I am in the Cave for always and always and always, I will hunt you till I catch you, and when I catch you I will bite you. And so shall all proper Dogs do after me."

"Ah," said the Woman, listening, "this is a very clever Cat, but he is not so clever as the Dog."

Cat counted the Dog's teeth (and they looked very pointed) and he said, "I will be kind to the Baby while I am in the Cave, as long as he does not pull my tail too hard, for always and always and always. But still I am the Cat that walks by himself, and all places are alike to me."

"Not when I am near," said the Dog. "If you had not said that last I would have shut my mouth for always and always and always; but now I am going to hunt you up a tree whenever I meet you. And so shall all proper Dogs do after me."

Then the Man threw his two boots and his little stone axe (that makes three) at the Cat, and the Cat ran out of the Cave and the Dog chased him up a tree; and from that day to this, Best Beloved, three proper Men out of five will always throw things at a Cat whenever they meet him, and all proper Dogs will chase him up a tree. But the Cat keeps his side of the bargain too. He will kill mice and he will be kind to Babies when he is in the house, just as long as they do not pull his tail too hard. But when he has done that, and between times, and when the moon gets up and night comes, he is the Cat that walks by himself, and all places are alike to him. Then he goes out to the Wet Wild Woods or up the Wet Wild Trees or on the Wet Wild Roofs, waving his wild tail and walking by his wild lone.

PUSSY can sit by the fire and sing,
Pussy can climb a tree,
Or play with a silly old cork and string
To'muse herself, not me.
But I like Binkie my dog, because
He Knows how to behave;
So, Binkie's the same as the First Friend was,
And I am the Man in the Cave.
Pussy will play man–Friday till
It's time to wet her paw
And make her walk on the windowsill
(For the footprint Crusoe saw);
Then she fluffles her tail and mews,
And scratches and won't attend.
But Binkie will play whatever I choose,
And he is my true First Friend.
Pussy will rub my knees with her head
Pretending she loves me hard;

But the very minute I go to my bed
Pussy runs out in the yard,
And there she stays till the morning-light;
So I know it is only pretend;
But Binkie, he snores at my feet all night,
And he is my Firstest Friend!

The Achievement of the Cat

Saki (H. H. Munro)

IN THE POLITICAL HISTORY OF NATIONS IT IS NO UNCOMMON EXPERI-
ence to find States and peoples which but a short time since were in
bitter conflict and animosity with each other, settled down comfortably
on terms of mutual goodwill and even alliance. The natural history of
the social developments of species affords a similar instance in the com-
ing-together of two once warring elements, now represented by civilized
man and the domestic cat. The fiercely waged struggle which went on
between humans and felines in those far-off days when sabre-toothed
tiger and cave lion contended with primeval man, has long ago been
decided in favor of the most fitly equipped combatant—the Thing with
a Thumb—and the descendants of the dispossessed family are relegated
today, for the most part, to the waste lands of jungle and veld, where
an existence of self-effacement is the only alternative to extermination.
But the felis catus, or whatever species was the ancestor of the modern
domestic cat (a vexed question at present), by a master-stroke of adap-
tation avoided the ruin of its race, and "captured" a place in the very
keystone of the conqueror's organization. For not as a bondservant or
dependent has this proudest of mammals entered the human fraternity;
not as a slave like the beasts of burden, or a humble camp-follower like
the dog. The cat is domestic only as far as suits its own ends; it will not
be kenneled or harnessed nor suffer any dictation as to its goings out or
comings in. Long contact with the human race has developed in it the

art of diplomacy, and no Roman Cardinal of medieval days knew better how to ingratiate himself with his surroundings than a cat with a saucer of cream on its mental horizon. But the social smoothness, the purring innocence, the softness of the velvet paw may be laid aside at a moment's notice, and the sinuous feline may disappear, in deliberate aloofness, to a world of roofs and chimney-stacks, where the human element is distanced and disregarded. Or the innate savage spirit that helped its survival in the bygone days of tooth and claw may be summoned forth from beneath the sleek exterior, and the torture-instinct (common alone to human and feline) may find free play in the death-throes of some luckless bird or rodent. It is, indeed, no small triumph to have combined the untrammeled liberty of primeval savagery with the luxury which only a highly developed civilization can command; to be lapped in the soft stuffs that commerce has gathered from the far ends of the world, to bask in the warmth that labor and industry have dragged from the bowels of the earth; to banquet on the dainties that wealth has bespoken for its table, and withal to be a free son of nature, a mighty hunter, a spiller of life-blood. This is the victory of the cat. But besides the credit of success the cat has other qualities which compel recognition. The animal which the Egyptians worshipped as divine, which the Romans venerated as a symbol of liberty, which Europeans in the ignorant Middle Ages anathematized as an agent of demonology, has displayed to all ages two closely blended characteristics—courage and self-respect. No matter how unfavorable the circumstances, both qualities are always to the fore. Confront a child, a puppy, and a kitten with a sudden danger; the child will turn instinctively for assistance, the puppy will grovel in abject submission to the impending visitation, the kitten will brace its tiny body for a frantic resistance. And disassociate the luxury-loving cat from the atmosphere of social comfort in which it usually contrives to move, and observe it critically under the adverse conditions of civilization—that civilization which can impel a man to the degradation of clothing himself in tawdry ribald garments and capering mountebank dances in the streets for the earning of the few coins that keep him on the respectable, or noncriminal, side of society. The cat of the slums and alleys, starved, outcast, harried, still keeps amid the prowlings of its adversity the bold, free, panther-tread with which it paced of yore the temple courts of Thebes, still displays the self-reliant watchfulness which man has never taught it to lay aside. And when its shifts and clever managings have not sufficed to stave off inexorable fate, when its enemies have proved too strong or too many for its defensive powers, it dies fighting to the last, quivering with the choking rage or mastered resistance, and voicing in its death-yell that agony of bitter remonstrance which human animals, too, have flung at the powers that may be; the last protest against a destiny that might have made them happy—and has not.

The Woman and the Cat

Marcel Prevost

"Yes," said our old friend Tribourdeaux, a man of culture and a philosopher, which is a combination rarely found among army surgeons; "yes, the supernatural is everywhere; it surrounds us and hems us in and permeates us. If science pursues it, it takes flight and cannot be grasped. Our intellect resembles those ancestors of ours who cleared a few acres of forest; whenever they approached the limits of their clearing they heard low growls and saw gleaming eyes everywhere circling them about. I myself have had the sensation of having approached the limits of the unknown several times in my life, and on one occasion in particular."

A young lady present interrupted him:

"Doctor, you are evidently dying to tell us a story. Come now, begin!"

The doctor bowed.

"No, I am not in the least anxious, I assure you. I tell this story as seldom as possible, for it disturbs those who hear it, and it disturbs me also. However, if you wish it, here it is":

In 1863 I was a young physician stationed at Orleans. In that patrician city, full of aristocratic old residences, it is difficult to find bachelor apartments; and, as I like both plenty of air and plenty of room, I took up my lodging on the first floor of a large building situated just outside the city, near Saint-Euverte.

It had been originally constructed to serve as the warehouse and also as the dwelling of a manufacturer of rugs. In course of time the manufacturer had failed, and this big barrack that he had built, falling out of repair through lack of tenants, had been sold for a song with all its furnishings.

The purchaser hoped to make a future profit out of his purchase, for the city was growing in that direction; and, as a matter of fact, I believe that at the present time the house is included within the city limits. When I took up my quarters there, however, the mansion stood alone on the verge of the open country, at the end of a straggling street on which a few stray houses produced at dusk the impression of a jaw from which most of the teeth have fallen out.

I leased one-half of the first floor, an apartment of four rooms. For my bedroom and my study I took the two that fronted on the street; in the third room I set up some shelves for my wardrobe, and the other room I left empty. This made a very comfortable lodging for me, and I had, for a sort of promenade, a broad balcony that ran along the entire front of the building, or rather one-half of the balcony, since it was divided into two parts (please note this carefully) by a fan of ironwork, over which, however, one could easily climb.

I had been living there for about two months when, one night in July on returning to my rooms, I saw with a good deal of surprise a light shining through the windows of the other apartment on the same floor, which I had supposed to be uninhabited. The effect of this light was extraordinary. It lit up with a pale, yet perfectly distinct, reflection, parts of the balcony, the street below, and a bit of the neighboring fields.

I thought to myself, "Aha! I have a neighbor."

The idea indeed was not altogether agreeable, for I had been rather proud of my exclusive proprietorship. On reaching my bedroom I passed noiselessly out upon the balcony, but already the light had been extinguished. So I went back into my room, and sat down to read for an hour or two. From time to time I seemed to hear about me, as though within the walls, light footsteps; but after finishing my book I went to bed, and speedily fell asleep.

About midnight I suddenly awoke with a curious feeling that something was standing beside me. I raised myself in bed, lit a candle, and this is what I saw. In the middle of the room stood an immense cat gazing upon me with phosphorescent eyes, and with its back slightly arched. It was a magnificent Angora, with long fur and a fluffy tail, and of a remarkable color—exactly like that of the yellow silk that one sees in cocoons—so that, as the light gleamed upon its coat, the animal seemed to be made of gold.

It slowly moved toward me on its velvety paws, softly rubbing its sinuous body against my legs. I leaned over to stroke it, and it permitted my caress, purring, and finally leaping upon my knees. I noticed then that it was a female cat, quite young, and that she seemed disposed to permit me to pet her as long as ever I would.

Finally, however, I put her down upon the floor, and tried to induce her to leave the room; but she leaped away from me and hid herself somewhere among the furniture, though as soon as I had blown out my candle, she jumped upon my bed. Being sleepy, however, I didn't molest her, but dropped off into a doze, and the next morning when I awoke in broad daylight I could find no sign of the animal at all.

Truly, the human brain is a very delicate instrument, and one that is easily thrown out of gear. Before I proceed, just sum up for yourselves the facts that I have mentioned: a light seen and presently extinguished in an apartment supposed to be uninhabited; and a cat of a remarkable color, which appeared and disappeared in a way that was slightly mysterious. Now there isn't anything very strange about that, is there?

Very well.

Imagine, now, that these unimportant facts are repeated day after day and under the same conditions throughout a whole week, and then, believe me, they become of importance enough to impress the mind of a man who is living all alone, and to produce in him a slight disquietude such as I spoke of in commencing my story, and such as is always caused when one approaches the sphere of the unknown. The human mind is so formed that it always unconsciously applies the principle of the *causa sufficiens*. For every series of facts that are identical, it demands a cause, a law; and a vague dismay seizes upon it when it is unable to guess this cause and to trace out this law.

I am no coward, but I have often studied the manifestation of fear in others, from its most puerile form in children up to its most tragic phase in madmen. I know that it is fed and nourished by uncertainties, although when one actually sets himself to investigate the cause, this fear is often transformed into simple curiosity.

I made up my mind, therefore, to ferret out the truth. I questioned my caretaker, and found that he knew nothing about my neighbors. Every morning an old woman came to look after the neighboring apartment; my caretaker had tried to question her, but either she was completely deaf or else she was unwilling to give him any information, for she had refused to answer a single word.

Nevertheless, I was able to explain satisfactorily the first thing that I had noted—that is to say, the sudden extinction of the light at the moment when I entered the house. I had observed that the windows next to mine were covered only by long lace curtains; and as the two balconies were connected, my neighbor, whether man or woman, had no doubt a wish to prevent any indiscreet inquisitiveness on my part, and therefore had always put out the light on hearing me come in.

To verify this supposition, I tried a very simple experiment, which succeeded perfectly. I had a cold supper brought in one day about noon by my servant, and that evening I did not go out. When darkness came on, I took my station near the window. Presently I saw the balcony shining with the light that streamed through the windows of the neighboring apartment. At once I slipped quietly out upon my balcony, and stepped softly over the ironwork that separated the two parts.

Although I knew that I was exposing myself to a positive danger, either of falling and breaking my neck, or of finding myself face to face with a man, I experienced no perturbation. Reaching the lighted window without having made the slightest noise, I found it partly open; its curtains, which for me were quite transparent since I was on the dark side of the window, made me wholly invisible to anyone who should look toward the window from the interior of the room.

I saw a vast chamber furnished quite elegantly, though it was obviously out of repair, and lighted by a lamp suspended from the ceiling. At the end of the room was a low sofa upon which was reclining a woman who seemed to me to be both young and pretty. Her loosened hair fell over her shoulders in a rain of gold. She was looking at herself in a hand mirror, patting herself, passing her arms over her lips, and twisting about her supple body with a curiously feline grace. Every movement that she made caused her long hair to ripple in glistening undulations.

As I gazed upon her I confess that I felt a little troubled, especially when all of a sudden the young girl's eyes were fixed upon me—strange eyes, eyes of a phosphorescent green that gleamed like the flame of a lamp. I was sure that I was invisible, being on the dark side of a curtained window. That was simple enough, yet nevertheless I felt that I was seen. The girl, in fact, uttered a cry, and then turned and buried her face in the sofa-pillows.

I raised the window, rushed into the room toward the sofa, and leaned over the face that she was hiding. As I did so, being really very remorseful, I began to excuse and to accuse myself, calling myself all sorts of names, and begging pardon for my indiscretion. I said that I deserved to be driven from her presence, but begged not to be sent away without at least a word of pardon. For a long time I pleaded thus without success, but at last she slowly turned, and I saw that her fair young face was stirred with just the faintest suggestion of a smile. When she caught a glimpse of me she murmured something of which I did not then quite get the meaning.

"It is you," she cried out; "it is you!"

As she said this, and as I looked at her, not knowing yet exactly what to answer, I was harassed by the thought: Where on earth have I already seen this face, this look, this very gesture?

Little by little, however, I found my tongue, and after saying a few more words in apology for my unpardonable curiosity, and getting brief but not offended answers, I took leave of her, and, retiring through the window by which I had come, went back to my own room. Arriving there, I sat a long time by the window in the darkness, charmed by the face that I had seen, and yet singularly disquieted.

This woman so beautiful, so amiable, living so near to me, who said to me, "It is you," exactly as though she had already known me, who spoke so little, who answered all my questions with evasion, excited in me a feeling of fear. She had, indeed, told me her name—Linda—and that was all. I tried in vain to drive away the remembrance of her greenish eyes, which in the darkness seemed still to gleam upon me, and of those glints which, like electric sparks, shone in her long hair whenever she stroked it with her hand.

Finally, however, I retired for the night; but scarcely was my head upon the pillow when I felt some moving body descend upon my feet. The cat had appeared again. I tried to chase her away, but she kept return-ing again and again, until I ended by resigning myself to her presence; and, just as before, I went to sleep with this strange companion near me. Yet my rest was this time a troubled one, and broken by strange and fitful dreams.

Have you ever experienced the sort of mental obsession which grad-ually causes the brain to be mastered by some single absurd idea—an idea almost insane, and one which your reason and your will alike repel, but which nevertheless gradually blends itself with your thought, fastens itself upon your mind, and grows and grows?

I suffered cruelly in this way on the days that followed my strange adventure. Nothing new occurred, but in the evening, going out upon the balcony, I found Linda standing upon her side of the iron fan. We chatted together for a while in the half darkness, and, as before, I returned to my room to find that in a few moments the golden cat appeared, leaped upon my bed, made a nest for herself there, and remained until the morning.

I knew now to whom the cat belonged, for Linda had answered that very same evening, on my speaking of it, "Oh, yes, my cat; doesn't she look exactly as though she were made of gold?" As I said, nothing new had occurred, yet nevertheless a vague sort of terror began little by little to master me and to develop itself in my mind, at first merely as a bit of foolish fancy, and then as a haunting belief that dominated my entire thought, so that I perpetually seemed to see a thing which it was in reality quite impossible to see.

"Why, it's easy enough to guess," interrupted the young lady who had spoken at the beginning of his story.

Linda and the cat were the same thing.

Tribourdeaux smiled.

I should not have been quite so positive as that, he said, even then; but I cannot deny that this ridiculous fancy haunted me for many hours when I was endeavoring to snatch a little sleep amid the insomnia that a too active brain produced. Yes, there were moments when these two beings with greenish eyes, sinuous movements, golden hair, and mysterious ways, seemed to me to be blended into one, and to be merely the double manifestation of a single entity.

As I said, I saw Linda again and again, but in spite of all my efforts to come upon her unexpectedly, I never was able to see them both at the same time. I tried to reason with myself, to convince myself that there was nothing really inexplicable in all of this, and I ridiculed myself for being afraid both of a woman and of a harmless cat.

In truth, at the end of all my reasoning, I found that I was not so much afraid of the animal alone or of the woman alone, but rather of a sort of quality which existed in my fancy and inspired me with a fear of something that was incorporeal—fear of a manifestation of my own spirit, fear of a vague thought, which is, indeed, the very worst of fears.

I began to be mentally disturbed. After long evenings spent in confidential and very unconventional chats with Linda, in which little by little my feelings took on the color of love, I passed long days of secret torment, such as incipient maniacs must experience. Gradually a resolve began to grow up in my mind, a desire that became more and more importunate in demanding a solution of this unceasing and tormenting doubt; and the more I cared for Linda, the more it seemed absolutely necessary to push this resolve to its fulfilment. I decided to kill the cat.

One evening before meeting Linda on the balcony, I took out of my medical cabinet a jar of glycerin and a small bottle of hydrocyanic acid, together with one of those little pencils of glass which chemists use in mixing certain corrosive substances.

That evening for the first time Linda allowed me to caress her. I held her in my arms and passed my hand over her long hair, which snapped and cracked under my touch in a succession of tiny sparks. As soon as I regained my room the golden cat, as usual, appeared before me.

I called her to me; she rubbed herself against me with arched back and extended tail, purring the while with the greatest amiability. I took the glass pencil in my hand, moistened the point in the glycerin, and held it out to the animal, which licked it with her long red tongue. I did this three or four times, but the next time I dipped the pencil in the acid. The cat unhesitatingly touched it with her tongue. In an instant she became rigid, and a moment after, a frightful tetanic convulsion caused her to leap thrice into the air, and then to fall upon the floor with a dreadful cry—a cry that was truly human. She was dead!

With the perspiration starting from my forehead and with trembling hands I threw myself upon the floor beside the body that was not yet cold. The starting eyes had a look that froze me with horror. The blackened tongue was thrust out between the teeth; the limbs exhibited the most remarkable contortions.

I mustered all my courage with a violent effort of will, took the animal by the paws, and left the house. Hurrying down the silent street, I proceeded to the quays along the banks of the Loire, and, on reaching them, threw my burden into the river. Until daylight I roamed around the city, just where I know not; and not until the sky began to grow pale and then to be flushed with light did I at last have the courage to return home.

As I laid my hand upon the door, I shivered. I had a dread of finding there still living, as in the celebrated tale of Poe, the animal that I had so lately put to death. But no, my room was empty. I fell half-fainting upon my bed, and for the first time I slept, with a perfect sense of being all alone, a sleep like that of a beast or of an assassin, until evening came.

Someone here interrupted, breaking in upon the profound silence in which we had been listening.

"I can guess the end. Linda disappeared at the same time as the cat."

You see perfectly well, replied Tribourdeaux, that there exists between the facts of this story a curious coincidence, since you are able to guess so exactly their relation. Yes, Linda disappeared. They found in her apartment her dresses, her linen, all even to the night-robe that she was to have worn that night, but there was nothing that could give the slightest clue to her identity.

The owner of the house had let the apartment to "Mademoiselle Linda, concert-singer," He knew nothing more. I was summoned before the police magistrate. I had been seen on the night of her disappearance roaming about with a distracted air in the vicinity of the river. Luckily the judge knew me; luckily also, he was a man of no ordinary intelligence. I related to him privately the entire story, just as I have been telling it to you. He dismissed the inquiry; yet I may say that very few have ever had so narrow, an escape as mine from a criminal trial.

For several moments the silence of the company was unbroken. Finally a gentleman, wishing to relieve the tension, cried out:

"Come now, doctor, confess that this is really all fiction; that you merely want to prevent these ladies from getting any sleep to-night."

Tribourdeaux bowed stiffly, his face unsmiling and a little pale.

You may take it as you will, he said.

TWENTY-NINE

The Demon Cat
Lady Jane Wilde

THERE WAS A WOMAN IN CONNEMARA, THE WIFE OF A FISHERMAN; AS he had always good luck, she had plenty of fish at all times stored away in the house ready for market. But, to her great annoyance, she found that a great cat used to come in at night and devour all the best and finest fish. So she kept a big stick by her, and determined to watch.

One day, as she and a woman were spinning together, the house suddenly became quite dark; and the door was burst open as if by the blast of the tempest, when in walked a huge black cat, who went straight up to the fire, then turned round and growled at them.

"Why, surely this is the devil," said a young girl who was by, sorting fish.

"I'll teach you to call me names," said the cat; and, jumping at her, he scratched her arm till the blood came.

"There, now," he said, "you will be more civil another time when a gentleman comes to see you."

And, with that, he walked over to the door, and shut it close to prevent any of them going out, for the poor young girl, while crying loudly from fright and pain, had made a desperate rush to get away.

Just then a man was going by, and, hearing the cries, he pushed open the door, and tried to get in; but the cat stood on the threshold and would let no one pass. On this the man attacked him with a stick, and gave him a sound blow; the cat, however, was more than a match in the fight, for

247

it flew at him, and tore his face and hands so badly that the man at last took to his heels, and ran away as fast as he could.

"Now, it's time for my dinner," said the cat, going up to examine the fish that was laid out on the tables.

"I hope the fish is good to-day. Now, don't disturb me, or make a fuss; I can help myself."

With that, he jumped up, and began to devour all the best fish, while he growled at the woman.

"Away out of this, you wicked beast!" she cried, giving it a blow with the tongs that would have broken its back, only it was a devil; "out of this; no fish shall you have to-day!"

But the cat only grinned at her and went on tearing and despoiling and devouring the fish, evidently not a bit the worse for the blows. On this both the women attacked it with sticks, and struck hard blows enough to kill it, on which the cat glared at them and spit fire; then, making a leap, it tore their heads and arms till the blood came, and the frightened women rushed shrieking from the house.

But presently the mistress of the house returned, carrying with her a bottle of holy water; and, looking in, she saw the cat still devouring the fish, and not minding. So she crept over quietly, and threw holy water on it without a word. No sooner was this done than a dense, black smoke filled the place, through which nothing was seen but the two red eyes of the cat burning like coals of fire.

Then the smoke gradually cleared away, and she saw the body of the creature burning slowly, till it became shrivelled and black like a cinder, and finally disappeared. And from that time the fish remained untouched and safe from harm, for the power of the Evil One was broken, and the Demon Cat was seen no more.

THIRTY

The Hypocritical Cat

W. H. D. Rouse

Once upon a time there was a troop of Rats that used to live in holes by a river side. A certain Cat often saw them going to and fro, and longed to have them to eat. But he was not strong enough to attack them all together; besides, that would not have suited his purpose, because most of them would have run away.

So he used to stand early in the morning, not far from their holes, with his face toward the sun, snuffing up the air, and standing on one leg.

The Rats wondered why he did that, so one day they all trooped up to him in a body, and asked the reason.

"What is your name, sir?" they began.

"Holy is my name," said the Cat.

"Why do you stand on one leg?"

"Because if I stood on all four, the earth could not bear my weight."

"And why do you keep your mouth open?"

"Because I feed on the air, and never eat anything else."

"And why do you face the sun?"

"Because I worship the sun."

"What a pious Cat!" the Rats all thought. Ever after that, when they started out in the morning, they did not fail first to make their bow to the Cat one by one, and to show thus their respect for his piety.

This was just what our Cat wanted. Every day, as they filed past, he waited till the tail of the string came up; then like lightning pounced upon the hindmost, and gobbled him up in a trice; after which he stood on one leg as before, licking his lips greedily.

For a while all went well for the Cat's plan; but at last the Chief of the Rats noticed that the troop seemed to grow smaller. Here and there he missed some familiar face. He could not make it out; but at last a thought came into his mind, that perhaps the pious Cat might know more about it than he chose to tell.

Next day accordingly, he posted himself at the tail of the troop, where he could see everything that went on; and as the Rats one by one bowed before the Cat, he watched the Cat out of the end of his eye.

As he came up, the Cat prepared for his pounce. But our Rat was ready for him, and dodged out of the way.

"Aha!" says the Rat, "so that is your piety! Feeds on the air, does he! and worships the sun—eh? What a humbug!"

And with one spring he was at the Cat's throat, and his sharp teeth fast. The other Rats heard the scuffle, and came trooping back; and it was crunch and munch, till not a vestige remained of the hypocritical Cat. Those who came first had cat to eat, and those who came last went sniffing about at the mouths of their friends, and asking what was the taste of catsmeat. And ever after the Rats lived in peace and happiness.

THIRTY-ONE

The Cat and the Dream Man

Charles J. Finger

THIS IS A TALE THAT I HEARD WHEN I WAS GOLD DIGGING IN TIERRA del Fuego, and if you want to get to the tale and skip the introduction, you may. To do that, stop here—and pass over everything until you come to the three stars * * * and begin at "Many years ago." But if you want information and all that kind of thing, read straight on and learn that the man who told me the tale was named Soto, Adolpho Soto.

He called himself a Bolivian and said that it was a tale of Bolivia, but he had never been to that country. His parents were Bolivian, but he had been born and reared in inland Patagonia, on the east side of the Cordilleras and north of the great shallow gulf that runs inland from the Strait of Magellan.

Anyway, he had heard the tale from others who knew all about the three great stones and how they looked. Certainly he had not read the story, for books meant nothing to him and he would not as much as look at a picture. And it was quite clear to me that he believed every word of the tale.

Indeed, I am almost sure that he was doubtful in his mind as to the wisdom of telling me all of it, thinking that I would not believe it. Perhaps that is why he told me the tale in two parts, as if in some manner I might thus get used to the shock of it. Mind you, on the other hand, I am certain that he did not believe all that I told him, though he was too polite to express unbelief.

For instance, he could not quite see how carriages went without horses, nor how men sent messages over miles of wire, nor how the sound of a human voice could come from a little box, without magic; for in the country that Adolpho came from there were no railways, no telegraphs, and no phonographs. So to the tale, or rather the first part of it, if you choose to hear it.

* * *

THE FIRST PART

Many years ago, said Soto, there came into the world a cat. It was in the days when all creatures were harmless; when the teeth and claws of the jaguar did not hurt; when the fang of the serpent was not poisonous; when the very bushes had no thorns. But this cat was of evil heart and unmerciful and a curse to the world, for she went about teaching creatures to scratch and to bite, to tear and to kill, to hide in shady places and leap out on unsuspecting things.

Even a sheep she did not leave to its own ways, but commenced to teach that gentle thing to fight by butting with its head, though as it came to pass most luckily, the cat came to a place where its mischief was stopped, as you shall hear soon, so that señor sheep was left with his lesson half or less than half learned, so that the youngest child now need not fear a whole flock.

But for the most part the cat slept in the daytime, so did not make all the mischief that she might have made, although she dreamed mischief, let it be remembered. But this was the bad thing of it: her dream came to life and walked the earth in the shape of a man with a fox-face, and a very terrible monster was he, for being a dream man he could not be killed. That you may see for yourself.

Sometimes he appeared among men, dressed in fine robes in a way of a rich man, clothes wonderfully fine, as fine as those that you may see about the men pictured on the playing cards. Sometimes it was otherwise and he came as one all worn and travel-stained. Sometimes he came as a head without a body, making mouths or looking slantwise; sometimes he ran at people, did this dream man, ran with hooked fingers and claw nails and made it so that the one he chased could not run at all, or running, moved but slowly.

For such must be the nature of the dreams of cats, as everyone knows who has seen a cat with a mouse. But whichever way the dream man came, mischief of some kind walked with him, and for the most part he did his evil work by granting men their wishes. For you must know that no man knows the thing that is best for him and for his welfare, and many are apt to see some little things as desirable, the which in time work out for their own undoing. Thus, once there was a man who was a wood-cutter, and growing weary of hard work he sat him down under a tree and sighed, saying that though he worked hard, yet his work was never done, and there were many mouths to feed. Then who should appear before him but the fox-faced man, which of course was but the cat-dream come to life, the cat meantime being asleep in the sun. So this happened:

"Why do you complain?" asked the fox-faced one, who knew very well what was afoot.

"All day I cut and chop, and chop and cut, but at the end of the day little is the work that I have done, and my very children for whom I toil, and for whom my wife toils, do but grumble that I am not rich," answered the poor fellow, who was indeed a very worthy man.

"Lucky for you, then, is it that you have seen me," said fox-face. "For know that I have it in my power to grant you a wish. What then would you have?"

Hearing that, the woodcutter was thoughtful, for, in the manner of those who see a dream man, everything seemed right and proper. Still, while he had in his life wished for many things from day to day, when the time came to make a wish he had none ready. Then his eye fell on his ax and he said without thinking: "For one thing I wish that my ax was an ax so that when I cut a stick or anything, I would have two as big as the first one."

To be sure, had he given thought he might have seen how foolish a wish was that, as both cat and fox-face knew. But he spoke as the wind blew. Then fox-face said some words which the woodcutter did not understand, and added:

"Try now your ax."

So the man took a stick about the size of a man's arm and brought down his ax in the middle of it, and lo, there were two sticks, each the size of a man's arm, instead of two pieces each the half of that. The man looked up, open-mouthed and surprised, to say something, but fox-face had vanished, for the cat had wakened and so her dream ceased.

But greatly amazed was the man, for, as he soon saw, all his chopping was of no account, for a tree cut down became at once two trees and one of those trees cut in halves became two trees again. As for cutting smaller wood, that, too, soon became impossible, seeing that each stick grew to two sticks, so that soon he had to cease work because of the wood all about him.

Worse still, as he went to the place where he lived, there came across his path a poisonous serpent, and forgetting for a moment the power of his ax he cut the snake in two, and there, hissing before him, were two snakes. So he fled to his people and told them the tale, at which they wondered greatly. But to make sure that the ax would do no mischief, and in truth somewhat fearing it, they hung it in a tree, and each man told his son the story of it, so that all might come to know it as a thing best left alone.

Now in the course of time there came to that place a very wise man who had seen many wonders. It had come to his ears that the cat was a creature of darkness, teaching harmless things evil tricks, but of the fox-faced man he knew nothing. The cat only, he considered. So the wise man walked the mountains for many days, and one day when the sky was low and it was a day of rain, an unpleasant day for the cat, he came upon the evil-minded creature hurrying somewhere.

"Why in so great a hurry?" asked the wise man. "Sit awhile with me and talk."

"No. No," said the cat. "I like not your water and I seek a place where there is shelter, so that I may be dry and warm." Indeed, the cat looked very miserable indeed.

"Well, how would you like to have a house of stone?" asked the wise man.

"That I should like very much indeed," answered the cat.

"But it must be a house large enough for me, and with no room for any other creature, for I am not fond of company. But a house in which I could sit and dream, and where no noises might disturb, would be very pleasant. Make me such a one and I shall teach you something. Or how about a wish? Would you like to have claws like an owl? Or would you like to drink blood like a vampire bat? Or would you like to spit poison? Or would you like to bristle like a porcupine?"

"Thank you, no," said the wise man. "I want nothing. But by to-morrow there shall be a house ready for you."

"Where is it to be built?" asked the cat. "First, it must be in a quiet place where men do not go."

"It shall be that," answered the wise man. "But just now I do not know where the place may be. I must seek a proper place."

"Then how shall I find it?" asked the cat.

"Attend," said the wise man. "I shall put a thread about the world, a thread that no man may break with his hands, and when you see that thread, follow it and so come to the stone house."

"Agreed," said the cat. "But let the house be just big enough for me. Let it be in a quiet place. Also, let it be of such fashion that I can slip out backward or leap out forward should an enemy come."

So that being said and no more to come, man and cat parted.

But mark well what followed. On the next day the cat chanced to see the thread and followed it, walking down hill and up hill, down mountain and up mountain, until she arrived at a high place where stood the wise man. At his feet were three flat stones, two standing upright, the third across the top of the two, so that it was like two sides of a little house, roofed and of a comfortable size for the cat.

So after looking about carefully and suspiciously, the cat entered into it and coiled her tail about her, blinked her eyes once, twice, thrice, then slept. And as soon as she was well asleep the wise man fastened the thread about her neck, the same thread which went about the world and which no man could break with his hands, there being magic about it, and señora cat was bound for years, and would have been bound for ever, had it not been for Nasca, about whom you shall hear.

255

That ends the tale of the cat, though there is much more to come. And if you are in a hurry to get to the rest of the tale, you may skip from this—to the three stars * * * again, without losing much.

I said that it ended the tale of the cat, but it does not. It ends the first part only, for Adolpho went only thus far, and the telling took the whole of an evening, for there was much looping and winding in his telling and he added much that had nothing to do with the tale. Indeed, you should be very grateful indeed to me for trimming all the uninteresting stuff away.

And let me tell you this: it was not at all easy to get Adolpho to tell the rest of the tale, and the place in which we sat when we talked was not comfortable. It was no house with radiators and electric lights, or bathtubs and bookshelves. Indeed, the only furniture that we had was a frying-pan without a handle and an iron pot.

As for our house, it looked more like a short stout bottle than a dwelling. For the truth is that we were careless builders and had made our house out of sods of earth; but while we started to build a square house, we did not take care of the corners, and the house came roundish and the walls leaned inward as they went higher, so we left the top open by way of chimney, for our fire was built in the middle of the floor. Thus such was the shape of our house that we had to sleep curved and we had to stand curved, though we rarely stood, because of the smoke, I assure you.

Almost three weeks passed away before Adolpho told me the rest of the tale and it was a cold night in June when he did. After supper he commenced, perhaps because it was the kind of stew that he liked best.

For the most of the stew was fish. I said "the most of the stew," because our stews were different from those you have. If on Monday we had a piece of huanaco meat, we put it in the iron pot to stew. There would be something left over, for we always made a little more than we required and we never wasted food.

So, supper being done, the iron pot with the remains of the stew was put aside. Perhaps next day we might have caught or shot a young goose, or something like that. Anyway, whatever we caught went into the pot by way of stew. So that day there would be goose stew with a flavour of huanaco. Next day we might add charqui, which is dried horse-flesh, to the stew, so while the chief thing would be charqui, there would be a decided flavor of goose and more than a trace of huanaco.

But if we had fish on the fourth day, then of course it would be strongly fishy stew, with a kind of side taste of charqui, a flavour of goose, and a mild trace of huanaco. On the whole it was satisfactory, for toward the end of the week anyone might find something to his liking, though on Saturday we always cleaned out the pot, as we needed it for our week's washing. And so, as I say, when we came one evening to fish stew, Adolpho was in high good humor and told me the rest of the tale, and this is how his story ran.

* * *

THE SECOND PART OF THE TALE

Now, began Soto, you must remember all that I have told you about the cat bound on the mountain top, the magic ax hanging in the tree, and the hundreds and hundreds of years that passed, with the cat growing larger and larger. As the cat grew, so did the house, for the wise man had promised that it should be just big enough for the cat, and he kept his word. But you must also remember that the cat could not move, but could certainly dream. So she dreamed of many lands, and the dream man was very active indeed, though he vanished whenever the cat woke.

When you come to think of it, you will see that it was a most excellent thing that the cat was bound, for had she not been, she would have worked her mischief on the world and a sheep might have been as terrible as a wild boar or flies as annoying as mosquitoes or horses as bold as wild bulls or the very fish as poisonous as serpents. While the cat did not dream, of course the fox-faced man was nowhere, and then all went very well and trees put out their blossoms and fruits, the grass was softly green, the rain was like silver, and gentle were the hearts of men as they went about their affairs.

But there was a day on which the cat dreamed and the fox-faced fellow was busy. To the place where lived the people who guarded the magic ax, there came a stranger. His eyes were aslant and little, the hair of him was reddish, and he was in rags and tatters and altogether dirty in appearance.

To be sure, no one would look twice at rags and tatters, for one coming through the forest must needs be torn by thorns and bushes in all that tangle, but dirt was quite another matter, especially when the dirt included blood stains, because in that place was much water and many running streams, nor was the water chill to the skin. So, because of the uncleanness of the man, people looked at him with unfriendly eyes, and though they were neither insolent nor rude they hoped that he would go farther and not stay there.

Nor would it have been any great hardship for him to do so, seeing that it was a place of much fruit and of many berries, and roots pleasant to the taste and full of nourishment. As for the night, any man might well stretch himself under that star-sprinkled sky, nor except for the beasts that the cat had made unfriendly were there creatures to do harm. But the stranger had no notion of doing anything to please the people, nor indeed could he do anything, seeing that he was the creature of the cat's dream, walking the world.

For a time then he stood under a tree bewailing his lot and crying out that all the world was against him and saying that none were kind to him. Strange things he did, too, as is the manner of dream people, making himself sometimes shoot far far away so that he looked small, then coming near again and getting big, or sometimes pointing his finger at someone, then throwing his arm round and round in great circles, the finger always pointing, the circles he made growing smaller and smaller, little by little, but his finger always pointing, until it came close to the watcher's eyes.

The people thought this an annoying thing for a stranger to do; but so it was. And always he woefully wailed. So those there stood about him in a little circle, none going close, but all wondering much at the great outcry, the like of which none there had heard before. Then he began to sing, noisily, wildly. This was his song:

"Over the world I walk,
Alone, for ever alone.

Trouble and trial and care,
Alone, I bear alone.
Torture and pain I bear,
Alone, for ever alone.
Wandering day and night,
Alone, for ever alone.
Sad and wretched my plight,
Alone, for ever alone."
Then he gave a long, long cry, like a wolf:
A—a—a—a—a——lone, Oo—oo—oo—oo!"

Nor did he stop at that, for his song done, he began to act stupidly, leaping from side to side in rage and fury, mouthing and grimacing, opening and closing his fists, but making no noise. Then he talked again, but it was a jabber of idle words, so presently those about him shook their heads at one another, looking at him as one who had lost his wits, never thinking of course that he was a cat's dream.

While all this was going on, there came from the little lake where he had been fishing a lad named Nasca, bearing a basket of fish, a happy fellow who always made music and song as he walked, and seeing the people gathered about the stranger he drew near.

No sooner did the stranger clap eyes on the fish than he leaped at the basket and began devouring the silvery things, eating them raw, heads, bodies, and tails, for thus ran the cat's dream and cattishness must out. But the meal being done, the stranger redoubled his lamentations, all the time swinging his arm in circles, sometimes great, sometimes small, with his finger pointed at the boy.

"A—a—a—a—a——lone, Oo—oo—oo—oo!" he screamed, and the boy thought that such a fellow well deserved to be alone, but he was too polite to say so.

"I am hungry and travel-worn," the stranger went on. "Is there no one here who will give me shelter? Is there no one in this place with a kind heart to pity me?"

Hearing that, the heart of Nasca was touched, for never had he, nor never had his grandmother with whom he lived, turned a hungry creature away empty. Indeed, so gentle in spirit was Nasca that if the stem of a flower was broken by a heedless creature he was full of grief.

Yet the doings of the stranger astonished him and troubled him, for the man without seeming to move his feet thrust his face close to the boy's, then somehow took his face far off. That silly trick he did again and again as dream creatures do, so that seeing him Nasca was well nigh made dizzy. Then the lad, blushing red as fire because of all the people thereabouts who did not offer what he offered, said:

"Come home, then, with me. Our house is small but there is room enough. Believe me, it is not that these people are hard-hearted that they do not seem to welcome you, but more because you must have been too weary with walking to wash yourself. But behind the hill and under a tree near where we live is a still pool, and there doubtless you will clean yourself."

Then Nasca led the way and the stranger went with him, yet not walking, but leaping up and down as he went, and sometimes not touching the ground at all. Nasca was not comfortable with the stranger by his side, for he felt him to be more like a shadow than a man, and a shadow that hung over him and tormented him, a shadow that might pounce upon him.

Having come to the place where his grandmother was, Nasca was sorely troubled to see the old woman fall to trembling when she heard the voice of the stranger, who was making an idle jabber of words again. Indeed, after a time she put her hands to her face and wept, though that was after the man having eaten had left the place to rest under a tree. Nasca comforted her as best he could, then asked her to tell him the cause of her grief. Be it remembered that she was very, very old and her eyes were weak and dim with age.

"Tell me," she said, taking Nasca's hand, "has this man eyes aslant, like the eyes of a fox?"

"Indeed and he has," answered Nasca. Then his heart bade him say some good of the fellow, and he added: "Yet no man makes his own face, wherefore must some be pitied."

"Tell me," said the grandmother eagerly, "has he sharp teeth like a cat?"

"That he has," said Nasca, then wondering, asked: "Have you seen this man, then, when your eyes were bright and strong?"

"No, Nasca," she answered, "never have I set eyes on him, yet I greatly fear him; and long, long ago I heard stories about such a creature and it was said that much evil he wrought, yet none could slay him." She was silent for a little, then again she asked this: "Did you see his ears, Nasca, and are they pointed, like those of a fox?"

"Yes," said Nasca.

At that answer the old woman was sad again and Nasca had to comfort her with sweet words, telling her that she should come to no hurt, since he was there, for he would die defending her.

"That I know, Nasca," she said. "If the hurt came to me alone, glad would I be, for I have seen my golden days and now there is little left for me but the brief sunset hour. But I fear for others. Of such a creature I have heard it said that he comes from nowhere and goes into nothing, but somehow looses evil upon men. Because of that I fear. So, Nasca, promise me that if this man asks anything of you, you will do nothing that promises hurt to any living thing."

That Nasca promised gladly enough, then said: "Yet it may be that this man is not the evil creature you have heard of. It may well be some unfortunate whose wits are loose. True, his face is far from pleasant to see, but a rough face may go with a good heart, and a man's face may change."

"Yes, with wickedness," said the old woman, "but in truth it has been said that a man's face and his character both go with him to the grave, if indeed there is any grave for such as this."

Now all that talk Nasca remembered well the next day when a strange thing happened. For the stranger went about among the people, asking this one and that what he most desired. But there were none to make a wish for a time, because life there was pleasant and easy and the possessions of men were few, so all that the stranger said went for nothing. Then, as it chanced, there came one of the people a little put out because he had lost sleep that morning.

He was a man much given to rest and slumber, a slow and heavy man, and that morning he had been awakened by the singing of the birds. To make matters worse, going away from the place where he had lain, in too great a hurry, he chanced to scratch himself on some thorns. So, taking it all in all, his humour was not a pleasant one; yet had it not been for the stranger, he might have forgotten his troubles. As it was, he heard the stranger's speech and the offer to grant any wish, so he spoke without considering his words.

"If you grant wishes, there is one that I would have," he said, nodding to his friends in the manner of one who had a matter of weight to tell of.

"Say it," said the stranger, and he grinned queerly so that his lip went up and his tusky teeth shone yellow.

"This morning I was disturbed by birds and scratched by thorns, so I wish that nothing might come near me to disturb me in the future."

"As you wish," said the stranger, and gabbled what seemed to be idle and meaningless words.

Then a strange thing happened, for as the man who had made the wish stood looking at the stranger, his mouth wide open, all living things about him suddenly fell away. Within the stretch of a man's arm from him the grass yellowed and died, and the flowers shrank and withered, and a butterfly that fluttered over him fell to earth, dead. And the people cried out, seeing that, but soon it became clear that not even sounds could come within that magic circle.

The air bore no noise to the charmed man, not even the sweet noise of the songs of birds nor the chirping of insects, and the man was, in very truth, in such case that nothing could be nigh him to disturb him. Indeed, as he moved, all things died within the stretch of his arms, seeing which his friends fled from him, all fearful of his nearness. Afraid of his loneliness the man walked to a tree, but no sooner did he touch it than the very leaves folded themselves and turned black, then dropped off and fluttered down, so that the arms of the good tree stood skeleton-bare against the sky. At that all hope in the man was gone and he turned and fled into the forest, a space opening before him as he ran, a track of death everywhere behind him.

Nasca saw all that, and his grandmother's fears came to his mind. Indeed, he told many there of what the old woman had said, but some of them held that the stranger had but granted the wisher his wish, and if there was fault in the matter the fault lay with the wisher, not with the granter of the wish. As for the grandmother, when she heard the tale she was in great trouble and threw herself on the ground weeping, and though Nasca did what he could to comfort her, yet she wept and wept.

"Nasca," she said presently, "surely we must do what we can to rid the place of this fearful creature. For it is as I thought, and he is a black-hearted thing, not of this world of men, and one who will assuredly bring hate and fear and trouble. Find, then, if there is any means by which he may be made to go away, even to the point of helping him, if need be, but see to it that you think not of yourself and your own gain, and see to it that anything that you do at his request will bring no harm to any living creature, even the smallest."

All this Nasca promised, and in the early dawn of the next day went up to the hills to see the sun rise, as indeed did all brave and strong men and fair maidens in that place. Then he swam a little while, and ate some fruit and thought a while, and after sought out the stranger.

"Stranger," said he, "be it known to you that there are many here who fear your presence among us and who would be glad to see you gone from here."

"Ho! Ho! What bold words are these I hear?" roared fox-face, full of wrath at Nasca's words.

"I speak but the truth," said the lad boldly enough, though his heart beat against his ribs. "Tell me, then, what can be done so that you may be persuaded to leave us."

Fox-face thought awhile, then he said: "On a far mountain is a gentle creature bound with a magic thread which no man's hand can break. Yet magic fights magic, and the magic ax can sever the thread. Also, at the moment the thread is cut, so will the man who is prisoned in air be free, but not before. Now the bound creature is my companion and no fierce thing at all. Come with me, Nasca, bringing the magic ax, and when you have seen the cat, then perchance shall the spell be broken."

All of that seeming fair to Nasca, he went to the tree where hung the magic ax, though he had much ado to climb through the tangle all about the tree, for no man had been there for many a year. He took the ax and fastened it well in his sash, and returned to the side of the stranger.

Then fox-face took a mat made of feathers of the night owl and the hair of the skunk, and spread it on the ground, but it was so small that there was scarce place for Nasca and the man too, so the lad cut it with the magic ax and there were two mats, which was more to Nasca's taste, for he had no liking to stand on the mat and hold on to fox-face. No sooner had they taken their places on the mats than they rose in the air, and in a swift moment both of them were so high that the country lay spread at their feet with trees like grass and with rivers that looked like silver threads. Nor could the swiftest condor move with the speed with which they flew through the air.

So at last they came to a place where everywhere were bare rocks and hard stone, with no blade of grass to be seen, and it was a place among mountain peaks, with stony ridge rising above stony ridge, and on a mountain peak the two rested.

"Now look away to the far hill," said the stranger, and while the place to which he pointed was very far off, yet because of the clearness of the air it seemed but a short distance away. Looking steadily Nasca saw the three great rocks, for they were tremendously grown now, after so many hundreds of years, but to Nasca they seemed no higher than a man's knee, and sitting under them was the cat.

"That is the companion I seek," said fox-face. "By magic she is bound and by magic only can she be loosed, and I promise you that if you will but loose her I shall be seen no more in your land."

"Fair enough," said Nasca. "But I must be assured of a return to my own place, for it is far from home on these hills."

"That is well enough," answered fox-face. "Have you not your flying mat? Though to be sure, as soon as you take your foot from it it will vanish."

Nasca thought for a little while, and the more he thought the more it seemed to him to be a good thing and not an evil to loose the cat, so he asked the stranger to show him the bond that held her. At that fox-face pointed, and there almost at his feet Nasca beheld a slender thread, like a hair, that ran this way and that as far as the eye could see.

So with a blow of the magic ax he cut the thread, and there was a noise like thunder and the thread ends slid away like swift snakes. Nor did the stranger play Nasca false, for in a flash he found himself back again at the foot of the tree where the magic ax had hung, and so swiftly had the journey been made that a man who had stooped to fill his calabash at a pool when Nasca left, was even then straightening himself to go away, his calabash being filled.

As for the fox-faced stranger, no one ever saw him again, for the cat being awakened, her dream had ended. And at the moment when the thread was cut, the man who had been bound in air came back again, his enchantment finished, and the things that had died about him, because of invisible forces, sprang to life again.

But what of the cat? For Nasca little thought that he had loosed a fearful thing on the world, a frightful form of giant mould of a size bigger than a bull. Nor did he know until one evening, as he sat by the fire, it being chill in that high place at times, he turned his head as the robe that hung at the door bulged into the house.

He looked to see his grandmother, but instead a great cat filled the doorway, a cat with green eyes, each the size of an egg. Indeed so great was the cat that it had to crouch low to enter. And when within, the room was filled with it, a sight that made the heart of Nasca stand still. A gloomy terror it was, and most fiendish was the look that it gave the lad.

But Nasca, though terror-stricken, yet showed no sign of fear. Instead, he made room for the cat by the fire as though he saw cats like that every day. So the cat sat by the fire and close to Nasca, sometimes looking at the blaze without winking, sometimes turning its great head to look for long and long at the boy. Once Nasca stood up, saying that he would go outside and bring in more wood for the fire, privately thinking to get out of the place in safety, but the great paw of the cat shot out with claws that looked like reaping hooks, whereupon Nasca sat down again saying that, after all, the fire would live awhile. But he thought and thought and the cat looked and looked, and the place was as still and quiet as a midnight pool.

Presently Nasca found heart to say something.

"If you want to stay here and rest," he said to the cat, "I shall go away."

"You must not go away," said the cat in a soft voice, stretching out one of her paws with the cruel claws showing a little.

After that a long time passed and the fire flamed only a little, and the shadow of the cat was big and black on the wall, and Nasca thought and thought and the cat looked and looked. Then the firelight danced and the big black shadow seemed to leap and then grow small, and the cat's eyes were full of a cold fire as they rested on Nasca.

Then suddenly Nasca broke into a laugh, though, to be sure, the laugh did not come from his heart.

"Why do you laugh?" said the cat.

"Because you are so big and I am so little, but for all that I can run ten times faster than you," answered Nasca, and his words sounded bold enough. He added: "All living creatures would agree in that."

"That is nonsense," said the cat, her jealousy at once aroused. "I am the fastest creature on earth. I can leap over mountains and I take rivers at a step."

"It does not matter what you can do," said Nasca, growing bolder every second. "Let me tell you this: While a man stooped to fill his cala-bash, I went from this place to a far mountain, cut the thread that bound you, and returned before the man with the calabash had straightened himself, and if you do not believe it, I will bring the man."

Nasca said all this with some idea of getting an excuse to go from there, but the words struck deep and the cat wondered.

"Why did you loose me?" asked the cat.

"Because I wanted to run a race with you," answered Nasca.

"If we run a race it must be for a wager," said the cat. "If you lose I make a meal of you. Is it agreed?"

"Fairly spoken," said Nasca, "though to be sure if you lose I make no meal of you."

"Let us run to-morrow then," said Nasca. "And I shall sleep well under the tree and be fresh in the morning."

"Not so," said the cat. "If we run, we run at midnight and under the cold white moon."

"So be it," answered Nasca. "Where shall we run?"

"Across the mountains and back again, seven times," said the cat, choosing the highlands, because she knew that she could leap over hills and cañons, while Nasca would have to climb up and down, and choosing night because she could see better in the dark than Nasca.

For the cat was very wise. But Nasca on his part thought of little more than getting away from the cat for a while. So he told the cat that he would bring a basket of fish for her supper, which he did, and while the cat ate he went outside and sought his grandmother.

The wise old woman laughed when she heard the story. "To a cat her cattishness," she said, "but to a woman her wit. All falls out well enough. Haste, run and bring me the magic ax."

"But no," said Nasca. "To use that would but make two terrible cats, and one is more than enough."

"Heed me, Nasca, and bring the ax," she repeated.

At that the boy ran swiftly and brought the ax.

"Now stand, Nasca, and fear not," said the old woman, and lifted the ax. So the lad stood, closing his eyes when he saw her raise the ax to strike.

Then with a swift blow she brought the weapon down on Nasca's head, cutting him in two, and in a moment there stood before her two Nascas, each as like the other as one blade of grass is like another. Surely and well had the ax done its work. One Nasca was as shapely as the other, one as fair-skinned as the other.

"Now," said the old woman, "happy was I with one Nasca, so doubly happy shall I be with two. So stay you here, Nasca the first, and Nasca the second must come with me. Oh, a merry world and a glad will it be now, since joy and gladness are doubled."

At that she remembered that she had told neither lad anything, in her delight, so she turned again to the first Nasca.

"Wait here for the great cat," she said. "Go with her to the great cañon where the race must start, and when the cat makes to leap across, which she will do, do you climb down a little way, then hide yourself until the cat returns. Doubtless we shall be able to manage matters at the other end. But see to it that you chide the cat for her slowness when she returns after the first run, and we shall see what we shall see."

Having said that, the old woman set off with Nasca the second, walking bravely over the ridges and hills that rose one behind the other like the waves of the sea. And when they had come to a far place where the mountain dropped down like a great stone wall to a fearful depth, they sat them down to wait, Nasca the second being in plain sight, the old woman hiding behind a rock.

But as soon as the moon rose the great cat walked to where Nasca the first stood, her eyes glaring terribly and her hair all a-bristle. So horrible a sight was she that for a moment Nasca went deadly pale, but he spoke boldly enough, nevertheless, for the brave one is not he that does not fear, but rather he that fears and yet does the thing that he has set out to do.

"One thing," said Nasca to the cat. "Is it right that you should leap over the cañon, going from one side to the other like a bird, while I must climb down and then up again? Let us make things fairer in the race, and do you climb down and up the other side with me." But all this he said in a kind of spirit of mischief, knowing full well that the cat would give him no chance at all.

"Ha! What is to do now?" said the cat with a hiss and a sneer. "Does your heart fail you already? Are you terror-tormented at the start? A fine racer, you, indeed! No, no, my fine lad. We race for a supper and you must supply the meal."

To that Nasca answered nothing, so there was a little silence, broken only by the hooting of the owl who was, indeed, trying to tell the cat the truth of matters. But the cat was too full of her own notions and had no ear for others. She lay crouched on the ground, ready to make a spring, and Nasca wondered whether her jump would be at him or across the cañon.

Suddenly, in a voice like thunder, the cat called: "START!" and at the word, leaped across the valley and was off and away, without as much as giving a glance at the lad. But he made a great deal of fuss on his part, climbing down the face of the cañon wall. The cat, on landing on the other side, looked back, then gave a cry of triumph, seeing the poor start that Nasca had made. "Come on! Come on!" she called. "The run will sharpen my appetite," and even as she said that, she was a distance off, then bounding away up hill and down hill, over the ridges, over the rocks, over the streams, taking a hundred yards at a bound. So in a very short space of time she came to the place where Nasca the second stood, and was mightily astonished to see her opponent, as she thought, there before her.

"Too easy, señora cat, too easy," said Nasca the second, speaking as the grandmother bade him. "I thought cats were swifter. Doubtless you play, though."

Hearing that speech the cat was full of anger and in a voice that shook the mountains, she roared: "BACK! BACK AGAIN! I'll show you."

Off ran Nasca the second then, but the cat passed him like lightning, her very whiskers streaming behind, and as soon as she was over the first hill the lad went back to the place where his grandmother was. Señora cat knew nothing of that, though, and went bounding as before, tearing up hill and down hill, over the ridges, over the rocks, over the streams, taking two hundred yards at a leap, and at last came to the place of beginning, to behold Nasca, who stood smiling and wiping his brow lightly, as if he had been running.

"Much better, señora cat," he said. "You almost caught me that time. A little faster and you would have won. But still I have more speed in me to let loose. Come on."

No sooner were the words out of his mouth than he started off, making as though to climb down the cañon wall, and the cat gave a screech that shook the very skies and made the pale moon quiver. So fast she went that the very trees and bushes that she passed were scorched, and as for the rocks over which she flew, they were melted by the heat of the air. Every leap that she took was four hundred yards. Up hill and down hill she went, over the ridges, over the rocks, over the streams, and so at last she came once more to where the second Nasca stood.

"A good run that, señora cat," he said. "I think that we shall finish the race soon and in a way that I may live and be happy, though for me you must go supperless. Certainly I must try, for to lose will profit me nothing."

But the cat was at her wits' end, supposing that Nasca ran faster than she. She opened her mouth to shriek, but fast upon her came a great feebleness, and she faltered and reeled and then fell down in a faint, seeing nothing at all. No time then did the second Nasca and the old woman lose. Putting themselves to the task, they rolled the cat to the edge of the great rock wall that ran down straight. Then after a pause to gain breath they gave another push, and the body of the giant cat fell over the edge and was broken to pieces on the sharp rocks below. So that was the end of the cat and the end of her dreams.

The two Nascas and the old woman went to their own place and told the people all that had happened, so there was great rejoicing, and laughter and song and weaving of garlands, and everybody was happy. And ever since there has been kindness and good fellowship in that land. And for those who would see signs of the tale there stand the three great rocks on the highlands, each so heavy that two hundred men could not lift them, and wise men wonder much what manner of men put them there. But only those who are not wise and learned know the truth of the matter, as you may test for yourself by asking any very wise men who come to visit you.

THIRTY-Two

Mr. Sweeney's Cat

Bill Nye

ROBERT ORMSBY SWEENEY IS A DRUGGIST OF ST. PAUL; AND THOUGH A recent chronological record reveals the fact that he is a direct descendant of a sure-enough king, and though there is mighty good purple, royal blood in his veins that dates back where kings used to have something to do to earn their salary, he goes right on with his regular business, selling drugs at the great sacrifice which druggists will make sometimes in order to place their goods within the reach of all.

As soon as I learned that Mr. Sweeney had barely escaped being a crowned head, I got acquainted with him and tried to cheer him up, and I told him that people wouldn't hold him in any way responsible, and that, as it hadn't shown itself in his family for years, he might perhaps finally wear it out.

He is a mighty pleasant man, anyhow, and you can have just as much fun with him as you could with a man who didn't have any royal blood in his veins. You would be with him for days on a fishing trip and never notice it at all.

But I was going to speak more in particular of Mr. Sweeney's cat. Mr. Sweeney had a large cat named Dr. Mary Walker, of which he was very fond. Dr. Mary Walker remained at the drug store all the time and was known all over St. Paul as a quiet and reserved cat.

If Dr. Mary Walker took in the town after office hours, nobody seemed to know anything about it. She would be around bright and cheerful the next morning and attend to her duties at the store just as though nothing whatever had ever happened.

One day last summer Mr. Sweeney left a large plate of fly-paper with water on it in the window, hoping to gather in a few quarts of flies in a deceased state. Dr. Mary Walker used to go to this window during the afternoon and look out on the busy street while she called up pleasant memories of her past life. That afternoon she thought she would call up some more memories, so she went over on the counter, and from there jumped down on the windowsill, landing with all four feet in the plate of fly-paper.

At first she regarded it as a joke and treated the matter very lightly, but later on she observed that the fly-paper stuck to her feet with great tenacity of purpose. Those who have never seen the look of surprise and deep sorrow that a cat wears when she finds herself glued to a whole sheet of fly-paper can not fully appreciate the way Dr. Mary Walker felt.

She did not dash wildly through a $150 plate-glass window, as some cats would have done. She controlled herself and acted in the coolest manner, though you could have seen that mentally she suffered intensely. She sat down a moment to more fully outline a plan for the future. In doing so she made a great mistake. The gesture resulted in gluing the fly-paper to her person in such a way that the edge turned up behind her in the most abrupt manner and caused her great inconvenience.

Some one at that time laughed in a coarse and heartless way, and I wish you could have seen the look of pain that Dr. Mary Walker gave him.

When she went away, she did not go around the prescription case as the rest of us did, but strolled through the middle of it, and so on out through the glass door at the rear of the store. We did not see her go through the glass door, but we found pieces of fly-paper and fur on the ragged edges of a large aperture in the glass, and we kind of jumped at the conclusion that Dr. Mary Walker had taken that direction in retiring from the room.

Dr. Mary Walker never returned to St. Paul, and her exact whereabouts are not known, though every effort was made to find her. Fragments of fly-paper and brindle hair were found as far west as the Yellowstone National Park, and as far north as the British line, but the

Doctor herself was not found. My own theory is that if she turned her bow to the west so as to catch the strong easterly gale on her quarter, with the sail she had set and her tail pointing directly toward the zenith, the chances for Dr. Mary Walker's immediate return are extremely slim.

The Cat and the Mouse

John R. Neill

ACCORDING TO THE DECREE OF HEAVEN, THERE ONCE LIVED IN THE
Persian city of Kerman a cat like unto a dragon—a longsighted cat who
hunted like a lion; a cat with fascinating eyes and long whiskers and
sharp teeth. Its body was like a drum, its beautiful fur like ermine skin.

Nobody was happier than this cat, neither the newly wedded bride,
nor the hospitable master of the house when he looks round on the smiling faces of his guests.

This cat moved in the midst of friends, boon companions of the
saucepan, the cup, and the milk jug of the court, and of the dinner table
when the cloth is spread.

Perceiving the wine cellar open, one day, the cat ran gleefully into
it to see if he could catch a mouse and hid himself behind a wine jar.
At that moment a mouse ran out of a hole in the wall, quickly climbed
the jar, and putting his head into it, drank so long and so deeply that he
became drunk, talked very stupidly, and fancied he was as bold as a lion.

"Where is the cat?" shouted he, "that I may off with his head. I would
cut off his head as if on the battlefield. A cat in front of me would fare
worse than any dog who might happen to cross my path."

The cat ground his teeth with rage while hearing this. Quicker than
the eye could follow, he made a spring, seized the mouse in his claws, and
said, "Oh, little mouse, now will you take off my head?"

"I am thy servant," replied the mouse; "forgive my sin. I was drunk. I am thy slave; a slave whose ear is pierced and on whose shoulder the yoke is."

"Tell fewer lies," replied the cat. "Was there ever such a liar? I heard all you said and you shall pay for your sin with your life. I will make your life less than that of a dead dog."

So the cat killed and ate the mouse; but afterward, being sorry for what he had done, he ran to the Mosque, and passed his hands over his face, poured water on his hands, and anointed himself as he had seen the faithful do at the appointed hours of prayer.

Then he began to recite the beautiful chapter to Allah in the Holy Book of the Persians, and to make his confession in this wise:

"I have repented and will not again tear the body of a mouse with my teeth. I will give bread to the deserving poor. Forgive my sin, O great Forgiver, for have I not come to Thee bowed down with sorrow?"

He repeated this so many times and with so much feeling that he really thought he meant it, and finally wept for grief.

A little mouse happened to be behind the pulpit, and overhearing the cat's vows, speedily carried the glad but surprising news to the other mice. Breathlessly he related how that the cat had become a true Mussulman; how that he had seen him in the Mosque weeping and lamenting, and saying:

"Oh, Creator of the world, put away my sin, for I have offended like a big fool." Then the mouse went on to describe how that the cat had a rosary of beads and made pious reflections in the spirit of a true penitent.

The mice began to make merry when they heard this startling news, for they were exceedingly glad. Seven chosen mice, each the headman of the village, arose and gave thanks that the cat should at last have entered the fold of the true believers.

All danced and shouted, "Ah! Ah! Hu! Hu!" and drank red wine and white wine until they were very merry. Two rang bells, two played castanets, and two sang. One carried a tray behind his back laden with good things, so that all could help themselves; some smoked water-pipes; another acted like a clown; others played various tunes on different instruments of music.

A few days after the feast, the King of the mice said to them, "Oh, friends, all of you bring costly presents worthy of the cat!" Then the mice scattered in search of gifts, but soon returned, each bearing something worthy of presentation, even to a nobleman.

One brought a bottle of wine; another a dish full of raisins; others came with salted nuts and melon seeds, lumps of cheese, basins of sugar-candy, pistachio nuts, little cakes iced with sugar, bottles of lemon juice, Indian shawls, hats, cloaks and many other things.

Discreetly they bore their gifts before the King of the Cats. When in the royal presence, they made humble obeisances, touching their foreheads on the ground, and saluting him, said:

"Oh, master, liberator of the lives of all, we have brought gifts worthy of thy service. We beseech thee to deign to accept of them."

Then the cat thought to himself, "I am rewarded for becoming a pious Mussulman. Though I have endured much hunger, yet this day finds me freely and amply provided for. Not for many days have I broken my fast. It is clear that Allah is appeased."

Then he turned to the mice, and bade them come nearer, calling them his friends. And they went forward trembling. So frightened were they that they were hardly aware of what they were doing. When they were close the cat made a sudden spring upon them.

Five mice he caught, each one the chief of a village; two with his front paws, two with his hind ones, and one in his mouth. The remaining mice barely escaped with their lives.

Picking up one of their murdered brothers, they quickly carried the sad news to the mice, saying: "Why do ye sit still, oh mice? Throw dust on your heads, oh young men, for the cruel cat has seized five of our unsuspecting companions with teeth and claws and has killed them."

Then for the space of five days they rent their clothes as do the mourners, and cast dust on their heads. Then they said: "We must go and tell our King all that has befallen the mice. We must not fail to tell him this calamity."

Whereupon they all rose up and went their way in deep sorrow; one beating the muffled drum, one tolling the bell; all had shawls around their necks; their tears the while running in little streams down their whiskers.

Arrived where the King was sitting on his throne, the mice paid homage to him, saying: "Master, we are subjects and thou art King. Behold the cat has treated us cruelly since he became a pious follower of Mahomet. Whereas, before his conversion he was wont to catch only one of us in a year, now that he is a sincere Mussulman his appetite has so increased that only five at a time will satisfy him."

Whereupon the King fell into such a violent rage that he resembled a saucepan boiling over. But to the deputation of mice he spoke very kindly, calling them his newly arrived and welcome guests, and to comfort them vowed that he would give the cat such a chastisement that the news of it should circulate through the world.

Then, observing their grief, he commanded that the dead mouse should be buried with all pomp and ceremony. Accordingly, they made lamentation for a whole week, as though it had been for one of royal degree; and having prepared delicious sweetmeats, they placed them in baskets and carried them with streaming eyes to the grave.

After the burial service, the King ordered the army to assemble on a given day on the great sandy plain that stretches as far as the eye can see around the city. Then he addressed them, saying:

"Oh, men and soldiers, inasmuch as the cat has so cruelly ill-treated our countrymen, he being a heretic and an evil doer, and brutal in nature, we must now go to the city of Kerman and fight him."

So three hundred and thirty thousand mice went forth, armed with swords, guns, and spears; and with flags and pennons bravely flying. A passing Arab from the desert, skilfully balancing himself on the back of a swift-traveling camel by means of a long pole, spied the great army in motion, and was so overcome with astonishment that he lost his balance and fell off. Several regiments of mice were put out of action by his fall; but nothing daunted, the army pressed on.

When the army was ready for battle, the King again addressed them saying: "O young men, an ambassador must be sent to the cat, one who is able, discreet, and eloquent." Then they all shouted: "The King's orders shall be carried out! Upon our heads be it."

Now, there was present a learned and eloquent mouse, the ruler of a province, and he it was that the King commanded to go as an ambassador to the cat in the city of Kerman. Almost before his name was out of the King's mouth, he had jumped out of his place in the ranks, and, traveling swiftly as the winds of the desert, he went in boldly before the cat and said:

"As an ambassador from the King of the Mice am I come, bowed down with grief and fatigue. Know this, my master has determined to wage war, and is even now come with his army to take off your head."

The cat roared out in reply, "Go tell your King to eat dust! I come not out of this city except at my good pleasure!" Then he sent messengers to bring up quickly some fighting and hunting cats from Khorassan—the land of the sun—to Kerman.

As soon as the cat's army was ready, the King of the Cats gave them marching orders, promising to come himself to the battle on the next day. The cats came out on horseback, each one like a hungry tiger. The mice also mounted their steeds, armed to the teeth, and boiling with rage. Shouting "Allah! Allah!" the armies fell upon each other with unsheathed swords.

So many cats and mice were killed that there was no room for the horses' feet. The cats fought valiantly, their fierce attacks carrying them through the first line of the mice, then through the second, and many Ameers and chiefs were killed. The mice, thinking the battle lost, turned to flee, crying out:

"Throw dust upon your heads, young men!"

But afterwards, rallying again, they faced their pursuers and attacked the right wing of the cat's army, shouting their battle cry of "Allah! Allah!"

In the thickest of the fray a mounted mouse speared the King of the Cats, so that he fell fainting to the ground. Before he could rise, the mouse leaped upon him and brought him captive to the King. So the cats were defeated on that day and sullenly retreated to the city of Kerman.

Having bound the cat, the mice beat him until he became unconscious. Then the plain echoed with the beating of tom-toms and shouts of joy. Then the King of the Mice seated himself on his throne and ordered the cat to be brought before him.

"Scoundrel!" he said to him, "Why hast thou eaten up my army? Hear now the King of the Mice." The cat hung his head in fear and remained silent. After a few minutes, he said: "I am thy servant, even to death." Then the King replied:

"Carry this black-faced dog to the execution ground. I will come in person without delay to kill him in revenge for the blood of my slaughtered subjects."

So he mounted his elephant, and his guard marched proudly before him. The cat, with his hands tied together, stood weeping. Upon arriving at the execution grounds and discerning that the cat was not yet executed, the King said angrily to the hangman: "Why is it this prisoner is still alive? Hang him immediately!"

At that very moment a horseman came galloping furiously from the city and besought the King, saying: "Forgive this miserable cat; in future he will do us no harm."

However, the King turned a deaf ear to his entreaties, ordering that the cat be killed at once. The mice hesitated, being unwilling, through fear, to carry out the order.

Of course, this made the King very angry. "O foolish mice!" he cried, "Ye will all take pity on the cat, in order that he may again make a sacrifice of you."

Directly the cat saw the horseman, his courage revived. With one bound he sprang from his place as does the tiger on his prey, burst his bonds asunder, and seized five unfortunate mice. The other mice, filled with dismay and terror, ran hither and thither, crying wildly:

"Allah! Allah! Shoot him! Cut off his head, as did Rastam his enemies on the day of battle!"

When the King of the Mice saw what, had happened, he fainted; whereupon the cat leaped on him, pulled off his crown, and placing the rope over his head, hanged him, so that he died immediately.

Then he darted here and there, seizing and slaying, and dashing mice to the earth, till the whole army of mice was routed, and there was none left to oppose him.

Johnny Reed's Cat

English Folk Tale

"YES, CATS ARE QUEER FOLK, SURE ENOUGH, AND OFTEN KNOW MORE than a simple beast ought to by knowledge that's rightly come by. There's that cat there, you've been looking at, will stand at a door on its hind legs with its front paws on the handle trying like a Christian to open the door, and mewling in a manner that's almost like talking.

He's a London cat, he is, being brought me by a cousin who lives there, and is called Gilpin, after, I'm told, a mayor who was christened the same. He's a knowing cat, sure enough; but it's not the London cats that are cleverer than the country ones. Who knows, he may be a relative of Johnny Reed's own tom-cat himself."

"And who was Johnny Reed? and what was there remarkable about his cat?"

"Have you never heard tell of Johnny Reed's cat? It's an old tale they have in the north country, and it's true enough, though folk may not believe it in these days when the Bible's not gospel enough for some of them. I've heard my father often tell the story, and he came from New-castle way, which is the very part where Johnny Reed used to live, being a parish sexton in a village not far away.

"Well, Johnny Reed was the sexton, as I've already said, and he and his wife kept a cat, a well enough behaved creature, sure enough, and a beast as he had no fault to set on, saving a few of the tricks which all cats play at times, and which seem born in the blood of the creatures.

It was all black except one white paw, and seemed as honest and decent a beast as could be, and Tom would as soon have suspected it of being any more than it really seemed to be as he would one of his own children themselves, like many other folk, perhaps, who, may be, have cats of the same kind, little thinking it.

"Well, the cat had been with him some years when a strange thing occurred.

"One night Johnny was going home late from the churchyard, where he had been digging a grave for a person who had died on a sudden, throwing the grave on Johnny's hands unexpectedly, so that he had to stop working at it by the light of a lantern to have it ready for the next day's burying.

Well, having finished his work, and having put his tools in the shed in a corner of the yard, and having locked them up safe, he began to walk home pretty brisk, thinking would his wife be up and have a bit of fire for him, for the night was cold, a keen wind blowing over the fields.

"He hadn't gone far before he comes to a gate at the roadside, and there seemed to be a strange shadow about it, in which Johnny saw, as it might be, a lot of little gleaming fires dancing about, while some stood steady, just like flashes of light from little windows in buildings all on fire inside. Says Johnny to himself, for he was not a man to be easily frightened, being accustomed by his calling to face things which might upset other folk—

"'Hullo! What's here? Here's a thing I never saw before,' and with that he walks straight up to the gate, while the shadow got deeper and the fires brighter the nearer he came to it.

"Well, when he came right up to the gate he finds that the shadow was just none at all, but nine black cats, some sitting and some dancing about, and the lights were the flashes from their eyes. When he came nearer he thought to scare them off, and he calls out—

"'Sh—sh—sh,' but never a cat stirs for all of it.

"'I'll soon scatter you, you ugly varmin,' says Johnny, looking about him for a stone, which was not to be found, the night being dark and preventing him seeing one. Just then he hears a voice calling—

"'Johnny Reed!'

"'Hullo!' says he, 'who's that wants me?'

"'Johnny Reed,' says the voice again.

"'Well,' says Johnny, 'I'm here,' and looking round and seeing no one, for no one was about 'tis true.

"'Was it one of you,' says he, joking like, to the cats, 'as was calling me?'"

"'Yes, of course,' answers one of them, as plain as ever Christian spoke. 'It's me as has called you these three times.'

"Well, with that, you may be sure, Johnny begins to feel curious, for 'twas the first time he had ever been spoken to by a cat, and he didn't know what it might lead to exactly. So he takes off his hat to the cat, thinking that it was, perhaps, best to show it respect, and, seeing that he was unable to guess with whom he was dealing, hoping to come off all the better for a little civility.

"'Well, sir,' says he, 'what can I do for you?'

"'It's not much as I want with you,' says the cat, 'but it's better it'll be with you if you do what I tell you. Tell Dan Ratcliffe that Peggy Poyson's dead.'

"'I will, sir,' says Johnny, wondering at the same time how he was to do it, for who Dan Ratcliffe was he knew no more than the dead. Well, with that all the cats vanished, and Johnny, running the rest of the way home, rushes into his house, smoking hot from the fright and the distance he had to go over.

"'Nan,' says he to his wife, the first words he spoke, 'who's Dan Ratcliffe?'

"'Dan Ratcliffe,' says she. 'I never heard of him, and don't know there's any one such living about here.'

"'No more do I,' says he, 'but I must find him wherever he is.'

"Then he tells his wife all about how he had met the cats, and how they had stopped him and given him the message. Well, his cat sits there in front of the fire looking as snug and comfortable as a cat could be, and nearly half-asleep, but when Johnny comes to telling his wife the message the cats had given him, then it jumped up on its feet, and looks at Johnny, and says—

"'What! is Peggy Poyson dead? Then it's no time for me to be here'; and with that it springs through the door and vanishes, nor was ever seen again from that day to this."

"And did the sexton ever find Dan Ratcliffe," I asked.

"Never. He searched high and low for him about, but no one could tell him of such a person, though Johnny looked long enough, thinking it might be the worse for him if he didn't do his best to please the cats. At last, however, he gave the matter up."

"Then, what was the meaning of the cat's message?"

"It's hard to tell; but many folk thought, and I'm inclined to agree with them, that Dan Ratcliffe was Johnny's own cat, and no one else, looking at the way he acted, and no other of the name being known. Who Peggy Poyson was no one could tell, but likely enough it was some relative of the cat, or may be some one it was interested in, for it's little we know concerning the creatures and their ways, and with whom and what they're mixed up."

An Idyll of Summer

Anne E. P. Searing

THE MINISTER OF BLUE MOUNTAIN CHURCH, AND THE MINISTER'S wife, were enjoying their first autumn fire, and the presence of the cat on the hearth between them.

"He came home this afternoon," the minister's wife was saying, "while I was picking those last peppers in the garden, and he jumped on my shoulder and purred against my ear as unconcernedly as if he'd only been for a stroll in the lower pasture, instead of gone for three months— the little wretch!"

"It does seem extraordinary"—the minister unbent his long legs and recrossed them carefully, in order to remove his foot from the way of the tawny back where it stretched out in blissful elongation—"very extraordinary, that an animal could lead that sort of double life, disappearing completely when summer comes and returning promptly with the fall. I daresay it's a reversion to the old hunting instinct. No doubt we could find him if we knew how to trail him on the mountains."

"The strangest thing about it is that this year and last he came back fat and sleek—always before, you know, he has been so gaunt and starved looking in the fall." She leaned over and stroked the cat under his chin; he purred deeply in response, and looked up into her eyes, his own like wells of unfathomed speech. "I have an eerie feeling," she said, "that if he could talk he'd have great things to tell."

The minister laughed, and puffed away at his corncob pipe. "Tales of the chase, my dear, of hecatombs of field-mice and squirrels!"

But she shook her head. "Not this summer—that cat has spent these last two summers with human beings who have treated him as a kind of fetich—just as we do!" As she rubbed his ear she murmured regretfully: "To think of all you've heard and seen and done, and you can't tell us one thing!"

The Yellow Cat's eyes narrowed to mere slits of black across two amber agates; then he shook his ears free, yawned, and gave himself up to closed lids and dreams. If he could have told it all, just as it happened, not one word of it could those good souls have comprehended—and this was the way of it.

It was near the close of a June day when the cat made his entrance into that hidden life of the summers from which his exits had been as sudden, though less dramatic. In the heart of the hills, where a mountain torrent has fretted its way for miles through a rocky gorge, there is a place where the cleft widens into a miniature valley, and the stream slips along quietly between banks of moss before it plunges again on its riotous path down the mountain. Here the charcoal-burners, half a century ago, had made a clearing, and left their dome-shaped stone kiln to cover itself with the green velvet and lace of lichen and vine. The man who was stooping over the water, cleaning trout for his supper, had found it so and made it his own one time in his wandering quest for solitude. The kiln now boasted a chimney, a door, and one wide window that looked away over the stream's next plunge, over other mountains and valleys to far horizons of the world of men. This was the hermitage to which he brought his fagged-out nerves from the cormorant city that feeds on the blood and brains of humans. Here through the brief truce of summer he found time to fish and hunt enough for his daily wants, time to read, to write, time to dream and to smoke his evening pipe, to think long thoughts, and more blessed than all—to sleep! When autumn came he would go back with renewed life and a pile of manuscript to feed to his hungry cormorant. He was chewing the cud of contentment as he bent to his fish cleaning, when, glancing to one side where the fire, between stones, was awaiting his frying-pan, he caught sight among the bushes of two gleaming eyes, and then the sleek back and lashing tail of the Yellow Cat. The man, being a cat lover was versed in their ways, so for a time he paid no attention, then began to talk softly.

"If you'd come out of that," he said, as he scraped the scales, "and not sit there watching me like a Comanche Indian, I'd invite you to supper!"

Whether it was the tone of his voice or the smell of the fish that conquered, the tawny creature was suddenly across the open with a rush and on the stooping shoulders. That was the beginning of the companionship that lasted until fall. The next season brought the animal as unexpectedly, and they took up the old relation where it had left off the previous summer. They trudged together through miles of forest, sometimes the cat on the man's shoulder, but often making side excursions on his own account and coming back with the proud burden of bird or tiny beast. Together they watched the days decline in red and gold glory from the ledge where the stream drops over the next height, or when it rained, companioned each other by the hearth in the hut. There was between them that satisfying and intimate communion of inarticulate speech only possible between man and beast.

There came a day when the man sat hour after hour over his writing, letting the hills call in vain. The cat slept himself out, and when paws in the ink and tracks over the paper proved of no avail, he jumped down and marched himself haughtily off through the door and across the clearing to the forest, tail in air. Late that afternoon the man was arrested midway of a thought rounding into phrase by the sudden darkness. There was a fierce rush of wind, as if some giant had sighed and roused himself. The door of the hut slammed shut and the blast from the window scattered the papers about the floor. As he went to pull down the sash the cat sprang in, shaking from his feet the drops of rain already slanting in a white sheet across the little valley. At the same moment there was a "halloo" outside, and a woman burst open the door, turning quickly to shut out behind her the onrush of the shower and the biting cold of the wind. She stood shaking the drops from her hair, and then she looked into the astonished face of the man and laughed.

She was as slim and straight as a young poplar, clad in white shirt-waist and khaki Turkish trousers with gaiters laced to the knee.

Her hair was blown about in a red-gold snarl, and her eyes looked out as unabashed as a boy's. The two stared at each other for a time in silence, and finally it was the woman who spoke first.

"This isn't exactly what I call a warm welcome—not just what the cat led me to expect! It was really the cat who brought me—I met him over on Slide Mountain—he fled and I pursued, and now here we are!"

She made a hasty survey of the hut, and then of its owner, putting her head on one side as she looked about her with a quick, bird-like movement, he still staring in stupefaction.

"Of course you detest having me here, but you won't put me out in the rain, again, will you?"

At once he was his courteous self. With the same motion he dumped the astonished cat from the cushioned chair by the writing table, and drew it forward to the fire. Then he threw on a fresh stick of pine that flared up in a bright blaze, and with deferring gentleness took the sweater that hung from her shoulders and hung it to dry over a section of tree-trunk that served as a chimney seat.

"You are as welcome to my hut as any princess to her palace," he smiled on her, "indeed, it is yours while you choose to stay in it!"

"Don't you think," she made reply, as he drew another chair up opposite to her, "that under the circumstances we might dispense with fine speeches? It is hardly, I suppose, what one would call a usual situation, is it?"

He looked at her as she stretched her small feet comfortably to the blaze, her face quite unconcerned.

"No," he acquiesced, "it certainly is not usual—or I should hate it—the 'usual' is what I fly from!"

She threw back her head, clasping her hands behind it as she laughed. She seemed to luxuriate as frankly in the heat and the dryness as the cat between them.

"And I"—she turned the comprehension of her eyes upon him—"I cross the ocean every year in the same flight!"

The storm drove leaves and flying branches against the window, while they sat, for what seemed a long time, in contented silence. He found himself as openly absorbing her charm as if she had been a tree or a mountain sunset, while she was making further tours of inspection with her eyes about the room.

"It is entirely adorable," she smiled at him, "but it piques my curiosity!"

"Ask all the questions you wish—no secrets here."

"Then what, if you please, is the object I see swung aloft there in the dome?"

"My canvas hammock which I lower at night to climb into and go to bed, and pull up in the daytime to clear the decks."

"And the big earthen pot in the fireplace—it has gruesome suggestions of the 'Forty Thieves!'"

"Only a sort of perpetual hot-water tank. The fire never quite goes out on this domestic hearth, and proves a very acceptable companion at this high altitude. There is always the kettle on the crane, as you see it there, but limitless hot water is the fine art of housekeeping—but, perhaps you don't know the joy there is to be found in the fine art of housekeeping?"

"No, I do not," her eyes took on a whimsical expression, "but I'd like to learn—anything in the way of a new joy! In the way of small joys I am already quite a connoisseur, indeed I might call myself a collector in that line—of *bibelot* editions, you understand, for thus far I seem to have been unable to acquire any of the larger specimens! Would you be willing to take me on as a pupil in housekeeping?"

"It would add to my employment a crowning joy—not a *bibelot*!"

"Pinchbeck fine speeches again," she shrugged. "Do you stop here all the long summer quite alone?"

"All the 'short summer,'" he corrected, "save for the society of the cat, who dropped down last year from nowhere. He must have approved of the accommodations, for he has chosen me, you see, a second time for a summer resort."

"Yes—I think he was trying to protest about you being his exclusive find, when I invited myself to follow him down the mountain—leading and eluding are so much alike, one is often mistaken, is it not so?"

She was sitting forward now, chin in hands, elbows on her knees, gazing into the flames where a red banner waved above the back log. When she turned to him again the westering sun had broken through the clouds and was sending a flare of rosy light in at the window. Studying her face more fully, he saw that she was years—fully ten years—older than he had supposed. The boyish grace that sat so lightly was after all the audacious ease of a woman of the world, sure of herself.

"I, too, am living the hermit life for the summer. I am the happy possessor of a throat that demands an annual mountain-cure. Switzerland with its perpetual spectacular note gets on my nerves, so last year we found this region—I and my two faithful old servitors. Do you know the abandoned tannery in the West Branch Clove? That has been fitted up for our use, and there we live the simple life as I am able to attain it—but you have so far outdone me that you have filled my soul with discontent!"

"Alas," said the man, "you have served me the very same trick! I could almost wish—"

"That I had not come!"

"Say, rather, that you would come again!"

She stood up and reached for her sweater, waiting for him to open the door. The round of the little valley was a glittering green bowl filled with pink cloud scuds. They stepped out into a jubilant world washed clean and freshly smiling. She put out her hand in good-bye.

"I almost think I shall come again! If you were a person with whom one could be solitary—who knows!"

When she appeared the next time she found him by the noise of his chopping. They climbed to the top of the moss-covered boulder that hangs poised over the ledge where the stream leaps into the abyss. Below them the hills rolled in an infinite recession of leaf-clad peaks to the sky line, where they melted to a blur of bluish-green mist.

"Oh, these mountains of America!" she cried, "their greenness is a thing of dreams to us who know only bare icy and alps!"

"Far lovelier," he said, "to look down upon than to look up to, I think. To be a part of the height comes pretty near to being happy, for the moment."

She turned from the view to study her companion. The lines in the corners of his kind, tired eyes, the lean, strong figure, hair graying about the temples. He grew a little impatient under it before she spoke.

"Do you know," she said slowly, "I am going to like you! To like you immensely—and to trust you!"

"Thank you, I shall try to be worthy"—even his derision was gentle—"I seem to remember having been trusted before by members of your sex—even liked a little, though not perhaps 'immensely'! At any rate this certainly promises to be an experience quite by itself!"

"Quite by itself," she echoed.

"Wouldn't it be as well for you to know my name, say, as a beginning?"

"No," she nodded, "that's just what I don't want! I only want to know you. Names are extraneous things—tags, labels—let us waive them. If I tell you how I feel about this meeting of ours will you try to understand me?"

The answer was less in words than in the assent of his honest gray eyes.

"I have been surfeited all my life," she went on, "with love—I want no more of it! The one thing I do want, more than anything else, is a man friend. I have thought a great deal about such a friendship—the give and take on equal terms, the sexless companionship of mind—what it could be like!"

He brushed the twigs from the lichens between them and made no answer.

"Fate—call the power what you will"—she met the disclaimer that puckered the corners of his mouth—"fate brought us together. It was the response to my longing for such a friendship!"

"It was the Yellow Cat!"

"The Yellow Cat plus fate! While I sat there by your fire I recognized you for that friend!"

Far below over the tree tops cloud shadows and sunlight were playing some wonderful game of follow-my-leader; a hawk hung poised on tilting wings; and on the veil of mist that was the spirit of the brook where it cast itself from the ledge curved the arch of a rainbow. The man pointed to the augury.

"You might try me," he said, and they shook hands on the compact, laughing half shamefacedly at their own solemnity.

"As woman to woman," he offered.

"Let it be rather as man to man," she shrugged.

"As you like—as women we should have to begin by explaining ourselves."

"Precisely, and men companion each other on impersonal grounds."

"Then it is a man's friendship?"

"Better still," she mused, "we'll pattern it after the ideals of the disembodied! We'll make this summer, you and I together, a gem from the heart of life—I will have it so!"

So it came about that like two children they played together, worked, walked, or read and talked by the open fire when cold storms came. Every morning she came over the wood-road that led by winding ways from her valley, and at sunset she went back over the trail alone. He might go as far as the outlook half way over the mountain where the path begins to go down, but no farther; as for any fear, she seemed to know nothing of its workings, and the revolver she wore in a case that hung from her belt was a mere convention.

One morning she came with eyes dancing—it was to be an especial day—a fête—and the gods had smiled on her planning and given them perfect weather. Never such sunshine, such crystal air, such high-hung clouds! Breakfast over, they hurried about the miniature housework, and packed the kit for a long day's tramp. Then they started forth, the cat following, tail aloft. Beyond a dim peak, where the clove opens southward, by the side of a tiny lake they lunched and took their noonday rest. She watched the smoke curl up from his pipe where he lay at peace with the scheme of things.

"Do you know, Man, dear," she said, "I am glad I don't in the least guess who you are! I have no doubt you write the most delightful stories in the world—but never put me in one, please!"

He took the pipe out of his mouth and looked at her long before he replied.

"Woman, dear," he said, "I have put you in a place—your own place—and it is not in my novels!"

She scrambled to her feet laughing.

"It's very well to make stories, but it is really more diverting to live them! Come, I must lead you now with your eyes shut tight to my surprise!"

So hand in hand they went along a smooth green wood-road until she stopped him.

"Look," she cried, "now look!"

Straight away till the road narrowed to a point of light against the sky where the mountain dipped down, banks of mountain laurel rose on either side in giant hedges of rose and white, while high above them waved the elms and beeches of the forest.

"It is the gardening of the gods!"

"It is my own treasure-trove! I found it last year and I have been waiting to bring you to it on my fête—what you call birthday! And now wish me some beautiful thing—it may come true! There is a superstition in my country—but I shall not tell you—unless the wish comes true!"

He broke off a spray of the waxen buds and crowned her solemnly where she stood.

"I have already wished for you—the most beautiful thing in the world!"

She shook her head, sorrowful. "Man, dear, the only thing in all the world I still want is the impossible!"

"Only the impossible is worthwhile—and I have wished!"

She shook her head again, laughing a little ruefully. "It could not arrive—my impossible—and yet you almost tempt me to hope!"

"Anything—everything may arrive! You once thought that such a friendship as this of ours could not, and lo, we have achieved it!"

"I wonder"—her eyes seemed fixed on some far prospect, a world beyond the flowery way—"I wonder if we have! And I wonder why you have never made a guess about my world when you have at least let me get a peep now and then into yours?"

"I don't care a rap about your 'world,'" he smiled into her eyes, "while I have you!"

"No curiosity about my—my profession?"

"Not a bit—though it was clear enough from the first that it was the stage!"

She made an odd little outcry at his powers of divination.

"Then I must look it—before the footlights from my birth! Since you are so clever, Mr. Man, will you also be merciful when you come to weigh me in those scales you try to hide beneath the garment of your kindness? Think, when you judge me, what it is for a woman never to be herself—always to have to play a part!"

He reached and took her hand suddenly, drawing her to him with a movement that was almost rough.

"This is no play acting—this is real! No footlights—no audience—only you and me in all this world!"

But she drew away, insistently aloof. She would have none of his caresses.

"This, too," she said, as she moved apart and stood waiting for him to follow, "is a part of the play—I do not deceive myself! When I go back to my world—my trade, I shall remember this little time that you and I have snatched from the grudging grasp of life as an act—a scene only! It's a perfect pastoral, Man, dear, but unreal—absurdly unreal—and we know it ourselves while we play the game!"

Down through the flower-bordered vista the cat went stalking his prey, his sinuous body a tawny streak winding along the green path. These trivial humans, with their subtle attractions and compunctions, were as though they never had been when the chase was on—the real business and purpose of life!

For the rest of the time they were together they avoided the personal. Each felt the threat in the air and tacitly averted it. For that one perfect day there should be no past, no future, nothing but the golden present.

Swinging in his breeze-rocked hammock between door and window the man lay awake through the long watches of the night, thinking, thinking, while his heart sang. Toward dawn he fell into a deep sleep from which he was only awakened by the cat springing up to lick his face in reminder of breakfast.

It was when he came back from his plunge in the pool that he first noticed a paper pinned to his door-post. Within its folds his doom was penned!

"Even you, dear Man, could not wish me the impossible! That superstition of my country is that to come true it must be the first wish of your fête day—and by one who loves you! Alas, my old servant had already wished—that he might get me started for home to-day! Clever

Friedrich—for he had also packed! When you read this I shall be far on my way. You could never find me though you searched the earth—but you will never try! It is well as it is, for you see—it was not friendship after all!"

And yet there was a sequel. During the following year there dropped to the man in his hard-pressed literary life, one of those errant plums from the political tree that now and then find their way to the right basket. He was named for an excellent diplomatic post. His friends congratulated him and talked a good deal about "material" and opportunities for "unique local color"; his wife chattered unceasingly about gowns and social details, while he armed himself, with the listless reticence that was become habit, to face new responsibilities and rather flavorless experiences. He had so withdrawn himself of late to the inner creative life that he moved in a kind of phantasmagoria of outer unrealities. It was the nearest to a comfortable adjustment for the mis-mating of such a marriage as his, but it was not the best of preparations for the discharge of public duties, and he walked toward his new future with reluctant feet, abstractedly. In some such mood as this, his mind bent on a problem of arrangement of fiction puppets, seeing "men as trees walking," he found himself one day making his bows at a court function. Along the line of royal highnesses and grand duchesses with his wife he moved, himself a string-pulled puppet, until—but who, in heaven's name is this?

For one mad moment, as he looked into her eyes, he thought the tightened cord he sometimes felt tugging at his tired brain had snapped, and the images of sight and memory gone hopelessly confused. She stood near the end of the line with the princesses of secondary rank, and the jewels in her hair were not more scintillant than her eyes as he bent over her hand. She went a little pale, but she greeted him bravely, and when they found themselves unobserved for a moment she spoke to him in her soft, careful English:

"You recognized me, you remember, for a play actor, and now you are come from the world's end to see me perform on my tiny stage! Alas, dear critic, since my last excursion, I am no longer letter perfect in my part!"

They met but once again. It was in the crush of guests in the great hall where her old Prince, in the splendor of his decoration-covered coat, was waiting to hand her to her carriage. There was a brief time in which to snatch the doubtful sweetness of a few hurried words. She was leaving in the early morning for the petty Balkan province where her husband held a miniature sway, over a handful of half-savage subjects. Hardly more than a renewal of greeting and a farewell, and she was gone!

As the old Prince wrapped her more carefully in her furs, and the carriage rolled away in the darkness, he spoke to her, somewhat puzzled:

"I should be sorry to think the American Ambassador has been taking too much wine—as you well know, my knowledge of the barbarous English tongue is but limited, and yet—I thought, as I joined you, he was talking some farrago of nonsense about a *Yellow Cat!*"

That year the Yellow Cat came home lean and gaunt, a chastened, humble creature, as one who has failed in a long quest, and is glad to stretch his weary length before the hearth and reap the neglected benefits of the domestic life.

"It is really very odd" said the minister, quite as if he were saying something he had never thought of saying before, "where that cat goes in the summer!"

"Isn't it?" responded the minister's wife—just as she always did. "It fires the imagination! He walks off some fine morning and completely shuts the door on our life here—as if he gave us notice not to pry into his movements. But this time"—she was leaning to stroke the tawny sides with a pitying touch—"this time you may be sure something very sad and disappointing happened to him—something in that other life went quite wrong! How I wish we could understand what it was!"

The Man Who Disliked Cats

P. G. Wodehouse

It was Harold who first made us acquainted, when I was dining one night at the Cafe Britannique, in Soho. It is a peculiarity of the Cafe Britannique that you will always find flies there, even in winter. Snow was falling that night as I turned in at the door, but, glancing about me, I noticed several of the old faces. My old acquaintance, Percy the bluebottle, looking wonderfully fit despite his years, was doing deep breathing exercises on a mutton cutlet, and was too busy to do more than pause for a moment to nod at me; but his cousin, Harold, always active, sighted me and bustled up to do the honours.

He had finished his game of touch-last with my right ear, and was circling slowly in the air while he thought out other ways of entertaining me, when there was a rush of air, a swish of napkin, and no more Harold.

I turned to thank my preserver, whose table adjoined mine. He was a Frenchman, a melancholy-looking man. He had the appearance of one who has searched for the leak in life's gas-pipe with a lighted candle; of one whom the clenched fist of Fate has smitten beneath the temperamental third waistcoat-button.

He waved my thanks aside. "It was a bagatelle," he said. We became friendly. He moved to my table, and we fraternized over our coffee.

Suddenly he became agitated. He kicked at something on the floor. His eyes gleamed angrily.

"Ps-s-st!" he hissed. "Va-t'en!"

I looked round the corner of the table, and perceived the restaurant cat in dignified retreat.

"You do not like cats?" I said.

"I 'ate all animals, monsieur. Cats especially." He frowned. He seemed to hesitate.

"I will tell you my story," he said. "You will sympathize. You have a sympathetic face. It is the story of a man's tragedy. It is the story of a blighted life. It is the story of a woman who would not forgive. It is the story—"

"I've got an appointment at eleven," I said.

He nodded absently, drew at his cigarette, and began:

I have conceived my 'atred of animals, monsieur, many years ago in Paris. Animals are to me a symbol for the lost dreams of youth, for ambitions foiled, for artistic impulses cruelly stifled. You are astonished. You ask why I say these things. I shall tell you.

I am in Paris, young, ardent, artistic. I wish to paint pictures. I 'ave the genius, the ent'usiasm. I wish to be disciple of the great Bouguereau. But no. I am dependent for support upon an uncle. He is rich. He is proprietor of the great Hotel Jules Priaulx. My name is also Priaulx. He is not sympathetic. I say, "Uncle, I 'ave the genius, the ent'usiasm. Permit me to paint." He shakes his head. He say, "I will give you position in my hotel, and you shall earn your living." What choice? I weep, but I kill my dreams, and I become cashier at my uncle's hotel at a salary of thirty-five francs a week. I, the artist, become a machine for the changing of money at dam bad salary. What would you? What choice? I am dependent. I go to the hotel, and there I learn to 'ate all animals. Cats especially.

I will tell you the reason. My uncle's hotel is fashionable hotel. Rich Americans, rich Maharajahs, rich people of every nation come to my uncle's hotel. They come, and with them they have brought their pets. Monsieur, it was the existence of a nightmare. Wherever I have looked there are animals. Listen. There is an Indian prince. He has with him two dromedaries. There is also one other Indian prince. With him is a giraffe. The giraffe drink every day one dozen best champagne to keep his coat good. I, the artist, have my bock, and my coat is not good. There is a guest with a young lion. There is a guest with an alligator. But especially there is a cat. He is fat. His name is Alexander. He belongs to an American woman. She is fat. She exhibits him to me. He is wrapped in a silk and fur creation like an opera cloak. Every day she exhibits him. It is "Alexander this" and "Alexander that," till I 'ate Alexander very much. I 'ate all the animals, but especially Alexander.

And so, monsieur, it goes on, day by day, in this hotel that is a Zoological Garden. And every day I 'ate the animals the more. But especially Alexander.

We artists, monsieur, we are martyrs to our nerves. It became insupportable, this thing. Each day it became more insupportable. At night I dream of all the animals, one by one—the giraffe, the two dromedaries, the young lion, the alligator, and Alexander. Especially Alexander. You have 'eard of men who cannot endure the society of a cat—how they cry out and jump in the air if a cat is among those present. *Hein?* Your Lord Roberts? Precisely, monsieur. I have read so much. Listen, then. I am become by degrees almost like 'im. I do not cry out and jump in the air when I see the cat Alexander, but I grind my teeth and I 'ate 'im.

Yes, I am the sleeping volcano, and one morning, monsieur, I have suffered the eruption. It is like this. I shall tell you.

Not only at that time am I the martyr to nerves, but also to toothache. That morning I 'ave 'ad the toothache very bad. I 'ave been in pain the most terrible. I groan as I add up the figures in my book.

As I groan I 'ear a voice.

"Say good morning to M. Priaulx, Alexander." Conceive my emotions, monsieur, when this fat, beastly cat is placed before me upon my desk!

It put the cover upon it. No, that is not the phrase. The lid. It put the lid upon it. All my smothered 'atred of the animal burst forth. I could no longer conceal my 'atred.

I rose. I was terrible. I seized 'im by the tail. I flung him—I did not know where. I did not care. Not then. Afterwards, yes, but not then.

Your Longfellow has a poem. "I shot an arrow into the air. It fell to earth, I know not where." And then he has found it. The arrow in the 'eart of a friend. Am I right? Also was that the tragedy with me. I flung the cat Alexander. My uncle, on whom I am dependent, is passing at the moment. He has received the cat in the middle of his face.

My companion, with the artist's instinct for the "curtain," paused. He looked round the brightly lit restaurant. From every side arose the clatter of knife and fork, and the clear, sharp note of those who drank soup. In a distant corner a small waiter with a large voice was calling the cook names through the speaking-tube. It was a cheerful scene, but it brought no cheer to my companion. He sighed heavily and resumed:

I 'urry over that painful scene. There is blooming row. My uncle is 'ot-tempered man. The cat is 'eavy cat. I 'ave thrown 'im very hard, for my nerves and my toothache and my 'atred 'ave given me the giant's strength. Alone is this enough to enrage my 'ot-tempered uncle. I am there in his hotel, you will understand, as cashier, not as cat-thrower. And now, besides all this, I have insulted valuable patron. She 'ave left the hotel that day.

There are no doubts in my mind as to the outcome. With certainty I await my *conge*. And after painful scene I get it. I am to go. At once. He 'ave assured the angry American woman that I go at once.

He has called me into his private office. "Jean," he has said to me, at the end of other things, "you are a fool, dolt, no-good imbecile. I give you good place in my hotel, and you spend your time flinging cats. I will 'ave no more of you. But even now I cannot forget that you are my dear brother's child. I will now give you one thousand francs and never see you again."

I have thanked him, for to me it is wealth. Not before have I ever had one thousand francs of my own.

I go out of the hotel. I go to a cafe and order a bock. I smoke a cigarette. It is necessary that I think out plans. Shall I with my one thousand francs rent a studio in the Quarter and commence my life as artist? No. I have still the genius, the ent'usiasm, but I have not the training. To train myself to paint pictures I must study long, and even one thousand francs will not last for ever. Then what shall I do? I do not know. I order one other bock, and smoke more cigarettes, but still I do not know.

And then I say to myself, "I will go back to my uncle, and plead with him. I will seize favourable opportunity. I will approach him after dinner when he is in good temper. But for that I must be close at hand. I must be—what's your expression?—"Johnny-on-the-spot."

My mind is made up. I have my plan.

I have gone back to my uncle's hotel, and I have engaged not too expensive bedroom. My uncle does not know. He still is in his private office. I secure my room.

I dine cheaply that night, but I go to theatre and also to supper after the theatre, for have I not my thousand francs? It is late when I reach my bedroom.

I go to bed. I go to sleep.

But I do not sleep long. I am awakened by a voice.

It is a voice that says, "Move and I shoot! Move and I shoot!" I lie still. I do not move. I am courageous, but I am unarmed.

And the voice says again, "Move and I shoot!" Is it robbers? Is it some marauder who has made his way to my room to plunder me?

I do not know. Per'aps I think yes.

"Who are you?" I have asked.

There is no answer.

I take my courage in my 'ands. I leap from my bed. I dash for the door. No pistol has been fire. I have reached the passage, and have shouted for assistance.

Hotel officials run up. Doors open. "What is it?" voices cry.

"There is in my room an armed robber," I assure them.

And then I have found—no, I am mistaken. My door, you will understand, is open. And as I have said these words, a large green parrot comes 'opping out. My assassin is nothing but a green parrot.

"Move and I shoot!" it has said to those gathered in the corridor. It then has bitten me in the 'and and passed on.

I am chagrined, monsieur. But only for a moment. Then I forget my chagrin. For a voice from a door that 'as opened says with joy, "It is my Polly, which I 'ave this evening lost!"

I turn. I gasp for admiration. It is a beautiful lady in a pink dressing-gown which 'ave spoken these words.

She has looked at me. I 'ave looked at her. I forget everything but that she is adorable. I forget those who stand by. I forget that the parrot has bitten me in the 'and. I forget even that I am standing there in pyjamas, with on my feet nothing. I can only gaze at her and worship.

I have found words.

"Mademoiselle," I have said, "I am rejoiced that I have been the means of restoring to you your bird."

She has thanked me with her eyes, and then with words also. I am bewitched. She is divine. I care not that my feet are cold. I could wish to stand there talking all night.

She has given a cry of dismay.

"Your 'and! It is wounded!"

I look at my 'and. Yes, it is bleeding, where the bird 'ave bitten it.

"Tchut, mademoiselle," I have said. "It is a bagatelle."

But no. She is distressed. She is what your poet Scott 'ave said, a ministering angel thou. She 'ave torn her 'andkerchief and is binding up my wound. I am enchanted. Such beauty! Such kindness! 'Ardly can I resist to fall on my knees before 'er and declare my passion.

We are twin souls. She has thanked me again. She has scolded the parrot. She has smiled upon me as she retires to her room. It is enough. Nothing is said, but I am a man of sensibility and discernment, and I understand that she will not be offended if I seek to renew our friendship on a more suitable occasion.

The doors shut. The guests have returned to bed, the hotel servants to their duties. And I go back to my room. But not to sleep. It is very late, but I do not sleep. I lie awake and think of 'er.

You will conceive, Monsieur, with what mixed feelings I descend next morning. On the one 'and, I must keep the sharp look-out for my uncle, for 'im I must avoid till he shall have—what do you say in your idiom? Yes, I have it—simmered down and tucked in his shirt. On the other 'and, I must watch for my lady of the parrot. I count the minutes till we shall meet again.

I avoid my uncle with success, and I see 'er about the hour of *dejeuner*. She is talking to old gentleman. I have bowed. She have smiled and motioned me to approach.

"Father," she has said, "this is the gentleman who caught Polly."

We have shaken hands. He is indulgent papa. He has smiled and thanked me also. We have confided to each other our names. He is English. He owns much land in England. He has been staying in Paris. He is rich. His name is 'Enderson. He addresses his daughter, and call her Marion. In my 'eart I also call her Marion. You will perceive that I am, as you say, pretty far gone.

The hour of *dejeuner* has arrived. I entreat them to be my guests. I can run to it, you understand, for there are still in my pockets plenty of my uncle's francs. They consent. I am in 'eaven.

All is well. Our friendship has progressed with marvellous speed. The old gentleman and I are swiftly the dear old pals. I 'ave confided to 'im my dreams of artistic fame, and he has told me 'ow much he dislikes your Lloyd George. He has mentioned that he and Miss Marion depart for London that day. I am desolate. My face tumbles. He has observed my despair. He has invited me to visit them in London.

Imagine my chagrin. To visit them in London is the one thing I desire to do. But how? I accept gratefully, but I ask myself how it is to be done? I am poor blighter with no profession and nine 'undred francs. He 'as taken it for granted that I am wealthy.

What shall I do? I spend the afternoon trying to form a plan. And then I am resolved. I will go to my uncle and say: "Uncle, I have the magnificent chance to marry the daughter of wealthy English landowner. Already I 'ave her gratitude. Soon—for I am young, 'andsome, debonair—I shall 'ave her love. Give me one more chance, uncle. Be decent old buck, and put up the money for this affair."

These words I have resolved to say to my uncle.

I go back to the hotel. I enter his private office. I reveal no secret when I say that he is not cordial.

"Ten thousand devils!" he has cried. "What do you here?"

I 'asten to tell him all, and plead with him to be decent old buck. He does not believe.

Who is he? he asks. This English landowner? How did I meet him? And where?

I tell him. He is amazed.

"You 'ad the infernal impudence to take room in my hotel?" he has cried.

I am crafty. I am diplomat.

"Where else, dear uncle?" I say. "In all Paris there is no such 'ome from 'ome. The cuisine—marvellous! The beds—of rose-leaves! The attendance—superb! If only for one night, I have said to myself, I must stay in this of all hotels."

I 'ave—what do you say?—touched the spot.

"In what you say," he has said, more calmly, "there is certainly something. It is a good hotel, this of mine!"

The only hotel, I have assured him. The Meurice? *Chut!* I snap my fingers. The Ritz? Bah! Once again I snap my fingers. "In all Paris there is no hotel like this."

He 'as simmered down. His shirt is tucked in. "Tell me again this plan of yours, Jean."

When I leave 'im we have come to an understanding. It is agreed between us that I am to 'ave one last chance. He will not spoil this promising ship for the 'a'porth of tar. He will give me money for my purpose. But he has said, as we part, if I fail, his 'ands shall be washed of me. He cannot now forget that I am his dear brother's child; but if I fail to accomplish the conquest of the divine Miss Marion, he thinks he will be able to.

It is well. A week later I follow the 'Endersons to London.

For the next few days, monsieur, I am in Paradise. My 'ost has much nice 'ouse in Eaton Square. He is rich, popular. There is much society. And I—I have the *succes fou*. I am young, 'andsome, debonair. I cannot speak the English very well—not so well as I now speak 'im—but I manage. I get along. I am intelligent, amiable. Everyone loves me.

No, not everyone. Captain Bassett, he does not love me. And why? Because he loves the charming Miss Marion, and observes that already I am succeeding with her like a 'ouse on fire. He is *ami de famille*. He is captain in your Garde Ecossais, and my 'ost told me 'e has distinguished himself as soldier pretty much. It may be so. As soldier, per'aps. But at conversation he is not so good. He is quite nice fellow, you understand—'andsome, yes; distinguished, yes. But he does not sparkle. He has not my *verve*, my *elan*. I—how do you say?—I make the rings round him.

But, *Chut*! At that moment I would have made the rings round the 'ole British Army. Yes, and also the Corps Diplomatique. For I am inspired. Love 'as inspired me. I am conqueror.

But I will not weary you, monsieur, with the details of my wooing. You are sympathetic, but I must not weary you. Let us say that I 'ave in four days or five made progress the most remarkable, and proceed to the tragic end.

Almost could I tell it in four words. In them one would say that it is set forth. There was in London at that time popular a song, a comic, vulgar song of the 'Alls, "The Cat Came Back." You 'ave 'eard it? Yes? I 'eard it myself, and without emotion. It had no sinister warning for me. It did not strike me as omen. Yet, in those four words, monsieur, is my tragedy.

How? I shall tell you. Every word is a sword twisted in my 'eart, but I shall tell you.

One afternoon we are at tea. All is well. I am vivacious, gay; Miss Marion, charming, gracious. There is present also an aunt, Mr 'Enderson's sister; but 'er I do not much notice. It is to Marion I speak—both with my lips and also with my eyes.

As we sit, Captain Bassett is announced.

He has entered. We have greeted each other politely but coldly, for we are rivals. There is in his manner also a something which I do not much like—a species of suppressed triumph, of elation.

I am uneasy—but only yet vaguely, you will understand. I have not the foreboding that he is about to speak my death-sentence.

He addresses Miss Marion. There is joy in his voice. "Miss 'Enderson," he has said, "I have for you the bally good news. You will remember, isn't it, the cat belonging to the American woman in the hotel at Paris, of which you have spoken to me? Last night at dinner I have been seated beside her. At first I am not certain is it she. Then I say that there cannot be two Mrs Balderstone Rockmettlers in Europe, so I mention to her the cat. And, to cut the long story short, I have ventured to purchase for you as a little present the cat Alexander."

I have uttered a cry of horror, but it is not 'eard because of Miss Marion's cry of joy.

"Oh, Captain Bassett," she has said, "how very splendid of you! Ever since I first saw him have I loved Alexander. I cannot tell you how grateful I am. But it amazes me that you should have been able to induce her to part with 'im. In Paris she has refused all my offers."

He has paused, embarrassed.

"The fact is," he has said, "there is between her and Alexander a certain coolness. He 'as deceived 'er, and she loves him no more. Immediately upon arrival in London, he had the misfortune to 'ave six fine kittens. 'Owever, out of evil cometh good, and I have thus been able to secure 'im for you. 'E is downstairs in a basket!"

Miss Marion 'as rung the bell and commanded for him to be brought instantly.

I will not describe the meeting, monsieur. You are sympathetic. You will understand my feelings. Let us 'urry on.

Figure yourself, monsieur, to what extent I was now 'arassed. I am artist. I am a man of nerves. I cannot be gay, brilliant, debonair in the presence of a cat. Yet always the cat is there. It is terrible.

I feel that I am falling behind in the race. 'Er gratitude has made her the more gracious to Captain Bassett. She smiles upon him. And, like Chanticleer at the sight of the sun, he flaps his wings and crows. He is no longer the silent listener. It is I who have become the silent listener.

I have said to myself that something must be done.

Chance has shown me the way. One afternoon I am by fortune alone in the 'all. In his cage the parrot Polly is 'opping. I address him through the bars.

"Move and I shoot!" he has cried.

The tears have filled my eyes. 'Ow it has brought the 'ole scene back to me!

As I weep, I perceive the cat Alexander approaching.

I have formed a plan. I have opened the cage-door and released the parrot. The cat, I think, will attack the parrot of which Miss 'Enderson is so fond. She will love him no more. He will be expelled.

He paused. I suppose my face must have lost some of its alleged sympathy as he set forth this fiendish plot. Even Percy the bluebottle seemed shocked. He had settled on the sugar-bowl, but at these words he rose in a marked manner and left the table.

"You do not approve?" he said.

I shrugged my shoulders.

"It's no business of mine," I said. "But don't you think yourself it was playing it a bit low down? Didn't the thought present itself to you in a shadowy way that it was rather rough on the bird?"

"It did, monsieur. But what would you? It is necessary to break eggs in order to make an omelette. All is fair, you say, in love and war, and this was both. Moreover, you must understand, I do not dictate his movements to the parrot. He is free agent. I do but open the cage-door. Should he 'op out and proceed to the floor where is the cat, that is his affair. I shall continue, yes?"

Alors! I open the cage-door and disappear discreetly. It is not politic that I remain to witness what shall transpire. It is for me to establish an alibi. I go to the drawing-room, where I remain.

At dinner that night Mr 'Enderson has laughed.

"In the 'all this afternoon," he has said, "I have seen by chance the dickens of a funny occurrence. That parrot of yours, Marion, had escaped once again from its cage and was 'aving an argument with that cat which Captain Bassett has given to you."

"Oh! I hope that Alexander 'as not hurt poor Polly, of whom I am very fond," she has said.

"The affair did not come to blows," has said Mr 'Enderson. "You may trust that bird to take care of himself, my dear. When I came upon the scene the cat was crouching in a corner, with his fur bristling and his back up, while Polly, standing before 'im, was telling 'im not to move or he would shoot. Nor did he move, till I 'ad seized the parrot and replaced him in the cage, when he shot upstairs like a streak of lightning. By sheer force of character that excellent bird 'ad won the bloodless victory. I drink to 'im!"

You can conceive my emotion as I listen to this tale. I am like the poet's mice and men whose best-kid schemes have gone away. I am baffled. I am discouraged. I do not know what I shall do. I must find another plan, but I do not know what.

How shall I remove the cat? Shall I kill 'im? No, for I might be suspect.

Shall I 'ire someone to steal 'im? No, for my accomplice might betray me.

Shall I myself steal 'im? Ah! that is better. That is a very good plan.

Soon I have it perfected, this plan. Listen, monsieur; it is as follows. It is simple, but it is good. I will await my opportunity. I will remove the cat secretly from the 'ouse. I will take him to an office of the District Messenger Boys. I will order a messenger to carry him at once to the Cats' House, and to request M. le Directeur immediately to destroy him. It is a simple plan, but it is good.

I carry it through without a 'itch. It is not so difficult to secure the cat. 'E is asleep in the drawing-room. There is nobody at hand. I have in my bedroom a 'at-box which I have brought from Paris. I have brought it with me to the drawing-room. I have placed in it the cat. I have escaped from the 'ouse. The cat has uttered a cry, but none has 'eard. I have reached the office of the District Messenger Boys. I have 'anded over the cat in its box. The manager is courteous, sympathetic. A messenger has started in a cab for the Cats' House. I have breathed a sigh of relief. I am saved.

That is what I say to myself as I return. My troubles are over, and once more I can be gay, debonair, vivacious with Miss Marion, for no longer will there be present the cat Alexander to 'arass me.

When I have returned there is commotion in the 'ouse. I pass on the stairs domestics calling "Puss, puss!" The butler is chirruping loudly and poking beneath the furniture with a umbrella. All is confusion and agitation.

In the drawing-room is Miss Marion. She is distressed.

"Nowhere," she has said, "can there be found the cat Alexander of whom I am so fond. Nowhere in the 'ouse is he, Where can he be? He is lost."

I am gentle, sympathetic. I endeavour to console her. I 'int to her that am I not sufficient substitute for a beastly cat? She is, however, inconsolable. I must be patient. I must wait my time.

Captain Bassett is announced. He is informed of what has 'appened. He is distressed. He has the air as if he, too, would endeavour to be gentle, sympathetic. But I am Johnny-on-the-spot. I stay till he 'as gone.

Next day again it is "Puss, puss!" Again the butler has explored under the furniture with the umbrella. Again Miss Marion is distressed. Again 'ave I endeavoured to console.

This time I think I am not so unsuccessful. I am, you understand, young, 'andsome, sympathetic. In another two ticks I am about to seize 'er 'and and declare my passion.

But, before I can do so, Captain Bassett is announced.

I gaze at him as at unsuccessful rival. I am confident. I am conqueror. Ah, I little know! It is in the moments of our highest 'ope, monsieur, that we are destroyed.

Captain Bassett, he, too, 'as the air of the conqueror.

He has begun to speak.

"Miss 'Enderson," he has said, "I have once more the bally good news. I rather fancy that I 'ave tracked down the missing Alexander, do you not know?"

Miss Marion 'as cried out with joy. But I am calm, for is not Alexander already yesterday destroyed?

"It is like this," he has resumed. "I have thought to myself where is lost cat most likely to be? And I have answered, 'In the Cats' House.' I go this morning to the Cats' House, and there I see a cat which is either lost Alexander or his living image. Exactly is he the same to all appearances as the lost Alexander. But there is, when I try to purchase 'im, some curious 'itch which they do not explain. They must 'ave time, they say, to consider. They cannot at once decide."

"Why, what nonsense!" Miss Marion 'ave cried. "If the cat is my cat, surely then must they return 'im to me! Come," she has said, "let us all three at once in a taxi-cab go to the Cats' House. If the all three of us identify the lost Alexander, then must they return 'im."

Monsieur, I am uneasy. I have foreboding. But I go. What choice? We go in a taxi-cab to the Cats' House.

The *directeur* is courteous and sympathetic. He has introduced us to the cat, and my 'eart 'as turned to water, for it is Alexander. Why has he not been destroyed?

The *directeur* is speaking. I 'ear him in a dream.

"If you identify 'im as your cat, miss," he has said, "the matter is ended. My 'esitation when you, sir, approached me this morning on the matter was due to the fact that a messenger was sent with instructions that he be destroyed at once."

"Rather rough, wasn't it, that, on the messenger, yes," Captain Bassett has said. He is facetious, you understand, for he is conqueror.

I am silent. I am not facetious. For already I feel—how do you say?—my fowl is cooked.

"Not the messenger, sir," the *directeur* has said. "You 'ave misunderstood me. It was the cat which was to be destroyed as per instructions of the anonymous sender."

"Who could have played such a wicked trick?" Miss Marion has asked, indignant.

The *directeur* has stooped, and from behind a table he has brought a 'at-box.

"In this," he has said, "the above animal was conveyed. But with it was no accompanying letter. The sender was anonymous."

"Per'aps," Captain Bassett has said—and still more in a dream I 'ear him—"per'aps on the 'at-box there is some bally name or other, do you not know—what?"

I clutch at the table. The room is spinning round and round. I have no stomach—only emptiness.

"Why, bless me," the *directeur* has said, "you're quite right, sir. So there is. Funny of me not to have before observed it. There is a name, and also an address. It is the name of Jean Priaulx, and the address is the Hotel Jules Priaulx, Paris."

My companion stopped abruptly. He passed a handkerchief over his fore-head. With a quick movement he reached for his glass of liqueur brandy and drained it at a gulp.

"Monsieur," he said, "you will not wish me to describe the scene? There is no need for me—*hein?*—to be Zolaesque. You can imagine?"

"She chucked you?" In moments of emotion it is the simplest language that comes to the lips.

He nodded.

"And married Captain Bassett?"

He nodded again.

"And your uncle?" I said. "How did he take it?"

He sighed.

"There was once more," he said, "blooming row, monsieur."

"He washed his hands of you?"

"Not altogether. He was angry, but he gave me one more chance. I am still 'is dear brother's child, and he cannot forget it. An acquaintance of his, a man of letters, a M. Paul Sartines, was in need of a secretary. The post was not well paid, but it was permanent. My uncle insist that I take it. What choice? I took it. It is the post which I still 'old."

He ordered another liqueur brandy and gulped it down.

"The name is familiar to you, monsieur? You 'ave 'eard of M. Sartines?'

"I don't think I have. Who is he?"

"He is a man of letters, a *savant*. For five years he has been occupied upon a great work. It is with that that I assist him by collecting facts for 'is use. I 'ave spent this afternoon in the British Museum collecting facts. Tomorrow I go again. And the next day. And again after that. The book will occupy yet another ten years before it is completed. It is his great work."

"It sounds as if it was," I said. "What's it about?"

He signalled to the waiter.

"*Garcon*, one other liqueur brandy. The book, monsieur, is a *'Istory of the Cat in Ancient Egypt*."

THIRTY-SEVEN

The Cat Came Back

Virginia West

LEONARD RAYMOND WAS TEMPERAMENTALLY A NATURALIST. HAD CIR-
cumstances not compelled him to make a living he would no doubt have
been an Audubon, or a Gray. He spent his spare moments studying the
habits of the living things about town, English sparrows, pigeons, stray
cats, homeless dogs, and so forth. Old man Peterkin, whose wife kept
the boarding-house at which Raymond was getting his meals, who did
nothing but collect the board bills, grow fat, and hold the position of
church deacon, had told him that the crows in the cupola of the Eutaw
Place synagogue had been nesting there for eleven years. Raymond did
not know whether to regard that as an interesting item about crows, or
as evidence against Mr. Peterkin's veracity. However, Mr. Peterkin and the
crows have nothing to do with this story.

In the backyard of the Linden Avenue house in which he lived with
his married sister Raymond raised flowers, and on Sundays and holidays
he would often go to the country to study the wild flowers and the birds.

One summer evening he sat in the backyard among the flowers. He
was hot and lonesome, the thermometer being close to ninety, the family
being out of town, and no vacation for himself in sight. To-morrow, he
reflected, he would return to his post of teller in the bank, and hand out
more money than he would ever own in a lifetime; the day after he would
do the same thing——

313

His melancholy reflections were broken in upon by what seemed to be a ball of fire on top of the tall board fence. In an instant it disappeared, and he saw the long black form of a cat slide down the fence, and light in the yard. The beast went to a garbage can in the corner of the yard, sniffed about it, observed that the lid was on, and then, turning the gleaming ball upon Raymond, sprang up the fence and disappeared.

The same thing happened the next evening. On the third evening when the cat appeared Raymond advanced cautiously, and tried to be friendly. The cat hesitated, but when the man's hand was almost on him he streaked up, and over the fence.

The following evening when Raymond walked uptown from the bank, as he approached Richmond market he thought of the cat, and stopping at a stall bought a small portion of meat.

The meat was put on the ground near the fence on which at the regular time the cat appeared. The eye gleamed. Raymond was wondering why both eyes did not gleam when the cat seemed to fall straight down upon the meat. Raymond sat as still as a stone, and heard the meat crunching between the cat's jaws. The animal was licking its chops when he advanced—it met him halfway, and while Raymond rubbed his fur, the cat purred. Sitting down upon a bench, the cat leaped into his lap, curled up, and settled down for a nap. Then it was that he found about the cat's neck a small chain with a tag on it.

When he went into the house the cat followed him, and by the gas light he read on the tag a Madison Avenue address. Also he observed that the cat had but one eye, and forthwith he christened him Cyclops. He wondered why a person who thought enough of the cat to provide him with a chain and tag should have left him to search for his victuals in alleys and backyards like an ordinary stray.

Cyclops stuck by Raymond like a twin brother. And every evening when Raymond came from business he stopped in Richmond market and bought meat for Cyclops. One day the man in the stall asked him if he were a family man.

One Sunday morning Raymond strolled across Eutaw Place and up to the Madison Avenue address. The house was closed for the summer, but the policeman on the post told him who lived there.

Summer was nearly at an end when Raymond happened to see in the paper that the people at the Madison Avenue house had returned to town. Now, Raymond was an honest man—had he been anything else he would not have been allowed to handle the bank's money, so on Saturday evening with Cyclops under his arm, he sadly went up Madison Avenue to return the cat to his lawful owner. Boys on the street made personal remarks about the man and the cat, and Cyclops's great eye turned green with wrath as he glared at them.

A woman answered his ring. She looked and gasped. Before Raymond could explain she thrust her head into the hall and shouted in strident tones:

"Come heah, Miss 'Liza! Bress de Lawd ef heah ain't yo' cat!"

In a moment appeared the prettiest girl that Raymond's eyes had ever rested upon. She had blue eyes and a mass of golden hair. Though comparatively young, and quite in the eligible class, Raymond was not a lady's man. With much embarrassment he told the history of the cat.

While she held Cyclops to her bosom, the girl explained that she had left him with a friend to keep for her during the summer, and he had run away. She had given him up for lost.

"Dat cat know whut he doin,'" snickered the woman.

Raymond went off catless. All the way home he was thinking of a way by which he might call on the beautiful Miss 'Liza. Sunday afternoon he went out to the country, to the woods, the flowers, the birds, and his soul was full of poetry and his mind of thoughts of the girl.

That evening old Cyclops was back on the fence! His great eye had a gleam of mischievousness. Down the fence he slid, and straight to Raymond, who decided that he must take the cat back to his owner immediately.

While Cyclops prowled about the parlor with tail erect, rubbing against every article of furniture, Raymond talked to Miss 'Liza.

Every evening Cyclops returned to Raymond, and every evening he as promptly took him home. Thus time passed from autumn into early winter.

One evening sitting before the little wood fire in her parlour, Raymond said to Miss 'Liza: "I don't see but one way to keep our cat in one place!"

Then Miss 'Liza blushed, and said she didn't see but one way either!

Then he kissed her!

And old Cyclops rubbed against both of them and purred to beat the band.

How Diana Made the Stars and the Rain

Charles G. Leland

DIANA WAS THE FIRST CREATED BEFORE ALL CREATION; IN HER WERE all things; out of herself, the first darkness, she divided herself; into darkness and light she was divided. Lucifer, her brother and son, herself and her other half, was the light.

And when Diana saw that the light was so beautiful, the light which was her other half, her brother Lucifer, she yearned for it with exceeding great desire. Wishing to receive the light again into her darkness, to swallow it up in rapture, in delight, she trembled with desire. This desire was the Dawn.

But Lucifer, the light, fled from her, and would not yield to her wishes; he was the light which flies into the most distant parts of heaven, the mouse which flies before the cat.

Then Diana went to the fathers of the Beginning, to the mothers, the spirits who were before the first spirit, and lamented unto them that she could not prevail with Lucifer. And they praised her for her courage, they told her that to rise she must fall; to become the chief of goddesses she must become a mortal.

And in the ages, in the course of time, when the world was made, Diana went on earth, as did Lucifer, who had fallen, and Diana taught magic and sorcery, whence came witches and fairies and goblins—all that is like man, yet not mortal.

And it came thus that Diana took the form of a cat. Her brother had a cat whom he loved beyond all creatures, and it slept every night on his bed, a cat beautiful beyond all other creatures, a fairy: he did not know it.

Diana prevailed with the cat to change forms with her, so she lay with her brother, and in the darkness assumed her own form, and so by Lucifer became the mother of Aradia. But when in the morning he found that he lay by his sister, and that light had been conquered by darkness, Lucifer was extremely angry; but Diana sang to him a spell, a song of power, and he was silent, the song of the night which soothes to sleep; he could say nothing. So Diana with her wiles of witchcraft so charmed him that he yielded to her love. This was the first fascination, she hummed the song, it was as the buzzing of bees (or a top spinning round), a spinning-wheel spinning life. She spun the lives of all men; all things were spun from the wheel of Diana. Lucifer turned the wheel.

Diana was not known to the witches and spirits, the fairies and elves who dwell in desert place, the goblins, as their mother; she hid herself in humility and was a mortal, but by her will she rose again above all. She had such passion for witchcraft, and became so powerful therein, that her greatness could not be hidden.

And thus it came to pass one night, at the meeting of all the sorceresses and fairies, she declared that she would darken the heavens and turn all the stars into mice.

All those who were present said—

"If thou canst do such a strange thing, having risen to such power, thou shalt be our queen."

Diana went into the street; she took the bladder of an ox and a piece of witch-money, which has an edge like a knife—with such money witches cut the earth from men's foot-tracks—and she cut the earth, and with it and many mice she filled the bladder, and blew into the bladder till it burst.

And there came a great marvel, for the earth which was in the bladder became the round heaven above, and for three days there was a great rain; the mice became stars or rain. And having made the heaven and the stars and the rain, Diana became Queen of the Witches; she was the cat who ruled the star-mice, the heaven and the rain.

Ye Marvellous Legend of Tom Connor's Cat

Samuel Lover

THERE WAS A MAN IN THESE PARTS, SIR, YOU MUST KNOW, CALLED TOM Connor, and he had a cat that was equal to any dozen of rat-traps, and he was proud of the baste, and with rayson; for she was worth her weight in gold to him in saving his sacks of meal from the thievery of the rats and mice; for Tom was an extensive dealer in corn, and influenced the rise and fall of that article in the market, to the extent of a full dozen of sacks at a time, which he either kept or sold, as the spirit of free trade or monopoly came over him.

Indeed, at one time, Tom had serious thoughts of applying to the government for a military force to protect his granary when there was a threatened famine in the county.

"Pooh! pooh! sir," said the matter-of-fact little man: "as if a dozen sacks could be of the smallest consequence in a whole county—pooh! pooh!"

"Well, sir," said Murphy, "I can't help if you don't believe; but it's truth what I am telling you, and pray don't interrupt me, though you may not believe; by the time the story's done you'll have heard more wonderful things than that,—and besides, remember you're a stranger in these parts, and have no notion of the extraordinary things, physical, metaphysical, and magical, which constitute the idiosyncrasy of rural destiny."

The little man did not know the meaning of Murphy's last sentence—nor Murphy either; but, having stopped the little man's throat with big words, he proceeded—

"This cat, sir, you must know, was a great pet, and was so up to everything, that Tom swore she was a'most like a Christian, only she couldn't speak, and had so sensible a look in her eyes, that he was sartin sure the cat knew every word that was said to her.

"Well, she used to sit by him at breakfast every morning, and the eloquent cock of her tail, as she used to rub against his leg, said, 'Give me some milk, Tom Connor,' as plain as print, and the plenitude of her purr afterwards spoke a gratitude beyond language. Well, one morning, Tom was going to the neighbouring town to market, and he had promised the wife to bring home shoes to the childre' out o' the price of the corn; and sure enough, before he sat down to breakfast, there was Tom taking the measure of the children's feet, by cutting notches on a bit of stick; and the wife gave him so many cautions about getting a 'nate fit' for 'Billy's purty feet,' that Tom, in his anxiety to nick the closest possible measure, cut off the child's toe.

"That disturbed the harmony of the party, and Tom was obliged to breakfast alone, while the mother was endeavouring to cure Billy; in short, trying to make a heel of his toe.

"Well, sir, all the time Tom was taking measure for the shoes, the cat was observing him with that luminous peculiarity of eye for which her tribe is remarkable; and when Tom sat down to breakfast the cat rubbed up against him more vigorously than usual; but Tom, being bewildered between his expected gain in corn and the positive loss of his child's toe, kept never minding her, until the cat, with a sort of caterwauling growl, gave Tom a dab of her claws, that went clean through his leathers, and a little further. 'Wow!' says Tom, with a jump, clapping his hand on the part, and rubbing it, 'by this and that, you drew the blood out o' me,' says Tom; 'you wicked divil—tish!—go along!' says he, making a kick at her.

"With that the cat gave a reproachful look at him, and her eyes glared just like a pair of mail-coach lamps in a fog. With that, sir, the cat, with a mysterious 'mi-ow' fixed a most penetrating glance on Tom, and distinctly uttered his name.

"Tom felt every hair on his head as stiff as a pump-handle; and scarcely crediting his ears, he returned a searching look at the cat, who very quietly proceeded in a sort of nasal twang—

"'Tom Connor,' says she.

"'The Lord be good to me!' says Tom, 'if it isn't spakin' she is!'

"'Tom Connor,' says she again.

"'Yes, ma'am,' says Tom.

"'Come here,' says she; 'whisper—I want to talk to you, Tom,' says she, 'the laste taste in private,' says she—rising on her hams, and beckoning him with her paw out o' the door, with a wink and a toss o' the head aiqual to a milliner.

"Well, as you may suppose, Tom didn't know whether he was on his head or his heels, but he followed the cat, and off she went and squatted herself under the edge of a little paddock at the back of Tom's house; and as he came round the corner, she held up her paw again, and laid it on her mouth, as much as to say, 'Be cautious, Tom.' Well, divil a word Tom could say at all, with the fright, so up he goes to the cat, and says she—

"'Tom,' says she, 'I have a great respect for you, and there's something I must tell you, becase you're losing character with your neighbours,' says she, 'by your goin's on,' says she, 'and it's out o' the respect that I have for you, that I must tell you,' says she.

"'Thank you, ma'am,' says Tom.

"'You're goin' off to the town,' says she, 'to buy shoes for the childre," says she, 'and never thought o' gettin' me a pair.'

"'You!' says Tom.

"'Yis, me, Tom Connor,' says she; 'and the neighbours wondhers that a respectable man like you allows your cat to go about the counthry bare-futted,' says she.

"'Is it a cat to ware shoes?' says Tom.

"'Why not?' says she; 'doesn't horses ware shoes?—and I have a prettier foot than a horse, I hope,' says she, with a toss of her head.

"'Faix, she spakes like a woman; so proud of her feet,' says Tom to himself, astonished, as you may suppose, but pretending never to think it remarkable all the time; and so he went on discoursin'; and says he, 'It's thrue for you, ma'am,' says he, 'that horses wares shoes—but that stands to rayson, ma'am, you see—seeing the hardship their feet has to go through on the hard roads.'

"'And how do you know what hardship my feet has to go through?' says the cat, mighty sharp.

"'But, ma'am,' says Tom, 'I don't well see how you could fasten a shoe on you,' says he.

"'Lave that to me,' says the cat.

"'Did any one ever stick walnut shells on you, pussy?' says Tom, with a grin.

"'Don't be disrespectful, Tom Connor,' says the cat, with a frown.

"'I ax your pard'n, ma'am,' says he, 'but as for the horses you wor spakin' about wearin' shoes, you know their shoes is fastened on with nails, and how would your shoes be fastened on?'

"'Ah, you stupid thief!' says she, 'haven't I illigant nails o' my own?' and with that she gave him a dab of her claw, that made him roar."

"'Ow! murdher!' says he.

"'Now, no more of your palaver, Misther Connor,' says the cat; 'just be off and get me the shoes.'

"'Tare an' ouns!' says Tom, 'what'll become o' me if I'm to get shoes for my cats?' says he, 'for you increase your family four times a year, and you have six or seven every time,' says he; 'and then you must all have two pair a piece—wirra! wirra!—I'll be ruined in shoe-leather,' says Tom.

"'No more o' your stuff,' says the cat; 'don't be stand in' here undher the hedge talkin,' or we'll lose our karacthers—for I've remarked your wife is jealous, Tom.'

"'Pon my sowl, that's thrue,' says Tom, with a smirk.

"'More fool she,' says the cat, 'for, 'pon my conscience, Tom, you're as ugly as if you wor bespoke.'

"Off ran the cat with these words, leaving Tom in amazement. He said nothing to the family, for fear of fright'ning them, and off he went to the town as he pretended—for he saw the cat watching him through a hole in the hedge; but when he came to a turn at the end of the road, the dickings a mind he minded the market, good or bad, but went off to Squire Botherum's, the magisthrit, to sware examinations agen the cat."

"Pooh! pooh!—nonsense!!" broke in the little man, who had listened thus far to Murtough with an expression of mingled wonder and contempt, while the rest of the party willingly gave up the reins to nonsense, and enjoyed Murtough's Legend and their companion's more absurd common sense.

"Don't interrupt him, Goggins," said Mister Wiggins.

"How can you listen to such nonsense?" returned Goggins. "Swear examinations against a cat, indeed! pooh! pooh!"

"My dear sir," said Murtough, "remember this is a fair story, and that the country all around here is full of enchantment. As I was telling you, Tom went off to swear examinations."

"Ay, ay!" shouted all but Goggins; "go on with the story."

"And when Tom was asked to relate the events of the morning, which brought him before Squire Botherum, his brain was so bewildered between his corn, and his cat, and his child's toe, that he made a very confused account of it.

"'Begin your story from the beginning,' said the magistrate to Tom.

"'Well, your honour,' says Tom, 'I was goin' to market this mornin',' to sell the child's corn—I beg your pard'n—my own toes, I mane, sir.'

"'Sell your toes!' said the Squire.

"'No, sir, takin' the cat to market, I mane—'

"'Take a cat to market!' said the Squire. 'You're drunk, man.'

"'No, your honour, only confused a little; for when the toes began to spake to me—the cat, I mane—I was bothered clane—'

"'The cat speak to you!' said the Squire. 'Phew! worse than before—you're drunk, Tom.'

"'No, your honour; it's on the strength of the cat I come to spake to you—'

"'I think it's on the strength of a pint of whisky, Tom—'

"'By the vartue o' my oath, your honour, it's nothin' but the cat.' And so Tom then told him all about the affair, and the Squire was regularly astonished. Just then the bishop of the diocese and the priest of the parish happened to call in, and heard the story; and the bishop and the priest had a tough argument for two hours on the subject; the former swearing she must be a witch; but the priest denying that, and maintaining she was only enchanted; and that part of the argument was afterwards referred to the primate, and subsequently to the conclave at Rome; but the Pope declined interfering about cats, saying he had quite enough to do minding his own bulls.

"'In the meantime, what are we to do with the cat?' says Botherum.

"'Burn her,' says the bishop, 'she's a witch.'

"'Only enchanted,' said the priest—'and the ecclesiastical court maintains that—'

"'Bother the ecclesiastical court!' said the magistrate; 'I can only proceed on the statutes'; and with that he pulled down all the law-books in his library, and hunted the laws from Queen Elizabeth down, and he found that they made laws against everything in Ireland, except a cat. The devil a thing escaped them but a cat, which did not come within the meaning of any act of parliament:—the cats only had escaped.

"'There's the alien act, to be sure,' said the magistrate, 'and perhaps she's a French spy, in disguise.'

"'She spakes like a French spy, sure enough,' says Tom; 'and she was missin,' I remember, all last Spy-Wednesday.'

"'That's suspicious,' says the squire—'but conviction might be difficult; and I have a fresh idea,' says Botherum.

"'Faith, it won't keep fresh long, this hot weather,' says Tom; 'so your honour had betther make use of it at wanst.'

"'Right,' says Botherum,—'we'll make her subject to the game laws; we'll hunt her,' says he.

"'Ow!—elegant!' says Tom;—'we'll have a brave run out of her.'

"'Meet me at the cross roads,' says the Squire, 'in the morning, and I'll have the hounds ready.'

"Well, off Tom went home; and he was racking his brain what excuse he could make to the cat for not bringing the shoes; and at last he hit one off, just as he saw her cantering up to him, half-a-mile before he got home.

"'Where's the shoes, Tom?' says she.

"'I have not got them to-day, ma'am,' says he.

"'Is that the way you keep your promise, Tom?' says she;—'I'll tell you what it is, Tom—I'll tare the eyes out o' the childre' if you don't get me shoes.'

"'Whisht! whisht!' says Tom, frightened out of his life for his children's eyes. 'Don't be in a passion, pussy. The shoemaker said he had not a shoe in his shop, nor a last that would make one to fit you; and he says, I must bring you into the town for him to take your measure.'

"'And when am I to go?' says the cat, looking savage.

"'To-morrow,' says Tom.

"'It's well you said that, Tom,' said the cat, 'or the devil an eye I'd leave in your family this night'—and off she hopped.

"Tom thrimbled at the wicked look she gave.

"'Remember!' says she, over the hedge, with a bitter caterwaul.

"'Never fear,' says Tom. Well, sure enough, the next mornin' there was the cat at cock-crow, licking herself as nate as a new pin, to go into the town, and out came Tom with a bag undher his arm, and the cat afther him.

"'Now git into this, and I'll carry you into the town,' says Tom, opening the bag.

"'Sure I can walk with you,' says the cat.

"'Oh, that wouldn't do,' says Tom; 'the people in the town is curious and slandherous people, and sure it would rise ugly remarks if I was seen with a cat afther me:—a dog is a man's companion by nature, but cats does not stand to rayson.'

"Well, the cat, seeing there was no use in argument, got into the bag, and off Tom set to the cross roads with the bag over his shoulder, and he came up, quite innocent-like, to the corner, where the Squire, and his huntsman, and the hounds, and a pack o' people were waitin.' Out came the Squire on a sudden, just as if it was all by accident.

"'God save you, Tom,' says he.

"'God save you kindly, sir,' says Tom.

"'What's that bag you have at your back?' says the Squire.

"'Oh, nothin' at all, sir,' says Tom—makin' a face all the time, as much as to say, I have her safe.

"'Oh, there's something in that bag, I think,' says the Squire; 'and you must let me see it.'

"'If you bethray me, Tom Connor,' says the cat in a low voice, 'by this and that I'll never spake to you again!'

"'Pon my honour, sir,' said Tom, with a wink and a twitch of his thumb toward the bag, 'I haven't anything in it.'

"'I have been missing my praties of late,' says the Squire; 'and I'd just like to examine that bag,' says he.

"'Is it doubting my charackther you'd be, sir?' says Tom, pretending to be in a passion.

"'Tom, your sowl!' says the voice in the sack, 'if you let the cat out of the bag, I'll murther you.'

"'An honest man would make no objection to be sarched,' said the Squire; 'and I insist on it,' says he, laying hold o' the bag, and Tom purtending to fight all the time; but, my jewel! before two minutes, they shook the cat out o' the bag, sure enough, and off she went with her tail as big as a sweeping brush, and the Squire, with a thundering view halloo after her, clapt the dogs at her heels, and away they went for the bare life.

"Never was there seen such running as that day—the cat made for a shaking bog, the loneliest place in the whole country, and there the riders were all thrown out, barrin' the huntsman, who had a web-footed horse on purpose for soft places; and the priest, whose horse could go anywhere by reason of the priest's blessing; and, sure enough, the huntsman and his riverence stuck to the hunt like wax; and just as the cat got on the border of the bog, they saw her give a twist as the foremost dog closed with her, for he gave her a nip in the flank.

"Still she went on, however, and headed them well, toward an old mud cabin in the middle of the bog, and there they saw her jump in at the window, and up came the dogs the next minit, and gathered round the house with the most horrid howling ever was heard. The huntsman alighted, and went into the house to turn the cat out again, when what should he see but an old hag lying in bed in the corner?

"'Did you see a cat come in here?' says he.

"'Oh, no—o—o—o!' squealed the old hag, in a trembling voice; 'there's no cat here,' says she.

"'Yelp, yelp, yelp!' went the dogs outside.

"'Oh, keep the dogs out o' this,' says the old hag—'oh—o—o—o!' and the huntsman saw her eyes glare under the blanket, just like a cat's.

"'Hillo!' says the huntsman, pulling down the blanket—and what should he see but the old hag's flank all in a gore of blood.

"'Ow, ow! you old divil—is it you? you ould cat!' says he, opening the door.

"In rushed the dogs—up jumped the old hag, and changing into a cat before their eyes, out she darted through the window again, and made another run for it; but she couldn't escape, and the dogs gobbled her while you could say 'Jack Robinson.' But the most remarkable part of this extraordinary story, gentlemen, is, that the pack was ruined from that day out; for after having eaten the enchanted cat, the devil a thing they would ever hunt afterwards but mice."

FORTY

The Cat the Mouse in Partnership

Anonymous

A CAT HAD MADE ACQUAINTANCE WITH A MOUSE, AND HAD SPOKEN SO much of the great love and friendship she felt for her, that at last the Mouse consented to live in the same house with her, and to go shares in the housekeeping. "But we must provide for the winter or else we shall suffer hunger," said the Cat. "You, little Mouse, cannot venture everywhere in case you run at last into a trap." This good counsel was followed, and a little pot of fat was bought. But they did not know where to put it. At length, after long consultation, the Cat said, "I know of no place where it could be better put than in the church. No one will trouble to take it away from there. We will hide it in a corner, and we won't touch it till we are in want." So the little pot was placed in safety; but it was not long before the Cat had a great longing for it, and said to the Mouse, "I wanted to tell you, little Mouse, that my cousin has a little son, white with brown spots, and she wants me to be godmother to it. Let me go out to-day, and do you take care of the house alone."

"Yes, go certainly," replied the Mouse, "and when you eat anything good, think of me; I should very much like a drop of the red christening wine."

But it was all untrue. The Cat had no cousin, and had not been asked to be godmother. She went straight to the church, slunk to the little pot of fat, began to lick it, and licked the top off. Then she took a walk on the roofs of the town, looked at the view, stretched herself out in the sun,

329

and licked her lips whenever she thought of the little pot of fat. As soon as it was evening she went home again.

"Ah, here you are again!" said the Mouse; "you must certainly have had an enjoyable day."

"It went off very well," answered the Cat.

"What was the child's name? asked the Mouse.

"Top Off," said the Cat drily.

"Topoff!" echoed the Mouse, "it is indeed a wonderful and curious name. Is it in your family?"

"What is there odd about it?" said the Cat. "It is not worse than Breadthief, as your godchild is called."

Not long after this another great longing came over the Cat. She said to the Mouse, "You must again be kind enough to look after the house alone, for I have been asked a second time to stand godmother, and as this child has a white ring round its neck, I cannot refuse."

The kind Mouse agreed, but the Cat slunk under the town wall to the church, and ate up half of the pot of fat. "Nothing tastes better," said she, "than what one eats by oneself," and she was very much pleased with her day's work. When she came home the Mouse asked, "What was this child called?"

"Half Gone," answered the Cat.

"Halfgone! what a name! I have never heard it in my life. I don't believe it is in the calendar."

Soon the Cat's mouth began to water once more after her licking business. "All good things in threes," she said to the Mouse; "I have again to stand godmother. The child is quite black, and has very white paws, but not a single white hair on its body. This only happens once in two years, so you will let me go out?"

"Topoff! Halfgone!" repeated the Mouse, "they are such curious names; they make me very thoughtful."

"Oh, you sit at home in your dark grey coat and your long tail," said the Cat, "and you get fanciful. That comes of not going out in the day."

The Mouse had a good cleaning out while the Cat was gone, and made the house tidy; but the greedy Cat ate the fat every bit up.

"When it is all gone one can be at rest," she said to herself, and at night she came home sleek and satisfied. The Mouse asked at once after the third child's name.

"It won't please you any better," said the Cat, "he was called Clean Gone."

"Cleangone!" repeated the Mouse. "I do not believe that name has been printed any more than the others. Cleangone! What can it mean?" She shook her head, curled herself up, and went to sleep.

From this time on no one asked the Cat to stand godmother; but when the winter came and there was nothing to be got outside, the Mouse remembered their provision and said, "Come, Cat, we will go to our pot of fat which we have stored away; it will taste very good."

"Yes, indeed," answered the Cat; "it will taste as good to you as if you stretched your thin tongue out of the window."

They started off, and when they reached it they found the pot in its place, but quite empty!

"Ah," said the Mouse, "now I know what has happened! It has all come out! You are a true friend to me! You have eaten it all when you stood godmother; first the top off, then half of it gone, then——"

"Will you be quiet!" screamed the Cat. "Another word and I will eat you up."

"Clean-gone" was already on the poor Mouse's tongue, and scarcely was it out than the Cat made a spring at her, seized and swallowed her.

You see that is the way of the world.

On Cats and Dogs

Jerome K. Jerome

WHAT I'VE SUFFERED FROM THEM THIS MORNING NO TONGUE CAN TELL. It began with Gustavus Adolphus. Gustavus Adolphus (they call him "Gusty" down-stairs for short) is a very good sort of dog when he is in the middle of a large field or on a fairly extensive common, but I won't have him indoors. He means well, but this house is not his size. He stretches himself, and over go two chairs and a what-not. He wags his tail, and the room looks as if a devastating army had marched through it. He breathes, and it puts the fire out.

At dinner-time he creeps in under the table, lies there for awhile, and then gets up suddenly; the first intimation we have of his movements being given by the table, which appears animated by a desire to turn somersaults. We all clutch at it frantically and endeavor to maintain it in a horizontal position; whereupon his struggles, he being under the impression that some wicked conspiracy is being hatched against him, become fearful, and the final picture presented is generally that of an overturned table and a smashed-up dinner sandwiched between two sprawling layers of infuriated men and women.

He came in this morning in his usual style, which he appears to have founded on that of an American cyclone, and the first thing he did was to sweep my coffee-cup off the table with his tail, sending the contents full into the middle of my waistcoat.

FORTY-ONE

I rose from my chair hurriedly and remarking "——," approached him at a rapid rate. He preceded me in the direction of the door. At the door he met Eliza coming in with eggs. Eliza observed "Ugh!" and sat down on the floor, the eggs took up different positions about the carpet, where they spread themselves out, and Gustavus Adolphus left the room. I called after him, strongly advising him to go straight downstairs and not let me see him again for the next hour or so; and he seeming to agree with me, dodged the coal-scoop and went, while I returned, dried myself and finished breakfast. I made sure that he had gone in to the yard, but when I looked into the passage ten minutes later he was sitting at the top of the stairs. I ordered him down at once, but he only barked and jumped about, so I went to see what was the matter.

It was Tittums. She was sitting on the top stair but one and wouldn't let him pass.

Tittums is our kitten. She is about the size of a penny roll. Her back was up and she was swearing like a medical student.

She does swear fearfully. I do a little that way myself sometimes, but I am a mere amateur compared with her. To tell you the truth—mind, this is strictly between ourselves, please; I shouldn't like your wife to know I said it—the women folk don't understand these things; but between you and me, you know, I think it does a man good to swear. Swearing is the safety-valve through which the bad temper that might otherwise do serious internal injury to his mental mechanism escapes in harmless vaporing. When a man has said: "Bless you, my dear, sweet sir. What the sun, moon, and stars made you so careless (if I may be permitted the expression) as to allow your light and delicate foot to descend upon my corn with so much force? Is it that you are physically incapable of comprehending the direction in which you are proceeding? you nice, clever young man—you!" or words to that effect, he feels better. Swearing has the same soothing effect upon our angry passions that smashing the furniture or slamming the doors is so well known to exercise; added to which it is much cheaper. Swearing clears a man out like a pen'orth of gunpowder does the wash-house chimney. An occasional explosion is good for both. I rather distrust a man who never swears, or savagely kicks the foot-stool, or pokes the fire with unnecessary violence. Without some

334

outlet, the anger caused by the ever-occurring troubles of life is apt to rankle and fester within. The petty annoyance, instead of being thrown from us, sits down beside us and becomes a sorrow, and the little offense is brooded over till, in the hot-bed of rumination, it grows into a great injury, under whose poisonous shadow springs up hatred and revenge.

Swearing relieves the feelings—that is what swearing does. I explained this to my aunt on one occasion, but it didn't answer with her. She said I had no business to have such feelings.

That is what I told Tittums. I told her she ought to be ashamed of herself, brought up in a Christian family as she was, too. I don't so much mind hearing an old cat swear, but I can't bear to see a mere kitten give way to it. It seems sad in one so young.

I put Tittums in my pocket and returned to my desk. I forgot her for the moment, and when I looked I found that she had squirmed out of my pocket on to the table and was trying to swallow the pen; then she put her leg into the ink-pot and upset it; then she licked her leg; then she swore again—at me this time.

I put her down on the floor, and there Tim began rowing with her. I do wish Tim would mind his own business. It was no concern of his what she had been doing. Besides, he is not a saint himself. He is only a two-year-old fox-terrier, and he interferes with everything and gives himself the airs of a gray-headed Scotch collie.

Tittums's mother has come in and Tim has got his nose scratched, for which I am remarkably glad. I have put them all three out in the passage, where they are fighting at the present moment. I'm in a mess with the ink and in a thundering bad temper; and if anything more in the cat or dog line comes fooling about me this morning, it had better bring its own funeral contractor with it.

Yet, in general, I like cats and dogs very much indeed. What jolly chaps they are! They are much superior to human beings as companions. They do not quarrel or argue with you. They never talk about themselves but listen to you while you talk about yourself, and keep up an appearance of being interested in the conversation. They never make stupid remarks. They never observe to Miss Brown across a dinner-table that they always understood she was very sweet on Mr. Jones (who has just married Miss

Robinson). They never mistake your wife's cousin for her husband and fancy that you are the father-in-law. And they never ask a young author with fourteen tragedies, sixteen comedies, seven farces, and a couple of burlesques in his desk why he doesn't write a play.

They never say unkind things. They never tell us of our faults, "merely for our own good." They do not at inconvenient moments mildly remind us of our past follies and mistakes. They do not say, "Oh, yes, a lot of use you are if you are ever really wanted"—sarcastic like. They never inform us, like our *inamoratas* sometimes do, that we are not nearly so nice as we used to be. We are always the same to them.

They are always glad to see us. They are with us in all our humors. They are merry when we are glad, sober when we feel solemn, and sad when we are sorrowful.

"Halloo! happy and want a lark? Right you are; I'm your man. Here I am, frisking round you, leaping, barking, pirouetting, ready for any amount of fun and mischief. Look at my eyes if you doubt me. What shall it be? A romp in the drawing-room and never mind the furniture, or a scamper in the fresh, cool air, a scud across the fields and down the hill, and won't we let old Gaffer Goggles' geese know what time o' day it is, neither! Whoop! come along."

Or you'd like to be quiet and think. Very well. Pussy can sit on the arm of the chair and purr, and Montmorency will curl himself up on the rug and blink at the fire, yet keeping one eye on you the while, in case you are seized with any sudden desire in the direction of rats.

And when we bury our face in our hands and wish we had never been born, they don't sit up very straight and observe that we have brought it all upon ourselves. They don't even hope it will be a warning to us. But they come up softly and shove their heads against us. If it is a cat she stands on your shoulder, rumples your hair, and says, "Lor,' I am sorry for you, old man," as plain as words can speak; and if it is a dog he looks up at you with his big, true eyes and says with them, "Well you've always got me, you know. We'll go through the world together and always stand by each other, won't we?"

He is very imprudent, a dog is. He never makes it his business to inquire whether you are in the right or in the wrong, never bothers as to whether you are going up or down upon life's ladder, never asks whether you are rich or poor, silly or wise, sinner or saint. You are his pal. That is enough for him, and come luck or misfortune, good repute or bad, honor or shame, he is going to stick to you, to comfort you, guard you, and give his life for you if need be—foolish, brainless, soulless dog!

Ah! old stanch friend, with your deep, clear eyes and bright, quick glances, that take in all one has to say before one has time to speak it, do you know you are only an animal and have no mind? Do you know that that dull-eyed, gin-sodden lout leaning against the post out there is immeasurably your intellectual superior? Do you know that every little-minded, selfish scoundrel who lives by cheating and tricking, who never did a gentle deed or said a kind word, who never had a thought that was not mean and low or a desire that was not base, whose every action is a fraud, whose every utterance is a lie—do you know that these crawling skulks (and there are millions of them in the world), do you know they are all as much superior to you as the sun is superior to rushlight you honorable, brave-hearted, unselfish brute? They are MEN, you know, and MEN are the greatest, and noblest, and wisest, and best beings in the whole vast eternal universe. Any man will tell you that.

Yes, poor doggie, you are very stupid, very stupid indeed, compared with us clever men, who understand all about politics and philosophy, and who know everything, in short, except what we are and where we came from and whither we are going, and what everything outside this tiny world and most things in it are.

Never mind, though, pussy and doggie, we like you both all the better for your being stupid. We all like stupid things. Men can't bear clever women, and a woman's ideal man is some one she can call a "dear old stupid." It is so pleasant to come across people more stupid than ourselves. We love them at once for being so. The world must be rather a rough place for clever people. Ordinary folk dislike them, and as for themselves, they hate each other most cordially.

But there, the clever people are such a very insignificant minority that it really doesn't much matter if they are unhappy. So long as the foolish people can be made comfortable the world, as a whole, will get on tolerably well.

Cats have the credit of being more worldly wise than dogs—of looking more after their own interests and being less blindly devoted to those of their friends. And we men and women are naturally shocked at such selfishness. Cats certainly do love a family that has a carpet in the kitchen more than a family that has not; and if there are many children about, they prefer to spend their leisure time next door. But, taken altogether, cats are libeled.

Make a friend of one, and she will stick to you through thick and thin. All the cats that I have had have been most firm comrades. I had a cat once that used to follow me about everywhere, until it even got quite embarrassing, and I had to beg her, as a personal favor, not to accompany me any further down the High Street. She used to sit up for me when I was late home and meet me in the passage. It made me feel quite like a married man, except that she never asked where I had been and then didn't believe me when I told her.

Another cat I had used to get drunk regularly every day. She would hang about for hours outside the cellar door for the purpose of sneaking in on the first opportunity and lapping up the drippings from the beer-cask. I do not mention this habit of hers in praise of the species, but merely to show how almost human some of them are. If the transmigration of souls is a fact, this animal was certainly qualifying most rapidly for a Christian, for her vanity was only second to her love of drink. Whenever she caught a particularly big rat, she would bring it up into the room where we were all sitting, lay the corpse down in the midst of us, and wait to be praised. Lord! how the girls used to scream.

Poor rats! They seem only to exist so that cats and dogs may gain credit for killing them and chemists make a fortune by inventing specialties in poison for their destruction. And yet there is something fascinating about them. There is a weirdness and uncanniness attaching to them. They are so cunning and strong, so terrible in their numbers, so cruel, so secret. They swarm in deserted houses, where the broken casements hang rotting to the crumbling walls and the doors swing creaking on their rusty hinges. They know the sinking ship and leave her, no one knows how or whither. They whisper to each other in their hiding-places how a doom will fall upon the hall and the great name die forgotten. They do fearful deeds in ghastly charnel-houses.

No tale of horror is complete without the rats. In stories of ghosts and murderers they scamper through the echoing rooms, and the gnawing of their teeth is heard behind the wainscot, and their gleaming eyes peer through the holes in the worm-eaten tapestry, and they scream in shrill, unearthly notes in the dead of night, while the moaning wind sweeps, sobbing, round the ruined turret towers, and passes wailing like a woman through the chambers bare and tenantless.

And dying prisoners, in their loathsome dungeons, see through the horrid gloom their small red eyes, like glittering coals, hear in the death-like silence the rush of their claw-like feet, and start up shrieking in the darkness and watch through the awful night.

I love to read tales about rats. They make my flesh creep so. I like that tale of Bishop Hatto and the rats. The wicked bishop, you know, had ever so much corn stored in his granaries and would not let the starving people touch it, but when they prayed to him for food gathered them together in his barn, and then shutting the doors on them, set fire to the place and burned them all to death. But next day there came thousands upon thousands of rats, sent to do judgment on him. Then Bishop Hatto fled to his strong tower that stood in the middle of the Rhine, and barred himself in and fancied he was safe. But the rats! they swam the river, they gnawed their way through the thick stone walls, and ate him alive where he sat.

"They have whetted their teeth against the stones,
And now they pick the bishop's bones;
They gnawed the flesh from every limb,
For they were sent to do judgment on him."

Oh, it's a lovely tale.

Then there is the story of the Pied Piper of Hamelin, how first he piped the rats away, and afterward, when the mayor broke faith with him, drew all the children along with him and went into the mountain. What a curious old legend that is! I wonder what it means, or has it any meaning at all?

There seems something strange and deep lying hid beneath the rippling rhyme. It haunts me, that picture of the quaint, mysterious old piper piping through Hamelin's narrow streets, and the children following with dancing feet and thoughtful, eager faces. The old folks try to stay them, but the children pay no heed. They hear the weird, witched music and must follow. The games are left unfinished and the playthings drop from their careless hands. They know not whither they are hastening. The mystic music calls to them, and they follow, heedless and unasking where. It stirs and vibrates in their hearts and other sounds grow faint. So they wander through Pied Piper Street away from Hamelin town.

I get thinking sometimes if the Pied Piper is really dead, or if he may not still be roaming up and down our streets and lanes, but playing now so softly that only the children hear him. Why do the little faces look so grave and solemn when they pause awhile from romping, and stand, deep wrapt, with straining eyes? They only shake their curly heads and dart back laughing to their playmates when we question them. But I fancy myself they have been listening to the magic music of the old Pied Piper, and perhaps with those bright eyes of theirs have even seen his odd, fantastic figure gliding unnoticed through the whirl and throng.

Even we grown-up children hear his piping now and then. But the yearning notes are very far away, and the noisy, blustering world is always bellowing so loud it drowns the dreamlike melody. One day the sweet, sad strains will sound out full and clear, and then we too shall, like the little children, throw our playthings all aside and follow. The loving hands will be stretched out to stay us, and the voices we have learned to listen for will cry to us to stop. But we shall push the fond arms gently back and pass out through the sorrowing house and through the open door. For the wild, strange music will be ringing in our hearts, and we shall know the meaning of its song by then.

I wish people could love animals without getting maudlin over them, as so many do. Women are the most hardened offenders in such respects, but even our intellectual sex often degrade pets into nuisances by absurd idolatry. There are the gushing young ladies who, having read "David Copperfield," have thereupon sought out a small, longhaired dog of nondescript breed, possessed of an irritating habit of criticising a man's trousers, and of finally commenting upon the same by a sniff indicative of contempt and disgust. They talk sweet girlish prattle to this animal (when there is any one near enough to overhear them), and they kiss its nose, and put its unwashed head up against their cheek in a most touching manner; though I have noticed that these caresses are principally performed when there are young men hanging about.

Then there are the old ladies who worship a fat poodle, scant of breath and full of fleas. I knew a couple of elderly spinsters once who had a sort of German sausage on legs which they called a dog between them. They used to wash its face with warm water every morning. It had a mutton cutlet regularly for breakfast; and on Sundays, when one of the ladies went to church, the other always stopped at home to keep the dog company.

There are many families where the whole interest of life is centered upon the dog. Cats, by the way, rarely suffer from excess of adulation. A cat possesses a very fair sense of the ridiculous, and will put her paw down kindly but firmly upon any nonsense of this kind. Dogs, however, seem to like it. They encourage their owners in the tomfoolery, and the consequence is that in the circles I am speaking of what "dear Fido" has done, does do, will do, won't do, can do, can't do, was doing, is doing, is going to do, shall do, shan't do, and is about to be going to have done is the continual theme of discussion from morning till night.

All the conversation, consisting, as it does, of the very dregs of imbecility, is addressed to this confounded animal. The family sit in a row all day long, watching him, commenting upon his actions, telling each other anecdotes about him, recalling his virtues, and remembering with tears how one day they lost him for two whole hours, on which occasion he was brought home in a most brutal manner by the butcher-boy, who had been met carrying him by the scruff of his neck with one hand, while soundly cuffing his head with the other.

After recovering from these bitter recollections, they vie with each other in bursts of admiration for the brute, until some more than usually enthusiastic member, unable any longer to control his feelings, swoops down upon the unhappy quadruped in a frenzy of affection, clutches it to his heart, and slobbers over it. Whereupon the others, mad with envy, rise up, and seizing as much of the dog as the greed of the first one has left to them, murmur praise and devotion.

Among these people everything is done through the dog. If you want to make love to the eldest daughter, or get the old man to lend you the garden roller, or the mother to subscribe to the Society for the Suppression of Solo-Cornet Players in Theatrical Orchestras (it's a pity there isn't one, anyhow), you have to begin with the dog. You must gain its approbation before they will even listen to you, and if, as is highly probable, the animal, whose frank, doggy nature has been warped by the unnatural treatment he has received, responds to your overtures of friendship by viciously snapping at you, your cause is lost forever.

"If Fido won't take to anyone," the father has thoughtfully remarked beforehand, "I say that man is not to be trusted. You know, Maria, how often I have said that. Ah! he knows, bless him."

Drat him!

And to think that the surly brute was once an innocent puppy, all legs and head, full of fun and play, and burning with ambition to become a big, good dog and bark like mother.

Ah me! life sadly changes us all. The world seems a vast horrible grinding machine, into which what is fresh and bright and pure is pushed at one end, to come out old and crabbed and wrinkled at the other.

Look even at Pussy Sobersides, with her dull, sleepy glance, her grave, slow walk, and dignified, prudish airs; who could ever think that once she was the blue-eyed, whirling, scampering, head-over-heels, mad little firework that we call a kitten?

What marvelous vitality a kitten has. It is really something very beautiful the way life bubbles over in the little creatures. They rush about, and mew, and spring; dance on their hind legs, embrace everything with their front ones, roll over and over, lie on their backs and kick. They don't know what to do with themselves, they are so full of life.

Can you remember, reader, when you and I felt something of the same sort of thing? Can you remember those glorious days of fresh young manhood—how, when coming home along the moonlit road, we felt too full of life for sober walking, and had to spring and skip, and wave our arms, and shout till belated farmers' wives thought—and with good reason, too—that we were mad, and kept close to the hedge, while we stood and laughed aloud to see them scuttle off so fast and made their blood run cold with a wild parting whoop, and the tears came, we knew not why? Oh, that magnificent young LIFE! that crowned us kings of the earth; that rushed through every tingling vein till we seemed to walk on air; that thrilled through our throbbing brains and told us to go forth and conquer the whole world; that welled up in our young hearts till we longed to stretch out our arms and gather all the toiling men and women and the little children to our breast and love them all—all. Ah! they were grand days, those deep, full days, when our coming life, like an unseen organ, pealed strange, yearnful music in our ears, and our young blood cried out like a war-horse for the battle. Ah, our pulse beats slow and steady now, and our old joints are rheumatic, and we love our easy-chair and pipe and sneer at boys' enthusiasm. But oh for one brief moment of that god-like life again!

FORTY-Two

Greta and the Black Cat

Abbie Phillips Walker

One day a woodsman named Peter was chopping down a tree when he saw swinging from one of the branches a bundle. Dropping his ax, he climbed up, and to his surprise, when he opened the bundle, he found in it a baby girl asleep. Peter hurried home with the baby to his wife. "Look, Martha," he said. "I have found a baby girl to be a sister to our son Robert. We will name her Greta and they shall grow up as brother and sister."

But Martha did not want the baby. "We have three mouths to feed now," she grumbled. "Why should we care for a child we know nothing of?"

But Peter would not hear of putting the child out-of-doors and so Greta lived with Peter and Martha and grew up with Robert.

Poor little Greta had anything but a happy life, for Martha treated her kindly only when Peter was in sight, and that was seldom.

Robert, seeing that his mother did not treat Greta well, began to order her to wait upon him as soon as he was old enough and treated her as a servant.

Greta had to weed the garden and bring in the water and the wood. She had to wash the dishes and make the beds and do all the work excepting when Peter was at home.

One day when Peter was going to the woods he told Robert to chop a pile of wood in the yard and have it finished by the time he came home.

When Peter was out of sight Robert told Greta to chop the wood. "That is what you are here for—to do the work," said Robert. "You would have been eaten up by the bears if we had not taken you in. Now go to work and chop that wood."

Greta began to cry and said she could not handle the ax; she was too small. But Martha boxed her ears and told her she should not have any dinner if she did not do as Robert told her.

Greta went to the woodpile and picked up the ax, but it was no use. She could not chop the wood. And fearing a beating if she did not do it, Greta ran away. On and on she ran until she came to a turn in the road which led into a forest. Here she decided to stop for the night, and she was just lying down by a rock when she heard a pitiful "me-ow."

Looking in the bushes close by, Greta saw a big black cat holding up one paw as though it was hurt. "Poor pussy!" said Greta, taking the cat in her arms. "You look as unhappy as I feel. Let me bind up your paw."

Greta tore off a piece of her dress and bound up the cat's paw, and then, to her surprise, the black cat spoke to her.

"Come with me and I will show you where to sleep. You will have to carry me, for my paw is very painful," said the cat.

Greta picked up the cat, too surprised to be frightened, and went through the woods as the cat directed her.

When they reached a big rock with an opening in it the cat said: "Here is my home. Take me in and you will find a place to sleep and food as well."

Creeping in on her hands and knees with the cat under her arm, Greta found herself in a big room with a table in the center and on it plenty of food.

In one corner of the room was a bed and on this Greta saw a queer-looking old woman with a hooked nose.

She was asleep and did not notice them until the cat said, "Eat your supper."

Up jumped the queer-looking old woman when she heard this, for she was the witch.

"You, and a mortal with you," she screamed, as she reached for her crooked stick.

Greta ran to the door, for she thought the old witch was about to strike her; but the black cat, who was sitting on the floor near by where Greta had put it, said: "Don't you dare touch this girl; she has saved my life, and from this hour you are in my power, for a mortal has held me in her arms.

"If you would live call the good fairy that has been looking for me all these years. I shall find her, anyway, but it will save time if you use your magic power, and you will regret it if you do not obey me."

When the old witch heard this she began to tremble and hobbled to the door of the cave and tapped it three times with her crooked stick.

The rock opened so she could walk out, and Greta followed to see what she did, for she was no longer afraid; she knew the black cat would protect her.

The old witch gave a peculiar cry when she was outside, and Greta saw the next instant a tiny creature dressed in pink gauze, holding a wand of gold in one little hand, standing on a bush beside the old witch.

"Here I am, Witch Terrible," said the fairy. "What can I do for you? You must be in great danger or you would not have called for one of us."

The cat when it heard the fairy speak ran out of the cave, limping, and lay down in front of the fairy. "Help me, my good fairy," said the black cat. "I am the Prince for whom you have looked so long. The old witch changed me into a black cat and took away my power to speak until I was held in the arms of a mortal.

"I know her secret, and, though she dared not kill me, she wanted me to die, so she turned me into the forest to starve, and if it had not been for this girl, good fairy, the old witch would have had her wish granted.

"When she changed me into a black cat she said I should never speak until a mortal held me, and that I could not regain my own shape until a fairy changed me, but something has happened since then, and to save herself she obeyed me and called you, for I know her secret, and that is why I did not have to hunt for you, my good fairy."

The fairy touched the black cat with her wand and Greta saw in place of the big black cat a handsome man dressed in black velvet, with gold trimmings. "Now tell me the secret you know about the witch," said the fairy.

The old witch threw up her arms and cried for mercy. "Remember, I called the fairy," she said; "you would have hunted a long time if I had not. Be merciful!"

"I shall not forget," said the Prince. "This woman is only half a witch," he said. "She is part mortal, and every night at twelve o'clock she has to become a mortal for an hour because she tried to change a water nymph into a frog. The river god, the water nymph's father, called on a very powerful ogre, who was his friend, and the ogre was about to change her into a rock, but she begged so hard he made her half mortal and left her to her fate."

"Which means she can never leave this forest," said the fairy, "and as she does many of her magic deeds at night when she rides abroad on her broomstick she is not a very powerful witch."

"Yes, that is it," said the Prince, "and she does not want it known among the fairies or the goblins or any of the magic-power folks. That is the mercy for which she begs.

"I hope you will keep her secret, good fairy, for she saved me so much time and trouble in calling you."

"I will keep her secret from all but the fairies, but one of the fairy family will come here every night to make sure no mortal has been harmed by her, for some one might stray in here just as this girl did and be changed into some other form."

"I have one more favor to ask of you, good fairy," said the Prince. "I wish to make this girl my wife if she will marry me, and I would like to have the proper clothes for a princess, so that I may take her to my palace at once."

"What do you say, my dear?" asked the fairy. "Will you marry the Prince?"

Greta felt she must be dreaming, but she was sure she would love the handsome Prince if she were awake, so she told the fairy she would, and the next instant her ragged clothes dropped from her and she stood before the Prince in a beautiful green velvet riding-habit, with a long feather in her hat, looking every inch a princess.

That night a great feast was held at the palace of the Prince in honor of his return and to celebrate their wedding, and the very next day Greta and the Prince rode to the home where she had once lived to give Peter a bag of gold.

"He was the only person who ever treated me kindly until I met you," Greta told the Prince, "and I shall never forget him."

Greta was not recognized by Martha or her son Robert, for they little thought the beautiful Princess was the poor girl that had once been their slave. But Peter, who had loved her, looked after the coach as it rolled away. "It looked a little like her," he said, "but, of course, it could not be." Many gifts did Greta and the Prince send to Peter, and in his old age he was given a comfortable house and plenty to eat, and, though Martha and Robert shared his good fortune, they never knew who sent it.

The Prince told Peter who the Princess really was one day, because the poor old man had never ceased to sorrow because Greta could not be found, but not a word did he tell of this to Robert or Martha, but kept his secret all to himself as long as he lived.

FORTY-THREE

The Slum Cat

Ernest Thompson Seton

"M-E-A-T! M-E-A-T!" CAME SHRILLING DOWN SCRIMPER'S ALLEY. Surely the Pied Piper of Hamelin was there, for it seemed that all the Cats in the neighborhood were running toward the sound, though the Dogs, it must be confessed, looked scornfully indifferent.

"Meat! Meat!" and louder; then the centre of attraction came in view—a rough, dirty little man with a push-cart; while straggling behind him were a score of Cats that joined in his cry with a sound nearly the same as his own. Every fifty yards, that is, as soon as a goodly throng of Cats was gathered, the push-cart stopped. The man with the magic voice took out of the box in his cart a skewer on which were pieces of strong-smelling boiled liver. With a long stick he pushed the pieces off. Each Cat seized on one, and wheeling, with a slight depression of the ears and a little tiger growl and glare, she rushed away with her prize to devour it in some safe retreat.

"Meat! Meat!" And still they came to get their portions. All were well known to the meat-man. There was Castiglione's Tiger; this was Jones's Black; here was Pralitsky's "Torkershell," and this was Madame Danton's White; there sneaked Blenkinshoff's Maltee, and that climbing on the barrow was Sawyer's old Orange Billy, an impudent fraud that never had had any financial backing,—all to be remembered and kept in account. This one's owner was sure pay, a dime a week; that one's doubtful.

There was John Washee's Cat, that got only a small piece because John was in arrears. Then there was the saloon-keeper's collared and ribboned ratter, which got an extra lump because the 'barkeep' was liberal; and the rounds-man's Cat, that brought no cash, but got unusual consideration because the meat-man did. But there were others.

A black Cat with a white nose came rushing confidently with the rest, only to be repulsed savagely. Alas! Pussy did not understand. She had been a pensioner of the barrow for months. Why this unkind change? It was beyond her comprehension. But the meat-man knew. Her mistress had stopped payment. The meat-man kept no books but his memory, and it never was at fault.

Outside this patrician "four hundred" about the barrow, were other Cats, keeping away from the push-cart because they were not on the list, the Social Register as it were, yet fascinated by the heavenly smell and the faint possibility of accidental good luck. Among these hangers-on was a thin gray Slummer, a homeless Cat that lived by her wits—slab-sided and not over-clean. One could see at a glance that she was doing her duty by a family in some out-of-the-way corner. She kept one eye on the barrow circle and the other on the possible Dogs.

She saw a score of happy Cats slink off with their delicious "daily" and their tiger-like air, but no opening for her, till a big Tom of her own class sprang on a little pensioner with intent to rob. The victim dropped the meat to defend herself against the enemy, and before the "all-powerful" could intervene, the gray Slummer saw her chance, seized the prize, and was gone.

She went through the hole in Menzie's side door and over the wall at the back, then sat down and devoured the lump of liver, licked her chops, felt absolutely happy, and set out by devious ways to the rubbish-yard, where, in the bottom of an old cracker-box, her family was awaiting her. A plaintive mewing reached her ears. She went at speed and reached the box to see a huge Black Tom-cat calmly destroying her brood. He was twice as big as she, but she went at him with all her strength, and he did as most animals will do when caught wrong-doing, he turned and ran away. Only one was left, a little thing like its mother, but of more pronounced color—gray with black spots, and a white touch on nose, ears, and tail-tip. There can be no question of the mother's grief for a few days; but that wore off, and all her care was for the survivor. That benevolence was as far as possible from the motives of the murderous old Tom there can be no doubt; but he proved a blessing in deep disguise, for both mother and Kit were visibly bettered in a short time. The daily quest for food continued. The meat-man rarely proved a success, but the ash-cans were there, and if they did not afford a meat-supply, at least they were sure to produce potato-skins that could be used to allay the gripe of hunger for another day.

One night the mother Cat smelt a wonderful smell that came from the East River at the end of the alley. A new smell always needs investigating, and when it is attractive as well as new, there is but one course open. It led Pussy to the docks a block away, and then out on a wharf, away from any cover but the night. A sudden noise, a growl and a rush, were the first notice she had that she was cut off by her old enemy, the Wharf Dog. There was only one escape. She leaped from the wharf to the vessel from which the smell came. The Dog could not follow, so when the fish-boat sailed in the morning Pussy unwillingly went with her and was seen no more.

The Slum Kitten waited in vain for her mother. The morning came and went. She became very hungry. Toward evening a deep-laid instinct drove her forth to seek food. She slunk out of the old box, and feeling her way silently among the rubbish, she smelt everything that seemed eatable, but without finding food. At length she reached the wooden steps leading down into Jack Malee's bird-store underground.

The door was open a little. She wandered into a world of rank and curious smells and a number of living things in cages all about her. A man was sitting idly on a box in a corner. He saw the little stranger enter and watched it curiously. It wandered past some Rabbits. They paid no heed. It came to a wide-barred cage in which was a Fox. The gentleman with the bushy tail was in a far corner. He crouched low; his eyes glowed. The Kitten wandered, sniffing, up to the bars, put its head in, sniffed again, then made toward the feed-pan, to be seized in a flash by the crouching Fox. It gave a frightened "mew," but a single shake cut that short and would have ended Kitty's nine lives at once, had not the man come to the rescue. He had no weapon and could not get into the cage, but he spat with such copious vigor in the Fox's face that he dropped the Kitten and returned to the corner, there to sit blinking his eyes in sullen fear.

The man pulled the Kitten out. The shake of the beast of prey seemed to have stunned the victim, really to have saved it much suffering. The Kitten seemed unharmed, but giddy. It tottered in a circle for a time, then slowly revived, and a few minutes later was purring in the man's lap, apparently none the worse, when Jap Malee, the bird-man, came home.

Jack was a full-blooded Cockney. He was not especially unkind to the birds and beasts whose sales were supposed to furnish his living, but his eye was on the main chance; he knew what he wanted. He didn't want the Slum Kitten.

The man who had rescued the kitten gave it all the food it could eat, then carried it to a distant block and dropped it in a neighboring iron-yard.

One full meal is as much as anyone needs in two or three days, and under the influence of this stored-up heat and power, Kitty was very lively. She walked around the piled-up rubbish, cast curious glances on far-away Canary-birds in cages that hung from high windows; she peeped over fences, discovered a large Dog, got quietly down again, and presently finding a sheltered place in full sunlight, she lay down and slept for an hour.

A slight "sniff" awakened her, and before her stood a large Black Cat with glowing green eyes, and the thick neck and square jaws that distinguish the Tom; a scar marked his cheek, and his left ear was torn. His look was far from friendly; his ears moved backward a little, his tail twitched, and a faint, deep sound came from his throat. The Kitten innocently walked toward him. She did not remember him. He rubbed the sides of his jaws on a post, and quietly, slowly turned and disappeared. The last that she saw of him was the end of his tail twitching from side to side; and the little Slummer had no idea that she had been as near death to-day, as she had been when she ventured into the fox-cage.

As night came on the Kitten began to feel hungry. She examined carefully the long invisible colored stream that the wind is made of. She selected the most interesting of its strands, and, nose-led, followed. In the corner of the iron-yard was a box of garbage. Among this she found something that answered fairly well for food; a bucket of water under a faucet offered a chance to quench her thirst.

The night was spent chiefly in prowling about and learning the main lines of the iron-yard. The next day she passed as before, sleeping in the sun. Thus the time wore on. Sometimes she found a good meal at the garbage-box, sometimes there was nothing. Once she found the big Black Tom there, but discreetly withdrew before he saw her. The water-bucket was usually at its place, or, failing that, there were some muddy little pools on the stone below. But the garbage-box was very unreliable.

Once it left her for three days without food. She searched along the high fence, and seeing a small hole, crawled through that and found herself in the open street. This was a new world, but before she had ventured far, there was a noisy, rumbling rush—a large Dog came bounding, and Kitty had barely time to run back into the hole in the fence. She was dreadfully hungry, and glad to find some old potato-peelings, which gave a little respite from the hunger-pang. In the morning she did not sleep, but prowled for food.

Some Sparrows chirruped in the yard. They were often there, but now they were viewed with new eyes. The steady pressure of hunger had roused the wild hunter in the Kitten; those Sparrows were game—were food. She crouched instinctively and stalked from cover to cover, but the chirpers were alert and flew in time. Not once, but many times, she tried without result except to confirm the Sparrows in the list of things to be eaten if obtainable.

On the fifth day of ill luck the Slum Kitty ventured forth into the street, desperately bent on finding food. When far from the haven hole some small boys opened fire at her with pieces of brick. She ran in fear. A Dog joined in the chase, and Kitty's position grew perilous; but an old-fashioned iron fence round a house-front was there, and she slipped in between the rails as the Dog overtook her. A woman in a window above shouted at the Dog. Then the boys dropped a piece of cat-meat down to the unfortunate; and Kitty had the most delicious meal of her life. The stoop afforded a refuge. Under this she sat patiently till nightfall came with quiet, then sneaked back like a shadow to her old iron-yard.

Thus the days went by for two months. She grew in size and strength and in an intimate knowledge of the immediate neighborhood. She made the acquaintance of Downey Street, where long rows of ash-cans were to be seen every morning. She formed her own ideas of their proprietors. The big house was to her, not a Roman Catholic mission, but a place whose garbage-tins abounded in choicest fish scrapings. She soon made the acquaintance of the meat-man, and joined in the shy fringe of Cats that formed the outer circle. She also met the Wharf Dog as well as two or three other horrors of the same class. She knew what to expect of them and how to avoid them; and she was happy in being the inventor of a new industry.

Many thousand Cats have doubtless hung, in hope, about the tempting milk-cans that the early milk-man leaves on steps and window-ledges, and it was by the merest accident that Kitty found one with a broken lid, and so was taught to raise it and have a satisfying drink. Bottles, of course, were beyond her, but many a can has a misfit lid, and Kitty was very painstaking in her efforts to discover the loose-jointed ones. Finally she extended her range by exploration till she achieved the heart of the next block, and farther, till once more among the barrels and boxes of the yard behind the bird-man's cellar.

The old iron-yard never had been home, she had always felt like a stranger there; but here she had a sense of ownership, and at once resented the presence of another small Cat. She approached this new-comer with threatening air. The two had got as far as snarling and spitting when a bucket of water from an upper window drenched them both and effectually cooled their wrath. They fled, the newcomer over the wall, Slum Kitty under the very box where she had been born. This whole back region appealed to her strongly, and here again she took up her abode. The yard had no more garbage food than the other and no water at all, but it was frequented by stray Rats and a few Mice of the finest quality; these were occasionally secured, and afforded not only a palatable meal, but were the cause of her winning a friend.

Kitty was now fully grown. She was a striking-looking Cat of the tiger type. Her marks were black on a very pale gray, and the four beauty-spots of white on nose, ears, and tail-tip lent a certain distinction. She was very expert at getting a living, and yet she had some days of starvation and failed in her ambition of catching a Sparrow. She was quite alone, but a new force was coming into her life.

She was lying in the sun one August day, when a large Black Cat came walking along the top of a wall in her direction. She recognized him at once by his torn ear. She slunk into her box and hid. He picked his way gingerly, bounded lightly to a shed that was at the end of the yard, and was crossing the roof when a Yellow Cat rose up. The Black Tom glared and growled, so did the Yellow Tom. Their tails lashed from side to side. Strong throats growled and yowled. They approached each other with ears laid back, with muscles a-tense.

"Yow-yow-ow!" said the Black One.

"Wow-w-w!" was the slightly deeper answer.

"Ya-wow-wow-wow!" said the Black One, edging up half an inch nearer.

"Yow-w-w!" was the Yellow answer, as the blond Cat rose to full height and stepped with vast dignity a whole inch forward. "Yow-w!" and he went another inch, while his tail went swish, thump, from one side to the other.

"Ya-wow-yow-w!" screamed the Black in a rising tone, and he backed the eighth of an inch, as he marked the broad, unshrinking breast before him.

Windows opened all around, human voices were heard, but the Cat scene went on.

"Yow-yow-ow!" rumbled the Yellow Peril, his voice deepening as the other's rose.

"Yow!" and he advanced another step.

Now their noses were but three inches apart; they stood sidewise, both ready to clinch, but each waiting for the other. They glared for three minutes in silence and like statues, except that each tail-tip was twisting.

The Yellow began again. "Yow-ow-ow!" in deep tone.

"Ya-a-a—a-a!" screamed the Black, with intent to strike terror by his yell; but he retreated one sixteenth of an inch. The Yellow walked up a long half-inch; their whiskers were mixing now; another advance, and their noses almost touched.

"Yo-w-w!" said Yellow, like a deep moan.

"Y-a-a-a-a-a!" screamed the Black, but he retreated a thirty-second of an inch, and the Yellow Warrior closed and clinched like a demon.

Oh, how they rolled and bit and tore, especially the Yellow One!

How they pitched and gripped and hugged, but especially the Yellow One!

Over and over, sometimes one on top, sometimes another, but mostly the Yellow One; and farther till they rolled off the roof, amid cheers from all the windows. They lost not a second in that fall to the junk-yard; they tore and clawed all the way down, but especially the Yellow One. And when they struck the ground, still fighting, the one on top was chiefly the Yellow One; and before they separated both had had as much as they wanted, especially the Black One! He scaled a wall and, bleeding and growling, disappeared, while the news was passed from window to window that Cayley's Black Tom had been licked at last by Orange Billy.

Either the Yellow Cat was a very clever seeker, or else Slum Kitty did not hide very hard; but he discovered her among the boxes, and she made no attempt to get away, probably because she had witnessed the fight. There is nothing like success in warfare to win the female heart, and thereafter the Yellow Tom and Kitty became very good friends, not sharing each other's lives or food,—Cats do not do that way much,—but recognizing each other as entitled to special friendly privileges.

September had gone. October's shortening days were on when an event took place in the old cracker-box. If Orange Billy had come he would have seen five little Kittens curled up in the embrace of their mother, the little Slum Cat. It was a wonderful thing for her. She felt all the elation an animal mother can feel, all the delight, and she loved them and licked them with a tenderness that must have been a surprise to herself, had she had the power to think of such things.

She had added a joy to her joyless life, but she had also added a care and a heavy weight to her heavy load. All her strength was taken now to find food. The burden increased as the offspring grew up big enough to scramble about the boxes, which they did daily during her absence after they were six weeks old. That troubles go in flocks and luck in streaks, is well known in Slumland. Kitty had had three encounters with Dogs, and had been stoned by Malee's servant during a two days' starve. Then the tide turned. The very next morning she found a full milk-can without a lid, successfully robbed a barrow pensioner, and found a big fish-head, all within two hours.

She had just returned with that perfect peace which comes only of a full stomach, when she saw a little brown creature in her junk-yard. Hunting memories came back in strength; she didn't know what it was, but she had killed and eaten several Mice, and this was evidently a big Mouse with bob-tail and large ears. Kitty stalked it with elaborate but unnecessary caution; the little Rabbit simply sat up and looked faintly amused. He did not try to run, and Kitty sprang on him and bore him off. As she was not hungry, she carried him to the cracker-box and dropped him among the Kittens. He was not much hurt. He got over his fright, and since he could not get out of the box, he snuggled among the Kittens, and when they began to take their evening meal he very soon decided to join them. The old Cat was puzzled. The hunter instinct had been dominant, but absence of hunger had saved the Rabbit and given the maternal instinct a chance to appear. The result was that the Rabbit became a member of the family, and was thenceforth guarded and fed with the Kittens.

Two weeks went by. The Kittens romped much among the boxes during their mother's absence. The Rabbit could not get out of the box. Malee, seeing the Kittens about the back yard, told the man to shoot them. This he was doing one morning with a 22-caliber rifle. He had shot one after another and seen them drop from sight into the crannies of the lumber-pile, when the old Cat came running along the wall from the dock, carrying a small Wharf Rat. He had been ready to shoot her, too, but the sight of that Rat changed his plans: a rat-catching Cat was worthy to live. It happened to be the very first one she had ever caught, but it saved her life. She threaded the lumber-maze to the cracker-box and was probably puzzled to find that there were no Kittens to come at her call, and the Rabbit would not partake of the Rat. Pussy curled up to nurse the Rabbit, but she called from time to time to summon the Kittens. Guided by that call, the man crawled quietly to the place, and peering down into the cracker-box, saw, to his intense surprise, that it contained the old Cat, a live Rabbit, and a dead Rat.

The mother Cat laid back her ears and snarled. The man withdrew, but a minute later a board was dropped on the opening of the cracker-box, and the den with its tenants, dead and alive, was lifted into the bird-cellar.

"Say, boss, look a-hyar—hyar's where de little Rabbit got to wot we lost. Yo' sho t'ought Ah stoled him for de 'tater-bake."

Kitty and Bunny were carefully put in a large wire cage and exhibited as a happy family till a few days later, when the Rabbit took sick and died.

Pussy had never been happy in the cage. She had enough to eat and drink, but she craved her freedom—would likely have gotten 'death or liberty' now, but that during the four days' captivity she had so cleaned and slicked her fur that her unusual coloring was seen, and Jack decided to keep her.

FORTY-FOUR

The Cat and the Fiddle

L. Frank Baum

Hey, diddle, diddle,

The cat and the fiddle,

The cow jumped over the moon!

The little dog laughed

To see such sport,

And the dish ran off with the spoon!

PERHAPS you think this verse is all nonsense, and that the things it mentions could never have happened; but they did happen, as you will understand when I have explained them all to you clearly.

Little Bobby was the only son of a small farmer who lived out of town upon a country road. Bobby's mother looked after the house and Bobby's father took care of the farm, and Bobby himself, who was not very big, helped them both as much as he was able.

It was lonely upon the farm, especially when his father and mother were both busy at work, but the boy had one way to amuse himself that served to pass many an hour when he would not otherwise have known what to do. He was very fond of music, and his father one day brought him from the town a small fiddle, or violin, which he soon learned to play

361

upon. I don't suppose he was a very fine musician, but the tunes he played pleased himself, as well as his father and mother, and Bobby's fiddle soon became his constant companion.

One day in the warm summer the farmer and his wife determined to drive to the town to sell their butter and eggs and bring back some groceries in exchange for them, and while they were gone Bobby was to be left alone.

"We shall not be back till late in the evening," said his mother, "for the weather is too warm to drive very fast. But I have left you a dish of bread and milk for your supper, and you must be a good boy and amuse yourself with your fiddle until we return."

Bobby promised to be good and look after the house, and then his father and mother climbed into the wagon and drove away to the town.

The boy was not entirely alone, for there was the big black tabby-cat lying upon the floor in the kitchen, and the little yellow dog barking at the wagon as it drove away, and the big moolie-cow lowing in the pasture down by the brook. Animals are often very good company, and Bobby did not feel nearly as lonely as he would have had there been no living thing about the house.

Besides he had some work to do in the garden, pulling up the weeds that grew thick in the carrot-bed, and when the last faint sounds of the wheels had died away he went into the garden and began his task.

The little dog went too, for dogs love to be with people and to watch what is going on; and he sat down near Bobby and cocked up his ears and wagged his tail and seemed to take a great interest in the weeding. Once in a while he would rush away to chase a butterfly or bark at a beetle that crawled through the garden, but he always came back to the boy and kept near his side.

By and by the cat, which found it lonely in the big, empty kitchen, now that Bobby's mother was gone, came walking into the garden also, and lay down upon a path in the sunshine and lazily watched the boy at his work. The dog and the cat were good friends, having lived together so long that they did not care to fight each other. To be sure Towser, as the little dog was called, sometimes tried to tease pussy, being himself very mischievous; but when the cat put out her sharp claws and showed her teeth, Towser, like a wise little dog, quickly ran away, and so they managed to get along in a friendly manner.

By the time the carrot-bed was all weeded, the sun was sinking behind the edge of the forest and the new moon rising in the east, and now Bobby began to feel hungry and went into the house for his dish of bread and milk.

"I think I'll take my supper down to the brook," he said to himself, "and sit upon the grassy bank while I eat it. And I'll take my fiddle, too, and play upon it to pass the time until father and mother come home."

It was a good idea, for down by the brook it was cool and pleasant; so Bobby took his fiddle under his arm and carried his dish of bread and milk down to the bank that sloped to the edge of the brook. It was rather a steep bank, but Bobby sat upon the edge, and placing his fiddle beside him, leaned against a tree and began to eat his supper.

The little dog had followed at his heels, and the cat also came slowly walking after him, and as Bobby ate, they sat one on either side of him and looked earnestly into his face as if they too were hungry. So he threw some of the bread to Towser, who grabbed it eagerly and swallowed it in the twinkling of an eye. And Bobby left some of the milk in the dish for the cat, also, and she came lazily up and drank it in a dainty, sober fashion, and licked both the dish and spoon until no drop of the milk was left.

Then Bobby picked up his fiddle and tuned it and began to play some of the pretty tunes he knew. And while he played he watched the moon rise higher and higher until it was reflected in the smooth, still water of the brook. Indeed, Bobby could not tell which was the plainest to see, the moon in the sky or the moon in the water. The little dog lay quietly on one side of him, and the cat softly purred upon the other, and even the moolie-cow was attracted by the music and wandered near until she was browsing the grass at the edge of the brook.

After a time, when Bobby had played all the tunes he knew, he laid the fiddle down beside him, near to where the cat slept, and then he lay down upon the bank and began to think.

It is very hard to think long upon a dreamy summer night without falling asleep, and very soon Bobby's eyes closed and he forgot all about the dog and the cat and the cow and the fiddle, and dreamed he was Jack the Giant Killer and was just about to slay the biggest giant in the world.

And while he dreamed, the cat sat up and yawned and stretched herself, and then began wagging her long tail from side to side and watching the moon that was reflected in the water.

But the fiddle lay just behind her, and as she moved her tail, she drew it between the strings of the fiddle, where it caught fast. Then she gave her tail a jerk and pulled the fiddle against the tree, which made a loud noise. This frightened the cat greatly, and not knowing what was the matter with her tail, she started to run as fast as she could. But still the fiddle clung to her tail, and at every step it bounded along and made such a noise that she screamed with terror. And in her fright she ran straight towards the cow, which, seeing a black streak coming at her, and hearing the racket made by the fiddle, became also frightened and made such a jump to get out of the way that she jumped right across the brook, leaping over the very spot where the moon shone in the water!

Bobby had been awakened by the noise, and opened his eyes in time to see the cow jump; and at first it seemed to him that she had actually jumped over the moon in the sky, instead of the one in the brook.

The dog was delighted at the sudden excitement caused by the cat, and ran barking and dancing along the bank, so that he presently knocked against the dish, and behold! it slid down the bank, carrying the spoon with it, and fell with a splash into the water of the brook.

As soon as Bobby recovered from his surprise he ran after the cat, which had raced to the house, and soon came to where the fiddle lay upon the ground, it having at last dropped from the cat's tail. He examined it carefully, and was glad to find it was not hurt, in spite of its rough usage. And then he had to go across the brook and drive the cow back over the little bridge, and also to roll up his sleeve and reach into the water to recover the dish and the spoon.

Then he went back to the house and lighted a lamp, and sat down to compose a new tune before his father and mother returned.

The cat had recovered from her fright and lay quietly under the stove, and Towser sat upon the floor panting, with his mouth wide open, and looking so comical that Bobby thought he was actually laughing at the whole occurrence.

And these were the words to the tune that Bobby composed that night:

Hey, diddle, diddle,

The cat and the fiddle,

The cow jumped over the moon!

The little dog laughed

To see such sport,

And the dish ran away with the spoon!

FORTY-FIVE

The Master Cat

Charles Perrault

THERE WAS A MILLER WHO LEFT NO MORE ESTATE TO THE THREE SONS he had than his mill, his ass, and his cat. The partition was soon made. Neither scrivener nor attorney was sent for. They would soon have eaten up all the poor patrimony. The eldest had the mill, the second the ass, and the youngest nothing but the cat.

The poor young fellow was quite comfortless at having so poor a lot.

"My brothers," said he, "may get their living handsomely enough by joining their stocks together; but for my part, when I have eaten up my cat, and made me a muff of his skin, I must die of hunger."

The Cat, who heard all this, but made as if he did not, said to him with a grave and serious air:

"Do not thus afflict yourself, my good master. You have nothing else to do but to give me a bag and get a pair of boots made for me that I may scamper through the dirt and the brambles, and you shall see that you have not so bad a portion in me as you imagine."

The Cat's master did not build very much upon what he said. He had often seen him play a great many cunning tricks to catch rats and mice, as when he used to hang by the heels, or hide himself in the meal, and make as if he were dead; so that he did not altogether despair of his affording him some help in his miserable condition. When the Cat had what he asked for he booted himself very gallantly, and putting his bag about his neck, he held the strings of it in his two forepaws and went into a warren where was great abundance of rabbits. He put bran and sow-thistle into his bag, and stretching out at length, as if he had been dead, he waited for some young rabbits, not yet acquainted with the deceits of the world, to come and rummage his bag for what he had put into it.

Scarce was he lain down but he had what he wanted. A rash and foolish young rabbit jumped into his bag, and Monsieur Puss, immediately drawing close the strings, took and killed him without pity. Proud of his prey, he went with it to the palace and asked to speak with his majesty. He was shown upstairs into the King's apartment, and, making a low reverence, said to him:

"I have brought you, sir, a rabbit of the warren, which my noble lord the Marquis of Carabas" (for that was the title which puss was pleased to give his master) "has commanded me to present to your majesty from him."

"Tell thy master," said the king, "that I thank him and that he does me a great deal of pleasure."

Another time he went and hid himself among some standing corn, holding still his bag open, and when a brace of partridges ran into it he drew the strings and so caught them both. He went and made a present of these to the king, as he had done before of the rabbit that he took in the warren. The king, in like manner, received the partridges with great pleasure, and ordered him some money for drink.

The Cat continued for two or three months thus to carry his Majesty, from time to time, game of his master's taking. One day in particular, when he knew for certain that he was to take the air along the river-side, with his daughter, the most beautiful princess in the world, he said to his master:

"If you will follow my advice your fortune is made. You have nothing else to do but go and wash yourself in the river, in that part I shall show you, and leave the rest to me."

The Marquis of Carabas did what the Cat advised him to, without knowing why or wherefore. While he was washing the King passed by, and the Cat began to cry out:

"Help! help! My Lord Marquis of Carabas is going to be drowned."

At this noise the King put his head out of the coach-window, and, finding it was the Cat who had so often brought him such good game, he commanded his guards to run immediately to the assistance of his Lordship the Marquis of Carabas.

While they were drawing the poor Marquis out of the river, the Cat came up to the coach and told the King that, while his master was washing, there came by some rogues, who went off with his clothes, though he had cried out: "Thieves! thieves!" several times, as loud as he could.

This cunning Cat had hidden them under a great stone. The King immediately commanded the officers of his wardrobe to run and fetch one of his best suits for the Lord Marquis of Carabas.

The King caressed him after a very extraordinary manner, and as the fine clothes he had given him extremely set off his good mien (for he was well made and very handsome in his person), the King's daughter took a secret inclination to him, and the Marquis of Carabas had no sooner cast two or three respectful and somewhat tender glances but she fell in love with him to distraction. The King would needs have him come into the coach and take part of the airing. The Cat, quite overjoyed to see his project begin to succeed, marched on before, and, meeting with some countrymen who were mowing a meadow, he said to them:

"Good people, you who are mowing, if you do not tell the King that the meadow you mow belongs to my Lord Marquis of Carabas, you shall be chopped as small as herbs for the pot."

The King did not fail asking of the mowers to whom the meadow they were mowing belonged.

"To my Lord Marquis of Carabas," answered they altogether, for the Cat's threats had made them terribly afraid.

"You see, sir," said the Marquis, "this is a meadow which never fails to yield a plentiful harvest every year."

The Master Cat, who went still on before, met with some reapers, and said to them:

"Good people, you who are reaping, if you do not tell the King that all this corn belongs to the Marquis of Carabas, you shall be chopped as small as herbs for the pot."

The King, who passed by a moment after, would needs know to whom all that corn, which he then saw, did belong.

"To my Lord Marquis of Carabas," replied the reapers, and the King was very well pleased with it, as well as the Marquis, whom he congratulated thereupon. The Master Cat, who went always before, said the same words to all he met, and the King was astonished at the vast estates of my Lord Marquis of Carabas.

Monsieur Puss came at last to a stately castle, the master of which was an ogre, the richest had ever been known; for all the lands which the King had then gone over belonged to this castle. The Cat, who had taken care to inform himself who this ogre was and what he could do, asked to speak with him, saying he could not pass so near his castle without having the honor of paying his respects to him.

The ogre received him as civilly as an ogre could do, and made him sit down.

"I have been assured," said the Cat, "that you have the gift of being able to change yourself into all sorts of creatures you have a mind to; you can, for example, transform yourself into a lion, or elephant, and the like."

"That is true," answered the ogre very briskly; "and to convince you, you shall see me now become a lion."

Puss was so sadly terrified at the sight of a lion so near him that he immediately got into the gutter, not without abundance of trouble and danger, because of his boots, which were of no use at all to him in walking upon the tiles. A little while after, when Puss saw that the ogre had resumed his natural form, he came down, and owned he had been very much frightened.

"I have been, moreover, informed," said the Cat, "but I know not how to believe it, that you have also the power to take on you the shape of the smallest animals; for example, to change yourself into a rat or a mouse; but I must own to you I take this to be impossible."

"Impossible!" cried the ogre; "you shall see that presently."

And at the same time he changed himself into a mouse, and began to run about the floor. Puss no sooner perceived this but he fell upon him and ate him up.

Meanwhile the King, who saw, as he passed, this fine castle of the ogre's, had a mind to go into it. Puss, who heard the noise of his Majesty's coach running over the draw-bridge, ran out, and said to the King:

"Your Majesty is welcome to this castle of my Lord Marquis of Carabas."

"What! my Lord Marquis," cried the King, "and does this castle also belong to you? There can be nothing finer than this court and all the stately buildings which surround it; let us go into it, if you please."

The Marquis gave his hand to the Princess, and followed the King, who went first. They passed into a spacious hall, where they found a magnificent collation, which the ogre had prepared for his friends, who were that very day to visit him, but dared not to enter, knowing the King was there. His Majesty was perfectly charmed with the good qualities of my Lord Marquis of Carabas, as was his daughter, who had fallen violently in love with him, and, seeing the vast estate he possessed, said to him, after having drunk five or six glasses:

"It will be owing to yourself only, my Lord Marquis, if you are not my son-in-law."

The Marquis, making several low bows, accepted the honor which his Majesty conferred upon him, and forthwith, that very same day, married the Princess.

Puss became a great lord, and never ran after mice any more but only for his diversion.

The Cat on the Dovrefell

George Webbe Dasent

ONCE ON A TIME THERE WAS A MAN UP IN FINNMARK WHO HAD CAUGHT
a great white bear, which he was going to take to the king of Denmark.
Now, it so fell out, that he came to the Dovrefell just about Christmas
Eve, and there he turned into a cottage where a man lived, whose name
was Halvor, and asked the man if he could get house-room there, for his
bear and himself.

"Heaven never help me, if what I say isn't true!" said the man; "but we
can't give any one house-room just now, for every Christmas Eve such a
pack of Trolls come down upon us, that we are forced to flit, and haven't
so much as a house over our own heads, to say nothing of lending one
to any one else."

"Oh?" said the man, "if that's all, you can very well lend me your
house; my bear can lie under the stove yonder, and I can sleep in the
side-room."

Well, he begged so hard, that at last he got leave to stay there; so the
people of the house flitted out, and before they went, everything was got
ready for the Trolls; the tables were laid, and there was rice porridge, and
fish boiled in lye, and sausages, and all else that was good, just as for any
other grand feast.

So, when everything was ready, down came the Trolls. Some were
great, and some were small; some had long tails, and some had no tails
at all; some, too, had long, long noses; and they ate and drank, and tasted

everything. Just then one of the little Trolls caught sight of the white bear, who lay under the stove; so he took a piece of sausage and stuck it on a fork, and went and poked it up against the bear's nose, screaming out:

"Pussy, will you have some sausage?"

Then the white bear rose up and growled, and hunted the whole pack of them out of doors, both great and small.

Next year Halvor was out in the wood, on the afternoon of Christmas Eve, cutting wood before the holidays, for he thought the Trolls would come again; and just as he was hard at work, he heard a voice in the wood calling out:

"Halvor! Halvor!"

"Well," said Halvor, "here I am."

"Have you got your big cat with you still?"

"Yes, that I have," said Halvor; "she's lying at home under the stove, and what's more, she has now got seven kittens, far bigger and fiercer than she is herself."

"Oh, then, we'll never come to see you again," bawled out the Troll away in the wood, and he kept his word; for since that time the Trolls have never eaten their Christmas brose with Halvor on the Dovrefell.

FORTY-SEVEN

Mistress Pussy's Mistake

Abbie Phillips Walker

A VERY KIND GENTLEMAN, WHO LIVED IN A BIG HOUSE WHICH WAS IN the midst of a beautiful park, had a handsome cat of which he was very fond. While he felt sure Pussy was fond of him, he knew very well she would hurt the birds, so he put a pretty ribbon around Pussy's neck, and on it a little silver bell which tinkled whenever she moved and this warned the birds that she was near.

Pussy resented this, but pretended she did not care. One day a thrush was singing very sweetly on the bough of a tree which overhung a small lake. Pussy walked along under the tree, and, looking up at the thrush, said: "Madam Thrush, you have a most beautiful voice, and you are a very handsome bird. I do wish I were nearer to you, for I am not so young as I was once, and I cannot hear so well."

The thrush trilled a laugh at Pussy, and said: "Yes, Miss Puss, I can well believe you wish me nearer, but not to see or hear me better, but that you might grasp me."

Pussy pretended not to hear the last remark, but said: "My beautiful Thrush, will you not come down where I can hear you better? I cannot get about as nimbly as I used to when I was young, or I would go to you."

"I cannot sing so well on the ground," replied the thrush. "You can come up here, even if you are not so spry as you were. But tell me, do you not find the bell you wear very trying to your nerves?"

"Oh no," answered sly Pussy. "It is so pretty that I'm glad to wear it, and my master thinks I am so handsome that he likes to see me dressed well. And then he can always find me when he hears the bell. That is why I wear it."

"I understand," answered the thrush, "and we birds are always glad to hear it, too." And she trilled another laugh at Pussy and added, "You are certainly a very handsome creature, Miss Puss."

Pussy all this time had very slowly climbed the tree, for she wanted the thrush to think she was old and slow, but the bird had her bright eyes upon her. When Pussy reached the branch the thrush was on she stopped and seated herself.

"Now, my pretty little friend, do sing to me your loudest song."

She hoped it would be loud enough to drown the tinkle of the bell. The thrush began and was soon singing very sweetly. Pussy took a very cautious step and then remained quiet. The thrush stopped singing and spread her wings.

"Oh, do not stop!" said Puss. "Your song was so soothing I was in a doze; do sing again." And she moved a little closer.

The thrush took a step nearer to the end of the bough and said: "I am glad you like my voice. I will sing again if it pleases you so much."

She began her song, but she kept her eyes on Puss, and as Puss drew nearer she moved closer to the end of the swinging bough.

She had reached a very high note when Puss gave a spring, but the thrush was too quick; she flew out of Pussy's reach, and splash went Pussy into the lake, for she had not noticed that the thrush was moving to the end of the bough, so intent was she on the thought of catching her.

Poor Pussy was very wet when she scrambled to the bank of the lake, and the birds were chirping and making a great noise.

"How did you like your bath, Miss Puss?" the thrush called to her. "You should never lay traps for others, for often you fall into them yourself."

What About the Cat?

Edith Eaton

WHAT ABOUT THE CAT?" ASKED THE LITTLE PRINCESS OF HER ELDEST maid.

"It is sitting on the sunny side of the garden wall, watching the butterflies. It meowed for three of the prettiest to fall into its mouth, and would you believe it, that is just what happened. A green, a blue, a pink shaded with gold, all went down pussy's red throat."

The princess smiled. "What about the cat?" she questioned her second maid.

"She is seated in your honorable father's chair of state, and your honorable father's first body-slave is scratching her back with your father's own back-scratcher, made of the purest gold and ivory."

The princess laughed outright. She pattered gracefully into another room. There she saw the youngest daughter of her foster-mother.

"What about the cat?" she asked for the third time.

"The cat! Oh, she has gone to Shinku's duck farm. The ducks love her so that when they see her, they swim to shore and embrace her with their wings. Four of them combined to make a raft and she got upon their backs and went down-stream with them. They met some of the ducklings on the way and she patted them to death with her paws. How the big ducks quacked!"

"That is a good story," quoth the princess.

She went into the garden and, seeing one of the gardeners, said: "What about the cat?"

"It is frisking somewhere under the cherry tree, but you would not know it if you saw it," replied the gardener.

"Why?" asked the princess.

"Because, Your Highness, I gave it a strong worm porridge for its dinner, and as soon as it ate it, its white fur coat became a glossy green, striped with black. It looks like a giant caterpillar, and all the little caterpillars are going to hold a festival tonight in its honor."

"Deary me! What a great cat!" exclaimed the princess.

A little further on she met one of the chamberlains of the palace. "What about the cat?" she asked.

"It is dancing in the ballroom in a dress of elegant cobwebs and a necklace of pearl rice. For partner, she has the yellow dragon in the hall, come to life, and they take such pretty steps together that all who behold them shriek in ecstasy. Three little mice hold up her train as she dances, and another sits perched on the tip of the dragon's curled tail."

At this the princess quivered like a willow tree and was obliged to seek her apartments. When there, she recovered herself, and placing a blossom on her exquisite eyebrow, commanded that all those of whom she had inquired concerning the cat should be brought before her. When they appeared she looked at them very severely and said:

"You have all told me different stories when I have asked you: 'What about the cat?' Which of these stories is true?"

No one answered. All trembled and paled.

"They are all untrue," announced the princess.

She lifted her arm and there crawled out of her sleeve her white cat. It had been there all the time.

Then the courtly chamberlain advanced toward her, kotowing three times. "Princess," said he, "would a story be a story if it were true? Would you have been as well entertained this morning if, instead of our stories, we, your unworthy servants, had simply told you that the cat was up your sleeve?"

The princess lost her severity in hilarity. "Thank you, my dear servants," said she. "I appreciate your desire to amuse me."

She looked at her cat, thought of all it had done and been in the minds of her servants, and laughed like a princess again and again.

FORTY-NINE

There Arose a King

E. F. Benson

AGAG, THOUGH OF UNDOUBTEDLY ROYAL BLOOD, WAS NEVER A REAL king. He was no more than one of the Hyksos, a shepherd-king, bound by the limitations of his race, and no partaker in its magnificence. Naturally, he did not work as the late housekeeper had done (and no one expected that of him), but he had neither the splendour nor the vivacity, possessed, let us say, by Henry VIII or George IV, to make up for his indolence in affairs of state.

Henry VIII, anyhow, busied himself in marriages, whereas Agag was merely terrified at the idea of wooing, not to say winning, any of the princesses that were brought to his notice; and they, on their part, only made the rudest faces at him. Again George IV, though unkingly in many respects, used to plunge about in the wild pursuit of pleasure, and was supposed to have a kind heart.

Agag, on the contrary, never plunged: a cushion and some fish and plenty of repose were the sum of his desires, and as for a kind heart, he never had a heart at all. An unkind heart would have given him some semblance of personality, but there was not the faintest room to suppose that any emotion, other than the desire for food and sleep and warmth, came within measurable distance of him.

He died in his sleep, probably of apoplexy, after a large meal, and beautiful in death as in life, was buried and forgotten. I have never known a cat so completely devoid of character, and I sometimes wonder whether he was a real cat at all, and not some sort of inflated dormouse in cat's clothing.

There followed a republican régime in this matter of cats. We went back, after Agag, to working cats, who would sit at mouse-holes for hours together, pounce and devour, and clean themselves and sleep, but among them all there was no "character" which ever so faintly resembled even Martha, far less Puss-cat.

I suppose the royalty of Agag, stupid and dull though he was, had infected me with a certain snobbishness as regards cats, and secretly— given that there were to be no more of those splendid plebeians, like Puss-cat—I longed for somebody who combined royal descent (for the sake of beauty and pride) with character, good or bad. Nero or Heliogabalus or Queen Elizabeth, or even the Emperor William II of Germany would have done, but I didn't want George I on the one side or a mere mild President of a small republic on the other.

Just after Agag's death I had moved up to London, and for a time there was this succession of unnoticeable heads of the state. They were born—those presidents of my republic—from respectable hard-working families, and never gave themselves out (though they knew quite well that they were the heads of the state) to be anything else but what they were: good, hard-working cats, with, of course, not only a casting, but a determining vote on all questions that concerned them or anybody else.

We were democratic in those days, and I am afraid "freedom broadened slowly down" from president to president. We were loyal, law-abiding citizens under their rule, but when our president was sitting at the top of the area steps, taking the air after his morning's work, it used to be no shock to me to see him tickled on the top of his head by people like tradesmen coming for orders, or a policeman or a nursery-maid. The president, in these circumstances, would arch a back, make poker of a tail, and purr. Being at leisure and unoccupied with cares of State, he did not pretend to be anything but *bourgeois*. The *bourgeoisie* had access to him; he would play with them, without any sense of inequality, through the area railings. There was a nursery-maid, I remember, whom our last president was very much attached to. He used to make the most terrific onslaughts at her shoelaces.

But now all that *régime* is past. We are royalist again to the core, and Cyrus, of undoubtedly royal descent, is on the throne. The revolution was accomplished in the most pacific manner conceivable. A friend, on my birthday, two years ago, brought a small wicker basket, and the moment it was opened the country, which for a month or two had been in a state of darkest anarchy, without president or any ruler, was a civilized state again, with an acknowledged king. There was no war; nothing sanguinary occurred. Only by virtue of the glory of our king we became a great Power again.

Cyrus had arranged that his pedigree should come with him; this was much bigger than Cyrus, and, being written on parchment (with a large gold crown painted at the head of it), was far more robust than he whose ancestors it enumerated. For his majesty, as he peered over the side of the royal cradle, did not seem robust at all. He put two little weak paws on the edge of his basket and tried to look like a lion, but he had no spirit to get farther. Then he wrinkled up his august face and gave a sneeze so prodigious that he tumbled out of the basket altogether, and by accident (or at the most by catarrh) set foot in the dominions where he still reigns. Of course, I was not quite so stupid as not to recognize a royal landing, though made in so unconventional a manner; it was only as if George IV, in one of his numerous landings on some pier (so fitly commemorated by the insertion of a large brass boot print), had fallen flat on his face instead, and was commemorated by a full-length brass, with top-hat a little separate.

Babies of the human species, it is true, are all like each other, and I would defy any professor of Eugenics or of allied and abstruse schools of investigation to say, off-hand, whether a particular baby, divorced from his surroundings, is the Prince of Wales or Master Jones. But, quite apart from his pedigree, there was never any question at all about Cyrus. There was no single hair on his lean little body that was not of the true and royal blue, and his ears already were tufted inside with downy growth, and his poor little eyes, sadly screened by the moisture of his catarrh, showed their yellow topaz irises, that were never seen on Master Jones.

So he tumbled upside down into his new kingdom, and, recovering himself, sat up and blinked, and said, "Ah-h-h." I took him up very reverently in both hands, and put him on my knee. He made an awful face, like a Chinese grotesque instead of a Persian king, but anyhow it was an Oriental face. Then he put a large paw in front of his diminutive nose and went fast asleep. It had been a most fatiguing sneeze.

Royal Persian babies, as you perhaps know, must never, after they have said good-bye to their royal mammas, be given milk. When they are thirsty they must have water; when they are hungry they have little finely chopped-up dishes of flesh and fish and fowl. As Cyrus slept, little chopped-up things were hastily prepared for him, and when he woke, his food and drink were waiting his royal pleasure. They seemed to please him a good deal, but at a crucial moment, when his mouth was quite full, he sneezed again. There was an explosion of awful violence, but the Royal baby licked up the fragments. . . . We knew at once that we had a tidy king to rule over us.

Cyrus was two months old when he became king, and the next four months were spent in growing and eating and sneezing. His general manner of life was to eat largely and instantly fall asleep, and it was then, I think, that he grew. Eventually a sneeze plucked him from his slumber, and this first alarum was a storm-cone, so to speak, that betokened the coming tornado. Once, after I began to count, he sneezed seventeen times. . . . Then, when that was over, he sat quiet and recuperated; then he jumped straight up in the air, purred loudly, and ate again. The meal was succeeded by more slumber, and the cycle of his day was complete.

His first refreshment he took about seven in the morning—as soon as anybody was dressed—and an hour later, heavily slumbering, he was brought up to my room when I was called, buttoned up in my servant's coat, and placed on my bed. He at once guessed that there must be a pleasant warm cave underneath the bedclothes, and, with stampings and purrings, penetrated into this abyss, curled himself against my side, and resumed his interrupted slumbers.

After a while I would feel an internal stirring begin in my bed, and usually managed to deposit the king on the floor before his first sneeze. His second breakfast, of course, had come upstairs with my hot water, and after the sneezing was over he leaped into the air, espied and stalked some new and unfamiliar object, and did his duty with his victuals. He then looked round for a convenient resting-place, choosing one, if possible, that resembled an ambush, the definition of which may be held to be a place with a small opening and spaciousness within.

That gave us the second clue (tidiness being the first) towards the king's character. He had a tactical mind, and should make a good general. As soon as I observed this, I used to make an ambush for him among the sheets of the morning paper, providing it with a small spy-hole. If I scratched the paper in the vicinity of the spy-hole, a little silver-blue paw made wild dabs at the seat of the disturbance. Having thus frustrated any possible enemy, he went to sleep.

But the ambush he liked best was a half-opened drawer, such as he found one morning for himself. There among flannel shirts and vests he made himself exceedingly comfortable, pending attacks. But before he went to sleep he made a point of putting out a small and awe-inspiring head to terrify any marauding bands who might be near. This precaution was usually successful, and he slept for the greater part of the morning.

For six months he stuffed and sneezed and slept, and then, one morning, like Lord Byron and the discovery of his fame, Cyrus woke and discovered the responsibilities of kingship. His sneezing fits suddenly ceased, and the Cyropaidaia (or education of Cyrus) began. He conducted his own education, of course, entirely by himself; he knew, by heredity, what a king had to learn, and proceeded to learn it. Hitherto the pantry and my bedroom were the only territories of his dominion that he had any acquaintance with, and a royal progress was necessary.

The dining-room did not long detain him, and presented few points of interest, but in a small room adjoining he found on the table a telephone with a long green cord attached to the receiver. This had to be investigated, since his parents had not told him about telephones, but he soon grasped the principle of it, and attempted to get the ear-piece off its hook, no doubt with a view to issuing orders of some kind. It would not yield to gentle methods, and, after crouching behind a book and wriggling his body a great deal, he determined to rush the silly thing. A wild leap in the air, and Cyrus and the green cord and the receiver were all mingled up together in hopeless confusion. . . . He did not telephone again for weeks.

The drawing-room was less dangerous. There was a bearskin on the floor, and Cyrus sat down in front of the head, prepared to receive homage. This, I suppose, was duly tendered, because he tapped it on the nose (as the King entering the City of London touches the sword presented by the Lord Mayor) and passed on to the piano. He did not care about the keyboard, but liked the pedals, and also caught sight of a reflection of himself in the black shining front of it.

This was rather a shock and entailed a few swift fandango-like steps with fore-paws waving wildly in the air. Horror! The silent image opposite did exactly the same thing; . . . it was nearly as bad as the telephone. But the piano stood at an angle to the wall, offering a suitable ambush, and he scampered behind it. And there he found the great ambush of all, for the back cloth of the piano was torn, and he could get completely inside it. Tactically, it was a perfect ambush, for it commanded the only route into the room from the door; but his delight in it was such that whenever he was ambushed there, he could not resist putting his head out and glaring, if anybody came near, thus giving the secret completely away. Or was it only indulgence towards our weak intellects, that were so incapable of imagining that there was a king inside the piano?

The exploration of the kitchen followed; the only point of interest was a fox-terrier at whom the king spat; but in the scullery there was a very extraordinary affair—namely, a brass tap, conveniently placed over a sink, half-covered with a board. On the nozzle of this tap an occasional drop of water appeared, which at intervals fell off. Cyrus could not see what happened to it, but when next the drop gathered he put his paw to it and licked it off. After doing this for nearly an hour he came to the conclusion that it was the same water as he drank after his meals. The supply seemed constant, though exiguous; . . . it might have to be seen to. After that he just looked in at the linen cupboard, and the door blew to while he was inside. He was not discovered till six hours later and was inclined to be stiff about it.

Next day the Royal progress continued, and Cyrus discovered the garden (forty feet by twenty, but large enough for Mr. Lloyd George to have his eye on it and demand a valuation of the mineral rights therein). But it was not large enough for Cyrus (I don't know what he expected), for after looking at it closely for a morning, he decided that he could run up the brick walls that bounded it.

This was an infringement of his prerogative, for the king is bound to give notice to his ministers, when he proposes to quit the country, and Cyrus had said nothing about it. Consequently I ran out and pulled him quietly but firmly back by the tail, which was the only part of him that I could reach. He signified his disapproval in what is called "the usual manner," and tried to bite me. Upon which I revolted and drove the king indoors and bought some rabbit wire. This I fastened down along the top of the wall, so that it projected horizontally inwards. Then I let the king out again and sat down on the steps to see what would happen.

Cyrus pretended that the walls were of no interest to him and stalked a few dead leaves. But even a king is bounded, not only by rabbit wire, but by the limitations of cat-nature, which compelled him to attempt again what he has been thwarted over. So, after massacring a few leaves (already dead), he sprang up the wall, and naturally hit his nose against the rabbit wire, and was cast back from the frontier into his own dominions.

Once again he tried and failed, appealed to an obdurate prime minister, and then sat down and devoted the whole power of his tactical mind to solving this baffling affair. And three days afterward I saw him again run up the wall, and instead of hitting his nose against the rabbit wire, he clung to it with his claws. It bent with his weight, and he got one claw on the upper side of it, then the other, wriggled round it, and stood triumphant with switching tail on the frontier.

So in turn I had to sit and think; but, short of building up the whole garden wall to an unscalable height, or erecting a *chevaux de fries* on the top of it, I had a barren brain. After all, foreign travel is an ineradicable instinct in cat-nature, and I infinitely preferred that the king should travel among small back-gardens than out of the area gate into the street. Perhaps, if he had full licence (especially since I could not prevent him) to explore the hinter-lands, he might leave the more dangerous coast alone. . . . And then I thought of a plan, which perhaps might recall my Reise-Kaiser, when on his travels. This I instantly proceeded to test.

Now I had been told by my Cabinet that the one noise which would pluck the king out of his deepest slumber, and would bring him bouncing and ecstatic to the place where this sound came from, was the use of the knife-sharpener. This, it appeared, was the earliest piece of household ritual performed in the morning, when Cyrus was hungriest, and the sound of the knife-sharpener implied to him imminent food. I borrowed the knife-sharpener and ran out into the garden.

Cyrus was already four garden walls away and paid not the slightest attention to my calling him. So I vigorously began stropping the knife. The effect was instantaneous; he turned and fled along the walls that separated him from that beloved and welcome noise. He jumped down into his own dominion with erect and bushy tail . . . and I gave him three little oily fragments of sardine-skin. And up till now, at any rate, that metallic chirruping of the sharpened knife has never failed. Often I have seen him a mere speck on some horizon roof, but there appears to be no incident or interest in the whole range of foreign travel that can compete with this herald of food.

On the other hand, too, if Cyrus is not quite well (this very seldom happens), though he does not care for food, he does not, either, feel up to foreign travel, and, therefore, the knife-sharpener may repose in its drawer. Indeed, there are advantages in having a greedy king that I had never suspected. . . .

As the months went on and Cyrus grew larger and longer-haired, he gradually, as befitted a king who had come to rule over men, renounced all connexion with other animals, especially cats. He used to lie *perdu* in a large flower-pot which he had overturned (ejecting the hydrangea with scuffles of backward-kicking hind legs), and watch for the appearance of his discarded race.

If so much as an ear or a tail appeared on the frontier walls, he hurled himself, his face a mask of fury, at the intruder. The same ambush, I am sorry to say, served him as a butt for the destruction of sparrows. He did not kill them, but brought them indoors to the kitchen, and presented them, as a token of his prowess as a hunter, to the cook. Dogs, similarly, were not allowed, when he sat at the area gate. Once I saw, returning home from a few doors off, a brisk Irish terrier gambol down my area steps (Cyrus's area steps, I mean), and quickened my pace, fearing for Cyrus, if he happened to be sitting there.

He was sitting there, but I need not have been afraid, for before I had reached the house a prolonged and dismal yell rent the air, and an astonished Irish terrier shot up, as from a gun, through the area gate again with a wild and hunted expression. When I got there I found Cyrus seated on the top step calm and firm, delicately licking the end of his silvery paw.

Once only, as far as I remember, was Cyrus ever routed by anything with four legs, but that was not a question of lack of physical courage, but a collapse of nerves in the presence of a sort of hobgoblin, something altogether uncanny and elfin. For a visitor had brought inside her muff an atrocious little griffon, and Cyrus had leaped on to this lady's knee and rather liked the muff.

Then, from inside it, within an inch or two of Cyrus's face, there looked out a half-fledged little head, of a new and nerve-shattering type. Cyrus stared for one moment at this dreadful apparition, and then bolted inside the piano-ambush. The griffon thought this was the first maneuvre in a game of play, so jumped down and sniffed round the entrance to the ambush. Panic-stricken scufflings and movements came from within. . . . Then a diabolical thought struck me: Cyrus had never yet been in his ambush when the piano was played, and the griffon being stowed back again in the muff, for fear of accidents, I went very softly to the keys and played one loud chord. As the Irish terrier came out of the area gate, so came Cyrus out of his violated sanctuary. . . .

Cyrus was now just a year old; his kitten-coat had been altogether discarded; he already weighed eleven pounds, and he was clad from nose to tail-tip in his complete royal robes. His head was small, and looked even smaller framed in the magnificent ruff that curled outward from below his chin. In colour he was like a smoky shadow, with two great topaz lights gleaming in the van; the tips of his paws were silvery, as if wood-ash smouldered whitely through the smoke.

That year we enjoyed a summer of extraordinary heat, and Cyrus made the unique discovery about the refrigerator, a large tin box, like a safe, that stood in the scullery. The germ of the discovery, I am afraid, was a fluke, for he had snatched a steak of salmon from the tray which the fishmonger had most imprudently left on the area steps, and, with an instinct for secrecy which this unusual treasure-trove awoke in him, he bore it to the nearest dark place, which happened to be the refrigerator.

Here he ate as much as it was wise to gobble at one sitting, and then, I must suppose, instead of going to sleep, he pondered. For days he had suffered from the excessive heat; his flower-pot ambush in the garden was unendurable, so also was his retreat under my bedclothes. But here was a far more agreeable temperature. . . . This is all the reconstruction of motive that I can give, and it is but guesswork. But day after day, while the heat lasted, Cyrus sat opposite the refrigerator and bolted into it whenever he found opportunity. The heat also increased his somnolence, and one morning, when he came up to breakfast with me, he fell asleep on the sofa before I had time to cut off the little offering of kidney which I had meant to be my homage. When I put it quite close to his nose he opened his mouth to receive it, but was again drowned in gulfs of sleep before he could masticate it. So it stuck out of the corner of his mouth like a cigarette. But eventually, I knew, he "would wake and remember and understand."

And now Cyrus is two years old, and has reigned a year and ten months. I think he has completed his own education, and certainly he has cleared his frontiers of cats, and, I am afraid, his dominion of sparrows.

One misguided bird this year built in a small bush in his garden. A series of distressing unfledged objects were presented to the cook. . . . He has appropriated the chair I was accustomed to use in my sitting-room, and he has torn open the new back-cloth that I had caused to be put on my piano. I dare say he was right about that, for there is no use in having an ambush if you cannot get into it. In other ways, too, I do not think he is strictly constitutional. But whenever I return to his kingdom after some absence, as soon as the door is open Cyrus runs down the steps to meet me (even as Puss-cat used to do) and makes a poker of his tail, and says "Ah-h-h-h."

That makes up for a good deal of what appears to be tyranny. And only this morning he gave me a large spider, precious and wonderful, and still faintly stirring. . . .

FIFTY

The Visitor from the Cellar

Amy Walton

THE WHOLE HOUSE IN LONDON WAS DULL AND GLOOMY, ITS LOFTY rooms and staircases were filled with a sort of misty twilight all day, and the sun very seldom looked in at its windows. Ruth Lorimer thought, however, that the very dullest room of all was the nursery, in which she had to pass so much of her time.

It was so high up that the people and carts and horses in the street below looked like toys. She could not even see these properly, because there were iron bars to prevent her from stretching her head out too far, so that all she could do was to look straight across to the row of tall houses opposite, or up at the sky between the chimney-pots. How she longed for something different to look at!

The houses always looked the same, and though the sky changed sometimes, it was often of a dirty grey colour, and then Ruth gave a little sigh and looked back from the window-seat where she was kneeling, into the nursery, for something to amuse her. It was full of all sorts of toys— dolls, and dolls' houses elegantly furnished, pictures and books and many pretty things; but in spite of all these she often found nothing to please her, for what she wanted more than anything else was a companion of her own age, and she had no brothers or sisters.

The dolls, however much she pretended, were never glad, or sorry, or happy, or miserable—they could not answer her when she talked to them, and their beautiful bright eyes had a hard unfeeling look which became very tiring, for it never changed.

There was certainly Nurse Smith. She was alive and real enough; there was no necessity to "pretend" anything about her. She was always there, sitting upright and flat-backed beside her work-basket, frowning a little, not because she was cross, but because she was rather near-sighted. She had come when Ruth was quite a baby, after Mrs. Lorimer's death, and Aunt Clarkson often spoke of her as "a treasure."

However that might be, she was not an amusing companion; though she did her best to answer all Ruth's questions, and was always careful of her comfort, and particular about her being neatly dressed.

Perhaps it was not her fault that she did not understand games and was quite unable to act the part of any other character than her own. If she did make the attempt, she failed so miserably that Ruth had to tell her what to say, which made it so flat and uninteresting that she found it better to play alone. But she often became weary of this; and there were times when she was tired of her toys, and tired of Nurse Smith, and did not know what in the world to do with herself.

Each day passed much in the same way. Ruth's governess came to teach her for an hour every morning, and then after her early dinner there was a walk with Nurse, generally in one direction. And after tea it was time to go and see her father—quite a long journey, through the silent house, down the long stairs to the dining-room where he sat alone at his dessert.

Ruth could not remember her mother, and she saw so little of her father that he seemed almost a stranger to her. He was so wonderfully busy, and the world he lived in was such a great way off from hers in the nursery.

In the morning he hurried away just as she was at her breakfast, and all she knew of him was the resounding slam of the hall door, which came echoing up the staircase. Very often in the evening he came hastily into the nursery to say good-bye on his way out to some dinner-party, and at night she woke up to hear his step on the stairs as he came back late.

But when he dined at home Ruth always went downstairs to dessert. Then, as she entered the large somber dining-room, where there were great oil paintings on the walls and heavy hangings to the windows, and serious-looking ponderous furniture, her father would look up from his book, or from papers spread on the table, and nod kindly to her:

"Ah! it's you, Ruth. Quite well, eh? There's a good child. Have an orange? That's right."

Then he would plunge into his reading again, and Ruth would climb slowly on to a great mahogany chair placed ready for her and watch him as she cut up her orange.

She wondered very much why people wrote him such long, long letters, all on blue paper and tied up with pink tape. She felt sure they were not nice letters, for his face always looked worried over them; and when he had finished he threw them on the floor, as though he were glad. This made her so curious that she once ventured to ask him what they were. They were called "briefs," he told her. But she was not much wiser; for, hearing from Nurse Smith that "brief" was another word for short, she felt sure there must be some mistake.

Exactly as the clock struck eight Nurse's knock came at the door, Ruth got down from her chair and said good-night.

Sometimes her father was so deeply engaged in his reading that he stared at her with a far-away look in his eyes, as if he scarcely knew who she was. After a minute he said absently: "Bed-time, eh? Good-night. Good-night, my dear." Sometimes when he was a little less absorbed he put a sixpence or a shilling into her hand as he kissed her, and added: "There's something to spend at the toy-shop."

Ruth received these presents without much surprise or joy. She was used to buying things and did not find it very interesting; for she could not hope for any sign of pleasure from her dolls when she brought them new clothes or furniture.

It is a little dull when all one's efforts for people are received with a perfectly unmoved face. She had once brought Nurse Smith a small china image, hoping that it would be an agreeable surprise; but that had not been successful either. "Lor,' my dear, don't you go spending your money on me," she said. "Chany ornaments ain't much good for anything, to my thinking, 'cept to ketch the dust."

Thus it came to pass that Ruth never talked much about what interested her either to her father or to Nurse Smith, and as she had no brothers and sisters she was obliged to amuse herself with fancied conversations. Sometimes these were carried on with her dolls, but her chief friend was a picture which she passed every night on the staircase.

It was of a man in a flat cap and a fur robe, and he had a pointed smooth chin and narrow eyes, which seemed to follow her slyly on her way. She did not like him and she did not actually fear him, but she had a feeling that he listened to what she said, and that she must tell him any news she had. There was never much except on "Aunt Clarkson's day," as she called it.

Aunt Clarkson was her father's sister. She lived in the country and had many little boys and girls whom Ruth had seldom seen, though she heard a great deal about them.

Once every month this aunt came up to London for the day, had long conversations with Nurse, and looked carefully at all Ruth's clothes.

She was a sharp-eyed lady, and her visits made a stir in the house which was like a cold wind blowing, so that Ruth was glad when they were over, though her aunt always spoke kindly to her, and said: "Some day you must come and see your little cousins in the country."

She had said this so often without its having happened, however, that Ruth had come to look upon it as a mere form of speech—part of Aunt Clarkson's visit, like saying "How d'ye do?" or "Good-bye."

It was shortly after one of these occasions that quite by chance Ruth found a new friend, who was better than either the dolls or the man in the picture, because, though it could not answer her, it was really alive. She discovered it in this way.

One afternoon she and Nurse Smith had come in from their usual walk, and were toiling slowly up from the hall to the nursery. The stairs got steeper at the last flight, and Nurse went more slowly still, and panted a good deal, for she was stouter than she need have been, though Ruth would never have dreamed of saying so. Ruth was in front, and she had nearly reached the top when something came hurrying towards her which surprised her very much. It was a long, lean, grey cat. It had a guilty look, as though it knew it had been trespassing, and squeezed itself as close as it could against the wall as it passed.

"Pretty puss!" said Ruth softly, and put out her hand to stop it.

The cat at once arched up its back and gave a friendly little answering mew. Ruth wondered where it came from. It was ugly, she thought, but it seemed a pleasant cat and glad to be noticed. She rubbed its head gently. It felt hard and rough like Nurse's old velvet bonnet; there was indeed no sleekness about it anywhere, and it was so thin that its sides nearly met.

"Poor puss!" said Ruth stroking it tenderly.

The cat replied by pushing its head gently against her arm, and presently began a low purring song. Delighted, Ruth bent her ear to listen.

"Whoosh! Shish! Get along! Scat!" suddenly sounded from a few steps below. Nurse's umbrella was violently flourished, the cat flew downstairs with a spit like an angry firework, and Ruth turned round indignantly.

"You *shouldn't* have done that," she said, stamping her foot; "I wanted to talk to it. Whose is it?"

"It's that nasty kitchen cat," said Nurse, much excited, and grasping her umbrella spitefully. "I'm not going to have it prowling about on *my* landing. An ugly thieving thing, as has no business above stairs at all."

Ruth pressed her face against the balusters. In the distance below she could see the small grey form of the kitchen cat making its way swiftly and silently downstairs. It went so fast that it seemed to float rather than to run, and was soon out of sight.

"I should like to have played with it up in the nursery," she said, with a sigh, as she continued her way. "I wish you hadn't frightened it away."

"Lor,' Miss Ruth, my dear," answered Nurse, "what can a little lady like you want with a nasty, low, kitchen cat! Come up and play with some of your beautiful toys, there's a dear! Do."

Nevertheless Ruth thought about the cat a great deal that afternoon, and the toys seemed even less interesting than usual. When tea was over, and Nurse had taken up her sewing again, she began to make a few inquiries.

"Where does that cat live?" she asked.

"In the kitchen, to be sure," said Nurse; "and the cellar, and coal-hole, and such like. Along with the rats and mice—and the beadles," she added, as an after-thought.

"The beadles!" repeated Ruth doubtfully. "*What* beadles?"

"Why, the *black* beadles, to be sure," replied Nurse cheerfully.

Ruth was silent. It seemed dismal company for the kitchen cat. Then she said:

"Are there many of them?"

"Swarms!" said Nurse, breaking off her thread with a snap. "The kitchen's black with 'em at night."

What a dreadful picture!

"Who feeds the cat?" asked Ruth again.

"Oh, I don't suppose nobody *feeds* it," answered Nurse. "It lives on what it ketches every now and then."

No wonder it looked thin! Poor kitchen cat! How very miserable and lonely it must be with no one to take care of it, and how dreadful for it to have such nasty things to eat! And the supply even of these must be short sometimes, Ruth went on to consider. What did it do when it could find no more mice or rats? Of the beetles she could not bear even to think.

As she turned these things seriously over in her mind she began to wish she could do something to alter them, to make the cat's life more comfortable and pleasant. If she could have it to live with her in the nursery for instance, she could give it some of her own bread and milk, and part of her own dinner; then it would get fatter and perhaps prettier too. She would tie a ribbon round its neck, and it should sleep in a basket lined with red flannel, and never be scolded or chased about or hungry any more. All these pictures were suddenly destroyed by Nurse's voice:

"But I hope you'll not encourage it up here, Miss Ruth, for I couldn't abide it, and I'm sure your Aunt Clarkson wouldn't approve of it neither. I've had a horror of cats myself from a gal. They're that stealthy and treacherous, you never know where they mayn't be hiding, or when they won't spring out at you. If ever I catch it up here I shall bannock it down again."

There was evidently no sympathy to be looked for from Nurse Smith; but Ruth was used to keeping her thoughts and plans to herself, and did not miss it much. As she could not talk about it, however, she thought of her new acquaintance all the more; it was indeed seldom out of her mind, and while she seemed to be quietly amusing herself in her usual way, she was occupied with all sorts of plans and arrangements for the cat when it should come to live in the nursery.

Meanwhile it was widely separated from her; how could she let it know that she wanted to see it again? When she went up and down stairs she peered and peeped about to see if she could catch a glimpse of its hurrying grey figure, and she never came in from a walk without expecting to meet it on her way to the nursery. But she never did. The kitchen cat kept to its own quarters and its own society. Perhaps it had been too often "bannocked" down again to venture forth. And yet Ruth felt sure that it had been glad when she had spoken kindly to it.

What a pity that Nurse did not like cats!

She confided all this as usual to the man in the picture, who received it with his narrow observant glance and seemed to give it serious consideration. Perhaps it was he who at last gave her a splendid idea, which she hastened to carry out as well as she could, though remembering Nurse's strong expression of dislike she felt obliged to do so with the greatest secrecy.

As a first step, she examined the contents of her little red purse. A whole shilling, a sixpence, and a threepenny bit. That would be more than enough. Might they go to some shops that afternoon, she asked, when she and Nurse were starting for their walk.

"To be sure, Miss Ruth; and what sort of shops do you want? Toy-shops, I suppose."

"N-no," said Ruth; "I think not. It must be somewhere where they sell note-paper, and a baker's, I *think*; but I'm not quite sure."

Arrived at the stationer's, Ruth was a long time before deciding on what she would have; but at last, after the woman had turned over a whole boxful, she came to some pink note-paper with brightly painted heads of animals upon it, and upon the envelopes also.

"Oh!" cried Ruth when she saw it, clasping her hands with delight. "*That* would do beautifully. Only—*have* you any with a cat?"

Yes, there *was* some with a nice fluffy cat upon it, and she left the shop quite satisfied with her first purchase.

"And now," said Nurse briskly, whose patience had been a good deal tried, "we must make haste back, it's getting late."

But Ruth had still something on her mind. She *must* go to one more shop, she said, though she did not know exactly which. At last she fixed on a baker's.

"What should you think," she asked on the way, "that a cat likes to eat better than anything in the world?"

"Why, a mouse to be sure," answered Nurse promptly.

"Well, but *next* to mice?" persisted Ruth.

"Fish," said Nurse Smith.

"That would never do," thought Ruth to herself as she looked at a fish-shop they were passing, "It's so wet and slippery I couldn't possibly carry it home. Perhaps Nurse doesn't *really* know what cats like best. Anyhow, I'm sure it's never tasted anything so nice as a Bath bun." A Bath bun was accordingly bought, carried home, and put carefully away in the doll's house. And now Ruth felt that she had an important piece of business before her. She spread out a sheet of the new writing-paper on the window-seat, knelt in front of it with a pencil in her hand, and ruled some lines.

She could not write very well, and was often uncertain how to spell even short words; so she bit the end of her pencil and sighed a good deal before the letter was finished. At last it was done, and put into the envelope. But now came a new difficulty: How should it be addressed? After much thought she wrote the following:

The Kitchen Cat, The Kitchen, 17 Gower Street.

After this letter had been dropped into the pillar-box just in front of the house, Ruth began to look out still more eagerly for the kitchen cat, but days passed and she caught no glimpse of it anywhere.

It was disappointing, and troublesome too, because she had to carry the Bath bun about with her so long. Not only was it getting hard and dry, but it was such an awkward thing for her pocket that she had torn her frock in the effort to force it in.

"You might a' been carrying brick-bats about with you, Miss Ruth," said Nurse, "by the way you've slit your pocket open."

This went on till Ruth began to despair. "I'll try it one more evening," she said to herself, "and if it doesn't come then I shall give it up."

Once more, therefore, when she was ready to go downstairs, she took the bun out of the dolls' house, where she kept it wrapped up in tissue paper, and squeezed it into her pocket. Rather hopelessly, but still keeping a careful look-out, she proceeded slowly on her way, when behold, just as she reached the top of the last flight, a little cringing grey figure crossed the hall below.

"It's come!" she exclaimed in an excited whisper. "It's come at last!"

But though it had come, it seemed now the cat's greatest desire to go, for it was hurrying toward the kitchen stairs.

"Puss! puss!" called out Ruth in an entreating voice as she hastily ran down. "Stop a minute! *Pretty* puss!"

Startled at the noise and the patter of the quick little feet, the cat paused in its flight and turned its scared yellow-green eyes upon Ruth.

She had now reached the bottom step, where she stood struggling to get the Bath bun out of her small pocket, her face pink with the effort and anxiety lest the cat should go before she succeeded.

"*Pretty* puss!" she repeated as she tugged at the parcel. "Don't go away."

One more desperate wrench, which gashed open the corner of the pocket, and the bun was out. The cat looked on with one paw raised, ready to fly at the first sign of danger, as with trembling fingers Ruth managed to break a piece off the horny surface. She held it out. The cat came nearer, sniffed at it suspiciously, and then to her great joy took the morsel, crouched down, and munched it up. "How good it must taste," she thought, "after the mice and rats."

By degrees it was induced to make further advances, and before long to come on to the step where Ruth sat, and make a hearty meal of the bun which she crumbled up for it.

"I'm afraid it's dry," she said; "but I couldn't bring any milk, you know, and you must get some water afterwards."

The cat seemed to understand, and replied by pushing its head against her, and purred loudly. How thin it was! Ruth wondered as she looked gravely at it whether it would soon be fatter if she fed it every day. She became so interested in talking to it, and watching its behavior, that she nearly forgot she had to go into the dining-room, and jumped up with a start.

"Good-night," she said. "If you'll come again I'll bring you something else another day." She looked back as she turned the handle of the heavy door. The cat was sitting primly upright on the step washing its face after its meal. "I expect it doesn't feel so hungry now," thought Ruth as she went into the room.

The acquaintance thus fairly begun was soon followed by other meetings, and the cat was often in the hall when Ruth came downstairs, though it did not appear every evening. The uncertainty of this was most exciting, and "Will it be there to-night?" was her frequent thought during the day.

As time went on, and they grew to know each other better, she began to find the kitchen cat a far superior companion to either her dolls or the man in the picture. True, it could not answer her any more than they did—in words, but it had a language of its own which she understood perfectly. She knew when it was pleased, and when it said "Thank you" for some delicacy she brought for it; its yellow eyes beamed with sympathy and interest when she described the delights of that beautiful life it would enjoy in the nursery; and when she pitied it for the darkness of its present dwelling below, she knew it understood by the way it rubbed against her and arched up its back. There were many more pleasures in each day now that she had made this acquaintance.

Shopping became interesting, because she could look forward to the cat's surprise and enjoyment when the parcel was opened in the evening; everything that happened was treasured up to tell it when they met, or, if it was not there, to write to it on the pink note-paper; the very smartest sash belonging to her best doll was taken to adorn the cat's thin neck; and the secrecy which surrounded all this made it doubly delightful. Ruth had never been a greedy child, and if Nurse Smith wondered sometimes that she now spent all her money on cakes, she concluded that they must be for a dolls' feast, and troubled herself no further.

Miss Ruth was always so fond of "making believe." So things went on very quietly and comfortably, and though Ruth could not discover that the kitchen cat got any fatter, it had certainly improved in some ways since her attentions. Its face had lost its scared look, and it no longer crept about as close to the ground as possible but walked with an assured tread and its tail held high.

It could never be a pretty cat to the general eye, but when it came trotting noiselessly to meet Ruth, uttering its short mew of welcome, she thought it beautiful, and would not have changed it for the sleekest, handsomest cat in the kingdom.

But it was the kitchen cat still. All this did not bring it one step nearer to the nursery. It must still live, Ruth often thought with sorrow, among the rats and mice and beetles. Nothing could ever happen which would induce Nurse Smith to allow it to come upstairs. And yet something did happen which brought this very thing to pass in a strange way which would never have entered her mind.

The spring came on with a bright sun and cold sharp winds, and one day Ruth came in from her walk feeling shivery and tired. She could not eat her dinner, and her head had a dull ache in it, and she thought she would like to go to bed. She did not feel ill, she said, but she was first very hot and then very cold. Nurse Smith sent for the doctor; and he came and looked kindly at her and felt her pulse and said she must stay in bed and he would send some medicine.

And she went to sleep and had funny dreams in which she plainly saw the kitchen cat dressed in Aunt Clarkson's bonnet and cloak. It stood by her bed and talked in Aunt Clarkson's voice, and she saw its grey fur paws under the folds of the cloak. She wished it would go away and wondered how she could have been so fond of it. When Nurse came to give her something she said feebly:

"Send the cat away."

"Bless you, my dear, there's no cat here," she answered. "There's nobody been here but me and Mrs. Clarkson."

401

At last there came a day when she woke up from a long sleep and found that the pain in her head was gone, and that the things in the room which had been taking all manner of queer shapes looked all right again.

"And how do you feel, Miss Ruth, my dear?" asked Nurse, who sat sewing by the bedside.

"I'm quite well, thank you," said Ruth. "Why am I in bed in the middle of the day?"

"Well, you haven't been just quite well, you know," said Nurse.

"Haven't I?" said Ruth. She considered this for some time, and when Nurse came to her with some beef-tea in her hand, she asked:

"Have I been in bed more than a day?"

"You've been in bed a week," said Nurse. "But you'll get along finely now and be up and about again in no time."

Ruth drank her beef-tea and thought it over. Suddenly she dropped her spoon into the cup. The kitchen cat! How it must have missed her if she had been in bed a week. Unable to bear the idea in silence, she sat up in bed with a flushed face and asked eagerly:

"Have you seen the cat?"

Nurse instantly rose with a concerned expression and patted her soothingly on the shoulder.

"There now, my dear, we won't have any more fancies about cats and such. You drink your beef-tea up and I'll tell you something pretty."

Ruth took up her spoon again. It was of no use to talk to Nurse about it, but it was dreadful to think how disappointed the cat must have been evening after evening. Meanwhile Nurse went on in a coaxing tone:

"If so be as you make haste and get well, you're to go along with me and stay with your Aunt Clarkson in the country. There now!"

Ruth received the news calmly. It did not seem a very pleasant prospect, or even a very real one to her.

"There'll be little boys and girls to play with," pursued Nurse, trying to heighten the picture; "and flowers—and birds and such—and medders, and a garding, and all manner."

But nothing could rouse Ruth to more than a very languid interest in these delights. Her thoughts were all with her little friend downstairs; and she felt certain that it had often been hungry, and no doubt thought very badly of her for her neglect. If she could only see it and explain that it had not been her fault!

The next day Aunt Clarkson herself came. She always had a great deal on her mind when she came up to town and liked to get through her shopping in time to go back in the afternoon, so she could never stay long with Ruth. She came bustling in, looking very strong, and speaking in a loud cheerful voice, and all the while she was there she gave quick glances round her at everything in the room.

Ruth was well enough to be up, and was sitting in a big chair by the nursery fire, with picture-books and toys near; but she was not looking at them. Her eyes were fixed thoughtfully on the fire, and her mind was full of the kitchen cat. She had tried to write to it, but the words would not come, and her fingers trembled so much that she could not hold the pencil straight. The vexation and disappointment of this had made her head ache, and altogether she presented rather a mournful little figure.

"Well, Nurse, and how are we going on?" said Aunt Clarkson, sitting down in the chair Nurse placed for her. Remembering her dream, Ruth could not help giving a glance at Aunt Clarkson's hands. They were fat, round hands, and she kept them doubled up, so that they really looked rather like a cat's paws.

"Well, ma'am," replied Nurse, "Miss Ruth's better; but she's not, so to say, as cheerful as I could wish. Still a few *fancies* ma'am," she added in an undertone, which Ruth heard perfectly.

"Fancies, eh?" repeated Aunt Clarkson in her most cheerful voice. "Oh, we shall get rid of them at Summerford. You'll have real things to play with there, Ruth, you know. Lucy, and Cissie, and Bobbie will be better than fancies, won't they?"

Ruth gave a faint little nod. She did not know what her aunt meant by "fancies." The cat was quite as real as Lucy, or Cissie, or Bobbie. Should she ask her about it, or did she hate cats like Nurse Smith? She gazed wistfully at Mrs. Clarkson's face, who had now drawn a list from her pocket, and was running through the details half aloud with an absorbed frown.

"I shall wait and see the doctor, Nurse," she said presently; "and if he comes soon I shall *just* get through my business, and catch the three o'clock express."

No, it would be of no use, Ruth concluded, as she let her head fall languidly back against the pillow—Aunt Clarkson was far too busy to think about the cat.

Fortunately for her business, the doctor did not keep her waiting long. Ruth was better, he said, and all she wanted now was cheering up a little—she looked dull and moped. "If she could have a little friend, now, to see her, or a cheerful companion," glancing at Nurse Smith, "it would have a good effect."

He withdrew with Mrs. Clarkson to the door, and they continued the conversation in low tones, so that only scraps of it reached Ruth:

"—excitable—fanciful—too much alone—children of her own age—"

Aunt Clarkson's last remark came loud and clear:

"We shall cure that at Summerford, Dr. Short. We're not dull people there, and we've no time for fancies."

She smiled, the doctor smiled, they shook hands and both soon went away. Ruth leant her head on her hand. Was there no one who would understand how much she wanted to see the kitchen cat? Would they all talk about fancies? What were Lucy and Cissie and Bobbie to her?— strangers, and the cat was a friend. She would rather stroke its rough head, and listen to its purring song, than have them all to play with. It was so sad to think how it must have missed her, how much she wanted to see it, and how badly her head ached, that she felt obliged to shed a few tears. Nurse discovered this with much concern.

"And there was master coming up to see you to-night and all, Miss Ruth. It'll never do for him to find you crying, you know. I think you'd better go to bed."

Ruth looked up with a sudden gleam of hope, and checked her tears.

"When is he coming?" she asked. "I want to see him."

"Well, I s'pose directly he comes home—about your tea-time. But if I let you sit up we mustn't have no more tears, you know, else he'll think you ain't getting well."

Ruth sank quietly back among her shawls in the big chair. An idea had darted suddenly into her mind which comforted her very much, and she was too busy with it to cry any more. She would ask her father! True, it was hardly likely that he would have any thoughts to spare for such a small thing as the kitchen cat; but still there was just a faint chance that he would understand better than Nurse and Aunt Clarkson.

So she waited with patience, listening anxiously for his knock and the slam of the hall door, and at last, just as Nurse was getting the tea ready, it came. Her heart beat fast. Soon there was a hurried step on the stairs, and her father entered the room. Ruth studied his face earnestly. Was he tired? Was he worried? Would he stay long enough to hear the important question?

He kissed her and sat down near her.

"How is Miss Ruth to-day?" he said rather wearily to Nurse.

Standing stiffly erect behind Ruth's chair, Nurse Smith repeated all that the doctor and Mrs. Clarkson had said.

"And I think myself, sir," she added, "that Miss Ruth will be all the better of a cheerful change. She worrits herself with fancies."

Ruth looked earnestly up at her father's face, but said nothing.

"Worries herself?" repeated Mr. Lorimer, with a puzzled frown. "What can she have to worry about? Is there anything you want, my dear?" he said, taking hold of Ruth's little hot hand and bending over her.

The moment had come. Ruth gathered all her courage, sat upright, and fixing an entreating gaze upon him said:

"I want to see my best friend."

"Your best friend, eh?" he answered, smiling as if it were a very slight affair. "One of your little cousins, I suppose? Well, you're going to Summerford, you know, and then you'll see them all. I forget their names. Tommie, Mary, Carry, which is it?"

Ruth gave a hopeless little sigh. She was so tired of these cousins.

"It's none of them," she said shaking her head. "I don't want any of them."

"Who is it, then?"

"It's the kitchen cat."

Mr. Lorimer started back with surprise at the unexpected words.

"The kitchen cat!" he repeated, looking distractedly at Nurse. "Her best friend! What does the child mean?"

"Miss Ruth has fancies, sir," she began with a superior smile. But she did not get far, for at that word Ruth started to her feet in desperation.

"It isn't a fancy!" she cried; "it's a *real* cat. I know it very well and it knows me. And I *do* want to see it so. *Please* let it come."

The last words broke off in a sob.

Mr. Lorimer lifted her gently on to his knee.

"Where is this cat?" he said, turning to Nurse with such a frown that Ruth thought he must be angry. "Why hasn't Miss Ruth had it before if she wanted it?"

"Well, I believe there *is* a cat somewhere below, sir," she replied in an injured tone; "but I'd no idea, I'm sure, that Miss Ruth was worritting after it. To the best of my knowledge she's only seen it once. She's so fond of making believe that it's hard to tell when she *is* in earnest. I thought it was a kind of a fancy she got in her head when she was ill."

"Fetch it here at once, if you please."

Nurse hesitated.

"It's hardly a fit pet for Miss Ruth, sir."

"At once, if you please," repeated Mr. Lorimer. And Nurse went.

Ruth listened to this with her breath held, almost frightened at her own success. Not only was the kitchen cat to be admitted, but it was to be brought by the very hands of Nurse herself. It was wonderful—almost too wonderful to be true.

And now it seemed that her father wished to know how the kitchen cat had become her best friend. He was very much interested in it, and she thought his face looked quite different while he listened to her to what it looked when he was reading his papers downstairs. Finding that he asked sensible questions and did not once say anything about "fancies," she was encouraged to tell him more and more, and at last leant her head on his shoulder and closed her eyes. It would be all right now. She had found someone at last who understood.

The entrance of the kitchen cat shortly afterward was neither dignified nor comfortable, for it appeared dangling at the end of Nurse's outstretched arm, held by the neck as far as possible from her own person.

When it was first put down it was terrified at its new surroundings, and it was a little painful to find that it wanted to rush downstairs again at once, in spite of Ruth's fondest caresses. It was Mr. Lorimer who came to her help, and succeeded at last in soothing its fears and coaxing it to drink some milk, after which it settled down placidly with her in the big chair and began its usual song of contentment.

She examined it carefully with a grave face, and then looked apologetically at her father.

"It doesn't look its *best*," she said. "Its paws are white *really*, but I think it's been in the coal-hole."

This seemed very likely, for not only its paws but the smart ribbon Ruth had tied round its neck was grimy and black.

"It's not *exactually* pretty," she continued, "but it's a *very* nice cat. You can't think how well it knows me—generally."

Mr. Lorimer studied the long lean form of the cat curiously through his eye-glass.

"You wouldn't like a white Persian kitten better for a pet—or a nice little dog, now?" he asked doubtfully.

"Oh, *please* not," said Ruth with a shocked expression on her face. "I shouldn't love it half so well, and I'm sure the kitchen cat wouldn't like it."

That was a wonderful evening. Everything seemed as suddenly changed as if a fairy had touched them with her wand. Not only was the kitchen cat actually there in the nursery, drinking milk and eating toast, but there was a still stranger alteration. This father was quite different to the one she had known in the dining-room downstairs, who was always reading and had no time to talk. His very face had altered, for instead of looking grave and far-away it was full of smiles and interest. And how well he understood about the kitchen cat! When her bed-time came he seemed quite sorry to go away, and his last words were:

"Remember, Nurse, Miss Ruth is to have the cat here whenever she likes and as long as she likes."

It was all so strange that Ruth woke up the next morning with a feeling that she had had a pleasant dream. The kitchen cat and the new father would both vanish with daylight; they were "fancies," as Nurse called them, and not real things at all. But as the days passed and she grew strong enough to go downstairs as usual, it was delightful to find that this was not the case. The new father was there still. The cat was allowed to make a third in the party, and soon learned to take its place with dignity and composure. But though thus honored, it no longer received all Ruth's confidences. She had found a better friend. Her difficulties, her questions, her news were all saved up for the evening to tell her father. It was the best bit in the whole day.

On one of these occasions they were all three sitting happily together, and Ruth had just put a new brass collar which her father had bought round the cat's neck.

"I don't want to go to Summerford," she said suddenly. "I'd much rather stay here with you."

"And the cat," added Mr. Lorimer as he kissed her. "Well, you must come back soon and take care of us both, you know."

"You'll be kind to it when I'm gone, won't you?" said Ruth. "Because, you know, I don't think the servants *understand* cats. They're rather sharp to it."

"It shall have dinner with me every night," said Mr. Lorimer.

In this way the kitchen cat was raised from a lowly station to great honor, and its life henceforth was one of peace and freedom. It went where it would, no one questioned its right of entrance to the nursery or dared to slight it in any way. In spite, however, of choice meals and luxury it never grew fat, and never, except in Ruth's eyes, became pretty. It also kept to many of its old habits, preferring liberty and the chimney-pots at night to the softly-lined basket prepared for its repose.

But with all its faults Ruth loved it faithfully as long as it lived, for in her own mind she felt that she owed it a great deal.

She remembered that evening when, a lonely little child, she had called it her "best friend." Perhaps she would not have discovered so soon that she had a better friend still, without the kitchen cat.

Uncle Wiggly and the Rich Cat

Howard R. Garis

ONCE UPON A TIME THERE WAS A VERY RICH CAT, BUT WITH ALL SHE had she was not happy. She owned an automobile and kept a little mouse servant girl to wait on her. And an old gentleman rat did all the heavy work around the house, such as putting out the ashes and cutting the grass.

"Heigh-ho!" sighed the rich cat lady one morning, after she had lapped up some thick, heavy cream, which was left on her doorstep each day.

"Heigh-ho! I am so tired!"

"Tired of what?" squeaked the little mouse servant, as she brought a paper napkin for the rich cat to wipe the cream from her whiskers. Even though she was well-off, the cat lady had whiskers, and she was very proud of them.

"Oh, I am tired of sitting around doing nothing!" purred the rich cat.

"Then why not go for a ride in your auto?" asked the poor little mouse servant girl.

"I am tired of that, too," spoke the rich cat. "It is the same old thing every day! Dress and go out. Come back and dress to eat! Dress to go out again! Come back and undress to go to bed and get up in the morning to dress and do it all over again! I—I'd like to have an *adventure*!" mewed the cat lady.

"Oh, mercy! An *adventure*!" squeaked the mouse. "Never!"

"Yes," went on the cat, "a real, exciting adventure. I saw a poor dog the other day—at least he used to be poor, and he is far from rich now. But he looked so well, and so lively, with such strong, white teeth! I heard him telling another dog he had had a most wonderful adventure in the woods with an old rabbit gentleman named Uncle Wiggily. I quite envied that poor dog!"

"Oh, and you so rich!" murmured the mousie girl.

"I don't care!" mewed the wealthy cat lady. "I'd almost be willing to be poor if I could have an adventure. Come, I'll go for a ride in the auto. It will be better than dawdling around the house."

So the cat lady ordered out her auto, with the rat gentleman to drive it, and the little mousie girl to sit beside her on the cushioned seat.

"Where shall I drive to, Lady Cat?" asked the old gentleman rat chauffeur.

"Oh, anywhere—to the woods—the fields—anywhere so that I may have an adventure—I don't care!" mewed the rich cat.

So the rat gentleman drove the auto through the village, and out into the forest. At first the roads were very good, but at last they became bumpy, and the cat lady and mousie girl were much shaken up and jiggled about, not to say joggled.

"Do you want to go on?" asked the rat.

"Oh, yes," answered the cat. "It shakes up my liver, and I seem to be feeling more hungry. Go on, perhaps I shall find an adventure."

The auto lurched and bumped on a little farther and, all of a sudden there was a crash.

"Oh!" screamed the little mousie girl.

"What is the matter?" asked the cat lady, looking through her fancy glasses.

"We have had an accident," answered the gentleman rat. "The auto is broken, and I shall have to go for help."

"Let us go, also," squeaked the mousie girl. "We don't want to stay here in the woods alone."

"*You* may not want to," said the cat with a smile. "But *I* am going to. Run along with Mr. Rat, Miss Mouse, and get help. I'll stay here!"

So the rich cat lady was left alone, sitting in the auto, one wheel of which was broken, while the rat gentleman and mousie girl went to look for a garage where they could get help.

"Perhaps this is the start of an adventure," thought the cat.

A moment later she heard a rustling in the bushes, and out popped a strange dog. Now the rich cat lady knew some rich dogs who wore silver and gold collars and were friends of hers. She was not afraid of them. But this was a dog without any collar, though he had on a suit of clothes. And, when the cat lady looked a second time, she saw that it was a boy dog and not a grown man dog.

"Bow! wow!" barked the boy dog. "You're a strange cat! What are you doing in these woods? Hi, Jackie!" howled the dog. "Come help me chase this strange cat up a tree!"

"All right, Peetie! I'm with you!" answered a voice, and out of the bushes came another boy dog. The two dogs rushed at the cat lady.

Now she might not have been afraid of *one* boy dog, but when *two* of them leaped toward her, this was enough to frighten almost any pussy! Don't you think so?

"Meaouw! Mew! Mee!" cried the cat, and before she knew it she was climbing a tree. Up she scrabbled, her claws tearing off bits of bark, until she was perched on a limb, high above her auto and the barking dogs down below.

"My goodness me, sakes alive, and a liver cream puff!" said the excited rich cat lady to herself, her heart beating like an alarm clock. "This is dreadful! To think of me, a wealthy cat, being chased up a tree by two poor dogs! What will my friends think?"

Then she looked down at the dogs and said:

"Run away if you please, little puppy boys!"

"No! No!" they barked. "Bow! Wow!"

"You run and tell him," said one puppy to the other. "Tell him there's a strange cat in his woods. I'll stay here at the foot of the tree so she can't get down until you come back with him!"

"I wonder whom they are going to bring back?" thought the rich cat up the tree. And she could not help laughing a little as she thought how strange she must look. "The mouse servant and rat chauffeur will be surprised when they come back and see me here," thought the cat.

One little puppy dog boy ran away, while the other remained on guard at the foot of the tree.

"May I come down?" asked the cat lady.

"No, indeed!" growled the dog, though he did not speak impolitely. "You must stay up there!"

"Dear me!" thought the cat lady. "This is quite an unexpected adventure!"

All of a sudden she saw the puppy at the foot of the tree jump up. At the same time there was a rustling in the bushes, and along came the other puppy, with an old gentleman rabbit, who wore a tall silk hat, who had a pair of glasses on his pink, twinkling nose and who walked with a red, white and blue striped rheumatism crutch.

"There she is, Uncle Wiggily!" barked a puppy dog. "We saw her in your woods, and chased her up a tree until you could look at her. Maybe she is the Woozie Wolf or the Fuzzy Fox, dressed up like a cat."

"Indeed I am not," said the rich pussy lady up the tree. "I am the Rich Mrs. Cat, and my auto has broken. When my mousie servant girl and the rat gentleman who drives my car return, they will tell you I never harm rabbits. But are you Uncle Wiggily Longears?" she asked.

"Yes," answered the bunny, "I am. And I know you, Mrs. Cat. I heard about you from the poor dog. I am very sorry Jackie and Peetie Bow Wow chased you up a tree. They meant no harm."

"I am sure they did not," mewed the cat politely.

"But they are always on the lookout so nothing will happen to me," went on Uncle Wiggily. "I would get up and help you down, only I can't climb a tree."

"Oh, I can easily get down," said the cat lady, and she did, though her rich clothes were rather ruffled. But she had plenty of money to buy more. So don't worry about that.

"Make yourself at home in these woods—the animal folk call them mine," said Uncle Wiggily kindly. "I am sorry you had this trouble. Now I must hop away. I hope your auto will soon be mended. Come, Jackie and Peetie, if you want to help me."

"Where are you going?" asked the rich cat.

"To help a poor cat family," said Uncle Wiggily. "The cat gentleman of the house has been out of work a long time, his wife is ill and he has a number of little kittens. I was on my way to see the family when Jackie came to tell me you were up a tree."

"Well, I'm down the tree now," laughed the rich cat lady. "And will you please let me help this poor family? I have a lot of money—see!" and she showed a purse full of golden leaves which the animal folk use for money. "I can buy them food, and if Mr. Cat wants work, let him take my auto, after it is fixed, and use it for a jitney."

"What!" cried Uncle Wiggily. "Aren't you going to use that fine car any more? All it needs is a new wheel."

"Give it to the poor cat," was the answer. "I am never going to ride in it again. I feel so much better since I came to the woods—and climbed a tree—that I am going to live here for the rest of my life. I'll buy a hollow stump bungalow near you, Uncle Wiggily. I know, now, I am going to be very happy."

"Well, you will make the poor cat family happy, at any rate," said Mr. Longears.

"And to make others happy is to be happy yourself," mewed the rich cat lady.

She went with Uncle Wiggily, Jackie and Peetie to the home of the poor cat family, and when the worried cat gentleman heard that he was to have the auto for a jitney, with which he could make money, he was so glad he almost stood on his head. And his wife and the kitten children were glad also.

When the rat gentleman chauffeur and the mousie servant girl came back, in another auto, to take the rich lady home, she said:

"I am going to stay with Uncle Wiggily. From now on I am going to live in the woods and be happy and poor."

"Oh, my!" squeaked the mousie servant. "Just fancy!"

"I never heard of such a thing," said the rat gentleman. "You had much better come home and live as you did before."

But the cat lady would not change her mind, and she built herself a bungalow near Uncle Wiggily's, and lived there happily forever after.

Sources

Elwes, Alfred. "Kittenhood." In *The Adventures of a Cat, And a Fine Cat Too!* London: Addey and Company, 1887.

Poe, Edgar Allen. "The Black Cat." In *Twenty-Five Ghost Stories.* New York: J.S. Olgivie and Company, 1904.

Morley, Charles. "Peter: A Cat O'One Tail." In *Peter: A Cat O'One Tail.* New York: G.P. Putnam's Son, 1891.

Stables, W. Gordon. "Is Cats to be Trusted?" In *Cats: Their Points and Characteristics.* London: Dean and Son, 1876.

Ross, Charles H. "The Case for Cats." In *The Book of Cats.* London: Griffin and Farran, 1878.

Paterson, Andrew Barton. "The Cat." In *Three Elephant Power and Other Stories.* 1917.

Dasent, G. W. "The Greedy Cat." In *Tales from the Field.* London: Chapman & Hall, 1874.

Benson, Arthur Christopher. "The Gray Cat." In *Paul the Minstrel and Other Stories.* London: Smith and Elder, 1911.

Weigall, Arthur. "The Home Life of a Holy Cat." In *Collier's Weekly.* 1933.

Lovecraft, H. P. "The Cats of Ulthar." In *Tryout.* 1920.

Blackwood, Algernon. "The Empty Sleeve." In *London Magazine.* 1911.

Stoker, Bram. "The Watchers." In *The Jewel of the Seven Stars.* London: Heinemann, 1903.

Greene, Frederick Stuart. "The Cat of the Cane-Brake." In *Metropolitan Magazine.* 1916.

Doyle, Arthur Conan. "The Brazilian Cat." In *Round the Fire Stories.* London: Smith, Elder and Company, 1908.

Jacobs, W. W. "The White Cat." In *Captains All and Others.* New York: Charles Scribner's Sons, 1905.

Chekhov, Anton. "Who Was to Blame?" In *Tales of Chekhov.* 1886.

Downs, A. S. "Plato: The Story of a Cat." In *The Junior Classics.* New York, 1912.

Twain, Mark. "Talk with Mark Twain's Cat, the Owner Being Invisible." In the *New York Times.* New York, 1905.

Bierce, Ambrose. "The Cat and the King." In *Fantastic Fables.* New York: G.P. Putnam's Sons, 1899.

Roberts, Charles G. D. "How a Cat Played Robinson Crusoe." In the *Ladies Home Journal.* 1910.

Alden, W. L. "The Yellow Terror." Circa 1900.

Adams, John Coleman. "Midshipman, the Cat." Circa 1890.

Saki (H. H. Munro). "The Philanthropist and the Happy Cat." In *Beasts and Super-Beasts*. London: John Lane, 1914.

Montaigne, Michel de. "My Cat." In *Essays*. 1588.

Warner, Charles Dudley. "Calvin: A Study of Character." In *Scribner's Monthly*. 1877.

Kipling, Rudyard. "The Cat that Walked by Himself." In *Just So Stories*. London: MacMillan & Company, 1902.

Saki (H. H. Munro). "The Achievement of the Cat." 1911.

Prevost, Marcel. "The Woman and the Cat." In *International Short Stories*. New York: Simon & Schuster, 1910.

Wilde, Lady Jane. "The Demon Cat." In *The Irish Fairy Tale Book*. London: Fisher and Unwin, 1892.

Rouse, W. H. D. "The Hypocritical Cat." In *The Giant Crab and Other Tales from Old India*. London: David Nutt, 1897.

Finger, Charles J. "The Cat and the Dream Man." In *Tales from Silver Lands*. New York: Doubleday & Company, 1924.

Nye, Bill. "Mr. Sweeney's Cat." In *Bill Nye's Cordwood*. Chicago: Rhodes and McClure, 1887.

Neill, John R. "The Cat and the Mouse." In *The Cat and the Mouse: A Book of Persian Fairy Tales*. Philadelphia: Henry Altemus Company, 1906.

"Johnny Reed's Cat." In *Folk-Lore and Legends*. London: W.W. Gibbings, 1890.

Searing, Anne E. P. "An Idyll of Summer." In *The Yellow Cat*. New York: The Short Stories Company, 1909.

Wodehouse, P. G. "The Man Who Disliked Cats." In *The Man Upstairs and Other Stories*.

West, Virginia. "The Cat Came Back." In *Short Stories from* Life *Magazine*. New York: Doubleday, Page & Company, 1916.

Leland, Charles G. "How Diana Made the Stars and the Rain." In *Aradia: The Gospel of Witches*. 1880.

Lover, Samuel. "Ye Marvellous Legend of Tom Connor's Cat." In *Handy Andy: A Tale of Irish Life*. 1842.

Anonymous. "The Cat the Mouse in Partnership." In *The Yellow Fairy Book*.

Jerome, Jerome K. "On Cats and Dogs." In *The Idle thoughts of an Idle Fellow*.

Walker, Abbie Phillips. "Greta and the Black Cat." In *Sandman's Rainy Day Stories*. New York: Harper & Brothers Publishers.

Seton, Ernest Thompson. "The Slum Cat." In *The Slum Cat*. New York: Curtis Publishing Company, 1904.

Baum, L. Frank. "The Cat and the Fiddle." In *Mother Goose in Prose*. New York: Bounty Books, 1901.

Perrault, Charles. "The Master Cat." In *Tales of Mother Goose*. Boston: D.C. Heath & Company Publishers, 1901.

Dasent, George Webbe. "The Cat on the Dovrefell." In *Popular Tales from the Norse*.

Walker, Abbie Phillips. "Mistress Pussy's Mistake." In *The Sandman's Hour: Stories for Bedtime*. New York: Harper & Brothers Publishers, 1917.

Eaton, Edith. "What About the Cat?" In *Mrs. Spring Fragrance*. Chicago: A.C. McClurg & Company, 1912.

Benson, E. F. "There Arose a King." In *The Countess and Lowndes Square and Other Stories*. London.

Walton, Amy. "The Visitor from the Cellar." In *The Kitchen Cat and Other Stories*. London: Blackie & Son Limited, 1890.

Garis, Howard R. "Uncle Wiggly and the Rich Cat." In *Uncle Wiggly's Story Book*. New York: Platt & Munk, 1921.